Japan Examined

Japan Examined

Perspectives on Modern Japanese History

Edited by
Harry Wray
and Hilary Conroy

University of Hawaii Press
Honolulu

Library of Congress Cataloging-in-Publication Data
Main entry under title:

Japan examined.

   Bibliography: p.
   1. Japan—History—1868–   . 2. Japan—History—
1868–   —Historiography.   I. Wray, Harry, 1931–
II. Conroy, Francis Hilary, 1919–
DS881.9.J29   1983   952.03   82–15926
ISBN 0–8248–0806–1
ISBN 0–8248–0839–8 (pbk.)

Printed by Versa Press, Inc.

To our children, Marceline, Jennifer,
Stephen, David, Sharlie, and Rusty;
to our grandchildren, Steven, Jennifer,
Allison, and Jessica; and to our students.

Contents

Acknowledgments

We wish to express our appreciation to Akiko Akita for her generous contribution that helped make the publication of this volume possible. Mrs. Akita's gift was made in memory of her father, Teiji Teshirogi.

We are grateful also to George Akita, Wray's former mentor, for his interest and encouragement of this undertaking.

We thank those scholars who wrote essays for this volume and the following scholars whose essays we hope to publish in a subsequent collection: Gail E. Bernstein, Gary Dean Best, Lois C. Dilatosh, John K. Emmerson, Masaru Ikei, Akira Iriye, Laura Jackson, Joyce Lebra, David Lu, Wayne McWilliams, Joy Paulson, Jun Tsunoda, and Sharlie C. Ushioda.

We owe deep gratitude to Dottie Haeffele, history department secretary, Illinois State University, for her cooperation and patience.

Note on Japanese Names

We hope the reader will bear with us on our decisions regarding Japanese names. All Japanese names in the text appear in the Japanese manner, that is, with the surnames first. The names of second and third generation Japanese scholars as well as those scholars born in Japan who have made their reputations outside Japan appear with the surname last, in the Western style.

Introduction

Scholarship on modern Japanese history in the English-speaking world has come of age. Twenty-five years ago a book of this kind could not have been envisaged; even ten years ago the background of specialized studies would have been insufficient. During the last two decades, however, the number of scholars of Japanese history and culture produced by American graduate institutions has increased remarkably. From the 1930s and 1940s, when a handful of specialists produced mostly general works on Japan, through the 1950s when the first significant monographs were written, now several hundred students of Japan have written doctoral dissertations and published articles and monographs probing in depth the many aspects of Japanese history, particularly the modern period. In the process they have developed many different points of view which have generated exciting intellectual controversy—even argument over when modern Japan begins.

The increasing scholarship and controversy have made the field stimulating not only to its practitioners but to the nonspecialist as well. In this volume specialists discuss the principal issues in ways which promise to be interesting and useful to nonspecialist scholars, undergraduate students, and general readers.

The genesis of the book lies in the personal experience of the authors of this introduction. As college teachers we have seen the usefulness of supplementary "problem books" for American and European history. Through them students see the mechanics of the historical process and the historian's work more clearly than through textbooks that merely give answers. In our graduate student and early teaching days we sorely missed in East Asian studies books that handled controversial topics of the sort available for European and American history courses. Their absence simply reflected the paucity of researchers in modern Japanese history.

The increase in the number of scholars in Japanese history since 1950 has resulted in the discovery of new materials, differing disciplinary approaches, and generational influences. Hence no two scholars analyzing the same topic or period will see things in exactly the same way. Names like Sansom, Norman, Borton, Brown, and Reischauer, however respected, can no longer be considered the final authorities in the field. Rather, they have been challenged or complemented by younger historians and political scientists and have themselves revised earlier interpretations in the light of new documentary evidence and fresh perspectives.

In this book the writing of five generations of American scholars of Japan can be found. Charles Fahs, one of the first Americans to receive a Ph.D. dealing with Japanese studies, represents the pre–Second World War scholar in an essay which appropriately assesses from his long acquaintance with Japan the question of whether that nation is East or West. Edwin Reischauer's two essays reflect the scholarship of over thirty years in the field, but his first writings in the late 1940s provided early interpretations for later historians to accept, reject, or modify. A third generation of scholars including Marius Jansen, Ardath Burks, W. G. Beasley, Roger Hackett, John Hall, James Morley, Thomas C. Smith, George Totten, and Hilary Conroy appeared on the scene in the mid 1950s. Many of this group had participated in the American occupation of Japan and were products of wartime language schools. It was they who introduced Japanese history in the major universities of the United States. A fourth generation, products of the new graduate programs of the postwar era, are also represented in this book. They appeared in the late 1950s and early 1960s plowing new ground and sometimes revising old interpretations. Among them were Jackson Bailey, Thomas Havens, Joyce Lebra, Peter Duus, Kenneth Pyle, George Akita, Marlene Mayo, Harry Harootunian, Bernard Silberman, Tetsuo Najita, James Crowley, and Conrad Totman. They, in turn, established or expanded programs at other institutions and have been training new scholars. In the late 1960s and early 1970s these young scholars examined narrower and more specialized topics such as Meiji journalism (James Huffman), Japanese colonialism (E. Patricia Tsurumi), Chōshū (Thomas Huber), labor (Stephen Large), the Meirokusha (Jerry Fisher), education (Harry Wray), and lesser known personalities than the giants of Meiji times (Wayne McWilliams and Gail Bernstein). Most of their scholarship has been steady, solid, and cautious though Richard Mitchell,

John Dower, and Richard Minear have been called revisionist. Many of this generation were trained by scholars concerned with Japan's modernization process; they are now trying to address themselves to other questions from other perspectives. Finally, a fifth generation of scholars has appeared since approximately 1975; they are represented here by Mark Michelson and Michael Barnhart. To some extent they seem to be returning to the broad topics and problems that attracted the interest of scholars of the late 1950s.

Something needs to be said about the format of this work. During the spring of 1976 the editors met at Illinois State University to discuss Wray's conceptualization and a tentative list of controversial issues in modern Japanese history. From an original selection of fifteen topics, eventually, at the urging of our publisher, we decided on twelve topics that would lend themselves ideally to the classroom teacher of a semester course on modern Japan. After enlisting the aid of recognized specialists as subeditors for most of these topics, we submitted names of likely contributors but gave them a free hand in making their own choices. In some cases it was necessary for us to make the invitations ourselves. Each subeditor was then asked to write a brief introduction to his or her topics. For the cooperation of the subeditors we are deeply grateful; it encouraged us to proceed with the project.

What makes this book unique is the approach we strongly recommended to the subeditors and individual essayists. We did not want a book of highly technical articles written for other scholars; we wanted essays which would have as their target a wider audience, including undergraduate students and lay readers. The authors were urged to adopt a persuasive—almost argumentative—tone in their essays. Moreover, they were asked to present their thesis in the first couple of paragraphs and then devote the rest of the essay to a relentless defense of their argument. The essays were to be the product of past or present scholarship; stress was to be placed on clarity of presentation as well as on content. Of course scholars are highly individualistic and some were more willing to be argumentative than others. But we editors think that the diversity of these essays is sufficient indication that modern Japanese history is neither a closed subject nor a dull one.

Another objective of this collection is to introduce students to Japanese scholars and to promote dialogue between them and their American counterparts. Originally it was hoped that at least one Japanese scholar would write on each topic. That objective was largely achieved, but distance, time considerations, language difficulties, and other projects made it difficult for some Japanese scholars to contribute. Those who were able to accept our invitation demonstrate clearly how the Japanese themselves think about certain topics.

Why study history at all? Given the multiplicity of views presented here, this query could become the refrain of readers bewildered by so many conflicting opinions and no firm conclusions. To such attitudes we should like to direct our concluding remarks. First, this book, although radical or at least innovative in its presentation of many perspectives but no answers, nevertheless follows the traditional chronological pattern from the mid-nineteenth century to the post–Pacific War era, and the standard periodization of Tokugawa, Meiji, Taishō, and Shōwa eras will be familiar to many readers or available from any standard Japanese history text to the complete newcomer to the study of Japan. The only section presented out of sequence, the one on Japanese colonialism, has been placed at a logical point for consideration.

This means that the book can be read not only consecutively but, for readers who wish to start with the present and seek out its roots, in reverse. Thus readers can travel a progression from, say, "Japan: East or West?" (Part XII) to "The Meiji Restoration" (Part III); the question "When Does Modern Japan Begin?" (Part I) could be taken up at some convenient point, perhaps midway or in conjunction with "The Allied Occupation: How Significant *Was* It?" (Part XI). Thus the book contains the logic of a two-way street but leaves open to the reader which side of the street one prefers to walk on and in which direction. We trust, therefore, that we have avoided intellectual chaos while opening up the reader's mind to the many divergent paths through Japanese history that are not only possible but plausible.

Editing this volume has been a tremendous task, and we are well aware of the many controversial decisions we have had to make in the process, some of which may not please every reader or contributor. But Clio is a wayward muse, and we can only say we have done our best and apologize for our shortcomings.

This has been a nonprofit enterprise for general editors, subeditors, and essayists alike, and it is with a deep sense of appreciation of the generosity of our colleagues in the field of Japanese studies that whatever profits accrue from the sale of this volume are to be assigned to the Interchange for Pacific Scholarship (IPS) and the Japanese-American Student Association.

—HARRY WRAY
—HILARY CONROY

PART I

When Does Modern Japan Begin?

THE TERM "MODERN" may seem like a relatively simple and straight-forward concept since the word is widely and commonly used. Actually it is a complex notion fraught with possibilities for misunderstanding and heated disagreement. Even when the term is used in connection with Western societies, vexing questions arise; when it is applied to non-Western societies it is like opening Pandora's Box or taking a broomstick to a hornet's nest. The difficulties and misunderstandings that beset the participants of a conference on the "modernization" of Japan, held in Japan in 1960, are discussed here and elsewhere by John W. Hall. The American scholars present sought to devise a value-free definition of the term "modern" while the Japanese scholars insisted, among other things, on including democracy as an essential component of the definition.

The essayists in this part of the book either explain their understanding of modern or define the way in which they use the term. Numerous authorities have offered other definitions, but two will be cited here to provide readers with additional frames of reference to facilitate their analysis of these essays.

C. E. Black in his *Dynamics of Modernization* asserts that modernization is "a process by which historically evolved institutions are adapted to the rapidly changing functions that reflect the unprecedented increase in man's knowledge, permitting control over his environment, that accompanied the scientific revolution." Black contends that, intellectually, modernization involves a new way of looking at the self and the world (the environment) and concerns the application of science "to the practical affairs of man in the form of technology." Political modernization means the consolidation of policymaking which entails in the public domain "increasing centralization of the administrative organs of the state." It also involves the rule of law maintained by a highly organized bureaucracy and the establishment of close ties between the state and the members of society. Economic modernization stems directly from the scientific and technological revolution which has dramatically increased productivity. In other words the industrial revolution marks a turning point in human economic history. Socially it means urbanization, a shift from the extended to the nuclear family, greater equality in income, education, and opportunities, changes in the relationship between men and women, social integration facilitated by better means of communication, and improved health. Psychologically, modernization leads to a greater sense of individual freedom.

Gunnar Myrdal, the Swedish social scientist, lists among his specifications for modernization such qualities as rationality, rise of productivity, higher levels of living, social and economic equalization, improved institutions and attitudes (which include such characteristics as efficiency, diligence, orderliness, and punctuality), national consolidation and independence, and political democracy.

If it is difficult to agree on a general definition of modernity or on the characteristics of a modern society, it is even more difficult to pinpoint the time when it can be said that a given society enters the modern age. An authority on Chinese history, Michael Gasster, writes, "The point in time at which these characteristics [the modern ones] overshadow traditional ones is said to mark the beginning of a country's modern history." This point, however, is extremely difficult to locate. Some historians tend to mark the rise of modernity in a given country with the appearance of a few significant changes in lifestyle. Others believe the modern age of a nation begins only when a complex pattern of changes develops. The difficulty here is that the viewer's focus determines what he or she sees as the beginning of modernization. The process of modernization does not affect all segments of a society uniformly and simultaneously. There are significant areas of retardation even in societies whose modernity is not usually questioned. There were major areas of retardation in Japan after the Meiji Restoration—a milestone generally accepted as the beginning of Japan's modern era—that persisted to the Second World War.

I contend in my essay that a new era did not begin for the Japanese peasantry (and it might be added for the Japanese woman) until postwar times. I do not argue that in the postwar era all the elements of what constitutes modernity have fully emerged. Rather, I maintain that the beginning of a new way of life—the "modern" way of life—started with the postwar era.

Koji Taira does not deny that the road to modernity in the economic realm was entered upon by Japan after the Meiji Restoration. But he holds that modern economic growth in Japan was severely hampered by the persistence of traditional forces in the prewar years. His essay is an experiment in the analysis of relationships between the political system and economic development based on Marxist methods of historical interpretation.

James Huffman contends that the leaders of Japan made a conscious decision to establish a new order—that is, to modernize Japan following the Meiji Restoration—and adopted measures that launched Japan on the road to modernity. For this reason he believes modernization in Japan begins in the first decade or so of the Meiji era.

John Hall offers a careful analysis of the question and comes to the conclusion that for the purposes of periodization the Meiji Restoration can be taken as the beginning of Japan's modern era. He believes that trends or conditions do not justify regarding the pre-Meiji era as the beginning of the modern era—despite the fact that Tokugawa Japan cannot be categorized as a feudal society. He sees the postwar era as a continuation and development of the modernization process that started after the Meiji Restoration.

—MIKISO HANE

The Problem:
When Did Modern
Japanese History Begin?

John W. Hall

A question of this sort can have no absolute answer, since any response to it is necessarily phrased within a context determined (in fact
predetermined) by the responder and not the questioner. To put it
another way, any answer is dependent upon the interpretation which
the responder gives to the question. Whether consciously or uncon-
sciously, any answer is shaped by the responder's premises (or biases)
regarding two open-ended parts of the question. One is the matter of
what is meant by modern; the other is the question of how modern a
society must be before it can be said to have begun its modern period.
The first poses a conceptual problem of historical generalization; the
second involves a problem of historical periodization. Since neither
has a simple, or absolute, solution, historians remain in disagreement
over them.

What is meant by "modern" as it applies to Japan? The range of
possible answers extends from the simple quality of up-to-dateness,
applied to such aspects of life as kitchens and bathrooms, to highly
technical descriptions of fundamental social and political conditions
throughout an entire society. As a term used by professional historians
for analytical purposes, it takes its place among a broad category of
middle-range generalizing concepts by which contemporary historians have tried to give meaning to the process of change in the world
around them. Even in this carefully restricted usage there exists a
wide variety of interpretations. Furthermore, since the conception of
modern is inevitably associated with the concept of modernization,
the controversy over meaning has taken on the same kind of politi-

cal and ideological implications as those engendered by terms like feudalism, absolutism, imperialism, fascism, and authoritarianism. Moreover, like these concepts, the idea of modernism has been drawn into controversies involving value judgments over whether to be modern is desirable or undesirable or whether the end product of modernization is to be predicted by extrapolation from current conditions in Western Europe and North America or the USSR and China.

Since the Second World War, the term modernization has taken on a number of negative connotations, especially in reference to Japan, due to the many unhappy experiences the Japanese people have undergone in the last hundred years. Imperialist expansion, social unrest, military defeat and foreign occupation, political and economic inequality, industrial pollution—all have been condemned as inevitable consequences of the course of national development taken by Japan's leaders following the Meiji Restoration, the effort to become modern in the style of the societies of Western Europe and North America. This disillusionment with the modern condition in the name of the agonies suffered by the Japanese people in the century following the restoration was all the more acute because of the once-confident assumption that modernization offered the prospect of continuous advance toward a world in which science and reason will have solved all human problems.

The meaning of modern has been debated since the middle of the nineteenth century but with a frequently changing vocabulary. The debate during the 1850s and 1860s over whether or not to end Japan's seclusion and to deal with Western powers was fundamentally a controversy over differing predictions about the world's future and what Japan should do about it. The early Meiji debates over conceptions of westernization and the meaning of "enlightened civilization" were basically attempts to establish priorities for national development. By the 1920s and 1930s, it was ideas such as representative government, imperialism, Japanism, socialism, democracy, and fascism that competed for influence over Japan's national policymakers. Following the Second World War, the key concepts became peace, democracy, and social equality. Controversies arose over whether to define these terms according to Marxist models or the normative criteria provided by the American presence as occupying power.

It was mainly in the United States, following the experience of the Second World War, that scholars from several academic disciplines began to work with the concept of modernization as a way of dealing with the changes which had been taking place with such force and complexity in the postwar world. For the most part, these scholars, having experienced the horrors of war, totalitarianism, atomic bombings, and racial prejudice, had been disabused of the certainty that modernization was handmaiden to progress. They were skeptical, as well, of the methods of analysis which relied exclusively on democratic or Marxist theory. It was out of this atmosphere that modernization theory, as it is sometimes called, emerged: an effort to achieve that illusory aim of "value-free" analysis.

An important event in the dialogue between American and Japanese historians on the issue of modernization took place in 1960 in Japan at the Hakone Conference, organized by members of the Conference on Modern Japan, an activity of the Association for Asian Studies. What had been planned as a fairly uncontroversial discussion to clarify theories and methodologies turned out to be both a highly stimulating experience and one that generated a great deal of debate in subsequent years. It is significant as well that the conference took place at the end of a summer when anti-Security Treaty demonstrations had momentarily disturbed Japanese-American relations. A noteworthy product of the modernization debate is the work of Kimbara Samon, whose *"Nihon kindaika" ron no rekishi zō* [History of the "modernization of Japan" controversy] appeared in 1968, was revised in 1971 and again in 1974, and has gone through eight printings to date. Although Kimbara did not attend the conference, his work begins essentially with Hakone and documents the exchange of interpretations among Japanese and American scholars in the years that followed.

Evident at the Hakone Conference, but even more in subsequent years, was the realization that there is not, nor can there be, a convergence of all opinions regarding the definition of modern. To place the most favorable light upon what American scholars were attempting to do, theirs was the effort to develop a broad, hypothetical concept with which to comprehend the great changes which were transforming societies the world over regardless of differences in social or political systems. Thus they attempted to break down the process of contemporary social change into component parts such as urbanization, industrialization, science, secularization, mass participation, bureaucratization, mass literacy, social mobility, and the like. These were phenomena which presumably could be measured empirically and, hence, could be assessed independent of differing cultural or political conditions. Opposed to this approach were those who focused, precisely on these cultural and political differences and so linked the

modern condition to a specific type of political system. To one like Inoue Kiyoshi, writing in the special 1963 issue of *Shisō* (an issue devoted to an analysis of modernization), the defining features of a
modern society were the complete abolition of feudalism in economic
and social relations, the acquisition of popular sovereignty, and the
assurance of complete individual freedom. He believed that these
conditions had yet to be achieved in Japan at the time of his writing.
It is possible, of course, to argue that the process defined by the "clus-
ter of symptoms" approach used by American social scientists would
result in the ideal conditions set forth by Inoue, but serious discussions on this possibility has not taken place.

One reason for this silence has been accidental. While American
scholars were claiming freedom from political bias for their value-free
approach, one of the original Hakone Conference participants became American ambassador to Japan. As a consequence there was an
immediate acceptance, particularly in the Japanese scholarly world, of
the assumption that modernization as social science theory was a tool
of American national (imperialist) policy. Just before and during the
Pacific War, American opinion about Japan had been extremely negative; Japan was depicted as militaristic, authoritarian, totalitarian,
and undemocratic. In the late 1950s that opinion was beginning to be
revised, and one began to hear, from American scholars especially, the
first formulations of the "successful modernization" evaluation of
Japan's post-Meiji history. For a prominent American official to praise
Japan's successful modernization was easily interpreted as a political
statement premised on the assumption that Japan was deemed successful for having remained within the "free world" and was therefore
a convenient model for developing nations.

There is no need to belabor the issue of what modern means except
to point out again how slippery the concept is, how subject to manipulation for political or ideological purposes, and how subject to reinterpretation generation by generation. Clearly no absolute answer to
the question of what constitutes modern society emerges spontaneously from the historian's so-called facts; rather the truth must be
sorted out by the historian as viewer. Thus any evaluation of Japanese
history over the last one or two centuries must make clear the premises
upon which it rests. Finally, it is evident that in no actual situation, in
Japan or any other society, does either the *process* of modernization or
the *end phase* of modernity necessarily conform to an ideal model. As
societies take on certain configurations at different rates and in different ways, at no time can two societies be expected to look absolutely

alike. There will be areas of advance and areas of retardation. And this brings us to the matter of beginnings.

When did modern Japanese history begin? We must start our inquiry with the understanding that there is a difference between beginning and fulfillment. Whichever definition of modern one chooses for purposes of historical periodization, there is little point to equating the moment of beginning with the fulfullment of *all* conditions of a proposed ideal type or, to put it more personally, the fulfillment of all the expectations in the mind of the viewer. Modern Japanese history is not still waiting "to begin" because there are social inequalities and injustices which have yet to be rectified. And the reverse of this proposition is also true: modern Japanese history did not start with, for instance, the first evidence of factory production in the silk spinning industry in eighteenth-century rural Japan.

What I am coming to, obviously, is what I presume to be a utilitarian approach to the question of periodization as seen from the generalist historian's point of view. And for this purpose I would start with some fairly noncontroversial observations. First, from the survey historian's point of view, Japanese society has clearly undergone three (and only three) major transformations (one might be tempted to say revolutions) in the last four hundred years. The first of these occurred in the latter half of the sixteenth century and gave rise to the sociopolitical structure which held through the Tokugawa era. The second took place as a result of the Meiji Restoration which brought the Tokugawa era to a close and led to the formation of the Meiji state. The third followed the military defeat and occupation of the Second World War, resulting in the new Shōwa Constitution. Having observed that periodizing names like "feudal" or "modern" do not emerge spontaneously from the raw data of national history, it is nonetheless true that such data do provide the historian with incontrovertible evidence that changes of fundamental scope did indeed take place at these three junctures and that the historical periods they define are sufficiently different from each other that each must be given a separate conceptual identity.

From the survey historian's position there is little need to make fine distinctions regarding the precise dating of these major turning points. Modern Japan has customarily been dated from the restoration with the full understanding that 1868 is a symbolic signpost and that the restoration cannot be explained without taking into account antecedent conditions that prepared Japan for modern change or that numerous holdovers from the Tokugawa era remained beyond 1868 to slow the fulfillment of modern change in certain important areas. Such qualifications need not disturb the symbolic usefulness of starting modern Japanese history with the concept, if not the precise date, of the Meiji Restoration.

No matter what definition of modern is taken, it is the natural tendency of those who would explain the apparent ease with which Japan went through the critical institutional changes which followed the restoration to look for preconditions of modern trends in the old regime. And it is characteristic of this tendency that they will claim to find the origins of such trends farther and farther back in history. This was true of the prewar search for a money economy or manufacturing in Tokugawa Japan, and it was true of the postwar search for modernizing trends leading up to the restoration. Obvious examples are T. C. Smith's quest in the Tokugawa era for the agrarian origins of modern Japan and Ronald Dore's study of the remarkable spread of literacy among Japanese of all classes before the end of the Tokugawa period.

At the other end of the interpretive spectrum, those who are reluctant to acknowledge the restoration as the true start of modernization in Japan because of the many "feudal legacies," which they assert were carried over into the postrestoration years, are prone to see such negative factors continuing later and later into the twentieth century. It is from this premise that a variety of antimodern aspects of Meiji Japan are identified: the absolutist nature of Meiji politics, the failure to change the traditional form of family law, the conservative statist nature of the Meiji Constitution, the slow start of modern economic growth, the lingering virulence of the so-called parasitic landlord phenomenon, and the like. But most of these negative qualifications have been put forth not to deny the assertion that modern history began at the time of the restoration but rather to attest the incompleteness of that event. The well-known interpretation that the restoration was an incomplete bourgeois revolution is the best example of this approach.

Historical studies in the last two decades have had a marked effect upon the periodizing concepts described above. Since the early 1950s, for instance, Japanese historians have given a great deal of attention to the sixteenth century, especially to the profound institutional changes brought about by Toyotomi Hideyoshi's domestic policies. These studies in turn have had an important effect on how historians now look upon the Tokugawa era. As I have written in *Studies in the Institutional History of Early Modern Japan*, the Tokugawa period has been regarded as basically feudal and it is often argued that whatever antifeudal tendencies might be identified in that period could only have come about in spite of the feudal order which persisted to the end. The most recent studies of the sixteenth century have shown, however, that in many ways Tokugawa Japan was not typically feudal even at the start. Thus increasingly it has become unacceptable to use the concept of feudalism as an automatic explanation of how things were in Japan's "old regime."

Where heretofore Hideyoshi's place in Japanese history was primarily that of military unifier, the new emphasis is on his domestic social measures. Of these, three have received the greatest attention. First was the dramatic movement within the countryside whereby the samurai became separated from the peasantry and the land and ended up in the castle towns of the daimyo. (This movement, known as *heino-bunri*, was carried out between roughly 1580 and 1590.) Second was the massive land survey (the Taikō *kenchi*) which registered all agricultural land. This survey resulted in the establishment of a new and more secure status for the cultivator (the *hyakushō*), the creation of a new method of taxation, and the formation of the *mura* (village) as the new unit of village life, taxation, and administration. Third was the nationwide swordhunt of 1588 which disarmed all but the samurai class. The effect of these changes was to transform relationships between government, the military aristocracy, and the peasantry into a structure very different from that found in a feudal society. The simple fact that the entire samurai class (often termed the feudal aristocracy) was removed from the land, and any direct ownership of land, constitutes one of the most profound differences between Tokugawa society and what we think of as typically feudal. Samurai, by the start of the Tokugawa regime, had almost to a man been drawn off the land and become urban-dwelling, stipended, patrimonial officials of the shogun and daimyo. The *hyakushō* class, though not given free tenures, were made secure in possession of their land by being listed on the village registers. While given few political rights of their own, other than village self-government, they were placed under a uniform public legal system. Such "peasants" were far from being feudal serfs.

These recent studies have effectively denied the historian of Tokugawa Japan the easy use of "feudalism" as a scapegoat explanation for the many presumed antimodern aspects of Tokugawa society. Family law, for example, which curtailed the free rights of individual family members in favor of the corporate household, while it persisted into the post-Meiji era and even today has not fully disappeared, is now looked at not as a feudal holdover but as a basic given of Japanese society. The lineage *ie* is now being studied objectively as a fundamental feature of traditional Japanese social behavior rather than as a practice imposed on Japan by the undesirable influence of feudalism. To take another example, explanations for why population in Japan trailed off after the middle of the Tokugawa period have recently been modified significantly. Proponents of the feudal scapegoat explanation assumed that the decline in population growth was the result of "feudal oppression" of the peasantry which led to widespread death from famine and resort to infanticide by the desperate poor. Recent studies have discovered that population control was more a practice of comfortable families who wished to safeguard a desired level of living. These and similar findings have shaped a very different picture of the old regime, one which could hardly be described as feudal in all its important characteristics and, hence, one which should not be considered so antithetical to modern change.

At the other end of the periodizing scale, the historian confronts the problem of how to interpret the post-1945 era. In this instance, most of us have in our lifetime been witness to the actual birth and acceptance of a new historical period. What had for a decade or so after 1945 been looked upon as the "postwar era" or the "occupation period" (simply an appendage to what had gone before) has now taken on its own identity under the provisions of the Shōwa Constitution and the achievements of the postwar economy. The growing recognition by historians that a new period has come into being has set up vibrations across the entire periodizing spectrum. The fact that the Allied Occupation came and went without the predicted surge toward nationalism and remilitarization has had the effect of making historians judgments less political for both the prewar and postwar periods. In particular it has made it easier to consider the 1868–1945 years dispassionately. It is no longer acceptable to describe shortcomings of the Meiji Constitution and the national structure it created without assuming that these defects were the inevitable result of some feudal legacy which remained unexorcised at the time of the restoration. Since many features of the modern condition appear to have been fulfilled (or are in the process of fulfillment) in the postwar era, it becomes easier for the historian of whatever persuasion to accept the Meiji Restoration as the beginning of modern Japanese history.

I began this analysis with the assertion that the beginning of modern Japanese history cannot be determined absolutely. Historians differ in their answers because of differing conceptions of what is modern and because of changing historical discoveries and circumstances which affect their conceptions of periodization. I have in this essay placed my main emphasis on the subject of periodization rather than on the question of what it means to be modern. In regard to periodization, we could have no better example of how the continuing process of historical reinterpretation affects a nation's historiographic structure. From one direction, recent reinterpretation of Japan's sixteenth-century transforamtions has had an important effect on how we now look upon the Tokugawa regime. From the other direction, the addition of an entirely new unit of history extending beyond 1945 has affected our assessment of the period from 1868 to 1945. Both these developments, I believe, reinforce the validity of the customary practice of beginning Japan's modern history with the Meiji Restoration.

Meiji 1–10:
Takeoff Time
for Modern Japan

James L. Huffman

There may never have been an era in which people did not regard their own world as modern; for the very word "modern," at its elementary level, simply connotes what Webster refers to as new-fashioned or up to date. In ancient Babylon, for example, modernity meant hanging gardens and arbitrary rule. In first-century China, it signified civil service exams and the writing of history and poetry. Thirteenth-century Mongolia saw the modern man as one who exhibited great skill in military horsemanship. And for the Japanese, modernity might variously have been defined as harmonious government, amorous gentility, or skill in the use of guns, depending on whether one lived in the age of Shōtoku Taishi, Genji, or Oda Nobunaga.

To be modern, in other words, is to be in tune with the basic themes and trends that mark one's own period of history as distinctive. Thus one might rephrase the question by asking: When did Japanese civilization begin to take on those special characteristics that can be considered uniquely typical of this historical epoch's more advanced societies?

Before answering this question, however, we must more precisely define the term modern, seeking an understanding of which special characteristics typify an advanced society. Such a definition is not easy to formulate in a brief essay, since debates on the topic often have produced as much confusion as they have consensus. But we must attempt at least a basic—if oversimplified—definition.

It seems to me that most of the writings on modernization converge in suggesting two basic features of the modern society. It is these two features that we shall take as the foundation of our discussion.

First: a modern (or "modernizing") society values secular rationality and the scientific approach to learning and order. In other words, the accumulation of knowledge and the ordering of institutions in the modern society depend on empirical observation and the exercise of rational thought rather than on uncritical acceptance of divine revelation or tradition. In such societies people generally control nature rather than the reverse. Education is basically secular, scientific, and empirical. Economic growth depends to a great extent on technological innovation and the harnessing of inanimate energy. Political styles are rationalized for the sake of accumulating and organizing power— usually in a bureaucratic form of government. Even the values of such a society are shaped by the notions of progress and change inherent in the scientific approach. Thus Everett M. Rogers has written that modernization is a process by which individuals become "psychologically nontraditional."

Second: the modern state is characterized by mass social institutions. The political-intellectual theorist S. N. Eisenstadt sees a "mass-consensual orientation" as the central characteristic of modern societies. By that he means that increasingly larger numbers of groups become actively involved in the central decision-making processes. Some scholars point out that a central educational system is essential for creating such a mass society. Others suggest the importance of a mass communications network. Economically the mass society involves an intricate and broad-based market system, as well as widespread industrialization and urbanization. Politically the development of a mass society depends on the emergence of several characteristics: a central administration or government; broad (though not necessarily democratic) participation in that government; widespread demands for services; acceptance of the nation-state concept; and interaction between that state and other states (international relations).

Some scholars, it should be noted, add as a third characteristic of modernity such concepts as the growth of democracy, the spread of individualism, and the full participation of all groups and classes in a society's social, economic, and political life. The denial of such rights and qualities to any major class, they maintain, is a sign that a society is not yet modern.

Words like democracy, individualism, and equality seem to me, however, to be too value-laden to be useful in formulating our definition. They turn the term "modern" into a polemical razor with which ideologues can attack societies that fall short of their own social goals. Such qualities may express laudable ideals, but they do not encapsulate the objective reality of this era's dominant societies. And thus they fail the test of being useful descriptive tools.

Having thus defined the modern society as one with a mass base and a scientific-rational approach to order and learning, we must now turn to the question of just when Japan had developed those characteristics to the extent that the nation could justifiably be called modern. It is at that point that we should be able to say with some confidence that modern history had begun.

The period that first draws our attention is likely to be the latter years of the Tokugawa era. This, after all, was the age in which modernizing forces were in full gale in several Western societies. It is the period most studied by scholars of the last two decades as the source of today's Japan. And there is no denying that it was the period in which Japan first exhibited numerous of its modern characteristics.

Governmental structures by late Tokugawa already had become highly bureaucratized, both within the feudal domains *(han)* and at the central *bakufu* level in Edo. The writings of Tokugawa theorists such as Ōgyu Sorai and Sakuma Shōzan had emphasized the need for an administration based on social utility and a rational understanding of contemporary realities, rather than on some absolute or normative ethical standard.

Several features of the mass society too had appeared by the early 1800s. Literacy rates (approximately 30 percent) were as high as in any European society. Commerce had become fairly widespread, especially on the main island of Honshu. Urbanization also was under way: Edo had a population of perhaps a million, while Osaka and Kyoto boasted 300,000 inhabitants each. And politically a number of early nineteenth-century intellectuals had begun to talk about the "nation" as a single entity, presaging the growth of genuine nation-state consciousness after the arrival of Perry in 1853.

It would be too much to say, however, that modernization had become a primary or pervasive characteristic of late Tokugawa Japan. For while its seeds were beginning to send their shoots through the soil, they were in fact only that—scattered sprouts that suggested what was to come, not developed plants able to support a genuine flowering of modernization.

The education received by most persons, for example, was still transmitted in tradition-bound temple schools; and it was based primarily on the premodern ethical norms of Neo-Confucianism. The central values underlying the social system were loyalty to superiors and achievement—values that emphasized conformity and continuity rather than individualism or change. And in the economic sphere, technology remained largely at a distinctly unmechanized, premodern level until the Meiji Restoration of 1868.

Indeed, even the impulse to industrialize was largely lacking until near the end of the period. As late as the 1850s the gunnery specialist Takashima Shūhan was kept in jail for supporting the use of Western technology to strengthen national defense. Though not all officials opposed the application of scientific methods or rational critical faculties, those who did were in the ascendancy throughout the late Tokugawa years. And the result was that modernizing efforts were spotty and disorganized, lacking in any unified or conscious direction from the top.

Nor could late Tokugawa Japan be said to have created anything approaching a mass society. Education was not centrally controlled; rather, each of ten thousand temple schools maintained its own curriculum, as did scores of private schools in the urban centers. Mass communications were almost completely lacking: intercity telegraphic service did not start until 1869; telephones and railroads were nonexistent. Modern newspapers, which by the time of Perry had a two-hundred-year history in England, had not even appeared in Japan.

The lack of mass social structure was even more apparent in the political sphere. The state, far from being unified, was divided into more than two hundred semiautonomous *han*. Only the adult male samurai, who comprised no more than 3 percent of the population, had any say in the decision-making process—and that only at the initiative of their feudal lords. Ideals of the nation as a single entity were generally submerged in a sea of loyalty to the domain. And even the most progressive intellectuals resisted notions of thoroughgoing internationalism until the eve of the restoration.

Tokugawa Japan was thus a premodern society largely devoid of either mass social structures or the scientific-rational approach to learning and order—and (perhaps even more important) equally devoid of conscious or unified governmental efforts to move forthrightly in the modernizing direction. If we want to begin a modern history by looking at the roots of modernity, we will find Tokugawa Japan a good starting point. But if we seek the onset of the modern order itself, we must move to a later period.

That period, I would suggest, arrived during the first decade of the Meiji era: 1868 to 1878. It was then that a small group of middle-level samurai, primarily from the western domains, staged a coup d'etat in January 1868 known as the Meiji Restoration. They overturned the

Tokugawa regime and established their own rule under the name of the young emperor, Meiji. Most scholars agree that, at that time, these men had little thought of replacing Tokugawa social or administrative structures. They simply wanted power. But they quickly found that if they were to succeed in consolidating their gains, a totally new system would have to be devised. Western influence had by now begun to permeate Japan. A new order had arrived. And the new day, they found, demanded solutions unavailable under the premodern social-political-economic order.

During the next decade these leaders engaged in a series of moves that obliterated the old, decentralized political structure (even if not all of its values) and established a new, rational, and highly centralized system of administration. In the process, they wiped out their own samurai class and abolished the time-honored feudal domain structure, replacing it in 1871 with a prefectural system. When several thousand samurai revolted against these reforms in 1877, the government crushed the revolt with a largely peasant-based army.

But it was not just the eradication of traditional structures that concerned these power consolidators. They were equally eager to devise a set of institutions which would propel Japan as rapidly as possible into a place of respect in the international community. Utilizing the slogan *Fukoku Kyōhei* (Rich Country, Strong Army), they instituted a series of reforms which transformed nearly every aspect of national life. In 1872 they scrapped the old temple schools and created a compulsory education system administered by the state. The samurai elite was replaced the next year with a peasant army recruited through a universal conscription law. Government income was regularized through a land tax; national banking and currency systems were set up. Newspapers were encouraged, too, for the dissemination of information. By the end of the decade, moves had been launched to begin the process of shaping a constitution.

The years 1868 to 1878 marked, in short, a revolutionary decade— one in which Japan began the conscious and rapid transition from the premodern to the modern era. This was the period that initiated Japan's "modern history." To understand just how true this was, we need to recall our definition of modernization.

Modernization, we said, first involved a scientific-rational approach —to education, to the position of values, to economics, and to politics. In each of these areas, early Meiji Japan met the test and then some. The initial aim of the Meiji education system was eminently utilitarian; officials sought to give the populace practical skills that would be useful in modern society. The prevailing attitude was summed up by the noted modernizer Fukuzawa Yukichi:

> A man who can recite the Chronicles but does not know the price of food, a man who has penetrated deeply into the classics and history but cannot carry out a simple business transaction—such people . . . are nothing but rice-consuming dictionaries, of no use to their country.

Likewise the government set out to rationalize not only its own administrative structure and power base but also the economy, sending fact-finding missions to the West to study American and European industrial systems, launching its own model industries, and encouraging the creation of private business. Fully modern economic growth might not be seen for another decade, but the early Meiji years witnessed the initiation of highly organized policies in that direction.

A prime symbol of the rational approach of early Meiji decision-makers was the establishment in 1873 of the Meirokusha, a society of officials and scholars who met twice a month to discuss the progress of Japanese civilization. Members debated everything from legislative assemblies to women's rights, from press freedom to church–state relations. One even suggested the abolition of the Japanese writing system. And if two features characterized their discussions more than any others, they were rationality and optimism about Japan's potential for rapid progress. No view was too extreme for discussion; but always the talks were calmly rational. The society's goals, said the writer of one of the Meirokusha's first published articles, included "establishing a model for the nation" and "opening the eyes of the ignorant with . . . elevated and penetrating opinions." One may question whether the same writer's optimistic forecast that "immortal theories" would emerge from the discussions was not a bit rose-tinted. But the fact that the Meirokusha included several leading intellectuals and influential officials bespeaks the heavy emphasis on the no-holds-barred, investigative orientation of the early Meiji leadership. And this approach permeated every area of national life.

Our second criterion for modernization was the creation of a mass society. Here again the first Meiji decade is typified by thoroughgoing, conscious movement toward that end.

Literacy grew rapidly under the centrally administered educational policies of the new government. It would take thirty years for the literacy rate to pass 90 percent, but the movement in that direction was quite steady after 1872. Even more important than the mere spread of literacy, however, was the fact that the government used the new educational system to inculcate in the Japanese people a loyalty to the nation-state. Through the schools, the people were expected to learn that they were part of a total society.

Progress in mass communication was equally striking, as we already have noted. Tokugawa Japan had no daily newspapers, no mass communication networks. That picture changed after the restoration. The first daily was launched in Yokohama in 1871, and within a few years newspapers, spurred by active government encouragement, had become a major force in national life. Indeed, by 1877 some forty-one of today's forty-seven prefectures had their own papers. And they were influential. Numerous persons who were eventually to become national leaders (including three future prime ministers) worked for these early papers. The nation's political debate centered in their editorial columns in the middle 1870s. As one observer then commented, they became "the eyes and ears of mankind"—creators, if one will, of a mass society.

The prime mover, however, in the creation of a mass society was the government itself. Its role in stimulating industrialization has already been noted, as has its creation of a unified educational system. But the efforts did not stop there. Every possible avenue was used to make people aware of their roles as citizens of a larger state. As the first decade progressed, the administration began increasingly to resurrect the imperial institution as a symbol of national unity and strength, a symbol with which loyal citizens could easily identify. The peasant conscripts were indoctrinated in ideas of national loyalty too, with the full expectation that they would take their new patriotism back to the villages from which they had come. Prefectural administrators were instructed to place copies of national newspapers in reading rooms throughout their regions. The government was, in other words, committed to the creation of a *national* populace, where people gave allegiance not so much to a local or state administration as to the nation-state at the top.

One offshoot of these efforts, which gave further evidence of the growing mass consciousness, was the rise in the 1870s of Japan's first nongovernmental, protomodern political organizations. Angered by certain bureaucratic policies, a number of former samurai and wealthy farmers joined together in 1874 to form a popular rights *(jiyūminken)* movement demanding the early creation of legislative assemblies. It can be argued that they were not really democratic since they sought the franchise for only a tiny minority of the wealthiest people. And their effectiveness is open to serious question. But their very existence proves that people outside the government were increasingly coming to identify with the national authority structure. They were, perhaps, Japan's first "interest group"—a key element in any modern society.

There is no denying that full modernization would have to await Meiji's later decades. The constitution would not come until 1889. Light industry would not take off until the Sino-Japanese War in 1894–1895. Nationalism would struggle against an overwhelming tide of westernization until the latter 1880s. And international interaction on an equal basis would have to await the final abrogation of unequal treaties in 1913.

But the highly conscious, unified effort of national leaders to modernize was well under way by the end of the first Meiji decade. As early as the Charter Oath of 1868, the new government had called for seeking knowledge "through the whole world" and for the utilization of "just universal principles" as the basis of government. That, I would maintain, was a modern approach to government. The fact that the leaders were able to move the nation so rapidly in that direction marks the 1868–1878 decade as the beginning of Japan's modern history.

Agrarian Japan and Modernization

Mikiso Hane

There are, as we see in my introduction to this part and James Huffman's essay, numerous ways of defining modern. Here we shall take it to mean basically Western—what Meiji enlightenment thinkers had in mind when they endeavored to "enlighten and civilize," that is, modernize, Japan. Economically it means the employment of the fruits of nineteenth- and twentieth-century science and technology; intellectually a balance in favor of rational, scientific, secular thinking and widespread literacy; politically a tendency toward freedom and democracy; socially a trend toward egalitarianism, individualism, and an open society; materially a life-style in which there is progressive improvement in comfort and health.

Conventional opinion holds that modern Japan begins with the Meiji Restoration of 1868. If we look at the salient aspects of the society—that is, the political system, the industrial sector, and the major cities—we might very well conclude that indeed the modern age in Japan commenced with the Meiji Restoration. But the process of modernization does not unfold uniformly in all sections of the society. As Herbert Passin observes, "Modernization does not mean the complete and instant displacement of the traditional. The progress is not uniform . . . it affects separate cultural elements, areas of thought and population groups in different ways." In other words, there are areas of "retardation." There were large segments of the Japanese population whose basic pattern of life and thought remained largely untouched by the process of modernization decades after the Meiji Restoration. If we agree with the thesis that "the point in time in which modern characteristics overshadow traditional ones is said to mark the beginning of a country's modern history," we can argue that the Japanese peasantry, who comprised the majority of the population, had not seen the beginning of the modern age in the prewar years. The same argument can be made about the female half of the population. In this sense we can agree with C. E. Black's contention that economic and social transformation in Japan does not start until 1945.

In this essay I uphold the thesis that traditional elements overshadowed the modern ones in rural Japan in the prewar years and hence the modern age for the vast majority of the Japanese peasants did not begin until after the Second World War. I agree with Fukutake Tadashi's contention that "although there are some signs of change, the fundamental character of Japanese farmers . . . did not change until the end of World War II."

Method of Farming and Economic Life

Thomas C. Smith judged that "in the course of its long history, Japanese agriculture has in some respects changed remarkably little." In fact little change has taken place in Japanese farming since the Ashikaga period (fourteenth to sixteenth centuries) when significant improvements in tools, irrigation, seeds, and fertilizers and greater use of draft animals took place. Even today much of the farm work depends on human muscle with some help from draft animals. Manure, firewood, rice, vegetables, and so on are transported on human backs or in baskets balanced by a shoulder beam. The tools used in the prewar years were the same as those used in the Ashikaga period, and very little chemical fertilizer was used, human and animal manure being the main source of fertility.

Aside from the fact that agricultural technique remained largely unchanged from the middle ages, the farm population stayed more or less stable between 1868 and 1940. More than 50 percent of the population was in farm work in 1930 compared with 6.2 percent in England in 1938. Moreover, contrary to earlier estimates it appears that agricultural production did not increase much in the post–Meiji Restoration years. According to James I. Nakamura the rate of production in late Tokugawa and early Meiji times seems to have been higher than previously estimated because of underreporting of production in those years. The annual growth rate of about 1 percent from the 1870s to 1920 barely kept up with the population growth in this period.

Moreover, the farmers' economic condition did not improve during the postrestoration years. During the 1870s more than 80 percent of the government's tax revenue came from the land tax. Further, the deflationary policy adopted by the government in the 1880s reduced the price farmers received for their products, causing many small farmers to fall heavily into debt. Continued agrarian poverty steadily increased the rate of tenancy. In early Meiji times 20 percent of the land under cultivation was farmed by tenant farmers but by 1910 the share had risen to 45 percent. In the Tokugawa era tenant farmers retained about 39 percent of their harvest; postrestoration tenants kept only about 32 percent.

After a major peasant uprising in Chichibu in 1884 was quashed, the peasants had little choice but to suffer in silence. The government extended little aid to the peasants in time of poor harvest and famine. In order to avoid starvation many peasants sent their daughters to the urban textile factories to work for cheap wages under conditions akin to indentured labor, and in times of extreme hardship they sold their daughters to the brothels in the cities or even overseas to Southeast Asia. Such practices persisted through the 1930s. A society in which parents have to sell their daughters into prostitution cannot be called modern.

Political Changes

Significant political and administrative changes were made at the center, but they affected the daily lives of the peasants very little. The exception was the introduction of compulsory military service. In the course of the years, particularly after the Russo-Japanese War of 1904–1905 when a large number of men were drafted into the army, veterans came to play an important political role. They were organized into military reserve associations and were used to marshal public opinion at the grass roots level to support the imperialistic and militaristic policies of the government.

So far as the extension of political rights was concerned, the peasants' gains were minimal. The government adopted a constitution in 1889 and held the first Diet election in 1890, but only 1.14 percent of the population—only those with a fixed amount of property—were given a franchise. Most of the peasants were unaffected and did not gain voting rights until 1925 when universal male suffrage was introduced. But even after 1925 power in the rural areas remained with the traditional village elites. The peasants continued to believe that political affairs should be left to government or village leaders. If we hold political democracy to be a requisite for a modern age, we must say that it had not arrived in rural Japan before the Second World War.

Social Conditions and Outlook

It cannot be denied that the policies adopted by the Meiji government and the introduction of the products of Western science and technology affected the way of life of rural Japan, but again their effects varied. Villages close to urban areas were, of course, more heavily influenced than out-of-the-way communities.

The significant legal change introduced by the Meiji government in this regard was the abolition of the feudal class system and the elimination of the castelike separation of the samurai and the common people. Freedom of occupation was granted; marriage between classes was now legal. But in fact class distinctions were retained, and little change occurred in the actual social relationship between upper and lower classes. The government classified people into the aristocracy or peers *(kazoku)*, the gentry or former samurai *(shizoku)*, and the commoners *(heimin)*. The former outcasts, the *eta*, were labeled as new commoners. These distinctions were recorded in the official family register which served the function that birth certificates do in the United States.

The traditional emphasis on social cohesion, order, and hierarchy persisted in prewar Japan. The common people retained their sense of deference toward their "betters." The spirit of independence and self-respect that Fukuzawa Yukichi sought to foster among the people did not penetrate into the countryside. Upward social mobility was still extremely limited though horizontal mobility, because of jobs in the urban factories, did occur. Most of the rural dwellers who took urban jobs commuted to work, however, and those who moved into the cities retained strong ties to their home villages and adhered to traditional ways.

The family system in the villages remained virtually unchanged from the pre-Meiji years. The collective interests of the family were supreme; individualism was stifled. The family line was continued by primogeniture, and a hierarchy of age and sex prevailed. The legal authority of the father remained supreme and ultimately he made the decisions about property, education, marriage, jobs, and so on for all family members. If any family member defied the father's authority he could disown that person and turn him or her into a legal nonentity.

The government held the family, not the individual, to be the basic legal entity. Vital statistics were recorded in the family register. Remnants of the concept of joint family responsibility persisted, for if a family member committed a crime it was recorded in the family register and stained the record of the entire family.

In the village traditional provincialism and parochialism persisted. Villagers remained suspicious of outsiders, and marriages were normally concluded within endogamous groups or within the village. People from other prefectures were regarded with as much distrust as foreigners.

In daily life the average peasant was governed largely by traditional beliefs and attitudes which can be labeled superstition. The peasant was credulous and believed in the existence of spirits which had to be exorcised by local Buddhist priests. Foxes, snakes, and badgers were believed to possess supernatural powers; certain inanimate objects, trees and stones, for example, were considered to be sacred. Lucky and unlucky days, fixed by the zodiac, determined whether one should get married or launch a special project on a given day. When soldiers went off to war they were given amulets from shrines and temples, and women collected "a thousand stitches" on sashes to be worn by the soldiers for protection.

A modern outlook also entails precision about time and number. Gunnar Myrdal lists punctuality as one of the requirements of modernity. The prewar Japanese peasants did not let the clock regulate their lives; they were casual about time. If a meeting was called for seven o'clock they might gather at eight. If a funeral was scheduled for three o'clock it might get started at four. They used the lunar calendar to mark important events of the year, and they counted their ages in the traditional way—a person was one at birth and two on the first New Year's Day.

In the realm of moral values, traditional ways persisted. Like their Tokugawa predecessors' the postrestoration government leaders sought to regulate the people's mores and values, particularly those of the peasants, in a paternalistic fashion. Fukutake maintains that they "intentionally prevented farmers from becoming modern citizens in a modern society by means of particular indoctrinations." This inculcation was accomplished not only through the public schools but through organizations like the Young Men's Association. Traditional values such as humility, respect, industry, frugality, loyalty, filial piety, self-denial, propriety, duty, and obligation were emphasized, and efforts were made to keep "the pristine ways" of the peasantry from contamination in the cities. A Tokugawa agrarian moralist, Ninomiya Sontoku, was held up as a model for farmers.

The government leaders believed that a solid agrarian base was needed for the construction of a strong Japan. For this a peasantry dedicated to their task, like the Tokugawa peasants, was needed. Hence the government stressed the importance of agriculture as a vocation and supported a Shintoistic, nationalist movement known as *Nōhonshugi* which considered agriculture to be the foundation of society.

Education and Cultural Life

One of the measures adopted by the Meiji government which must be counted as a potent instrument for modernizing the peasantry was the introduction of compulsory universal education provided by the Education Act of 1872. Initially, however, the compulsory aspect of the program was largely ignored. Since fees were charged until 1898, many rural families did not send their children, especially their daughters, to school. This situation remained true well into the 1890s. Consequently illiteracy among rural children born before 1900 remained high. During the 1930s many rural dwellers in their forties and fifties were illiterate. Even those who attended school before the century did so only for a few years, and many remained functionally illiterate. Only in 1907 was compulsory education extended to six years. By the 1930s, however, practically all school age children were in school for at least six years.

In early Meiji times the content of education was designed to foster modernization because the emphasis was on "civilization and enlightenment." But in the 1880s reaction set in and a more traditionalist philosophy began to permeate the educational system. Greater emphais was placed on Confucian and Shinto values in the textbooks on moral education. The teachers themselves failed to foster a modern attitude among the students; much like traditional Confucian scholars, they placed themselves above the students as absolute authorities whose opinions could not be challenged. In effect a feudal relationship characterized the teacher–student relation up and down the education system. The children were taught they owed three great obligations: to the emperor, to their parents, and to their teachers.

The cultural life of the peasantry remained limited and simple. Although newspapers had penetrated into the rural areas in the prewar years, hardly any farm families had a radio and few read magazines or books. Movies seldom came to the villages. The more *"haikara"* (high-collared) elements had phonographs but they were a rarity.

Physical Conditions

The introduction of the postal system, telegraph, railroad, and better roads facilitated transportation and communications, but for villages not on the mainline the means of transportation remained traditional —that is, people walked and carried things on their backs. But communication certainly was facilitated by the introduction of the postal system.

In terms of housing, clothing, and food there was little significant improvement. One notable exception was the introduction of electricity. Most villages had electric light, however dim, by the 1930s. But the peasants still wore traditional work clothes and home-made straw sandals. Sanitation remained primitive. The privies were holes in the floor; human waste was collected for use in the fields as manure. Water that ran through rice paddies fertilized with human waste flowed into streams in which villagers washed clothes, kitchenware, and vegetables. Lice, fleas, bedbugs, and other vermin were commonplace in peasant homes. As a result, cholera, typhus, typhoid, diptheria, dysentery, and smallpox broke out frequently and communicable diseases like trachoma, tuberculosis, veneral diseases, and skin infections were prevalent. Children were afflicted with hookworms and other parasites. Malnutrition and inadequate health care kept the incidence of tuberculosis high to the end of the Second World War. In 1935 the death rate by tuberculosis was 1,908 per million population compared to 104 in 1974. Beriberi was another widespread sickness caused by poor diet.

The government did take steps to curb communicable diseases by vaccination and inoculation, but the measures were hardly adequate; it was not until the postwar period when the occupation authorities implemented a massive health program that most of these diseases were reduced significantly or eliminated entirely.

Although modern medicine had come to the villages before the war, the peasants still relied heavily on traditional cures such as moxa burning, herbs, and medicines provided by peddlers who left paper bags filled with old remedies. Babies were delivered by amateur midwives; broken bones were set by local judo experts; dental care was practically nonexistent.

The backwardness of health care in the country as a whole is reflected in the relative lack of improvement in life expectancy between the Meiji Restoration and the Second World War. Life expectancy in 1891–1898 was 42.8 years for men and 44.3 years for women. In 1926–1930 the figures were 44.82 and 46.54. Compare these with the figures for 1975: 71.75 for men and 76.95 for women.

Conditions changed drastically after the Second World War. The land reforms introduced by the occupation authorities have resulted in an end to absentee landlordism, more equitable landholding, and general prosperity of the farmers. The younger generation is better educated. The urban influence that prewar leaders sought to prevent from infiltrating the rural areas has penetrated the countryside. Even a cursory look at rural Japan today reveals striking changes. Cars, televisions, and electrical gadgets have inundated the villages. Traditional values and attitudes still survive but they have been modified. There is greater equality, freedom, openness, individualism, mobility, and sophistication. Now perhaps we can say that the modern age has begun in rural Japan. But it is debatable that the modern age had dawned upon the vast majority of the prewar Japanese villages. The modern elements had not yet overshadowed the traditional ones, and the feel and texture of the prewar village were still traditional.

Japan's Modern Economic Growth: Capitalist Development Under Absolutism

Koji Taira

Japan's modern economic growth is believed to have begun in the late 1880s, curiously coinciding with the preparation and promulgation of the Meiji Constitution which defined the character of the Japanese state. The system in which modern economic growth was generated was a variant of capitalism, although the state was powerful enough to violate the rules of capitalist economy by mobilizing large proportions of human and material resources from time to time. Because the Meiji Constitution concentrated the powers of the state in the monarch, the Japanese state between 1889 and 1947 can be considered a type of absolutism. The combination of an absolutist state and a capitalist economy during this period has been an enigma, far from fully unraveled, among scholars interested in Japanese economic history.

In Western history, absolutism gave way to a form of government dominated by a commercial bourgeoisie long before modern economic growth started as the industrial revolution. In the process of modern economic growth, therefore, bourgeois industrialists (now called capitalists) and industrial wage earners (now called the proletariat) confronted each other and interacted to generate between them a rising volume of output which was shared as wages to workers and profits to capitalists. Profits were reinvested and capital accumulation took place. Owing to the prior bourgeois revolution which overturned absolutism, capitalists and workers involved in modern economic growth were free individuals in the sense that they had been freed from premodern constraints on their persons, beliefs, and occupational choices. The blessings of liberty, first enjoyed by a few, were in due course generalized for all as the uninterrupted growth turned out a larger and larger output. The class struggle between capitalists and proletariat over respective shares in the ever-expanding output generated social progress.

In Japan, absolutism had just come into being when that nation's industrial revolution began. This peculiar historical equation lacked the crucial medium between economy and polity that Western capitalist development enjoyed—namely, a commercial and industrial bourgeoisie as a leading class. In short, Japan's modern economic growth was an industrialization without a bourgeoisie or a proletariat, that is, economic growth without personal freedom or civil liberties. Japan's capitalist development, unchecked by adequate constitutional and civilian restraints and made to serve the glory of the monarch, eventually resulted in an overextension of the dynastic military adventurism, which ceased in 1945 when Japan was beaten at her own game by the superior military power of her opponents.

The origins of Japan's anomalous modern economic growth may be sought in the sudden opening of feudal Japan to the West in the 1850s and 1860s. By this time, leading Western countries had passed through the industrial revolution. Japan could not manage the socioeconomic chaos brought about by this unequal confrontation. The feudal state system *(bakuhan taisei)* which had lasted in peace for more than two hundred years collapsed in 1867 within less than ten years of the opening of Japanese ports to foreign commerce. A new state system was worked out in the ensuing twenty years and solidified by the Meiji Constitution of 1889. How unprepared Japan initially was for a fruitful relationship with the West may be seen from many features of backwardness that characterized her feudal economy. The Japanese economy was not yet an integrated national economy; although local markets had developed to a certain extent, interregional linkages were distorted or hampered by political barriers and technical difficulties. Markets for factors of production such as land, capital, and labor were even more severely underdeveloped. The monetary system had barely advanced beyond the use of gold, silver, and copper coins, although promissory notes and bills of exchange were used to some extent among merchants of major cities.

Economic activities of individuals were determined by the class inheritance of occupation. Socially, individuals were presumed unfree and unequal. Feudal laws differentiated rights and obligations, or immunities and penalties, broadly by class (shogun, lord, samurai, peasant, artisan, merchant, and outcast) and in particular by personal status (sex, age, rank order in the family, social standing of the family, and so on). The common human denominator applicable to all was never discovered as it was buried under particular characteristics of individuals. There was no effective vocabulary to express the notion that "all men are created equal" or the concept of unalienable rights to "life, liberty, and the pursuit of happiness." There were no free individuals. There was no freedom of conscience. This legacy of feudalism was skillfully manipulated by the new absolutist regime. The result, as we shall see, was defective capitalist development.

In rural Japan where a great majority of Japanese lived and worked, the distribution of the basic resource, land, was highly unequal. There was no capitalism in Japanese agriculture. Insofar as laws and institutions were concerned, those of the feudalist nature inimical to the market economy were swept away. The Meiji land tax reforms, implemented in the years from 1873 to 1882, created peasant proprietors with full property rights over the holdings they were cultivating. At this time, land tilled by nonowning peasants (tenants) may have been about 30 percent of all cultivable land in Japan. The ratio rose to 40 percent by 1892. The prewar peak of 48 percent overall (53 percent for rice fields) was reached in 1930, reflecting a progressive dispossession of proprietory peasants. Few peasants had large enough holdings to employ themselves and their family fully, however. More than two-thirds of the peasants depended upon rented land in varying degrees of combination with their own holdings. Even so, more than half of the peasant families had to supplement their farm incomes by revenues from nonfarm sources; earnings and remittances from young children working in textile mills and other urban enterprises accounted for a large part.

All told, Japan's agrarian society looked like a system dominated by rentier-landlords called "parasite landlords" by Japanese economic historians, perhaps unsympathetically. This condition implies an enigmatic pattern of historical transition: from feudalism to parasitic landlordism via the forced creation of smallholder peasants. The rise of capitalist agriculture or even the rise of viable, market-oriented family agriculture was aborted.

In industry and commerce, an enormous diversity in the organization of production and marketing and in the pattern of business ownership and control became conspicuous in the course of Japan's capitalist development. A few giant state enterprises and *zaibatsu* combines towered over myriads of small workshops and family stores; enterprises of infinite varieties and sizes filled the interstices of the unequal system. The unequal industrial structure was associated with an unequal distribution of economic and political power. It also produced a grossly unequal distribution of personal income.

The variety of industrial organization indicates that the ability to organize production and marketing on a large scale and the resources by which to actualize entrepreneurial ability were in short supply. Once exposed to the Western standard and style of life, it was easy for the Japanese to see the range of things they did not have but wanted. The contact with the West thus created a great disequilibrium between realities and aspirations. This, in turn, meant unlimited opportunities for entrepreneurship. The supply of entrepreneurship fell far short of the size of disequilibrium to be filled, however. The few entrepreneurs who happened to be around enjoyed the advantage of a head start and exploited the most favorable opportunities. They were the Japanese counterpart of the West's robber barons. Another difficulty which constrained capitalist development was the scarcity of managerial ability needed for the organization and administration of modern technology, production, and marketing. Entrepreneurs who were quick to see profitable opportunities, adept at manipulating political and social connections, and daring enough to pursue their objectives on a large scale were not necessarily competent managers of going concerns. Modern industry required engineers and managers in addition to entrepreneurs. The few engineers and managers who were available at the right time were quickly monopolized by the government and major robber barons. The result was a concentration of great fortunes in the hands of a few in the midst of an economically backward populace.

The rapid emergence of economic inequalities of this type points up the relative narrowness of Japan's technological and organizational base relevant to modern industrial activities. For more than two hundred years prior to its own industrial revolution, the West had accumulated technological and organizational expertise which produced early capitalists and enabled them to organize large-scale workshops based on the division and coordination of labor. These workshops were called "manufactories" or "manufactures." When the instruments of work used in a series of various but coordinated operations were technologically organized into one large mechanized process driven by steam power, modern factories were born and with them the industrial revolution.

A question of great importance with respect to the extent of Japan's success with its own industrial revolution then is whether, and

to what extent, manufactories had developed prior to Japan's expo-
sure to the West's factory system. Historical research indicates that
workshops deserving to be called manufactories in pre-Meiji Japan
were probably sparse indeed. This finding suggests that Meiji Japan
started on the road to industrialization with deficient preconditions
and preparations. On a narrow base, it was possible to construct only
a small building. Japan's industrial revolution, hardly comparable to
the West's in scale or depth, installed the factory system in cotton
spinning, silk reeling, and selected processes of shipbuilding, paper
production, and the state-run armaments industry. In terms of output and labor force employed, the three branches of the textile industry—cotton spinning, silk reeling, and weaving—dominated Japanese
industry well into the 1920s. The invasion of the factory system was
very limited in weaving, however. On the eve of the First World War,
several forms of organization of production were visible in this field:
(1) weaving factories belonging to modern cotton-spinning firms, (2)
small and medium enterprises modernized enough to use power
looms, (3) classic manufactories with hand looms, and (4) cottage industry or domestic industry under the control of wholesale merchants
(ton'ya), who supplied raw materials to people who did the processing in their own homes. This type of industrial structure, in different
degrees, applied to many manufacturing industries.

The phenomenon of inequalities in industrial organization and
structure may also be discussed with special reference to the problems
of small and medium enterprises. Millions of working proprietors,
their family members, and a few hired hands per enterprise literally
sweated under hazardous working conditions. Together with small
peasants, these small operators and their employees accounted for a
great majority of the working population of Japan. The persistence of
these numerous smaller units has produced various interpretations.
The population pressure, relative ease of entry into these activities,
and intense competition among them have been mentioned by many.
These are certainly some of the necessary conditions for the persistence of a vast sea of small and medium enterprises.

To understand the plight of small and medium enterprises as a
problem of inequalities, however, a more dynamic structural view of
the whole economic system is needed. In fact, the stratification of
economic units by size may be viewed as a consequence of competition in the pursuit of profits among the participants in the market
economy. Even if a given number of competitors started on an equal
footing, the outcome of competition would be (1) the decimation

and dispersion of capital by the losing enterprises and (2) the concentration of capital in victorious and growing enterprises through the absorption of resources released by the losers. In reality, the equal start rarely obtains. Privileges under one system of inequalities can be turned into capital for buying new privileges under another system. Inequalities of any kind, therefore, tend to be hardened into a rigid stratification modified only marginally by the limited chance occurrences of extraordinary talent among the disadvantaged or gross incompetence among the privileged. In the case of inequalities among enterprises, the structure is strengthened by relations between powerful and weak enterprises in various forms, especially subcontracting by the weak for the powerful. At the same time, the growth of the population and the relative ease of entry keeps the smaller enterprises in excessive competition among themselves for favors of subcontracting from large and powerful concerns. Thus the large and the powerful profit from the struggling small enterprise. They also gain monopolistic profit from consumers. Furthermore, they are influential over public policy. By their superior ability to pay for whatever they consider desirable, moreover, they enjoy a nearly exclusive use of innovations for profitable technology, production, and marketing.

The structure of inequalities was exacerbated by Japan's reluctance to use foreign capital and by repeated wars followed by the acquisition of additional colonial dependencies. A liberal use of foreign capital by the government and big business would have allowed more resources from the domestic sources to remain in the hands of small producers and thereby would have helped them share more in the process and outcome of economic development. The government's borrowing abroad was limited to emergencies; private borrowing or direct foreign investment in Japan was discouraged or forbidden. In the early Meiji years, the government issued two foreign loans to raise capital for railroad construction and to finance the creation of jobs for the dispossessed samurai. The fear of dependence on foreign capital was so great, however, that borrowing abroad was suspended for more than twenty years until the end of the nineteenth century.

Despite Japan's victory, the Sino-Japanese War (1894–1895) drained Japanese resources because of the necessity of managing Taiwan as a newly acquired colony, bringing Korea under the Japanese sphere of influence, and investing in Southern Manchuria. The Russo-Japanese War (1904–1905) was even more expensive. It was fought by incurring additional heavy debts to foreigners. As a consequence of the war, southern Sakhalin was added to the Japanese empire, investment in Manchuria was accelerated, and Korea soon came into the empire. The components of the Japanese sphere of influence required heavy costs of government, social overhead capital, private direct investment, and so forth. True, economic growth resulting from initial resource inputs into these areas produced an additional foreign demand for exports from Japan proper. The structure of comparative advantage forged between Japan and the colonies, however, well nigh destroyed Japanese agriculture because of the impact of low-cost food imports from the colonies. The damage done to the still dominant base needed for the subsistence of a large proportion of the Japanese labor force intensified the pressure on nonagricultural employment, resulting in massive unemployment after the First World War.

What modern economic growth achieved between 1890 and 1940 for Japan was twofold: (1) the reorganization of the preceding feudal structure of inequalities into a capitalist structure generally associated with an early phase of capitalist development and (2) the emergence of international inequalities within the Japanese empire and adjacent areas. This double outcome issued from the peculiarities of Japan's economic growth, which combined dynastic absolutism and nascent capitalist development. Under this style of economic development, unfair competition characterized the economic process and differential gains made through unfair means were used for solidfying the dynastic stratification. In place of genuinely competitive capitalist markets, a concentration of economic power emerged. In place of international trade among economies of sovereign nations, colonialism emerged. The merits of economic achievement were directly translated into status rewards under the dynastic, aristocratic system of honors and ranks. Even academic achievements were drawn into this system of status rewards—for example, "doctor's degree" (*hakasei-go*; not to be confused with the Western professional degree like the Ph.D.), the privilege of appointment to a chair by the monarch, entitlement to a seat in the House of Peers, and, finally, ennoblement to join the galaxy of illustrous personages around the majestic throne. Co-opted into the status structure of the absolutist regime, businessmen never aspired to a bourgeois republic; nor did scholars forge an appropriate ideology about it. Japan failed to achieve a Western-style enlightenment.

In an unequal society, privileges at one end are usually counterpoised by deprivations at the other end. Japan's structure of inequalities did call forth criticism from a small group of awakened intellectuals as well as protest movements from the dispossessed and dishonored segments of the society. To these forces of opposition the government responded with a skillful manipulation of minor concessions and reckless repression. When first signs of the labor movement arose after the Sino-Japanese War, the government reacted with the Peace Policing Law (1900) which banned all peaceable assemblies in order to prevent the disruption of law and order. On the other hand, the need for the protection of industrial workers against occupational hazards and employer abuses was grudgingly recognized and provided for by the Factory Law (1911) which was put into effect in 1916. The renewed labor movement of the interwar period never obtained legal recognition, despite Japan's international obligation to encourage a free labor movement and to send freely elected representatives of worker organizations to the international labor conferences. Furthermore, the government massively intervened in all social movements to rid them of communist infiltration under the terms of the newly enacted Peace Preservation Law (1925). At the same time, elementary schemes of health insurance and retirement allowances were instituted for the benefit of industrial workers.

By the 1920s, postrestoration Japan was more than fifty years old and the spirit of the times after the First World War generated a hope for greater democracy among the Japanese. The ordinary Japanese had been disenfranchised by a highly restrictive election law which enabled only a handful of the well-to-do to elect members for the House of Representatives. In 1925, universal male suffrage was finally enacted into law accompanied by the Peace Preservation Law which empowered the government to maintain close surveillance over the people's thoughts and actions. The repression of "dangerous" thoughts (socialism and communism) and restrictions on freedom of speech were intensified. In the 1930s Japan came under the sway of the militarists. All protest movements were strangled, and in December 1941 the divine emperor declared war on America, Britain, and their allies. In August 1945, atomic bombs fell on Hiroshima and Nagasaki. The emperor terminated the war on 15 August. A prospect of genuine modernization with emphasis on liberty, humanity, and peace then arose from the ruins of war. The Meiji Constitution was replaced by the new constitution of 1947.

PART II

Have "Modern" and "Modernization" Been Overworked?

THE PRECEDING ESSAYS on "When Does Modern Japan Begin?" contain a number of references to the problem of modernization as a theme for modern Japanese history. As stated in Mikiso Hane's introduction and elaborated in John Hall's essay, the idea of using modernization as a "value-free" yardstick for studying Japanese history of recent centuries emerged from the Hakone Conference of 1960. Though widely accepted as a yardstick for years, it became in the 1970s highly suspect in some historians' quarters as by no means value-free and hence unsuitable for the role in which it was being utilized.

Indeed, in the two essays presented here, Thomas Havens and Ardath Burks argue that the time has come to move beyond modernization and even beyond modern in approaching the study of Japanese history. Serving as an excellent counterpoint to the *when* question posed in Part I, they ask here *whether* we should be talking about modern and modernization so much. The authors are less concerned with locating specific origins in the Meiji era, or before, or beyond, than in trying to see how the course of Japanese history will look in the future. Whether they are errant futurologists or not we leave for the reader to ponder.

—HILARY CONROY

Beyond Modernization: Society, Culture, and the Underside of Japanese History

Thomas R. H. Havens

Modernization is no longer the main thread of writings on recent Japanese history—not because the theme is trivial or overfamiliar but because it has succeeded in meeting its limited goals. Since the late 1950s, a generation of non-Marxist social scientists have used the concept of modernization to explain how Japan developed a powerful state and economy during the past century. Their findings have illuminated a lot of murky problems that were previously unrecognized in Japan or abroad: the nature of late feudal politics and production, who led the Meiji Restoration in 1868 and why, how decisions were reached in domestic and foreign policy, where capital was accumulated and invested, and dozens of other details about how Japan turned so rapidly into an influential and prosperous country. But, like any tool, modernization was intended for only certain defined tasks. Because it has done its job so competently, the theme has probably reached the limits of its effectiveness and has nearly vanished as a model for fresh investigation.

Historians are preoccupied with changes that occur in individuals and groups. The concept of modernization often troubles them because it seems to prize stability and order while overlooking process and change. Tokugawa Japan (1603–1868) has been sketched as a stable, functioning society that fell into "dysfunction" in the mid-nineteenth century. The image of modernization is the portrait of how Japanese leaders created a new, secure structure and put it in smooth running order. Lost in this view of function–dysfunction–new function is the dynamism, perplexity, and ceaseless change of ordinary life everywhere in Japan.

Also missing is the sharp break with the past that happened in 1868. Modernization has directed general attention to the elements that persisted from the old order to the new—entrepreneurship, schools, talented leadership, the throne, and so forth. The years after 1868 were of course a period of enormous change. And it is also true that modernization has never quite explained what it is to be modern. The concept has been far more useful in understanding politics and economics than in clarifying the psychological and intellectual question of modernity—what it means to be a modern person, how being modern differs from the past, whether the Japanese today are modern, nonmodern, or simply contemporary.

A vogue of structuralism has recently helped displace modernization as the main organizing thread of Japanese history. Writers under the influence of the anthropologists Claude Lévi-Strauss and Mircea Eliade believe that fundamental social structures—above all, the family patterning of society—have endured in Japan from earliest times to the present. This emphasis on social continuities is welcome because they seem to be true and real. But historians cannot find in structuralism any more attention to the idea of change than in modernization. (In fact there may be even less.) And structuralists usually assert the fundamental oneness of all human social patterns everywhere in the world, whereas historians are often concerned with the particularities that make Japan's recent experience distinctive, perhaps even unique.

Structuralism in a general sense is still useful because it indirectly invites attention to a problem too little explained by modernization: the history of society. Now that the political and economic framework for Japanese development is well understood, local history, the history of social groups and classes, and the record of daily life in recent decades can reveal a great deal that escaped the net of modernization. Field surveys, computerized analyses, oral history, family reconstitution, and even psychoanalytic techniques (if not rigidly deterministic) are new instruments that transcend and supplant the device of modernization. But without the prior mapwork by scholars of modernization, the fresh terrain would be much harder to scout.

The history of society is one of three important aspects of recent Japanese life that modernization has been powerless to explain. A second is the more foreboding side of Japanese life since the late nineteenth century: political terrorism, chauvinism in foreign policy, ultranationalism amid economic depression, and the bizarre schemes of political and social controls during wartime, 1937 to 1945. Because of its focus on leaders and elites, modernization has also deflected attention from citizens' movements, pacifism, utopian communities, and nonconformist dogmas in religion, politics, and philosophy—vital components of the underside of recent Japanese history.

A third matter beyond the grasp of modernization is the cultural transformation that has taken place in two stages. The first is the efflorescence of creativity in Japanese literature and painting during the first quarter of this century—the revolution in "higher culture" among privileged urban classes familiar with both the Japanese artistic heritage and Western ideas. The second stage is the massive internationalization of the arts since the mid-1950s and their diffusion to every village and social class. Music, architecture, painting, sculpture, fiction, poetry, drama, and the dance are widely known, patronized, and appreciated throughout the country. This change stems from affluence, a high-technology information society based on the media, and a long-standing aesthetic sensitivity among the public. Higher culture and mass culture have largely merged into a broad popular mode in food, fashion, and the arts, creating a cultural style closer to the twenty-first century than to the years before 1945 with which modernization has been concerned.

Beyond Modern

Ardath W. Burks

It cannot be stated with certainty that modernization was an over-worked theme. It could have been, it probably was, a dated approach. Although the theme was first sounded by the historians, they themselves were tremendously influenced by the counterpoint provided by the social scientists. And when modernization was most popular, the latter were mainly concerned with development, specifically with culture change and culture contact.

Despite all the disclaimers, modernization did imply something of patterned change. For some of the social scientists, it was yet another aspect of search which placed emphasis on the scientific rather than the social. In one field, political science, great effort was devoted to finding the truly comparative. That is to say, the social scientist would be more comfortable approaching the *universal;* at the opposite extreme is the traditional historian, who would continue to be fascinated by the *unique* in cultures. At the time, this author wrote: "In fact, data to support an evolutionary theory in the realm of social change may be harder to come by than experimental data which demonstrate the force of evolution in biology."

Moreover, the concept of modernization really did imply a patterned progress toward "modern and Western." Modernization theorists were quick to point out the seductive simplicity of such popularizations and "the non-Western world." Sophisticated observers of Japan escaped from the crude concept "westernization." They took refuge in more accurate, if more difficult, phrases like "the impact of the West." The two—modernization and the impact—were doubtless related, but they were seen as independent variables. Finally, casual but shrewd visitors to Tokyo came to recognize that, whatever did happen in Japanese society since the nineteenth century, the culture was neither westernized nor, later, Americanized. Tokyo culture may have come to represent one of the few "worldized" styles: with a vertical society adapted over centuries from Chinese Confucianism; with vestigial religious beliefs adapted from Indian Buddhism; with basic arts and crafts filtered through Korea; with a faith in consumerism and reliance on marketing adapted from America; with a basic administrative structure remodeled from German, British, and American plans; and with an aesthetic sense which is characteristically Japanese, perhaps most closely attuned to French style. Technology and airport culture have been adapted from no one, of course, since they belong to all.

Usually the skilled observer escaped from this dilemma—that Japan constantly changed and yet remained the same—by stating that the society has Japanized all the imports. Or, to cite a Japanese author writing in *Bungei Shunju,* Japanese modernization has shown "abnormal adaptability." It was hard to figure out from this description whether modernization was good or bad.

Furthermore, just as westernization implied an ethnocentric view, a culture bias, so modernization suggested a temporicentric view, a time bias. Modernization was temporal in two senses of the word. First, the modern era had lasted only for a time; the concept tried unsuccessfully to exclude all the elements that were traditional. And, second, modern was of this world, worldly as distinguished from spiritual. Again sophisticated observers recognized the problem: that somehow modernized Japanese culture included a number of highly functional traditional elements. Robert Ward, for example, stated: "The history of the modernization of Japan . . . demonstrates in many ways not only the ability of 'modern' institutions and practices to coexist with 'traditional' ones for substantial periods of time, but also the manner in which 'traditional' attitudes and practices can be of great positive value to the modernization process "

One difficulty, which on reflection we can now perhaps recognize, lies in the subtly different uses of these terms. Tradition, if sharply defined, is used in an anthropological sense: it can encompass persistent values, norms, and attitudes (as well as the process of socialization) within a fuedal, a postfeudal, or developed society; it can be found in village Japan, in preindustrial, urban Japan, or in contemporary industrial, urban Japan. The term "modern" always has a more limited meaning; it never quite escapes from imprecise and careless usage in the hands of the ordinary layman. It is temporal and therefore dated.

If our concept of modernization had difficulty including traditional elements inherited from the past by the modern society, how much more troublesome it is to think of the other end of the continuum. Is modernization the be-all and end-all of the society? Does Norman's "modern state" emerge and then freeze? Does Kahn's "superstate" explode into orbit and then resolve endlessly? The problem is, of course, that historical time is no respecter of terminology. Ideas themselves—for example, concepts of modernization—are no sooner defined and set into place than the pace of development outdistances theory. Let us turn now to a rather more concrete example.

The phenomenon of the city (and the process of urbanization) reinforces the assumption that ideas need constant refining. In a somewhat crude fashion, we have come to realize that modernization has something to do with urbanization—whether cause, effect, or both, we are not quite sure. The vast majority of "nonmodernized" people live in rural, agricultural rather than in urban, industrial environments. In Japan, the migration of villagers from Agraria to Industria has been spectacular and has occurred in our time. Now shrewd analysts like Gideon Sjoberg have tempered this concept by usefully visualizing non-Western urban complexes or, more accurately, pre-industrial cities. We have become familiar with the remarkable emergence of the castle town (*jōkamachi*) and the Genroku urban style and their role in laying down the foundations for the modern, megalopolitan structure of Japan.

Once again, however, contemporary urban culture in Japan illustrates how ideas about modernization were culturally determined and time-bound. The fact is, urban culture in Japan may already have moved from a postfeudal past through the modernizing, transitional period to and beyond the modern, industrial stage.

Modern (if we may use that word) observers are beginning to use quite different terms, which may well leave modernization in the dim past. It is just as well: modernization was a useful, if temporary, frame. We knew what it was. We could describe "the modern condition." Wryly we admitted we did not quite understand the process that brought it about. And we never felt comfortable with the word. (The devil theory that modernization was a carefully wrought approach used by scholars of The Establishment to justify contemporary policy, which in turn was designed to recreate a familiar pluralism out of Western, capitalist democracy into developing, dependent societies, can readily be dismissed as without foundation in fact.)

The concept of the postindustrial society was applied first within a familiar, largely Western context. It was inconceivable that Japan could have entered a stage of development *before* Western societies. In any case, the phenomenon was classified under different, highly imaginative rubrics: David Riesman (who *had* visited Japan) rather casually coined the term "postindustrial" in 1958. Daniel Bell then seized upon that word and popularized it. Some observers referred rather to "the temporary society," and a brace of authors (including Gideon Sjoberg) called it the postwelfare state. Meanwhile John Galbraith was writing about "the new industrial state" and "the age of uncertainty," while Zbigniew Brzezinsky (who had described Japan in *The Fragile Blossom*) spoke of "the technetronic era." Even before *gaijin*, the outsiders, recognized the implications for theory of Japan's experience, Japanese themselves spoke of their "information society" *(kahō shakai)*. The term "postindustrial" has, however, become popular and now social scientists have begun systematically to apply the concept to Japan. Indeed, on occasion Japanese society has been recognized as prologue to the future.

The idea of a postindustrial society may, of course, be dated too, but the concept at least carries a good deal more precision than the term "modern." A set of relatively simple economic guidelines may be used to identify the postindustrial society and quite clearly to place Japan within the category.

In 1958 Walt W. Rostow offered a new twist on stages-of-economic-growth theory by characterizing the "mass consumption society." In technical terms it was a matter of the level of capital accumulation and per capita national income. Certainly by the 1960s not only had the Japanese economy won membership in the exclusive growth club but also the Japanese themselves were fully aware of the GNP Game. In general terms poverty was no longer an economic problem of production, although of course it may have remained a social problem of distribution. Alongside this objectively observed fact was the related movement of the postindustrial society into a tertiary stage of development.

Those who studied the history of Japan and got caught up in the fad of modernization were familiar with the dramatic transition from primary, agrarian to secondary, industrial pursuits. The movement had its own indicator: the growth of the industrial-urban settlements, Manchester and Pittsburgh in the West, Tokyo, Nagoya, and Yawata in Japan. It was then noted that as GNP and income rose, there was a parallel rise in the service sector. A. G. B. Fisher, Colin Clark, Simon Kuznets, and others began to refer to primary (agricultural), secondary (industrial), and tertiary (service) sectors. Probably by the late

1960s, certainly by the early 1970s, well over 50 percent of Japan's labor force was already in the service sector. By 1963 the output by the service sector in Japan (as a proportion of GNP) had passed the 50 percent level. In Japan, of course, as in many other countries, the various sectors continued to coexist: preindustrial, agrarian rice culture in the villages; industrial, blue-collar culture in the cities; and postindustrial, white-collar *sarari man* culture in the bedroom suburbs of megalopolis.

It is sometimes useful, at this stage of an argument, to refocus from the macrolevel to the microlevel, to descend from the grand-abstract to the mundane-concrete. One has only to pay a backstage visit to the Tokyo Broadcasting Center of Nippon Hōsō Kyōkai to witness effects of the significant transition to the tertiary stage, the era of service-centered employment, and postindustrial style. The NHK Center is one of the temples dedicated to technetronic religion.

Completed in June 1968, the center in Shibuya is, of course, the product of a highly advanced, industrial society. It consists of a 23-story building, with two 8-story wings, housing 22 television studios and 23 radio stations and occupying some 23,000 square meters. Most striking is NHK–TOPICS (total on-line program and information control system), a completely computerized system for implementing program production and automatic transmission. TOPICS has two children in the NHK family: SMART (schedule management and allocating resource technique), which arranges necessary schedules, automatically allocates facilities, and assigns skilled staff; and ABC (automatic broadcast control), which automatically carries out switching and control of production and transmission. Impressive as the hardware is, in other words, the software is far more significant. Most employees at the center are highly skilled, white-collar, service specialists. And the product is a service.

As is well known, most Japanese households have television (and most of them have color). A 1975 NHK survey indicates that 93 percent of all Japanese watch television at least once a day (95 percent on Sunday). The average viewing time per person is 3 hours and 19 minutes a day (4 hours and 11 minutes on Sunday). Respondents covered by the survey indicate that news comes to Japanese mostly through television; and television has a desirable cultural and educational influence, conserving traditional Japanese culture, spreading new ways of thinking, and allowing deeper understanding of conditions overseas. By the way, backstage the players in the daily historical drama on what looks like a kabuki set are, of course, older, experienced actors.

On the fringes of the set, the directors, crews, and technicians are very young. In the hallways of NHK are middle-aged white-collar planners, coordinators, computer specialists, and researchers.

This scene, which could be repeated in many fields, simply symbolizes the drift of highly skilled Japanese labor into the service-software sector: communications, government service, education, research and development, medical care, pollution control, entertainment, banking, real estate sales, marketing, insurance, and foreign trade. The industrial city, which could have been and should have been decentralized, is supplanted by the postindustrial city, which thrives on the concentration of neotechnical skills.

If one more brief digression be permitted, it might be noted that Japan's celebrated and articulate critic-authors have been slow to pick up the implications of Japan's plunge into the postindustrial environment. One writer has likened Japan to a black-hole star, composed of matter which has shrunk to the point of maximun density. Although information-gathering at home and mass transmission services are highly sophisticated, very little of this immense energy is devoted to overseas communication. Japan is thus a highly sensitive receiver, as opposed to an efficient transmitter civilization, according to this social critic.

Meanwhile scholars, both Japanese and Westerners, have begun to explore the implications of the newly identified transition into the postindustrial era. In very brief summary, first there is an air of confusion, consisting of both a popular ambivalence as among traditional, preindustrial, industrial, and postindustrial values and a failure of leadership to recognize new issues. Indeed new problems—distribution of wealth, fiscal policy and inflation, the costs of industrialization (mainly pollution), and the quality of life after growth—completely transcend the stances, platforms, and rhetoric of the familiar political parties of right, left, and center. Party problems are still the product of an earlier industrial age of scarcity and competition. New modes of dissent appear, some violent, as brand-new urban coalitions struggle to provide additional channels for citizens' participation in politics. The alternative is pragmatism and even skepticism verging on withdrawal, perhaps the end of ideology. Even the political scientists, equipped with the most up-to-date and sophisticated survey techniques, take refuge in such phrases as "persistent tradition," "modern attitudes," "nonpartisans," "the floating vote," "urban communes," "alienation," and "cultural politics." Political prediction becomes peril.

At the time of this writing we cannot foresee the outcome of the transition into the postindustrial era. It might even be possible to apply to this development, too, the term modernization. The theme is not overworked or dated, provided it allows for change beyond the familiar "modern" of our industrial revolution. There is an interesting historical parallel here, but we may not be able to understand it until later. Now we know that many features of Japan's celebrated Edo era, particularly during the waning of Tokugawa power *(bakumatsu)*, bore a remarkable resemblance to the matrix known in the West as feudalism. As Edwin O. Reischauer pointed out, however, those characteristics were in fact better described as postfeudal. We also know that, soon thereafter, Japan entered upon a remarkable process of what has been called modernization. Perhaps the mature stage of this change will be known as postmodern.

PART III

The Meiji Restoration: Product of Gradual Decay, Abrupt Crisis, or Creative Will?

IN EARLY 1868 the leaders of the Tokugawa shogunate *(bakufu)* were swept from their positions of hereditary power, and in following months hereditary leaders of most daimyo domains *(han)* followed their former superiors into obscurity. In their place other men forged a new governing system, the Meiji political order, in which samurai status was abolished and a unified imperial government ruled a nation of diligent subjects.

This change in political system has been treated in many ways by historians. It has been viewed as the product of a confrontation between Western imperialism and Japanese nationalism. It has been treated in terms of a confrontation between feudalism and capitalism: some writers see bourgeois elements displacing anachronistic feudal forces while others see a sinister outcome in which feudal and bourgeois elements struck an unholy alliance at the expense of the masses. Some have linked the themes of capitalism and imperialism in terms of international monopoly capitalism confronting Japanese feudalism. Others have analyzed the Meiji Restoration more precisely in terms of dissatisfied lower-ranking samurai overthrowing their masters and forging a new polity. The themes of internal decay and external threat have been integrated in intellectual terms as the collapse of one normative order and its replacement by another or as a process in which culturally enlightened elements displaced reactionary forces. In another formulation the domestic and foreign themes have been linked in terms of dissident feudal groups—leaders of the daimyo domains prompted by domanial ambition and by alarm at the imperialist intrusion—rebelling against their decadent liege lord the Tokugawa shogun and doing so successfully precisely because of the solidity of the feudal order in their domains.

These formulations differ in their particulars, but they all perceive Japanese society essentially in terms of three basic configurations. One configuration depicts Japan as an entity interacting with external entities. Another portrays Japan divided vertically into feudal domains. The third pictures Japan riven horizontally along class or status lines. Most studies of the restoration regard all three configurations as real; differences of interpretation arise primarily in terms of their specific manifestations, patterns of interaction, and relative importance to the political outcome.

These three basic configurations appear in the essays presented here, and with modest exaggeration the essays can be juxtaposed to each other starkly in terms of the three. Harold Bolitho sees considerations of self-interest, expressed most fully as domanial interest, as decisive in the restoration; the emperor, symbol of the nation, is invoked consciously as political rhetoric. For Thomas Huber class consciousness wedded to an elemental sense of social justice is decisive; domanial and national political considerations are marginal. In my essay, national political considerations are crucial in goading people to act; questions of domain and status are only of instrumental consequence, shaping the form, not the purpose, of political action.

There are other areas of disagreement among the essays. One well-worn problem is whether the Tokugawa system collapsed because of complications created by the imperialist intrusion of the mid-nineteenth century or whether it was falling apart anyway. On that issue I argue the former position, Bolitho and Huber the latter. We three differ also in our assessments of the major political initiatives of the 1860s. Bolitho regards the "Union of Court and Camp" (*Kōbu Gattai*) movement as a futile decentralizing initiative of daimyo seeking to replace *bakufu* hegemony with a coalition regime of independent domains. He sees it being followed by the "Revere Emperor, Expel Barbarians" (*Son'nō Jōi*) movement, a movement of middle and lower samurai from all over Japan, which overthrew the old regime in 1868. I see both *Kōbu Gattai* and *Son'nō Jōi* as voluntaristic movements of the early sixties that came to nought, giving way to more ruthless strategies of radical change in which national unification would be achieved by armed force. Huber is in essential agreement with me that *Son'nō Jōi*—the "Heaven's Revenge" of his Choshu activists—developed into a more ruthless strategy during the late sixties. However, he is at odds with both Bolitho and me insofar as we both see reformist movements emerging within the *bakufu* as well as elsewhere in Japan while Huber regards the *bakufu* as the bastion of conservatism protecting the interests of privileged upper samurai.

More important, all three of us differ in our sense of how profound was the change being sought by those who overthrew the older order. Bolitho asserts that Japan of the 1860s needed more central coordination than the Tokugawa political system (*bakuhan taisei*) could provide, but he indicates that it was the pursuit of personal self-interest rather than any national goal that motivated political actors of the day. Huber speaks directly of lower-ranking samurai seeking a more equitable society governed by more competent people. I am more explicit yet, attributing to radicals a clear intention of building a unified imperial regime dedicated to substantial social change and industrial development.

In one basic way we three essayists are in agreement. We all focus on the samurai class. Bolitho refers to peasant discontent at one point, but in the end he joins Huber and me in regarding the restoration as a samurai achievement with no noteworthy contribution from commoners. Huber's distinction between upper and lower samurai notwithstanding, the picture that emerges from the essays is that of an "aristocratic revolution," which is what T. C. Smith called the Meiji Restoration in 1961. The reader may well ask, therefore, how a political reorganization engineered by samurai could end up with the abolition of hereditary samurai status and security. Was it because the samurai had seen their world gradually decaying for decades anyway, because they saw it swept abruptly into unmanageable crisis by the mid-century imperialist intrusion, or because they possessed the ingenuity and will to create a new and better order with or without provocation? I believe it is the historian's task to grasp these—and other—dimensions of the experience and understand how they fitted together to eventuate in modern Japan.

—CONRAD TOTMAN

The Meiji Restoration

Harold Bolitho

Two processes were involved in the Meiji Restoration. The first, culminating in the overthrow of the Tokugawa *bakufu*, was a gradual, cumulative, and almost total erosion of authority. The second, launched in the decade after the *bakufu* was overturned, was the construction, piece by piece, of forms of authority far more effective than any previously seen in Japan. My interest lies in the former process, the erosion of authority, together with its consequences.

By the beginning of the nineteenth century, it had become plain to a great many Japanese that the Tokugawa system was no longer functioning properly—if, indeed, it ever had. In the abstract, it had offered a remarkably tidy form of government. The notion of a shogunate, at the center, directing national policy in the emperor's name while, in the provinces, obedient and cooperative daimyo cared for the samurai and farmers entrusted to them was undeniably a beguiling one. Unfortunately it was also unreal.

As the Tokugawa period wore on, this *bakuhan taisei* system revealed unmistakable symptoms of an administrative paralysis from which few of its elements proved immune. In the country, the authority of shogun and daimyo alike was successfully flouted by farmers pursuing land reclamation schemes, commercial agriculture, small-scale industry, and usury with an enthusiasm exceeded only by the energy with which they fought against government restraints. Matters were no better in the cities and castle towns, where the various local governments found commercial control increasingly difficult.

The samurai class too were much less amenable to authority than they had once been. They were, after all, the victims not only of a general financial malaise but of profound social and economic changes to which neither ideology nor training had accustomed them. At best, in a time of rising prices, they lived on fixed incomes; all too often those incomes were further diminished by the demands of their lords. The samurai were therefore restive, prepared to be more critical of established authority, and much more anxious to exert upon it what influence they could gather.

Similarly there had been an open deterioration in relations between the daimyo domains and the Tokugawa government. Of course all daimyo, and their senior administrators, were prepared to pledge alliance to the Tokugawa house as they had always done; but like so much else, this vow had become a formality. Neither *bakufu* nor daimyo domains could interfere with each other or make demands. For one thing, they did not have the money. For another, they could not be sure of the cooperation of their samurai.

With large sections of the system effectively out of control, the Japanese had to face two unpalatable consequences. The first was that no superior had any more than a nominal, or at best conditional, authority over those for whom he was responsible. The likely outcome in a crisis, therefore, would be the end of restraint and the collapse of law and order. The second, no less ominous, was that when the power to command obedience vanished so too did the ability to protect. In a crisis, therefore, few could look to their superiors to help them if law and order went.

One by one the control mechanisms of the system failed: in the countryside the frequency, and the scale, of agrarian risings mounted and banditry reappeared; in the towns and cities reports of riots and looting told a similar story; among the domains it grew easier than ever before for the large and powerful to dominate their smaller neighbors without fear of *bakufu* restraint; on the national level, the foreign policy crisis after 1853 made it clear that the Tokugawa government, entrusted with the duty of protecting emperor and empire from foreign aggression, was unable to do anything of the kind.

Such pressures obliged the people of Tokugawa Japan to look to their own protection. In the countryside it became not uncommon for farmers to organize militia forces, or *nōhei*, for their own protection, whether against bandits, rioters, rebels, or foreigners. At a higher level, daimyo domains developed elaborate defense policies of their own, quite independent of a *bakufu* from which they could expect no protection and to which they were prepared to offer only token assistance. Some formed militia units; others produced arms or imported them, secretly and illegally, from gunrunners in Nagasaki; still others did all three. Diplomatically, too, the domains became openly independent, negotiating first with each other, then with the imperial court, and finally with foreign representatives. All three forms of diplomacy contravened the practice of more than two centuries, but they were nevertheless avenues to security which few domains could afford to ignore.

The general decline in authority, and its accompanying political fragmentation, did not escape the attention of nineteenth-century Japanese, but the system was too well established to be toppled without considerable expense and risk, and none of its constituent elements was assertive enough to force anybody to bother. In 1840, however, once the troubling reports of British victories in the Opium War arrived, the situation changed. Inevitably it would merely be a matter of time before the foreigners turned their acquisitive gaze from hapless China to defenseless Japan.

Once they did so, as many responsible Japanese were aware, then Japan would have cause to regret her want of internal cohesion. Accordingly, from 1850 onwards Japanese were searching tentatively for solutions to their dilemma—how best to organize against certain foreign pressure and even foreign invasion.

Of the three strongest plans to emerge after 1840, the earliest came from inside the Tokugawa *bakufu* itself in the guise of a reform movement aimed at producing a coordinated and effective response to foreign interference. Many *bakufu* administrators recognized a need for a form of government far stronger, and with a far greater degree of coercive power, than Japan had yet seen. Naturally, as *bakufu* officials, they thought first of restoring the lapsed powers of their government and then, with that achieved, of proceeding to win other powers—particularly in relation to the daimyo domains—of a new and different kind. This policy surfaced first in the Tempō Reforms, later in the government of Ii Naosuke, and finally—desperately—with Oguri Tadamasa in 1865.

A movement toward a refurbished and reinvigorated *bakufu*, while it clearly offered the Japanese one form of escape from their dilemma, proved far from universally acceptable. The dismissal of Mizuno Tadakuni, architect of the Tempō Reforms, the assassination of Ii Naosuke, and the summary execution of Oguri Tadamasa all demonstrate just how unacceptable it was. Its unpopularity came from the demands it seemed likely to make upon various sections of the community. The daimyo, the samurai, and the common people all valued their independence far too much to surrender it meekly; nor were they willing to relinquish it to a government which, like the Tokugawa *bakufu*, seemed so closely identified with the interests of one particular group—the senior branch of the Tokugawa family. It may be that the *bakufu*'s very modest record of administrative efficiency also robbed that particular solution of such little charm as it had. Whatever the reason, the movement was mortally stricken by Ii Naosuke's assassination; the wounding of Andō Nobumasa in 1862 was merely the *coup de grâce*. Thereafter it won no support beyond lower-echelon *bakufu* bureaucrats. It found its leaders then among men like Oguri Tadakan, who, isolated from all other sources of power, was willing to ally himself with the French in an effort to revive the *bakufu*.

Rejecting *bakufu* authority, however, while it undeniable preserved local independence, took Japan no further toward the central coordination she so urgently needed. This was one predicament which would not go away. Consequently, even the opponents of a revitalized *bakufu* were forced into some positive response. It was in this context that the second plan appeared. This was the *Kōbu Gattai* solution—allegedly a compromise between two conflicting diplomatic positions but in fact a movement to eviscerate the Tokugawa *bakufu* while retaining only its administrative carapace to conceal a totally different form of government. Policy was to be determined by a number of people previously unconnected, in any formal sense, with the Tokugawa *bakufu:* Tokugawa Nariaki, Matsudaira Yoshinaga, Yamanouchi Toyōshige, and Date Munenari are perhaps the most notable. Their concern was for regional independence—at least for the large domains —but with a far greater degree of cooperation and consultation among daimyo than the old *bakufu*, malleable though it was, could ever have countenanced. They also shared an implacable opposition to Tokugawa authority and a resolute hostility to the political activities of their samurai subordinates.

Although the term *Kōbu Gattai* was not to appear until the beginning of the 1860s as a policy, it had had a lengthy history, having surfaced most recently in the government of Abe Masahiro. Abe, it will be recalled, had abandoned the *bakufu*'s ancient restrictions on shipbuilding and thus opened the door for the expansion of the regional navies. In 1862, some of Abe's spiritual successors—among them Matsudaira Yoshinaga, Matsudaira Katamori, and Tokugawa Yoshinobu —came to hold influential positions from which they, too, further curtailed what remained of *bakufu* authority; the relaxation of *sankin kōtai* obligations in 1862 must be seen in this light. The other main area of *Kōbu Gattai* concern—the growing political involvement of disaffected samurai—also produced some notable victories in the 1860s, beginning symbolically with the Teradaya massacre.

Despite such successes, however, the *Kōbu Gattai* approach offered no real solution to Japan's problems. By its very nature it depended on a degree of mutual trust, cooperation, and power sharing among daimyo and their senior advisors for which none of them was prepared. The movement came to an end among a welter of personal differences in 1865. Only its negative aspects—hostility to the Tokugawa *bakufu* and reluctance to share inherited power with either samurai or common people—remained.

The final, and successful, approach to emerge from Japan's difficulties in the years after Perry was that of the *Son'nō Jōi,* or loyalist movement, by which the Tokugawa *bakufu* was utterly destroyed, even to the dismantling of its shell. In its place was insinuated a government with a degree of authority not very dissimilar to that urged by *bakufu* reformers. Its adherents, largely from the lower and middle ranks of samurai society, were drawn from all over Japan, in particular from Satsuma, Chōshū, and Tosa. They were opposed equally to a refurbished Tokugawa *bakufu* and to any government dominated by daimyo. The former sentiment was openly acknowledged. But the latter, wisely, was not revealed until some time after the *bakufu* had been overturned; for without a measure of daimyo acquiescence, if not cooperation, the enterprise would have failed.

As it was, the *Son'nō Jōi* group was able to push through a coup d'état at the end of 1867, thereby accomplishing the first stage of the Meiji Restoration. It is perhaps worth emphasizing that few took part in the coup, so few that any combination of daimyo and samurai, if determined to save the *bakufu,* could have done so. They did not bother, however, simply because they did not feel they had anything to fear from its passing. Such resistance as there was to the coup and its aftermath came almost entirely from those—for the most part from the rank of *hatamato* and *gokenin*—whose estates, stipends, and offices were put at risk by the ending of Tokugawa authority.

Certainly it would be difficult to argue that significant numbers of daimyo were greatly concerned with anything other than their security of tenure. Their chief interest lay in their domains, to preserve which they were prepared to take whatever steps appeared necessary. Naturally the paths open to them varied from case to case, according to considerations like the size and location of each domain. The leaders of many large domains, such as Kaga, Echizen, and Tosa, while they viewed the coup and its makers with substantial misgivings, preferred the safety of total inactivity.

The leaders of the new government, all of whom (save for a handful of courtiers) were samurai, and most of whom came from the great domains of the southwest, lost no time in building the sort of nation they wanted. In the face of dangerous pressures from abroad and mounting unrest at home, they could afford no delay. So they moved quickly to affirm their control, obliterating all traces of daimyo authority, making an end to the samurai class, creating a conscript army, and using this army, in combination with the newly established police force, to reduce the considerable pockets of tension which remained. Consequently they were able to make Japan a fairly united and stable country at a time when unity and stability were at a premium. By giving strong and authoritarian direction to Japan's affairs, and restoring law and order, they could be said to have saved their country from her late Tokugawa *(bakumatsu)* predicament—and saved her, too, from the worst consequences of her weakness. There is little doubt, however, that a reformed Tokugawa *bakufu,* had one ever been developed, would have followed similar policies.

It will be noticed that this account of the Meiji Restoration has neglected the question of the emperor. I have done so deliberately. True, the imperial institution was the focus of opposition to the *bakufu* in the 1850s and 1860s. It could hardly have been otherwise. In the lexicon of Tokugawa Japan no political action, no matter how clear-cut its practical objective, could be sustained without recourse to the concept of loyalty: the standard political reflex was to declare oneself loyal and one's opponents disloyal. Opposition to the *bakufu,* therefore, had to be justified by a plea, whether genuine or not, to a higher loyalty—and that was, inevitably, to the emperor. Of course, the events I have described took place at the same time as a philosophical movement endowing the imperial institution with a completely new significance. This movement, confined largely to libraries, did not affect the political developments of which I have written save only to furnish them with a more extravagant vocabulary.

This account of the restoration ignores two other considerations beloved of historians. One of these is the question of ability, a quality which, while never assessed by any objective criteria, is notwithstanding customarily reserved for those who overthrew the *bakufu.* Ability is no more reliable a yardstick than loyalty, however; one is naturally able, and one's opponent just as naturally stupid. Ability ranked second only to loyalty in the Tokugawa lexicon; each was a quality restricted to winners. The possibility of any political figure being at the same time loyal and incompetent was not one which a Japanese of the Tokugawa period would willingly contemplate; still more unthinkable would have been the defeat of anyone both loyal and able.

The second of the two considerations I have excluded is that of daimyo status, specifically the influence of *fudai* status on the behavior of those who held it. I have suggested at length elsewhere that labels like *fudai*, *tozama*, and *kamon* had long outlived any tangible meaning they may once have had. There seems little reason to believe that *fudai* status, however much invoked, determined domain behavior during the *bakumatsu* years. Far more significant were considerations like domain size and location. Small domains, many of which were *fudai*, had neither the resources nor the will to jeopardize their existence by supporting a losing cause. Accordingly they sided with whichever party seemed most likely to win.

I also believe that, in the course of these events, there is little point in asking whether any of the actors were more or less socially progressive than any other. Scholars have contended that the *Son'nō Jōi* movement, because of its links with farmers and rural businessmen, was more democratic than any other political group at the time. On this issue it is difficult to see anything to choose between them. Nor do I consider it useful to examine the influence of popular opinion on the course of the restoration. No doubt popular unrest injected an element of urgency into political deliberations, but there is nothing to suggest that it influenced the direction of those deliberations. If nothing else, the later development of the Meiji state confirms this.

The Chōshū Activists and 1868

Thomas M. Huber

Many factors converged to bring about the establishment in Japan of the new Meiji government in 1868. Still, the most essential and dynamic of those factors was probably the group of men known to history as the Chōshū activists. They came from the southwestern domain of Chōshū and were at first only a circle of scholars and administrators concerned over the social injustice within and the foreign threat without. In the turbulent decades of the 1850s and 1860s, this loose association of Chōshū's thoughtful professional men was antagonized, provoked, and transformed into an insurrectionary cadre dedicated to the restructuring of society as they knew it. Some of their more youthful and idealistic members involved themselves in the strenuous contest of ideas which took place in the 1850s, and this commitment led all of them gradually but inexorably into a far more hazardous struggle on the battlefield. In 1866, having by then little choice, they dealt a swift and stunning defeat to the massive *bakufu* armies sent to suppress them. This victory, perhaps more than anything else, made construction of the Meiji state possible, and it would be farsighted leaders from Chōshū—Kido Kōin, Itō Hirobumi, and Yamagata Aritomo—who would serve for several generations as the vital nucleus of the Meiji government.

While Chōshū men were at the forefront of the particular combination of reformers which prevailed in 1868, countless other leaders from scores of domains besides Chōshū shared reformist perceptions and interests similar to those of their peers in Chōshū. These other reformers outnumbered the Chōshū leadership many times over, even though they lacked the opportunities of their Chōshū counterparts to lead the last decisive campaigns against the old regime. These numerous reformist sympathizers also contributed importantly to the Meiji outcome—by influencing the climate of public opinion throughout, by providing the Chōshū movement with ideas in the fifties and men in the sixties, and by joining the Chōshū leaders in the new Meiji government after 1868.

There is abundant evidence to indicate that both the Chōshū rebels and many of their allies were motivated primarily by a gnawing sense of social grievance. Although Tokugawa Japan is said to have been ruled by the samurai class, there were in reality two distinct kinds of samurai. John Hall has referred to them as "legitimizing" samurai and "service" samurai. According to the contemporary observer Fukuzawa Yukichi, these two categories of samurai were characterized by different modes of dress, different patterns of speech, and different standards of living. They were strictly forbidden to intermarry. Fukuzawa once described the social distance between the two strata in this way:

> A lower samurai might aspire to promotion within his own class, but he would no more hope to enter the ranks of the upper samurai than would a four-legged beast hope to fly like a bird. . . . Even in cases of adultery, both parties nearly always came from the same class. [*Monumenta Nipponica* 9(1)(April 1953):310–311]

The legitimizing samurai, the upper stratum, were a privileged minority who received princely incomes from the domanial treasury and were, as a matter of lineage, appointed almost automatically to the most prestigious and influential positions in domanial governments. The service samurai, the lower stratum, represented a much larger number of persons who lived frugally themselves and were as a group the most highly educated and professional element in Tokugawa society. It was this class of disciplined and literate service operatives who carried out the complicated and increasingly technical business of government and who, as part of their sober vocation, nourished, reaped, and gathered a steadily growing harvest of social treasure. As master technicians of political economy, they managed an increasingly prosperous society and were able to draw increasing wealth from that society in the form of taxes and other levies. This substantial tax yield, having no other socially approved use, then constituted a lavish fund which the nobiliary legitimizing samurai habitually consumed in elaborate display and the pursuit of luxury.

A household of the service samurai depended for its livelihood and survival on its adult male member's winning an official position in the domanial bureaucracy. The number of these positions was limited, and appointment depended on the demonstration of superior ability during a young samurai's education at his domain's academy (the Meirinkan, for example, in the case of Chōshū). Although intense competition placed great psychological strain on the samurai, it did produce a capable group of men from whom each domain's professional administrators, physicians, and scholars could be drawn. Aristocratic samurai were of course spared this competition; nor did they acquire as a rule the fine edge of mental discipline which was often associated with it.

There were thus two classes of samurai in most Tokugawa domains. The "upper" samurai, despite their notorious mediocrity, enjoyed large incomes and were secure in the domain's highest ceremonial and supervisory posts. The "lower" samurai, although they demonstrated a much greater capacity for social creativity, were made to compete for a meager livelihood and then to devote themselves to a life of subordinate toil. In the eyes of many lower samurai, the meritorious were cast down and the undeserving raised up.

It had occurred to a number of social philosophers in the last half century of the Tokugawa era, men like Aizawa Yasushi, Rai Sanyō, and Takano Chōei, that this arrangement did not represent the best of all possible worlds. In Chōshū especially the injustices which operated between the two tiers of samurai seem to have been deeply felt. Even before Perry's arrival in 1853, professional men in Chōshū were acutely sensitive to this problem of stratum-related inequity—not only because it made their daily sacrifices ridiculous but also because the society of which they were the stewards had crying needs which could be met only by applying some of the surplus wealth which had traditionally gone to an aristocratic few. Chōshū's lean professional elite had understood for many years the need for major structural reform. Leaders in other domains shared this perception, and many of them would join the Chōshū men in their struggle in the 1860s. These non-Chōshū leaders would include established scholarly theoreticians like Sakuma Shōzan and Yokoi Shōnan, but also active younger men like Nakaoka Shintarō of Tosa.

It was Perry's arrival which finally made it possible for serious reformers in Chōshū and elsewhere to convert their theoretical understanding into an urgent public demand for change. When the "black ships" of the American Pacific squadron dropped anchor at Uraga in 1853, reformist ideologues no longer had to argue in such vague quantities as social justice. Now they could argue, and many did with compelling eloquence, that unless the realm's grave internal ills were rectified immediately, Japan would fall precipitously into degrading subservience to the Westerner.

Between 1853 and 1858 a vigorous polemical exchange took place in which a few outspoken reformers argued resolutely for the creation of a new order while other leaders argued out of weary sincerity in defense of the old. By 1858 public criticism of the prevailing order of things had become so shrill that the conservative *bakufu* government under Ii Naosuke, the chancellor, sought to suppress political dissent by force. For the better part of a year, *bakufu* police agents combed the metropolis and dealt out severe punishments to outspoken dissidents. This policy is known in history as the Ansei Purge.

The Ansei repression left a residue of bad feelings toward Ii, and early in 1860 he was attacked by a band of dissidents and killed while on his way to the shogunal palace. Even before the chancellor's death, the *bakufu*'s harsh policies of Ansei had been moderated, but this attenuation was not sufficient to mollify the resentment stirred by earlier *bakufu* action. In the early sixties, reformist sympathizers in the street, many of whom had lost friends during Ansei, acted independently to deal out severe punishments to the prominent conservative officials who in their minds had been responsible for the harshness of Ansei and who continued to support conservative policies.

These were the years of "Heaven's Revenge." A portion of Chōshū's leadership was aware of these extralegal activities and sought to promote them here and restrain them there in a manner calculated to advance Chōshū's own reformist interests. During these years a loose but powerful radical coalition gradually took shape. This alliance embraced three elements: small groups of loyalist assassins in the street, the dominant reformist faction of the Chōshū leadership, and reformist nobles in the court.

The emperor, Kōmei, finding himself uncomfortably pressed by this pattern, contacted powerful conservative domains and arranged a palace coup for 18 August 1863 which relied on troops to exclude the Chōshū reformers and other radicals first from the imperial presence and then from the entire city of Kyōto. This conservative coup of 1863 marked the end of the second and most troubled stage of the restorationist struggle. By the early 1860s the forceful debate of the 1850s had given way to force proper. Although the years between 1858 and 1863 had been disorderly years of repression and terror, the violence was still on a limited *ad personam* scale.

The conservative coup of 1863 represented the beginning of a third phase in the reformist movement, one which would prove less disorderly than "Heaven's Revenge" though not less violent. After 1863, the shifting mutual antagonisms of the terror would be replaced by a simpler phenomenon: civil war. Once troops had been used to guarantee the coup of 1863, the encounter would come between armies in the field.

Chōshū's radical leadership found that they must march domanial military forces to Kyōto if they wished to regain the influence they had lost in 1863 when conservative troops had sealed off the imperial abode and capital at their expense. Late in the summer of 1864 Chōshū's insurgent soldiers did reach the outskirts of the imperial city; but there they were badly defeated in a battle called the Incident of the Forbidden Gate and had to withdraw once more to their own territory. Subsequently in 1866 the *bakufu* sent a full-scale expedition to Chōshū's borders with the mission of definitively rooting out that domain's recalcitrant leadership. The result was a conflict called the Four-Sided War, a conflict in which Chōshū, having reorganized her military along Western lines, achieved a complete and decisive victory over the forces of conservatism.

The triumphant reformist leadership in Chōshū had relied throughout on a flexible combination of thought and action. Ideologues like Yoshida Shōin were active in the polemical stage. Men with a taste for diplomacy and politics, like Kusaka Genzui and Sufu Masanosuke, took the lead during the fluid years of the terror. Soldiers like Takasugi Shinsaku and Yamagata Aritomo came to the fore during the years of armed strife. Chōshū was the only great domain where reformist elements in the professional echelon were able to act decisively through the apparatus of a domanial government—perhaps because a professional ethos was stronger in Chōshū than elsewhere, or because the strain of social philosophy cultivated there was more vital than in other domains, or merely because Chōshū had a stronger tradition of power sharing and policy consensus.

At the same time, throughout the long struggle, Chōshū men were in touch with hundreds of leaders from other domains who assisted the movement generously with their aid and council. In 1863, dissidents from all parts of Japan went to Chōshū to join her armies and fight for national reform. After 1868, Chōshū statesmen readily joined with sympathetic elements of other domains, especially Satsuma, Tosa, and Hizen, to establish the new government of Meiji.

It was largely the reformist leadership's mastery of a wide array of power-molding techniques, from polemic to diplomatic maneuvering to warfare, which made the emergence of a new regime in 1868 possible. The availability of the entire Chōshū government as a vehicle for reform was also important, and the catalytic impact of Perry's intrusive arrival in 1853 can hardly be overestimated.

Yet the fundamental dynamic underlying the daring efforts of reformists from Chōshū and elsewhere was one of acute social discontent. The restorationists believed that they and the society as a whole were the victims of a demeaning pattern of exploitation whereby power and wealth were lavished on a few at the expense of all. The program they strived to realize was one of restoring power to those who could use it responsibly and reallocating wealth to serve the nation's needs for safety and achieve a greater prosperity for all. They wanted social justice and well-being in a more ample and unprecedented magnitude. In the end they were successful.

The Meiji Restoration: From Obsolete Order to Effective Regime

Conrad Totman

The Meiji Restoration occurred because sufficient numbers of Japanese in positions to shape national affairs resolved to replace what they saw as the obsolete political order of the Tokugawa era (the *baku-han* system) with one that seemed adequate to the requirements of the day. Accordingly, the questions that need answering are these: What made the old order seem obsolete? Who perceived it as obsolete? And why did they go about replacing it as they did?

The Tokugawa political order was a highly compartmentalized structure based on a finely calibrated hereditary status order and legitimized by a reasonably well-integrated bundle of Confucian and historicist propositions. The emperor in Kyoto had his proper symbolic function as sanctifier of the polity; the shogun in Edo, his proper task actively preserving the peace of both the realm and his own domain; and each daimyo, his proper task serving the shogun upon call and keeping the peace within his own *han* or domain. Each advisor to shogun or daimyo had his proper task advising his lord on appropriate matters; and each lesser samurai, his proper task carrying out the duties of his office and his position as head of his own household. At yet lower levels city fathers, village elders, and others performed their assigned duties—all in ways designed to preserve the social order and sustain the polity.

During the late eighteenth and nineteenth centuries the Tokugawa regime faced severe domestic difficulties. The fiscal condition of the *bakufu*, *han* governments, and samurai in general had been a matter of concern for generations, and by the nineteenth century difficulties in government financing seem to have exacerbated relations between high and low-ranking samurai, between *han* and *bakufu*, and between taxpayers and tax collectors. As long as tax income could be used to meet customary costs, that problem did not render the polity obsolete, but it did deprive the system of the capacity to assume any major new expenses or undertake any major reallocation of resources. To do so would certainly precipitate resistance proportional to the extremity of the undertaking.

While not leading to political upheaval, these domestic tensions did foster political reflection, critiques of the established order, and proposals for political reform. Commentators became more conscious of the interrelated character of society's problems, and this consciousness found expression in new lines of political thought. Intellectuals and officials such as Fujita Tōko, Hirata Atsutane, Honda Toshiaki, Oshio Heihachirō, and Satō Nobuhiro increasingly spoke of problems and their solutions in terms of nationwide perceptions and alternative strategies—whether in reference to fiscal policies, personnel recruitment and employment practices, military matters, foreign policy, or imperial-*bakufu* relations.

Because of the compartmentalized structure of the polity these strands of thought did not converge into an integrated program supported by a broad public. Rather, those whose interests seemed best served by the established order—daimyo, their senior advisors, the core of *bakufu* officialdom, senior courtiers, higher clergy, wealthy segments of the common people—were able to isolate and neutralize dissatisfied elements by such simple expedients as forbidding them to leave their own castle towns or placing them under house arrest. Nevertheless, by the mid-nineteenth century cumulative problems and alternative perceptions had created a situation in which any contextual change that placed major new financial burdens on the regime, split its supporters, or led its critics into joint action could quickly tip the balance of forces in favor of a drastic restructuring of the system.

As matters worked out, it was the Western imperialist intrusion of mid-century that created the unmanageable problems. The complications created by that intrusion were of such number and magnitude that they utterly displaced the cumulative domestic factors of fiscal and conceptual change as the cause of political disintegration and replacement. Those domestic changes contributed to the crisis, however, by enhancing the sense of urgency, by depriving the system of means of delaying its final collapse, and by suggesting important elements of the solution.

The imperialist encroachment first became a political issue in Japan when Russian explorers, adventurers, and traders appeared in coastal waters during the 1790s. In succeeding decades minor foreign incidents led to periodic policy changes designed to preserve intact the established foreign policy of seclusion *(sakoku)* and thereby minimize domestic repercussions of the foreign visitations. After 1853, however, Commodore Matthew C. Perry's demands for a consular treaty and subsequent foreign demands for trade arrangements abruptly wrecked the policy of seclusion. The new pattern of treaty relations *(kaikoku)* presented political complications that quickly subverted the old regime.

The most immediate requirement of the new diplomatic situation was a massive strengthening of national defenses. That task entailed not only extensive technological change, with the acquisition of up-to-date rifles, cannon, and warships, but also basic reorganization of the military system so that the new technology could be used effectively for national purposes. Merely paying for the new weaponry was beyond the capacity of the polity, but in addition the organizational changes required by that weaponry destroyed the whole intricate samurai status system. These changes humiliated and antagonized large numbers of samurai—the very people whose loyal support was most essential to the old order's survival. Worst of all for the *bakuhan* system, effective military reorganization for purposes of national defense required an administratively unified polity. And that Japan lacked.

The *bakufu* was a regional structure that occupied and administered much of central Japan while the rest of the country was governed by the daimyo. Furthermore the *bakufu* had not even purported to be a genuine national government. Its national writ had always been limited to the negative duties of enforcing the policy of seclusion and preventing civil unrest. The court constituted a symbolic representation of Japanese ethnic identity, but it had neither an institutional structure of national governance nor a staff prepared to assume such duties. Neither did the daimyo nor any other group have sufficient authority or suitable personnel for the task. In a phrase, the necessity for a cohesive national polity constituted a demand for the creation of something that did not exist. It implied, therefore, a systemic reorganization that presented two basic questions: What form would the new unified order take? And who would construct it, thereby securing his own private interests while fulfilling his public duty?

The dilemma presented by imperialism had other ramifications as well. The educational system, the rigidly stratified, hierarchical, Confucian class system, and even the economic system of the Tokugawa order were all affected by the crisis of the age, and the successful forging of a new order would, of necessity, entail changes in those aspects of society. The mid-century crisis, then, left not only the polity but the overall socioeconomic configuration of Tokugawa Japan obsolete. The dimension of crisis that stood out most clearly, however, was the compelling need for military reform and its radical corollary: the need for fundamental reorganization of the political system.

One can argue that obsolescence created by the imperialist intrusion led to systemic change in the 1860s only if one can show that problems stemming from it generated the action that replaced one regime with another. After all, critics of the regime and even proponents of major change had been visible long before the mid-century crisis. Nevertheless, in view of the seriousness of the regime's problems—during the famine and turmoil of the 1780s and 1830s, for example—it was the relative scarcity and ineffectiveness of radical critics that most impresses one. When the crisis of 1853 struck, moreover, the overwhelming response in Japan was a closing of ranks in defense of the *bakuhan* order. Bitter disagreements over policy certainly erupted among political leaders, notably between such men as Tokugawa Nariaki of Mito and Ii Naosuke of Hikone, but the bitterness was, at heart, a measure of their concern to preserve the Tokugawa order, with or without modest adjustments. Others, including scholars such as Sakuma Shōzan and Yoshida Shōin, as well as most daimyo and their advisors, initially gave their support to the regime, assuming that *han* and samurai alike would cooperate with the *bakufu* in addressing the foreign menace.

During the years after 1853, however, it became ever more apparent that the *bakufu* with its limited writ and limited power could not, in fact, manage the foreigners and that the whole *bakuhan* order was indeed endangered. The political principles and interests of many influential people were at stake. Frustration, fury, and fear combined to precipitate a domestic power struggle that pitted Ii Naosuke and others in the *bakufu*, the court, and among daimyo against rival elements in the *bakufu*, the court, and other daimyo. That confrontation led in 1858–1859 to Ii's seizure of power and harsh repression of his opponents. Ii's repression, in turn, exacerbated domestic tensions. Lesser samurai, who had no legitimate way to shape affairs, began to communicate and cooperate with one another as never before. They turned to radical activism in the name of *Son'nō Jōi*—"Revere the Emperor, Expel the Barbarian"—and in early 1860 carried out successfully a plot to murder Ii.

By 1860 the prime beneficiaries of the established order were thus becoming deeply divided and activists *(shishi)* were experimenting with violent forms of political persuasion. These they justified in terms that were themselves a menace to the regime: *jōi*, a menace because it invited men to abandon their sense of place in a hierarchical loyalty structure in favor of direct service to the emperor. The system was threatened, then, because in face of the foreign danger its core of worried defenders had begun to turn against one another and its critics had begun to acquire reasons, rationales, and ways of acting in coalition against it.

In general those who engaged in political struggle during the 1860s adopted postures that seemed best to accommodate the interests of their positions while meeting the needs of the crisis as they understood them. What that meant was that domanial leaders in both the *bakufu* and major *han* tried to achieve the needed political unity without sacrificing their own domanial autonomy. To that end they adopted a policy of coalition called *Kōbu Gattai*, or "Union of Court and Camp." For some, most notably *bakufu* leaders, that meant unity of court and *bakufu*; but for others, primarily great daimyo and their advisors, it came to mean unity of court and *han*. Activists of lesser status, as noted above, most commonly stood for a more diffuse coalition of emperor and subject, *son'nō*, in which domanial interests were not really a matter of concern but personal participation in the national struggle was.

During the early 1860s these two formulas for political action were invoked to justify new political procedures and arrangements. The undertakings came to nought, however. Attempts at driving out or otherwise controlling the foreigners were repeatedly thwarted and resulted in severe reprisals by foreign naval squadrons in 1863 and 1864 and a more exploitative treaty settlement in 1865. Most attempts at military strengthening yielded little real gain despite the severe costs in wealth and hardship to all domains that undertook it. The attempts at unity through coalition, both the unity of *Kōbu Gattai* and the unity of restoration, repeatedly foundered and only exacerbated mutual distrust and internal struggle.

In the crisis of the sixties political alignments were not congruent with intellectual alignments. Those who first and most fully grasped the general implications of the crisis were not limited to the proponents of one or another form of *Kōbu Gattai* or *Son'nō Jōi*. Rather, those who emerged as the intellectual vanguard were intellectuals and officials who, regardless of their institutional and political location, had direct involvement with foreigners and foreign ideas. Early proponents of radical change included the scholars Sakuma Shōzan, Yokoi Shōnan, and, before his death, Yoshida Shōin. Their studies of the West led them to appreciate the magnitude of both the danger and the needed reforms. Sakuma and Yokoi were associated with *Kōbu Gattai;* Yoshida, with *Son'nō Jōi.* Among *bakufu* officials, such men as Kurimote Kon and Katsu Kaishū led the search for feasible policies and new organizational struggles.

Because of this disjunction between a person's political perception and political location, movements such as *Son'nō Jōi* and *Kōbu Gattai* lacked internal cohesion and consistency of purpose and were much less effective in consequence. While these two formulas for political action were being applied uncessessfully during the early 1860s, however, events were bringing more and more men into contact with the foreigners—in the process giving them, willy-nilly, an ever richer appreciation of their dilemma and greater readiness for radical action. By 1865–1867 a significant number of samurai in critical positions in the *bakufu* and in some major *han,* such men as Ōkubo Toshimichi of Satsuma, Kodo Kōin of Chōshū, and Oguri Tadamasa of the *bakufu,* shared a conviction that the whole decentralized *bakuhan* order must be discarded. In its place, they believed, the age required some sort of effective state controlling a unified army and navy and committed to some measure of social change and industrial development. They were in agreement on two further points: that the order must be rooted one way or another in the imperial institution and that it would have to be achieved by force and in the face of vigorous resistance.

As the scope and requirements of the crisis came to be more fully understood, men were driven to address the question of what instrumentality would resolve the crisis. Following the discrediting of the coalition formulas of the early 1860s, the only vehicles of political action that still held promise were domanial entities. Of them, only the *bakufu* and the largest of the *han* were really in positions to serve as instruments for national unification. Consequently during the last three years of the Tokugawa period the political process boiled down to a struggle for supremacy in which leaders of rival domains raced to develop the strength necessary to subdue one another and deter any others who might try to stop their unification of the country. One of those domains was the Tokugawa at Edo, the *bakufu,* which was in military terms basically a domain centered on the Kantō Plain in eastern Japan. The other was an alliance of Satsuma and Chōshū, two domains situated in southwestern Japan. The rivalry was fierce, and in the civil war that erupted near Kyoto early in 1868, the armies of Satsuma and Chōshū proved the more effective. In consequence it was they who unified the country and forged the new regime.

The political order of Tokugawa Japan had been overwhelmed by the imperialist intrusion. Previously weakened by domestic problems, by 1860 it was severely hampered by quarrels among its defenders, assaults by its critics, and a declining commitment among those who were most fully aware of what the foreign encroachment involved. This combination of factors led to attempts at compromise—*Kōbu Gattai*—that were designed to limit the foreign problem while shoring up the polity by modest changes. Simultaneously it fostered political activism—*Son'nō Jōi*—that sought to reverse the flow of diplomatic history by replacing the existing chain of command with an imperial regime to which the samurai public would patriotically rally. Both efforts came to nought, however, and escalating failure drove more and more men to accept the inevitability of fundamental change and to seek ways of securing their own interest in this new situation. That perception of the problem then forced—or freed—people to address the instrumental question of how to attain that goal. Domanial power became the vehicle; the restoration was its outcome.

PART IV

The Meiji Government and Its Critics: What Is Best for the Nation?

IN 1876 MODERN JAPAN'S first Western historian, William Elliot Griffis, posed the question, "Can a nation be born at once?" In the decades to follow it became increasingly clear that the Japanese nation had been built and with remarkable speed. This is a point upon which all Japanese historians agree. There is much disagreement, however, about the exact way in which modern Japan was built as well as the wisdom and motives of those who did the building. It is difficult to analyze Meiji Japan without examining the life and thought of individuals. Certainly a very small group of men dominated the political, economic, and even the social life of the nation. The insiders as well as most of the outsiders in the Meiji political process were all members of this elite. For the most part the debates on the establishment of a parliamentary assembly, the responsibility of the government to the people, and the people to the government, as well as the advisability of certain government policies, were pursued only among the members of this elite.

In the first essay on the Meirokusha, I examine a significant segment of the Meiji intellectual elite which supported modernization. I conclude that unlike their counterparts in many other nations undergoing rapid change they did not advocate fundamental modifications in their contemporary society. Even those outside the government, such as Nakamura Keiu and Fukuzawa Yukichi, who had little faith in its ability to engineer progressive change, saw the slow process of education as the ultimate answer to Japan's fundamental problems.

The motives of the Meiji elite, both those within and those outside the government, is a concern of several of the writers presented here. In his defense of Matsukata Masayoshi's economic policies Jackson H. Bailey contends that Matsukata, as well as "virtually all the Meiji leaders, was guided first and last by a commitment to the twin objectives of *Fukoku Kyōhei*. He further maintains that this interest in what was "best for the country" was not a mere slogan masking self or class interests: "The Meiji leaders adhered to it fiercely and made most of their political and economic decisions on the basis of what they believed would contribute to its fulfillment." I do not comment directly on the motives of the Meirokusha intellectuals in my essay, but I do observe that like most of the Meiji elite they were able to combine their vision of a strong and prosperous Japan with a perception of their forthcoming role in that future.

James L. Huffman, in his essay on the popular rights debate, strongly objects to the position taken by Bailey. He contends that to suggest the Meiji leaders were self-sacrificing giants who always kept

the best interests of country in mind "distorts our understanding of
Meiji Japan." Huffman maintains that such a view obscures the "selfish interests" and "the struggles for personal or factional power that
lay behind most of the Meiji political debates" and "gloss over the
ugly power struggles that marked every stage of Meiji development."
In his essay, Huffman focuses on the arguments presented in the Japanese press concerning popular rights and the advisability of establishing a parliamentary government. He concludes that ideology was
clearly secondary to practical political considerations and self-serving
power plays by the Meiji elite both inside and outside the government.

Mikiso Hane in his essay on the movement for popular rights also
questions the motives of those involved in this movement. He further
contends that the whole idea of popular rights was alien to Japan.
Hane maintains that the ideas its leaders propagated, as well as the
examples they cited, were mainly from the West and ultimately failed
to appeal to the masses. Victor Carpenter's study of Tanaka Shōzō
both agrees and differs on many of the points stated or implied by
Hane and Huffman. For one, Tanaka Shōzō, an outspoken critic of
his time, condemned both those in the ruling oligarchy and the party
politicians as self-seeking individuals who had little interest in the
needs of the common people. But though he eventually left his political party and even resigned his seat in the Diet, he had long been a
regional activist in the popular rights movement. Indeed, he found
the ideology of the popular rights movement quite congenial with his
own views of the inviolability of local government and pursued a long
and vigorous career endeavoring to guard against encroachment upon
popular rights by the objectionable alliance of big government and
big business.

—Jerry K. Fisher

The Meirokusha and the Building of a Strong and Prosperous Nation

Jerry K. Fisher

The Meirokusha, founded on 1 February 1874 for the purpose of "promoting civilization and enlightenment," was Meiji Japan's most prominent intellectual society. Among its members were many of the top educators, bureaucrats, and thinkers of the day. Most of the society's thirty-three members were samurai intellectuals who acquired knowledge of Western languages during the late Tokugawa era and ascended to prominence in the early Meiji period when Japan turned its eyes sharply westward in search of ways to modernize the nation quickly. This unique group of men, born and educated in Tokugawa Japan, served as an important intellectual link between traditional society and the new, modern age they so strongly promoted. Intellectuals do not always affect their times profoundly, but these men, bestriding their times, charted the path toward national strength, prosperity, and independence with a degree of self-confidence rarely found among men of letters.

One of these self-confident intellectuals was Mori Arinori, founder and first president of the society. Mori, who began his tenure as Japan's first envoy to the United States at the age of twenty-five, apparently conceived the idea of forming a society of leading Japanese intellectuals while in the United States from 1871 to 1873. Though a diplomat, Mori was also interested in education, especially the practical but value-oriented universal education with which educators such as Horace Mann hoped to unify America. Mori saw in the American system a possible model for Japan which could weld together a nation of well-educated men and women dedicated to serving their country. To promote modern education, Mori felt it advisable to join with

others of like mind, and six months after he returned home the
Meirokusha was formally established. Its bylaws stressed the society's
role in "furthering education in Japan" and established bimonthly
meetings for the purpose of exchanging views "to broaden knowledge
and illuminate understanding."

The most surprising thing about the Meirokusha was the diversity
of its membership. Among those who joined the society were physicians, Confucian scholars, merchants, and large numbers of samurai
bureaucrats. They ranged in age from twenty-seven to fifty-six and
came from a wide variety of *han,* both Tokugawa-related and anti-
Tokugawa *han.* Even today when social relationships are less struc-
tured than in the Meiji era it would be difficult to find such a diverse
group of important men willing to spend half a day together twice a
month. The quick lunch, speech, and run programs of the Japanese
Rotary International are probably the closest equivalent. But despite
the Meirokusha's diverse ages and social background they shared a
very similar intellectual background. All the members, with possibly three exceptions, had studied both *jugaku* (Confucian studies)
and *yōgaku* (Western studies) by 1874. Twenty had studied Dutch;
twenty-two, English; three, French; one, German; and two, Russian.
Fifteen had traveled abroad and twenty-five had at one time been
teachers before joining the society. Perhaps most important, in the
course of their *yōgaku* studies many of them had studies with the
same teachers.

"Civilization" and Independence

A few hundred prominent men and women (mostly men) dominated
the social, political, and economic life of Meiji Japan. It would be a
mistake to consider the Meiji elite as self-sacrificing servants of their
nation—nearly all had strong personal ambitions which they pursued
with great vigor. But most were able to combine their vision of a
strong and prosperous Japan with a personal view of the role they
should play in that future. The Meirokusha was no exception. To a
man they agreed that Japan was in peril of being passed by or, worse,
swallowed up by the West. To defend Japan against this possibility
she must be guided to a position of strength among the nations of the
world as quickly as possible. Furthermore, they strongly felt that they
themselves had a key role in Japan's quest for equality with the West
and superiority in the East. As the nation's leading intellectuals it was
their responsibility to introduce the fruits of Western civilization to

their countrymen and instruct them how to become concerned, inde-
pendent-minded, spirited citizenry. They called for a cultural revolution which would bring the Japanese people to the level of "civilization"—a word they often used—equal to that of the most advanced
Western nations. Only when this was accomplished would Japan become fully independent.

Moral and Institutional Reform

Among the Meirokusha there were several different but not necessarily mutually exclusive views regarding the basis of this new "civilized" culture. A group of Confucian humanists headed by Nakamura
Keiu, Nishimura Shigeki, and Sakatani Rōro reasoned that Western
strength and prosperity resulted from the moral strength of its people. To come abreast of the West, therefore, the Japanese must understand the nature of Western morality and strive to make it functional
in their own society.

The Confucian humanists as well as other Meirokusha members
found the general moral level of their countrymen appalling. In the
society's organ, the *Meiroku Zasshi,* they penned articles on "How to
Change the Character of the Japanese People," "Theory on Nourish-
ing the Spirit," and "Two Items Which Are Necessary for Moral Government." In their advocacy of a morality to uplift and unify the nation, these Confucian humanists were neither iconoclastic nor were
they simply mouthing the "Eastern Ethics, Western Technique" argument of the late Tokugawa era. Nakamura Keiu, eminent Confucian
scholar and the first well-known Japanese to become a Christian, best
represents the blend of Eastern and Western ethics. Through his
translations of such works as John Stuart Mill's *On Liberty* and Samuel Smiles' *Self Help* he endeavored to show his countrymen that
only through self-reliance combined with a high standard of individual morality could Japan hope to achieve the level of civilization already attained by the most advanced Western nations. His attraction
to Western ethics came about not despite, but because of, his Confucian training. In Nakamura's mind neither time nor geographic location altered universal moral truths. The Japanese lagged far behind
their Western counterparts because they were "still illiterate and culturally blind . . . indulged in wine and women . . . didn't pay attention to their work . . . [and] hated to read things." Only if the
Japanese people improved the degenerate state of their personal morality could the country hope to become strong and prosperous.

Other Meirokusha thinkers such as Katō Hiroyuki, Tsuda Mamichi, and Nishi Amane emphasized the organic nature of society and held that the West's strength was derived from rationally constructed and operated institutions and societies. *Kokutai* (national polity), constitutional government, and universal education were the topics they addressed. Nishi's long series in the *Meiroku Zasshi*, "*Jinsei sanpōsetsu*" [Man's three treasures], emphasized the importance of social welfare from a utilitarian point of view. His careful analysis of individual conduct and human needs set the stage for a presentation of the government policies he thought were needed to protect and promote health, knowledge, and wealth—his three treasures. For Nishi, a nation's level of civilization could be judged by the efficiency with which its government protected and nurtured the three treasures.

Among the Meirokusha members who emphasized institutional change in Japan's modernization process, Tsuda most clearly enunciated the nature and importance of developing enlightened legal structures and bureaucratic organizations. In Tsuda's mind a nation's legal system reflected its level of civilization. Katō, on the other hand, focused on the importance of *kokutai*, the universal principles underlying the relationship between emperor and people, and *seitai*, the governmental form for carrying out those principles. Unlike *kokutai*, *seitai* differed from country to country and from time to time, and it behooved Japan to adopt a system of government suited to her own conditions. Like Tsuda, Katō considered a British-style parliament far too advanced for Japan's low level of enlightenment in the mid-nineteenth century. Responding to the call made by Itagaki, Soejima, Etō, and Gotō, Katō wrote:

> In a country like Japan especially, where there has never been a revolution and the warm, friendly relations between the ruler and the people go very deep, it is necessary for many years of enlightenment to elapse before even a constitutional government which would be the basis of a strengthened monarchy can be established.

The two most prominent members of the Meirokusha, Mori Arinori and Fukuzawa Yukichi, had their own approaches to the task of making Japan strong and prosperous. They agreed with the Confucian humanists that individual morality in Japan was appalling and that self-reliance, industry, and moral uprightness must predominate if Japan had any hope of catching up with the West. But in their effort to reform men they also believed, as did the institutionalists, that the structures of government, industry, and education must be attuned to the challenge of producing a civilization equal to the West.

The Responsibility of the Scholar

Both Mori and Fukuzawa were educators, and it was in the area of education that these two giants of Meiji Japan were in closest agreement. In 1875 their common concern for the important but neglected field of commercial education in Japan led them to work together to found the Shōhō Kōshūjo (Commercial Institute), the forerunner of Hitotsubashi University, Japan's leading school of economics and finance. At the time Fukuzawa was already busy with his own private school (Keiō Gijuku), and a decade later Mori became Japan's first cabinet level minister of education. But the nature of their major involvement in education also underscored their primary disagreement about how to make Japan strong and prosperous. Fukuzawa insisted that intellectuals like those in the Meirokusha should shun government service to devote themselves fully to the task of raising the level of Japan's civilization; Mori and most of the other Meirokusha members maintained that qualified intellectuals were desperately needed in government to lead the nation forward.

The disagreement between Fukuzawa and Mori, which may have contributed to the delay in formally establishing the Meirokusha in January 1874, became public when Fukuzawa departed from the planned format of his serialized best seller, *Gakumon no susume* [Encouragement of learning], and wrote parts four and five in a manner necessary "to contend with scholars." Setting aside the simple writing style which made the book an ideal text for lower schools, he used more scholarly language to discuss the questions "Is Japan Independent?" and "The Task of the Scholar." His answer to the first question was a resounding no. The reason why Japan was not yet independent, contended Fukuzawa, was not because the Meiji government had not done well by its people. "In less than ten years," he wrote, "it has revolutionized the educational and military systems; it has built railroads and telegraphs; it has constructed stone buildings and iron bridges; the intensity of its determination and splendor of its success are simply astonishing." The fundamental weakness of the Japanese nation was not its government but its citizenry. Fukuzawa maintained that the people of Japan were not providing sufficient stimuli to the government to keep the nation in a state of dynamic economic, social, and political development. As a result, according to Fukuzawa, "the government is still as despotic as always, and the people are still the spiritless, powerless, ignorant masses that they have always been."

For Fukuzawa, the only hope for Japan's salvation was the "middle class" intellectual elite comprised of the Meirokusha and others like them: "This group alone advocates modern civilization and supports national independence." Calling the common people "intransigent idiots" and bureaucrats "short-sighted individuals" more interested in advancing their own careers than the civilization of their country, Fukuzawa instructed his Meirokusha colleagues:

> We must stand in the forefront of our nation's citizenry, assisting the government by joining on an equal basis the power of the bureaucracy and the power of the private citizen to increase the strength of the entire nation. In this way we will arrest the erosion of our people's independence and construct an immovable foundation which will allow us to face war with a foreign country without yielding.

As one might expect, the Meirokusha members who immediately responded to Fukuzawa's immoderate views about bureaucrat-intellectuals were themselves bureaucrats. At the time their rebuttals were published in the *Meiroku Zasshi,* Katō held an important position in the Department of the Imperial Household, Mori was a top officer in the Department of Foreign Affairs, and Tsuda and Nishi had responsible posts in the Department of War. There is little wonder that these men balked at Fukuzawa's contention that "the government was simply a place where many people of intelligence gather to carry on their work like one stupid person."

Mori, the highest-ranking bureaucrat in the Meirokusha at the time of the debate, directly attacked Fukuzawa's fundamental thesis that two separate elements, the government and the people, constituted the nation-state. For Mori, no distinction could be made between the *seifu* (government) and the *tami* (people). He insisted that there was not a single Japanese who could not be classified a member of the *tami*—bureaucrats, peers, and commoners all were *tami.* Furthermore, the government was not a separate entity operating independently of the people. The Meiji government was a government of the people established by them and working for them. Mori viewed the bureaucracy as nothing more than a community of people engaged in the common task of uplifting the nation. Since Fukuzawa agreed that governmental failing resulted from the weaknesses in individual men responsible for its operation, Mori maintained that it was absolutely necessary to have highly qualified people willing to serve in government. Above all, the Meiji government needed the superior knowledge and experience of intellectuals such as the Meirokusha members. It was fine, stated Mori, for Fukuzawa to work as a private citizen to promote civilization, but it was also important for Japan's intellectual elite to help guide the government by serving in it.

The Meaning of the Meirokusha

The fact that the Meirokusha's critiques always addressed what was or was not "best for the nation" limited criticism of Japanese government and society throughout the Meiji era. Civil rights, parliamentary government, and freedom of the press were all debated in the context of what would make the nation stronger. The Meirokusha not only set the tone of criticism but also helped define the fundamental issues to be debated. Inalienable rights, power, and class struggle were not part of the Meirokusha's vocabulary. Morality was. The Confucian humanists addressed themselves to the question of personal morality while the institutionalists spoke of the government's moral responsibility to operate efficient institutions.

"Promoting civilization and enlightenment" was a prerequisite to building a strong and independent nation, and virtually every Meirokusha member believed that the most essential element in furthering civilization was education. They had confidence that if the Japanese people acquired a sound moral education together with quality universities and technical schools to construct a strong modern nation, Japan could soon take her place among the most advanced countries of the world. Whether working within or outside the government they further believed that as Japan's leading intellectuals it was their responsibility not only to help build the structures but also to furnish the content necessary for their countrymen's enlightenment.

The Movement
for Liberty
and Popular Rights

Mikiso Hane

The beginning of the *jiyū minken* (liberty and popular rights) movement can be marked with the submission to the government by Itagaki Taisuke and others of the Memorial of 1874, and its termination can be marked by the temporary dissolution of the Jiyūtō (Liberal Party) in 1884. Of course the ideals of freedom and people's rights had been introduced to Japan earlier (by such works as *Seiyō Jijō*—Conditions in the West—by Fukuzawa Yuichi and the translation of John Stuart Mill's *On Liberty* by Nakamura Keiu) but the term *minken* ("popular rights") was not used as a political slogan until the memorial was submitted and a movement to establish a national assembly got started.

Minken Leadership and Objectives

The key figure initially associated with the *minken* movement was Itagaki Taisuke (1837–1919) of Tosa (now Kōchi Prefecture). He was a councilor of state in the Meiji government but left his post in 1873 together with Saigō Takamori (1827–1877) and others when their proposal to send a military expedition into Korea was rejected. He then returned to Tosa and organized the Risshisha, a local political association, and the Aikokukosha, a patriotic society, in order to establish a political base. In 1874 he and his political allies submitted the memorial mentioned above and launched a campaign to gain popular support for the establishment of a national assembly. The ostensible objective of the movement was "liberty and people's rights," but the true aim was to gain a share of the power held by the oligarchs and also find a way to provide jobs for the unemployed former samurai (the *shizoku*). The desire to alleviate the plight of the *shizoku* who had lost the privileged places they had held in the Tokugawa era was one of the reasons why Saigō, Itagaki, and the others favored sending an expeditionary force into Korea. This venture would have provided the jobless *shizoku* with an undertaking suited to their training and status.

The impetus for the *minken* movement, then, was provided by those who had practical political objectives, and the struggle between the *minken* faction and the oligarchy was in essence a contest between the ins and the outs. Such expediency turned out to be the Achilles' heel of the *minken* movement because the advocates could easily be bought off by being absorbed into the governmental bureaucracy. Moreover, because their primary objective was the advancement of the *shizoku*'s welfare, they failed to turn the movement into a truly popular cause.

That the movement was basically a struggle for power was revealed in the way in which the advocates of *minken* wavered between support and opposition to Saigō when he and his followers rebelled against the Meiji government in 1877. The fact that some were willing to support Saigō, who cannot be called a supporter of freedom and popular rights, belies the *minken* advocates' claim that their goal was the fulfillment of the ideals of freedom and people's rights.

Even at the rhetorical level the mainstream of the *minken* movement did not advocate the establishment of a republic. In general they professed their loyalty to the imperial throne and reproached the oligarchs for encroaching upon the royal prerogative. The political system they favored was a constitutional monarchy. Aside from being good monarchists they claimed to be just as patriotic as the wielders of power. Their advocacy of *minken*, they argued, was founded upon the desire to strengthen *kokken* (state authority or national sovereignty). This, it appears, was not merely a ploy designed to appeal to the nationalistic sentiments of the populace. The *minken* advocates and their successors remained consistent in their espousal of *kokken*, especially its extension abroad.

The entire movement had its genesis in the proposal to invade Korea. The *minken* advocates continued to favor an aggressive policy toward that country. In a memorial the Risshisha submitted in 1877, a call for intervention in Korea was inserted; a similar demand was made by the *minken* advocates in 1884–1885 when that country was undergoing internal strife. In the late 1880s, they joined the right-wing nationalists in strenuously opposing the government's efforts to revise the treaties with the Western powers because the proposed treaties still contained clauses that compromised Japan's sovereignty. They wholeheartedly supported the Sino-Japanese War of 1894–1895, and many proved to be more jingoistic than the government leaders themselves. In the Russo-Japanese War of 1904–1905 the old *minken* advocates emerged as fervent flag-wavers. When the Portsmouth Treaty was concluded, they incited the populace to stage massive protest demonstrations against the government for failing to win greater concessions from Russia. During the First World War the former leader of the political party movement, Ōkuma Shigenobu (1838–1922) as prime minister, thrust the Twenty-one Demands upon the hapless Chinese, and in the late twenties and early thirties the Seiyūkai (the successor to the Jiyūtō) led the critics of the "weak-kneed" Shidehara diplomacy and gave vocal support to the military in Manchuria.

All this indicates that the advocates of *minken* and their successors in the political parties were true believers when it came to the extension of *kokken* at home and abroad. They generally endorsed Fukuzawa Yukichi's (1835–1901) contention that liberal ideals such as freedom and independence had to be instilled in the people in order "to fortify our nationality and give added luster to our imperial dynasty." The newspapers calling for the establishment of a national assembly insisted that "without popular rights the nation cannot preserve its independence. In order to regain our national rights we must establish a national assembly." The Memorial of 1874 declares that "the state will be ruined" unless a national assembly is established. They were speaking out, they asserted, because they were "unable to resist the promptings of our patriotic feelings."

Minken liberalism, in retrospect, seems shallow and weak in contrast to nationalism. Not even Kōno Hironaka, who was more deeply committed to popular rights than most *minken* advocates, turned away from the ideals of "filial piety and loyalty" and the concept of *kokutai* (national polity) with the imperial system at its core. The presence of Tōyama Mitsuru (1855–1944), the arch conspirator of the ultranationalists of modern Japan, among the early advocates of *minken* symbolizes the linkage between the *minken* advocates and right-wing nationalists.

The Scope of the Minken Movement

The Tosa *minken* advocates were in the main members of the *shizoku* and their chief aim was to serve the *shizoku*'s interests. They spoke eloquently of "people's rights" but did not aim to extend political rights to the masses. Not even Ueki Emori, one of the most liberal of the *minken* proponents, favored granting the franchise to the commoners. He observed that the common people may be capable of managing their household and business but lack knowledge of public affairs. Thus "they are neither capable of gaining their rights on their own initiative nor extending the freedom that should be extended."

But the upper-class segments of the agrarian and merchant classes did join the *minken* movement, especially in central and northern Japan, as associations similar to the Risshisha came to be organized throughout the land. The wealthier farmers and merchants joined the *minken* movement primarily because they wished to preserve the vested interests and privileged positions they had traditionally held in their home towns and villages. The extension of the central government's authority into the local areas following the establishment of the prefectural system posed a threat to their old power base. The *minken* movement offered them a means to protect their interests against the centralizing tendencies of the Meiji government. The alliance that was effected in 1882 between the sake brewers, who were dissatisfied at the series of taxes being imposed on them, and the *minken* proponents led by Ueki is illustrative of this convergence of interests. Because they were primarily concerned about protecting their local interests they concentrated on gaining control of the prefectural assemblies. Here too the masses were given little voice. During 1880–1888 the franchise in the prefectural assemblies was limited to 4 or 5 percent and the right to run for the assemblies to about 2 percent of the population.

The diffusion of *jiyū minken* ideas was facilitated by the emergence of newspapers and journals in early Meiji. These publications served as the chief medium for the propagation of liberal political concepts. The advocates of *jiyū minken* also traveled around the countryside delivering speeches to gain public support. The government attempted to curtail these activities by passing laws restricting the press and political associations. Although it failed to contain the movement, its depiction of *minken* as a subversive activity aroused the rightists to commit such acts as the attempted assassination of Itagaki in 1882.

The *minken* movement at the local level became increasingly conservative as agrarian distress caused the impoverished peasants to turn to violence. Frequently the wealthy farmers and merchants became targets of attack. Rural discontent culminated in the Kabayama Incident of 1884 when a handful of men, led by Kōno Hironaka's nephew who favored recourse to terroristic methods, challenged the government. In the Chichibu Uprising during the same year, thousands of hard-pressed rural dwellers rioted and marched against the government authorities in Chichibu, about forty miles northwest of Tokyo. Because a number of radical members of the Jiyūtō were involved in these incidents, many upper-class farmers and merchants left the party to support the more moderate Kaishintō (Progressive Party) which had been organized by Ōkuma Shigenobu in 1882. Numerous supporters of the *minken* camp, among them Fukuzawa Yukichi, began to denounce the radical elements in the movement. There was dissension in the Jiyūtō itself as well as interparty strife between the Jiyūtō and the Kaishintō. Thus the movement as an organized affair fell into trouble, and Itagaki initiated the temporary dissolution of the Jiyūtō in 1884.

Ueki Emori: Spokesman for the Movement

One of the most articulate spokesmen for the cause was Ueki Emori (1857–1892), who wrote extensively on behalf of the movement. Ueki came from a middle-level samurai family of Tosa. He received a traditional Confucian education and studied largely on his own by reading translations of works on Western political thought. His interest in liberal political philosophy led him to join Itagaki Taisuke's movement to establish a national assembly, and he played an active role in the organization of the Jiyūtō. In 1884, after the temporary dissolution of the party, he returned to Tosa and became a member of the Kōchi prefectural assembly and also wrote editorials for a newspaper in Tosa. He returned to the national political scene in 1888 and helped to revive the Jiyūtō. In 1890 he ran for a seat in the first Diet election and won. He died at the age of thirty-five just prior to the second Diet election.

Ueki began publishing tracts, pamphlets, and newspaper articles on behalf of the *jiyū minken* movement around 1877. He argued in a logical, persuasive fashion, quoting from Western thinkers and citing examples from the West—particularly England and the United States, where, he noted, the people had fought for their political rights.

Even though Ueki and other advocates of freedom pleaded for the rights of the people, they usually had in mind the rights of the *shizoku* and upper-level farmers and merchants when they spoke of "the people." Occasionally Ueki did sound as if he favored extending political rights to the lower classes. In a series of articles he wrote in 1886 he argued that the lower classes should be granted political rights also. But here too he qualified his position by saying that political rights should be restricted to taxpayers. Ueki was also ahead of his time in favoring women's suffrage. But his main concern was the *shizoku*. When he argued on behalf of the rights of the poor he seems to have had in mind the propertyless *shizoku*. When wealthy commoners criticized the *shizoku* for their impecuniosity he denied that they were without property. They may not possess material property, he reasoned, but they did hold property in the form of "knowledge, moral principles, and honor." The *shizoku*, he pointed out, comprised the nucleus of feudal Japan and in the postrestoration years held more than half the important positions in the country. "In all countries and in all ages," he insisted, "the progressive persons have been members of the middle class." The *shizoku* constituted this class in Japan. They are what the Confucians call *ryōmin* (law-abiding people), for they possess "knowledge, vigor, the spirit of freedom and independence, a sense of patriotism and loyalty." In contrast the common people, he contended, were devoid of these qualities. The Risshisha memorial of 1874, which Ueki helped to draft, states: "A great mistake has been made in endeavoring to lower the samurai to the level of the common people. Encouragement should have been given to the latter to raise themselves to the level of the samurai."

Ueki, like the other *minken* advocates, coupled *minken* ("people's rights") with *kokken* ("national sovereignty"), but later in his life he became concerned about the direction that nationalism was taking and renounced this linkage. *Minken*, he argued, should not be turned into a handmaiden of *kokken*. It is more important to fight for freedom and popular rights than to clamor about the nation and the state. In this sense he was an exception among popular rights advocates; if anything, his cohorts became even more vociferous defenders of *kokken* with each passing year.

Why the Movement Failed

The arguments which the advocates of popular rights propounded in their voluminous writings may appear logical and convincing to people acclimated to Western liberal thought, but for the Japanese masses of the Meiji era they remained abstract concepts unrelated to the realities of their daily life. The ideas being propagated and the examples being cited came mainly from the West. Thus they failed to appeal to the innermost sentiments of the masses. The values they cherished were still traditional ones like social harmony, self-denial, moderation, humility, courtesy, deference, duty, obedience, and self-discipline. Liberty was equated with license. Insistence on individual rights seemed to be a sign of selfishness. In the battle for the minds of the masses, the *jiyū minken* advocates lost out to the proponents of *chūkun* (loyalty to the sovereign) and *aikoku* (love of nation).

Another flaw in the popular rights movement was the dichotomy of theory and practice that characterized the behavior of the proponents. They advocated liberalism but in most cases they continued to behave in traditional authoritarian fashion. In his writings Ueki championed the cause of women's rights and dignity, for example, but he himself was a regular patron of the brothels and at one time even took a woman by force. After having devoted most of his life fighting for popular rights and criticizing the authoritarianism of the Meiji oligarchs, he joined those who broke rank with the party members in the first Diet session and voted for the government's military budget—an issue which the opposition leaders deemed vital in checking the oligarchs' power. His critics hinted darkly that he and the others had been bribed by government leaders. Thus he helped set the precedent which enabled the Meiji oligarchs to split and manipulate the opposition.

Because many of the *minken* leaders were motivated by the desire to gain power rather than uphold theoretical principles they were easily persuaded to split off from the movement with offers of posts in the government. Gotō Shōjirō (1838–1897), sponsor of the Memorial of 1874, moved in and out of the government. Itagaki himself took a post in the Itō cabinet as home minister in 1896, and Ōkuma took his first cabinet post in 1888 as foreign minister. Less prominent men were often absorbed into the lower depths of the bureaucracy. It would not be unjust to say that the motives and thinking of the mainstream *minken* movement were in essence little different from those of the Meiji oligarchs. It can be argued that the government faction, led by Prince Itō Hirobumi (1841–1909), did as much in laying the groundwork for constitutional and parliamentary government as did the *minken* advocates. In fact the government faction may even have been a step ahead of the latter. George Akita has written, "the thinking of the oligarchy on the subject [of parliamentary government] plainly antedated the demands of the outs and was at times much more 'liberal'."

At the same time, however, the continuous pressure that the *minken* advocates applied on the oligarchs forced them to move more quickly than they had expected. Moreover, even though many were motivated by selfish ends, others were sincere, especially men like Fukuzawa Yukichi and Nakae Chōmin (1847–1901), who harbored no political ambitions. And their writings, whether sincere or mere verbiage, did influence the thinking of the literate public and enhance the political sophistication of the thinking public.

The Popular Rights Debate: Political or Ideological?

James L. Huffman

The Meiji years mark one of history's most dynamic eras, a time of breathtakingly rapid change in nearly all aspects of Japan's national life. As a result, the men who guided and challenged the national transformation have become the subjects of more than an ordinary amount of scholarly attention. They are usually viewed as giants—individuals with special talents, unique vision, overarching influence, extraordinary administrative skills, even unusual sexual prowess—the stuff, in many cases, of myth and legend. While the more fantastic aspects of these myths are scorned (or, more appropriately, ignored) by scholars, there nevertheless remain several areas in which the "bigger-than-life" syndrome seems to have affected even scholarly analyses of the overall period, thus distorting our understanding of Meiji Japan. I seek, in this discussion, to challenge—or at least to bring into balance—two such areas.

First, there is an unfortunate tendency to dwell on the early Meiji leaders' special sense of nation. More than their counterparts in other lands, we are told, these men operated in an overwhelmingly *national* context, basing their arguments and decisions on a single question: What is best for the nation? A leading Meiji historian, Marius B. Jansen, has written in this vein: "The samurai provided Japan with single-minded, nation-directed leadership. The phrase *kuni no tame* ('for the sake of the country') was a constant in political discussions. . . . The argument was not whether the nation needed building, but how it could be built most rapidly and effectively."

This theme dominates many of the texts on the era, often to the point of excluding less idealistic motivations. A related generalization is the oft-repeated (or silently accepted) idea that the government's critics, whether on the right or on the left, were inspired to an unusual degree by unmitigated ideological commitment. Saigō Taka-mori, for example, is depicted as believing so deeply in the feudal samurai ethic that he felt compelled to resign from office when he saw the government "prostituting" that ethic in 1873. Members of the "liberal" opposition, from Ōi Kentarō to the Chichibu freedom fighters, are similarly portrayed as near-zealots, dedicated so completely to their causes that they would accept death or defeat more easily than compromise. The "liberals" of early Meiji, says Joseph S. Pittau, "were in general large-minded and optimistic seekers after freedom and progress, confident that individual freedom would result in national freedom.

There is, without question, considerable truth in both these generalizations. Meiji leaders did concern themselves consistently with questions regarding the national good, even as many of their opponents argued their causes with such consistency and fervor as to suggest genuine ideological conviction. I would suggest, however, that a scholarly preoccupation with the leaders' nation orientation or with the ideological statements of the critics (a preoccupation, that is, with surface rhetoric that ignores subsurface motivations) has tended to obscure an equally important component of the Meiji political mix. It has ignored the more selfish interests: the struggle for personal or factional power that lay behind most Meiji political debates.

Examples of calculating power politics abound in the Meiji archives —in government efforts to control the opposition by bribery and brutality, in the theoretical flip-flops of liberals as diverse as Itagaki Taisuke and Ōkuma Shigenobu, in the oligarchs' successful attempts to pack the bureaucracy with men from their own *han* of Satsuma and Chōshū. But one need not rely only on actions. An analysis of rhetoric, too, even the carefully calculated rhetoric of the era's leading debates, reveals a great deal of the self-interested side of leadership. One of the more striking examples lies in the highly ideological popular rights *(jiyū minken)* debate of 1874–1875, a debate sparked by the "optimistic seekers after freedom and progress" referred to above and carried on in the editorial columns of the day's leading newspapers. It is this debate that I wish to analyze here.

The popular rights discussions were sparked by the Memorial of 1874 calling for the immediate creation of a popularly elected national assembly. Drawn up by Itagaki and a number of other former officials who had left office with Saigō the previous autumn, it accused the government of arbitrariness and predicted that unless popular reforms were initiated soon, the state would be ruined. The memorial reportedly stunned the government, coming as it did from several of the nation's prominent leaders, and sparked the most intense public policy discussion since the Meiji Restoration.

The newspaper debate of the issue appeared in segments. An initial outburst came early in 1874, just after the publication of Itagaki's memorial; the furor died down in the spring as national attention turned to the government's plans to send a military expedition to Taiwan; then it flared up again during the latter part of 1874, continuing into the next spring. During the initial months, the government organ, *Nisshin Shinjishi,* edited by the Englishman J. R. Black, generally took the progovernment, anti-*minken* position whereas the Tokyo *Nichi Nichi Shimbun* ran articles on both sides of the issue. One interesting characteristic of this first period was that most articles were run not as editorials but in correspondence columns; newspapers, still in their infancy, had not yet developed either a consistent editorial line or a format for editorials. Another characteristic was the rancor with which both sides often took to the attack; Black described the early 1874 press as a "battleground go-between."

By the time the popular-assembly debate had resumed later in 1874, the generals leading the battle had changed, however, and so had the battle itself. During the summer and early autumn, two new voices had entered the press world—Fukuchi Gen'ichirō at *Nichi Nichi* and Kurimoto Joun at *Yūbin Hōchi Shimbun,* which until mid-1874 had been a progovernment paper. Both men had already become opinion leaders, Fukuchi as a Finance Ministry official with close ties to the government's Chōshū faction, Kurimoto as a private spokesman with links to Fukuzawa Yukichi and his Keiō school. And both used the popular rights fight to turn their papers into highly influential voices of political opinion by running regular front-page editorials on the issue. As a result, the newspaper debate became a major focus and stimulus of national political discussion: *Nichi Nichi* supported the progovernment position known as gradualism *(zenshin-shugi)* while *Hōchi* led the *minken* cause.

On the surface, the positions of each camp were reasonably straightforward. The *minken* faction argued with a passion born of apparent conviction: (1) that current government policies amounted to a "continuation of official despotism, which would cause the people not to believe in official decrees or to submit to the government," (2) that a popularly elected assembly must be created immediately to forestall disillusionment and possible chaos, and (3) that the assembly should be composed of the national elite—members of the former samurai and noble classes. (*Shizoku* was the term generally used to encompass both nobles and samurai.) The heart of this position lay in the second demand—that an assembly be created *now*. As a *Hōchi* editorialist declared on 29 January 1875, the only political leaders in all Japan worthy of the name "true statesman" were those "former lords and councillors who wanted to open an assembly immediately." But if the bulk of copy was devoted to the call for an assembly, the greatest heat was generated by the *minken* camp's insistence that *shizoku* alone make up the legislative body. Nothing, apparently, angered—or frightened—them more than several official moves afoot to dilute their strength and undermine their economic status by raising the nation's 30 million commoners *(heimin)* to equal legal status by taking away the annual hereditary stipends that all samurai were used to receiving from the government. As a result, repeated articles during the early months of 1875 berated the *heimin* as "ignorant," "unlearned," "weakhearted people" or "powerless fools incapable of guiding the nation." Moreover, these editorials added, the elite *shizoku* class *deserved* its annual stipends. As a *Hōchi* writer declared on 20 March 1875, the *shizoku* in recent years "had earned great merit, maintaining the country's independence and honor, carrying out the restoration, bringing European and American culture to Japan, and masterminding national progress." The merit thus attained, he argued, demanded a continuation of special privileges, both political and economic.

Fukuchi at *Nichi Nichi,* on the other hand, defended the government's gradualist position. He agreed that an assembly was needed but maintained that since most citizens still were unskilled in the arts of self-government, they should be educated through cooperative ventures (both economic and political) at the local and prefectural levels before a national assembly was created. To move too rapidly toward a national popular assembly, he argued on 6 December 1874, would be to invite disruptive change, thus making it "impossible to maintain national tranquility." Did not the most perceptive Western statesmen all maintain that radical political shifts represented a "gamble, a race between national peace and national chaos"? Basic to this argument was his further contention that all the people—commoners as well as *shizoku*—should be included in the assembly. "Is it logical," he asked in a *Nichi Nichi* editorial on 12 March 1875, that stipend-receiving former samurai "who are parasites sustained by the people . . . should have more rights than rich or good commoners?" On 25 March he said the only reason why many *heimin* were spiritless today was that in previous eras they had been forced "to live in servitude under an oppressive governmental system." Trained in the arts of local public service, they would soon become just as capable of legislative service as the *shizoku*. Such training would, however, take time: "Vitality is a quality that does not develop in an instant. But as we increase the rate of the restoration of popular rights, their spirit will increase commensurately" (27 March 1875).

That the debaters on both sides felt deeply about their ideological positions is indisputable, as is the fact that men on both sides were genuinely concerned about what was best for the nation. But it is equally significant that each side took only those positions most likely to enhance its own chances in the struggle for power. While the "nation's interests" dominated the rhetoric, the *faction's* interests dictated the underlying positions. And though this fact hardly sets Japan apart from other lands, it nevertheless demands notice in light of the almost exclusive emphasis placed by most scholars on the "nation-centered" concerns of Meiji leaders.

Let us look at Fukuchi's position. Not surprisingly, a careful reading of his 1874–1875 gradualist articles reveals not a single argument likely to have seriously threatened the power of the government. The assembly system that he advocated was regarded by all as necessary to the eventual rationalization of what was essentially an ad hoc regime. Deliberate movement toward the creation of that assembly would enable the oligarchs to stay in power for a time while giving them an opportunity to develop methods to control the assembly system. Even his "liberal" insistence on including commoners in the government, though probably not insincere, was replete with advantages for the Meiji establishment. It would justify postponement of the day when an assembly would be feasible; it would undermine the powerful ex-samurai class, which was small enough and prestigious enough to serve as the regime's most potent opposition; and it would lend support to government arguments that the samurai class did not deserve special privileges—especially the annual stipends that had become such a drain on the national treasury. Commoners, moreover, made up almost half of *Nichi Nichi*'s subscribers; to advocate their cause was hardly an ideological act of economic self-sacrifice.

But the gradualists were not alone in tailoring logic to expediency. The opposition, which sometimes is considered to have been more thoroughly ideological in its orientation, apparently played the same game. *Minken* arguments that the current government was despotic, for example, carried with them the corollary that "honest" servants of the national will (that is, *minken* leaders) should be brought into the government to effect proper changes. And what tool could have given Itagaki and Kurimoto greater leverage than the early election of a popular assembly—an assembly to which only individuals from their own small class would be selected? Perhaps the most obviously self-serving aspect of the *minken* position was the sustained defense of the idea of granting governing rights only to the elite *shizoku*. The *Hōchi* editorials made it absolutely clear that when *minken* theorists spoke of popular rights they had in mind rights for their own social stratum and no other. Popular rights, in other words, meant elite rights—rights for the class represented by Itagaki, Kurimoto, and most of the *Hōchi* readers.

The fact that the *minken* disputants suddenly abandoned the debate in mid-April of 1875, when the government announced that a "conference of local officials" *(chihōkan kaigi)* would be convened and that Itagaki had been asked to reenter the government, simply heightens the impression that their arguments were, to a significant degree, political. The promised conference was not to be popularly elected; nor was there assurance that it would carry any clout. But the fact that it was an assembly and that the *minken* clique's leading spokesman had been invited back into the government was apparently enough to cause *Hōchi* to exult on 14 April: "It is splendid. It is good. . . . It is for the good of the people." One is hardly surprised to hear Fukuchi sneering some weeks later that the *minken* had been "swallowed whole by its god and general" Itagaki.

It seems clear that, at least in the 1874–1875 debate over a popular assembly, neither side operated simply on the basis of ideological conviction. This is not to suggest that the debaters were cynics; nor is it to argue that they were less sincere than typical leaders in any other time or place. I wish merely to emphasize that while the leading spokesmen of Meiji Japan may have *talked* more about the nation's good than have those of many lands, they nevertheless acted as typically human, political individuals with an abundance of ego and an intense craving for power. As Albert Craig has noted: "The desire for success is strong in most Japanese. Only a few can attain it. Those who do must exhibit drive to an exceptional degree." Only as we deal with this easily accepted but little examined fact of personal ambition and factional power struggle can we expect to bring Meiji history out of the two-dimensional world of the Modernizing Hero and into the complex universe of human struggle—good, bad, and neutral.

The Meiji Leadership: Matsukata Masayoshi

Jackson H. Bailey

Financial wizard, political autocrat, perpetrator of arbitrary oligarchic control: these are the clichés in modern Japanese history that are attached to Matsukata Masayoshi. Yet to New Left revisionist historians of the early 1970s and to traditionalist Marxist historians in Japan he epitomized many of the evils of Meiji politics and the Meiji period. Much writing about Meiji history in Japan and in the West has been colored by a priori ideological assumptions. Even detailed discussions of Meiji political and economic development devote little space to serious evaluation of Matsukata's role in that process. W. W. Lockwood's standard history of Japan's modern economic development seldom mentions him by name.) So, paradoxically, we find Matsukata cited as the paradigm of all that was bad about Meiji leadership *and* referred to only briefly as the able architect of Japan's modern system of government finance.

It is time to explore Matsukata's role in modern Japan history in a much less superficial way. While there are biographies and research volumes in Japanese which develop this role in great detail, few of them have a substantial interpretive thrust. It is the thesis of this essay that Matsukata, like virtually all the Meiji leaders, was guided first and last by a commitment to the twin objectives of *Fukoku Kyōhei.* This slogan was not a facade masking self-interest or class interest; indeed the Meiji leaders made most of their political and economic decisions to contribute to its fulfillment from a sense of urgency. Otherwise Japan, which was patently far behind the advanced nations of the West, would be swallowed up in the intense competition for markets and colonies that marked the world of the late nineteenth century.

Matsukata's commitment to Japanese economic development was deep and his talent substantial. He was a hybrid typical of the Meiji leadership. Of samurai stock and a patriotic Japanese to the core, he acquired Western knowledge and experience and dedicated them and talent to building a great nation. Was he a liberal? Yes, in terms of late-nineteenth-century economic thinking, and certainly in terms of his samurai background. Was he autocratic? Yes, in terms of democratic principles and processes, and especially in terms of late-twentieth-century practice.

Matsukata was born in 1835 in Kagoshima, Kyushu, the capital of the Satsuma *han*. His family, lower-rank samurai, was not prosperous and as the fourth son (some sources say fifth) he was forced to make his own way in a world that was falling apart as he reached adulthood in the 1850s. At that point he managed to attach himself to the staff of the daimyo of Satsuma, Shimazu Hisamitsu; there he drew the attention of one of Hisamitsu's able young lieutenants, Ōkubo Toshimichi. Matsukata's accomplishments resulted from this connection and the opportunities which it and Ōkubo and, later, Itō Hirobumi provided him. He was a less colorful figure than other Meiji leaders, and his interests were not as broad as those of Itō or Ōkuma Shigenobu, who seemed to revel in politics and took a hand in every aspect of national life.

Matsukata played an active role in the events of the Meiji Restoration, working devotedly for the elimination of shogunal rule. He was rewarded in 1868, at the age of thirty-three, by a governorship in northern Kyushu. There he endeavored to put the affairs of that part of Japan in order after the chaotic years of the anti-Tokugawa movement. This practical experience in local government became the basis for his later work at the national level. His approach to local government was simple and direct: keep expenses to a minimum, stabilize government policy so people will know what to expect, and attack local problems directly and efficiently. During his two-year tenure Matsukata devised several plans for local welfare work which later became models for national policy planning.

Once the authority of the Meiji government had been established, Matsukata was drawn into national administration and joined Ōkuma in the Finance Ministry as one of Ōkubo's trusted assistants. With Ōkuma he devised plans for commuting stipends for ex-samurai into single-payment bonds. By 1873 they had designed the conversion of the national economy to a regular money tax system based on assessed land values to replace the feudal system of taxes on crops. This new tax system provided the foundation for Meiji government finances; yet it is often singled out as one of the great evils perpetrated by the

Meiji leaders since it burdened the farmers with the weight of taxes for the whole modernization process. Although that issue is too complex to be dealt with here, it should be noted that there were few alternatives available to the Meiji government and, further, that in the twentieth century other regimes, of the left as well as the right, have in effect done much the same.

Matsukata's interests became more and more focused on government finance and in the late 1870s he made his first trip abroad, spending part of a year in Europe. His assignment was to represent Japan in the planning for a world trade fair in France. It appears that his ideas about fiscal management and broad economic policy took final shape at this time. He had lengthy conversations with Leon Say, the French minister of finance, and some of his associates, and this informal training in government finance seems to have established for Matsukata his basic approach to Japan's economic problems. It was an approach characterized by laissez-faire, capitalist economic principles and infused with a deep personal sense of patriotism, devotion to the emperor, and a desire to make Japan a strong state and a world power.

Fukoku Kyōhei expressed the sort of fierce and urgent nationalism that characterized the West in the late nineteenth century when Japan reentered the mainstream of events. The world was a fiercely competitive place as the advanced Western nations vied for new colonies, resources, and markets in Asia and Africa. Matsukata reflected this reality when he wrote "there is no quick way to achieve national power other than through planning for the development of industry and relying upon it for fiscal strength. To do this we must make overseas trade prosper, greatly expand our exports, and reduce our imports." Such words express economic nationalism with overtones that persist in Japanese thinking even today. On his return from Europe in late 1878 Matsukata gave a speech at a reception which reflected the fierce pragmatism he had acquired. He said, "People's eyes are usually caught by the beauty of the flowers. Few focus their attention on the fruit. We Japanese must put aside our preoccupation with the flowers of civilization. We must realize the fruits of wealth and power." Matsukata returned home to seek the fruits of national power for Japan.

The political crisis of October 1881, which had been brewing for some time, led to the removal of Ōkuma from government leadership and opened the way for Matsukata to assume the key role in government fiscal planning and administration. From then until 1900 his was the dominant voice in economic matters in the Japanese government. He set the goals, devised the means to reach them, convinced his colleagues of their appropriateness, and gave a tone to the whole government operation which produced fiscal stability at home, inspired confidence abroad, and outraged opposition leaders and later historians. From 1900 to his death in 1924, as a member of the genro, he continued to be a powerful, though gradually muted, force in all matters related to the national economic life of the country. His advice and his approval were sought by politicians and bureaucrats alike.

What did Matsukata do? How should we assess his work and his role as a Meiji leader? In late 1881 when he took over as state minister of finance succeeding Ōkuma Shigenobu, the nation's financial condition was desperate. Inflation was rampant at home; the yen was not accepted as sound currency abroad; the Meiji state was virtually bankrupt. The reasons for this state of affairs were easy to find. The Satsuma Rebellion of 1877 on top of the early reforms of the Meiji period (the universal education law, for example, and the bond issue floated to commute samurai stipends) had strained government financial capacity beyond the breaking point. Currency had been printed as a short-term palliative but had only added to the problems of inflation and instability. Matsukata had already quarreled with Ōkuma over the selection of means to deal with the crisis. Ōkuma had advocated foreign loans to shore up the money supply and stabilize the yen. Matsukata was unalterably opposed to such action, fearing foreign interference or control like that which obtained in China

Once in charge Matsukata moved swiftly and effectively on two fronts. On the one hand he cut government expenses drastically and immediately began to sell government-sponsored enterprises; on the other he made plans for domestic loans which would be used to retire some of the inflated currency and stabilize the remainder. His actions were dramatic and daring. Before he took them he had carefully made the rounds of the top leadership to be sure he had full support. He received assurance from Itō, Iwakura, and Sanjō as well as the emperor himself. He called together the officials of the Finance Ministry and sketched his plans, receiving promises of support from them in the implementation of the new approach.

Once the policies of retrenchment and currency reform were under way Matsukata turned to what he considered the positive task of building new institutions. First came establishment of a national bank. The Bank of Japan began operation on 10 October 1882. Matsukata was responsible for its basic conception and design, and it remains the greatest monument to his leadership.

These first steps, bold and dangerous as they were, were consistent and received wide support. The sense of urgency felt by most Japanese in the face of a presumed foreign threat and internal financial chaos was sufficient to produce this support. Consistency in policy is difficult to maintain, however, and nowhere more than in politics. Matsukata and his colleagues were soon under pressure to expand budgetary commitments to the military. This proposal flew in the face of his retrenchment policy, but the pressures of geopolitical realities in Korea as viewed from Tokyo convinced him and the other Meiji leaders that they must continue the buildup of Japan's armed forces. (Some historians would call this the reflection of a plan for imperialist activity. I reject that explanation. There was no grand design.) Such was the force of Matsukata's leadership and fiscal skills that in spite of these added expenses he was able to keep government spending in balance, though he had to raise taxes further in the mid-1880s. Simultaneously, the tax burden of the 1880s fell heavily on the agricultural population and future problems such as farm debt and rising tenancy among farmers appear at this time.

"Matsukata fiscal policy" *(Matsukata Zaisei)* was in economic terms a success. By 1886 inflation and government spending were under control and, perhaps the most dramatic evidence of its success, the currency was sound and convertible at home and abroad. Ground had been cleared for a sound budgeting and accounting system in preparation for the establishment of constitutional government. These were no small achievements. At the same time there were social costs which were not evenly shared but, rather, were borne disproportionately by the agricultural segment of the population.

In the late 1880s, with domestic finances stable and the plans for the new constitution nearing completion, the Meiji government again turned its attention to foreign affairs, specifically the revision of the unequal treaties. Without the fiscal reform and institution-building that Matsukata had accomplished in the first half of the decade Japan would not have had the stability or the strength to mount the campaign for treaty revision which culminated in July 1894 with the agreement with Britain for full and comprehensive revision. The reforms also provided the fiscal base on which Japan was able to mount her successful war with China, thereby joining the Western nations as a major colonial power in Asia.

Though Matsukata was dramatically successful as the architect of fiscal reform and economic policy in the 1880s he was singularly unsuccessful as politician and prime minister in the 1890s. His first premiership ended in utter disaster and he was forced to resign after fourteen months in office. He failed to understand the nature and potential of parliamentary government—indeed he failed to accept the process of parliamentary government as legitimate. This attitude led to serious and violent abuses of state power to restrict political activity by the opposition. In fact it led him to condone, if not actively promote, bribery and intimidation by government officials in the second general election under the new constitution in January and February 1892. Throughout the 1880s in the constitution-making process he had thrown his weight behind the need to strengthen state power to maintain central fiscal control and prevent the political parties from acquiring significant power over state finances. A careful reading of the Meiji Constitution reveals the way in which this approach was implemented. The Diet had only a negative veto power over the budget. Initiative and positive control lay within the government. As one of his biographers, Fujimura T., put it, "he attacked the parties fiercely. He showed no understanding of their role. He did not have the political flexibility that Itō had."

Matsukata made one more foray into active politics, heading a cabinet in 1896, but his interests and his talents clearly were not in this broader role of general political leadership. His lack of breadth and flexibility as a politician have tended to obscure the significance of his role in the economic life of Japan from 1880 to 1900. These two facets of his career need to be assessed separately.

The political crisis of 1881 has been interpreted largely as the first great test in the struggle for popular rights. Ōkuma's ouster from the government has been seen as primarily a political event. It is useful to regard it also as a key move in economic policy. Matsukata and Ōkuma, as chief assistants to Ōkubo, had worked together on the tax reforms of the mid-1870s. Ōkuma's interests were broadly political; Matsukata's were economic and financial. Behind the political maneuvering between Itō and Ōkuma, behind the scandal in Hokkaido over development practices, lay the economic crisis of inflation and fiscal chaos. Matsukata and Ōkuma were at odds over policies to deal with the crisis, especially the issue of foreign loans. One could view the events of October 1881 as determined primarily by these economic considerations. Matsukata believed that Ōkuma's policies, far from solving the crisis, would add to it the danger of foreign intervention. He convinced Itō that he was right and was given essentially a free hand to apply his own methods to find a solution. By any standard one could use, in the short run, his policies were signally successful. Within five years effective reforms had been implemented and sound institutions and fiscal practices established.

Both his Japanese experience and his Western practice confirmed Matsukata in his policy commitments. He saw sound fiscal practice and capitalist-oriented economic policy as the twin pillars of those government policies. Politically, he viewed party activity and popular participation in government not only as inappropriate but an evil to be avoided. Such activities would interfere with sound management and healthy economic growth. Matsukata's focus was narrowly on the economic and fiscal realities as he knew them. Politics should be subordinate to economics.

The economic and political issues were so interrelated, however, that they could not be separated and Matsukata's inability to come to terms with that reality led him to adopt politically inappropriate and ineffective means. One analysis of this interrelationship puts the matter this way:

> On the one hand *Matsukata Zaisei* fulfilled a major role in the process of savings (and capital) accumulation. At the same time it also served to prepare the mechanism for financial administration and the fiscal system under the Meiji Constitution. Further, it established a fiscal policymaking structure which could be protected (from the parties) in the consultations regarding budget which would take place after the opening of the Diet. As a result, all of these mechanisms and structure—the modern tax administration, a unified national treasury, the budgetary process which had developed as a method to produce democratic fiscal policy (and control) in the Diet—served instead to fulfill the objectives of strengthening the power structure of the emperor system and the state.

Here we find the historian's dilemma in interpretation. In the decade of the 1880s Matsukata took vigorous steps to reform and build a sound financial structure for the state. He did this out of a sense of patriotic devotion to Meiji Japan. The institutions he established were viable and effective. In the 1890s, however, within a parliamentary system this new structure inhibited the development of democratic control of national finances.

Matsukata was a modern bureaucrat imbued with nineteenth-century liberal economic principles. How could one run national finances effectively if meddling politicians had the power to block or disrupt the process? Since he viewed political parties as illegitimate, they and their activities should be dealt with summarily by any means at hand, including the police power of the state. Fujimura says:

Matsukata in this way devoted himself to modernizing the country's finances. His economic ideas clearly were modern but his political ideas were both reactionary and antidemocratic. Herein lies the contradiction in his thinking. Whereas Itō was prepared to become a man of the political parties, Matsukata found this repulsive. He put greater emphasis on economics than on politics.

Matsukata's contribution to modern Japan was not just positive in economic terms; it was monumental. In political terms it was negative. What had been bold, liberal, and successful economic leadership in the 1880s became autocratic political obstructionism in the 1890s.

Tanaka Shōzō: Champion of Local Autonomy

Victor Carpenter

Tanaka Shōzō (1840–1913) became one of the major antigovernment figures of the Meiji period. He drew from his own rural beginnings, his involvement in the popular rights movement of the 1880s, and his encounter with the Ashio Copper Mine poisoning issue while a national Diet member in the 1890s to fashion an attack on the policies and ideological orthodoxies of the Meiji government. For Tanaka, an ardent supporter of local autonomy, local rights, and the primacy of agriculture, Meiji economic polity, with its heavy emphasis on industrialization and political centralization, was undermining the rural foundations of the country. So strong were Tanaka's commitments that he broke with the rest of the Diet over them and eventually quit that body altogether. His story, and his critique, serve as poignant illustrations of the underside of Meiji modernization.

Tanaka Shōzō was born in Konaka, a small rice-growing village located in Shimotsuke-no-kuni (modern Tochigi prefecture) northeast of Edo. Konaka, like many other villages in the Kantō region, was characterized by fragmented ownership. This situation could be traced back to the Tokugawa settlement of 1601 when the *bakufu* consciously created a landholding system around Edo which assured that no single house could concentrate its resources and pose a threat to the capital. Land rights were given only to direct retainers of the *bakufu*. Holdings were kept small and often were scattered among several villages while the retainers themselves were required to reside in Edo.

Konaka itself was half owned by a *bakufu* bannerman *(hatamoto)* house, the Sano; most of the remainder was under the control of the Rokkaku, an aristocratic family *(kōke)* with origins in the Muromachi period which managed to secure a hereditary bureaucratic position under the Tokugawa. The Rokkaku and the Sano both lived in Edo, far from their Shimotsuke domains. Because their incomes and means were limited and their rule circumscribed by Tokugawa law, they had little direct say in the innerworkings of the villages under their control. As a result these villages, although responsible for collecting and submitting taxes to their overlords, were left to manage their own affairs independent of higher authority. Thus the cultivators in Konaka village, as in other Kantō villages, developed a strong sense of independence and self-reliance while the village itself evolved customs and institutions of self-rule *(jichi)*. The cooperative institutions at the *han* level, where the warrior *(samurai)* class ruled over a political and social hierarchy defined in rigid class terms.

In 1857 Tanaka Shōzō's father, the headman *(nanushi)* of the Rokkaku half of the village, was named as the official liaison *(warimoto)* for the seven Shimotsuke villages under Rokkaku control. The villagers, in accordance with established procedure, gathered to elect a new headman and chose the seventeen-year-old Shōzō to succeed his highly regarded father. The son served the Konaka villagers as headman for the next twelve years.

Because Tanaka was elected directly by fellow villagers and continued to farm among them, he had to view himself variously as leader, cultivator, and part of the communal self-rule village. His sense of leadership was molded by his Confucian training and the precept that it was an official's duty to rule in an enlightened and responsible manner. His day-to-day duties as cultivator and elected headman demanded that these ideas be put into practice.

Tanaka was also firmly committed to the autonomy of the village itself. He believed that the custom of self-rule was inviolable and that it was the obligation of one with public responsibility to defend it. Much of his twelve-year headmanship was taken up in a long dispute over levies assessed by an ambitious Rokkaku official in Edo.

After the Meiji Restoration, Tanaka served briefly as a minor official in northeastern Japan. Shortly after assuming office, however, he was falsely accused of the murder of another official and imprisoned for more than two years. After his release he returned to Konaka, to farming, and to local politics. After a successful land speculation venture he acquired the financial means to engage full time in regional politics. When he decided to enter the world of politics he resolved to rid himself of all other commitments, including his personal property and children, and completely immersed himself in politics.

He quickly became involved in the local popular rights movement *(jiyū minken undō)*. Ex-samurai, the rural elite *(gōnō)*, and small landowners were all involved in local popular rights groups, although the *gōnō* usually dominated. This loose and ill-defined alignment fell apart in the mid-1880s due largely to the conflict between the *gōnō* and the smaller landholders, reflecting the growing polarization between hard-pressed small-scale cultivators and the *gōnō* whose land and financial holdings were rapidly expanding at the former's expense. After the dissolution of the popular rights movement, *gōnō* popular activists continued as the core of the political parties which dominated prefectural assemblies and prepared for the creation of the national Diet in 1890. They also carried on the popular rights movement's hostility to the government.

Tanaka Shōzō was an early activist in the popular rights politics of Tochigi prefecture. First he became editor of *Tochigi Shimbun*, a popular rights newspaper, in 1879. Shortly thereafter, in 1881, he was named to the Tochigi Prefectural Assembly, where he spearheaded a drive to oust Mishima Michitsune, the prefectural governor dispatched from Tokyo. Mishima came promoting an ambitious road-building project which exacted a heavy price from prefectural taxpayers. After a bitter struggle, Tanaka and other assemblymen succeeded in having the governor recalled to Tokyo.

Tanaka's grasp of law and politics, still grounded in his experience in the autonomous village, differed greatly from the autocratic and bureaucratic consciousness of the Meiji leadership. Like other rural leaders, he opposed the land tax. Put into effect by the Meiji oligarchy to consolidate government control over the countryside and to create stable revenues for industrial growth, the land tax did little to enhance local prosperity or encourage local participation in national affairs.

His position in the conflict between the *gōnō* and the smallholders was ambivalent. Tanaka's family had only modest wealth, but because they had held the village leadership from the time of his grandfather, their status and influence were greater than one might imagine. He did, however, remain in the party movement after the dissolution of the popular rights movement (belonging to Ōkuma Shigenobu's Progressive Party) and did not break with *gōnō* politics until after his confrontation with the Ashio Mine case in the 1890s.

Tanaka's tenure in the prefectural assembly and his participation in the popular rights and early party movements exposed him to regional and national problems. Nevertheless, despite his involvement in the larger political conflict with the central government, he never

lost sight of the village as the major source of his strength and the focus of his loyalty. In 1890 he was elected as a representative from Tochigi prefecture to the first national Diet, where he and other party
members carried on their fight against the oligarchs. In 1891 he was
first informed of a pollution crisis developing in the Watarase River
Valley in his district. Thus began the Ashio Mine affair.

The development of the Ashio Copper Mine was intimately connected with the Meiji government's drive to modernize the country
and increase exports of industrial products in order to keep the balance of payments disequilibrium as small as possible. The Ashio
Mine, located in Tochigi prefecture, was the most productive copper
mine in Japan. Its owner, Furukawa Ichibei, one of Japan's most successful financial entrepreneurs, amassed an empire around his mining
interests. He astutely cultivated contacts with the Meiji oligarchs in
securing and mechanizing his holdings while the oligarchs, in turn,
protected his interests for the sake of the national economy. Furukawa's quest for profits and the oligarchs' encouragement of expanded
production thus generated a natural symbiosis of economic and political interests.

With the tremendous increase in the mine's output in the late
1880s, greater and greater amounts of poison effluents seeped into
the Watarase River, which drained the area. First the river's fish died;
then crops failed from the effects of the river's poisoned floodwater;
finally, unusual illnesses appeared among people living along the
river. The Meiji government, however, took no action against the
mine. It refused to recognize the clear evidence that the mine was responsible for the distress along the river. When the government finally admitted that the mine was responsible, it pressured affected
villages to make out-of-court damage settlements with the mine. In
spite of the promises by both the government and the mine that measures would be taken to curtail the population, the poisoning continued.

Unlike the Meiji government, Tanaka Shōzō focused on the needs
and rights of the people. For the villagers along the Watarase, solution of the poisoning problem was a life and death matter. Tanaka
therefore considered it the responsibility of the government, the
Diet, and the political parties to redress the suffering caused by the
polluting mine.

Hoping the domination of the Diet by political parties that were
thought to be more responsive to public opinion would help his
cause, Tanaka took the copper poisoning problem to the Diet; but his

efforts met with little success. For the parties, dominated by emerging landlord and small middle-scale manufacturing interests, popular participation meant securing a voice for their own demands as well as the ouster of the oligarchs. After the opening of the Diet they continued their all-out struggle against the oligarchy by refusing to pass the government's budgets. The parties demanded an end to the land tax, or at least a reduction, and pushed for the elimination of the oligarchs. The oligarchs countered by dissolving the Diet, three times in the first four years of its existence, thus forcing new elections. Eventually party members wearied of this frustrating struggle and sought power through compromise rather than confrontation. In turn the oligarchs, particularly Itō Hirobumi, gradually decided to integrate the parties into the political structure.

Two parties dominated in the early 1890s: Itagaki Taisuke's Liberal Party (Jiyūtō) and Ōkuma Shigenobu's Progressive Party (Kaishintō). By 1894 both Itagaki and Ōkuma were actively arranging alliances with oligarchic factions, and after 1895 they were able to capture cabinet posts in successive governments. In 1898 they collaborated to form Japan's first party cabinet. The Ōkuma–Itagaki government, however, lasted only four months. This brief exercise in party government was dominated by infighting between the two factions, the intense efforts of party members to establish themselves in influential and lucrative governmental positions, and the hostility of the Meiji oligarchy. Subsequently the two parties again competed with one another to establish coalitions with whichever oligarchic faction was in power. Finally, in 1901, the Liberal Party dissolved and joined forces with Itō to form the Seiyūkai. The parties were after power; collaboration and even amalgamation with the Meiji rulers to obtain it—even at the expense of an opposition political party—were their practices.

While other party politicians were joining forces with the oligarchs, Tanaka Shōzō continued his attacks on the government. He refused to compromise with the Meiji government because he was absorbed in the problems of the people along the Watarase and their battle against the Ashio Mine. Viewing the ties between mine and government as the reason behind the government's refusal to stop mine production, he therefore continued to press for removal of the oligarchs. As headman of Konaka village, he felt compelled to protect the interests of his fellow villagers and the integrity of the village itself. Tanaka's encounter with the copper poisoning issue revived his agrarian hostility toward central authority and reinvigorated his populism.

The parties' lack of concern for the copper poisoning problem increasingly isolated Tanaka within the Diet. His frustration intensified as conditions along the Watarase worsened. Yet he never ceased to struggle outside the Diet as a lobbyist or to make speeches in the Diet demanding that the mine be closed. He orchestrated rallies, made speeches, and headed a loosely organized movement including farmers from the Watarase River Valley, students, and intellectuals and journalists, like Kinoshita Naoe, from the emerging left. He was also one of the most charismatic orators of his time. He would arrive at a rally in his black robe, disheveled hair, and graying beard and thoroughly move the crowd with his theatrics. By the turn of the century, the Ashio Mine case was one of the most controversial political issues in the nation. The Meiji government, hesitant to move directly against a person of Tanaka's fame, yet concerned over the growing public outcry over Ashio and other issues, enacted a series of laws restricting freedom of assembly and written expression. The efforts of persons like Tanaka were clearly having an effect.

Tanaka was also concerned over the plight of the village itself. The Meiji government, in an effort to rationalize and thus strengthen control over the countryside, enacted a series of reforms in 1889–1890 which consolidated villages into larger administrative units. One purpose was to undermine the autonomy of the self-rule village and integrate it into the centralized Meiji bureaucratic system. There was considerable resistance to these reforms, especially in villages like Konaka, where the tradition of self-rule was deeply engrained.

The Meiji government's alliance with the Ashio Mine and its neglect of the Watarase River Valley inhabitants offered concrete proof to Tanaka that the government was engaged in a systematic effort to destroy the village. Consequently, his defense of self-rule (jichi) became more strident. Yet it took the direct action of distraught Watarase River Valley cultivators to force Tanaka into finally accepting that the interests of the Meiji government and the party-dominated Diet were irreconcilably opposed to those of the villages along the Watarase.

In September 1898, several thousand afflicted villagers, frustrated by the empty promises of the government and the mine and desperate over the continued destruction of their crops and livelihood by the copper poisons, set out en masse toward Tokyo to petition the government to close the mine. Tanaka met them at Hokima, on the outskirts of Tokyo, and begged them to return home. He suggested that they select fifty representatives to accompany him back to Tokyo to lobby with him against the mine. He emphasized that, as their Diet representative, it was his responsibility to lead the effort against the government. As the Ōkuma–Itagaki cabinet had just come into power he reasoned with them: "It is our government. We must believe in it and work to correct its weaknesses." He also promised to lead the next march if his efforts failed to move the government. Tanaka's arguments won out and only fifty representatives went with him to Tokyo.

The party government ignored the marchers' pleas just as the oligarchs had done. This treatment furthered Tanaka's disillusionment and hardened his conviction that the Meiji government would destroy the Watarase River complex. In February 1900, when Watarase River Valley villagers again organized a mass protest march on Tokyo, Tanaka offered no resistance. The marchers were met at the Kawamata crossing of the Tone River by government troops and dispersed by force.

For Tanaka this was the last straw. Two days after the Kawamata Incident he announced that he was dropping his party affiliation and becoming an independent. On 19 September he delivered his famous "Death of the Country" speech *(Bōkoku no Ron)*. In it he reiterated his position that the Meiji government's policies were destroying the agricultural base of the nation. This, he continued, would bring about the eventual destruction of the nation itself.

In late 1901, Tanaka quit the Diet altogether. In leaving he charged that any political body which ignored the rights and needs of the people and pursued only its self-seeking interests could no longer be considered a "government" or "Diet." According to Tanaka, the government had neither the ability nor the will to save the inhabitants along the Watarase.

At about the same time Tanaka was quitting the Diet, the government announced its solution for the copper poisoning problem. Instead of forcing a halt to mine production, they would improve flood control techniques along the Watarase, thus keeping poisoned waters out of the farmers' paddies. But one village, Yanaka, would have to be abandoned in order to create a floodplain. Many Yanaka residents, whose attachment to the village ran back countless generations, resisted the evacuation order and refused to move out.

Tanaka, moved by their resolve, decided to aid the doomed village. As government pressure on the inhabitants increased, however, the population dwindled. Finally only eighteen households remained to carry the struggle to the end. Tanaka Shōzō stayed until his death in 1913.

For Tanaka, Yanaka exemplified the fate which awaited other villages in Japan. The "self-rule" system devised by the Meiji government was designed to make the village completely subservient to central control. In practice, as well as in theory, the village had become the smallest cog in a centralized bureaucratic hierarchy—subject, like Yanaka, to the arbitrary whims of the central government. Therefore Tanaka joined forces with the remaining inhabitants to fight for the inviolable right of the village to its land and its autonomy.

By moving into Yanaka village, Tanaka Shōzō reestablished a link with his past. Once again he was immersed in the simple communal politics of the village. But he also saw in the cohesion and the commitment of this tiny group of people the spark of example which could catalyze a revival of local community throughout Japan: a revival which could shake the Meiji government from its destructive course and back to one which recognized and defended the rights of the people. As a result, Tanaka became one of the most influential outsiders of his time.

PART V

Meiji Imperialism: Planned or Unplanned?

THE TITLE of this part suggests that there has been a considerable scholarly debate concerning Meiji imperialism. Was it the result of long-time planning or, as in Akira Iriye's judgment, a reaction to "various unexpected happenings"? The four essays by Hilary Conroy, Ann Harrington, Shumpei Okamoto, and myself disclose a surprising turn of events, however. Despite the disparaging pronouncements—Conroy and Harrington for the "unplanned" theory—a remarkable degree of agreement runs beneath the apparent controversy. This consonance of opinion might indicate a greater maturity in current American scholarship on Japan than was witnessed in the 1960s.

All of the authors seem to agree that Meiji Japan was imperialistic, imperialism being defined here as extension of control over alien peoples and territories either by conquest or by economic and cultural penetration. In the long reign of Emperor Meiji, Japan emerged from a feudalistic state to become an imperial power whose control extended deep into the Asiatic continent as well as to the Pacific islands.

Even Conroy and Harrington, who deny the existence of long-sustained plans for imperialistic expansion during the Meiji period, are not dogmatic. In fact Conroy has modified his stand somewhat since his publication of *The Japanese Seizure of Korea*, which created one of the most heated debates in the recent history of East Asian studies. Although still holding firmly to the view that Korean annexation itself was not long in planning and occurred only after Ito's assassination, he nevertheless concedes that Japanese foreign policy seems to have followed a concerted plan after 1905.

Harrington follows a familiar line of argument based on Japan's desire for national security and equality with the West. She discusses these issues by reviewing mainly Japan's policy toward Korea—from the *seikanron* (Conquer Korea) argument all the way to the annexation of Korea by Japan in 1910. She notes at the outset that the "issue of Korea and Korean independence dominated Meiji foreign policy" and that a war was fought in 1894–1895 to ensure Korean independence. She notes further that it is tempting to "argue that Japan achieved in 1910 what she had set out to do in the early years of Meiji." But she concludes there was no grand design: "Whatever design we might see in hindsight was either not available . . . or else they succeeded well in hiding their pattern." Does she suspect, then, that there might have been a design although the pattern is not very clear?

Okamoto Shumpei examines the question of imperialism more obliquely. By examining Foreign Minister Komura Jutarō's records of activities and attitudes, Okamoto finds that the Japanese government consciously encouraged Asiatic continental expansion. Disagreeing with a much-discussed view of the noted historian Akira Iriye, Okamoto concludes that the Japanese government concentrated on substantial gains on the Asiatic continent in order to discourage transpacific migration and thus ease tension with the United States over Japanese immigration. Okamoto contends that Japan sought only form in the treaty of 1911 with the United States whereas substance was sought in negotiations with China. The Japanese government could afford to compromise with the United States, Okamoto reasons, because Japan could expand into Asia. Thus Japan pursued imperial expansion into Asia to avoid another imperial expansion coming from the other side of the Pacific.

I too have modified my past views somewhat. While I am still convinced that Japan had deliberate plans to expand into the Asiatic continent, for whatever reasons, further research by myself and others has caused me to reconsider certain past assumptions. I have found it difficult to present a clear-cut argument on an issue as complicated as Meiji imperialism. For instance, an abstracted goal cannot be pursued ruthlessly without regard to compromise. If one genuinely wanted to achieve the end, one needed, on occasion, to be realistic enough to abandon that long-range goal temporarily. Furthermore, given the nature, personalities, and structure of the Meiji leadership, I found it hard to believe that they were either blindly pursuing ultimate goals, disregarding realities, or abandoning them altogether because of unforeseen difficulties.

This part affords the reader an opportunity to examine the arguments of both sides and yet find that the two sides are not so far apart as it might seem.

—BONNIE B. OH

Meiji Imperialism: "Phenomenally Rapid"

Bonnie B. Oh

During the forty-four-year reign of Emperor Meiji, Japan expanded from a closed feudal state to an empire with colonies extending from semiarctic to tropical regions in East Asia. Within a decade of the Meiji Restoration, the newly established modern state of Japan succeeded in incorporating the Ryukyu and Bonin Islands and extended its authority over the Kurils. As the result of two major wars, fought with China and Russia, Japan acquired Taiwan as a colony, obtained an extensive leasehold and economic privileges in southern Manchuria, won the southern half of Sakhalin, and assumed a preponderant position in Korea. Finally, in 1910, Japan annexed Korea. The directly ruled colonies alone increased Japanese territorial holdings from less than 142,000 square miles of the four main islands to over 242,000 square miles, an increase of more than one and a half times. The colonies of Taiwan and Korea added some 15 million to a Japanese population which was already growing rapidly to almost 50 million by the end of the Meiji period.

As the preceding sketch shows, the Meiji expansion was phenomenally rapid. Even if one accepts the thesis that expansion is a pervasive phenomenon of human history, as swift a growth as that of Meiji Japan cannot be construed as natural. Nor can the expansion be interpreted as nonimperialistic, although not all of early Meiji expansion was imperialistic. It is even harder to view the Meiji expansion as the result of Japanese leaders adapting realistically to "various unexpected happenings" without any goals and plans.

Whether or not the Japanese empire, established during the Meiji era, was the result of a long-range plan has been the subject of controversy for the past couple of decades. Nevertheless, it has become increasingly fashionable to deny any long-sustained plans behind Japanese empire building while the traditional view that Japan pursued her imperialistic aims according to a plan has been dismissed as uninformed or prejudiced. In this author's opinion, the issue has been confused and the debate has become heated because of certain assumptions regarding the planned or unplanned nature of Meiji imperialism.

In explaining my position I shall try to clarify the assumptions which have colored a true understanding of the Meiji expansion. Certainly the term "planned," as associated with Meiji imperialism, has long held the connotation of sinister plots and aggression whereas "unplanned" suggests innocence provoked to action. A plan does not have to be sinister, of course, and having no plan is not necessarily more desirable—as demonstrated by the fates of Japan's neighbors, China and Korea. A newly emerging nation could not have survived without far-sighted, comprehensive plans for national reconstruction and defense given the intense international rivalry of the late nineteenth century when a nation became either an imperialist or a victim. Buttressed with the ideology of social Darwinism imperialism was lauded rather than condemned; imperialism was a sign of a strong country. For Japan, especially, imperialism was a means of attaining equality with the West, one of the primary goals of Meiji Japan. Both sides of the scholarly argument appear oblivious of the fact that current perceptions of imperialism differ drastically from those of the turn of the century.

Another area of confusion lies in the question of *whose* plans are being considered in the discussion of Meiji imperialism. A great deal of confusion could be avoided by citing whether the plans of the core leaders of government, former officials, military leaders, intellectuals, or the ultranationalists are being considered. Meiji Japan was blessed especially with an abundance of expansionists—ultranationalist societies as well as military leaders—whose views were at odds with government leaders. The differences among these groups have been discussed with varying degrees of emphasis.

"No plan" advocates stress the existence of a wide gap between the government and the societies; "plan" advocates minimize the ideological distance. According to Shumpei Okamoto, a noted historian and a contributor to this section, the societies were unruly and troublesome and opposed to government policies from time to time; nevertheless, he argues, their "nationalistic stand and expansionist aspirations were, in essence, shared also by the leaders of the government." Furthermore, the societies' support for the imperial institution and the creed of *kokutai* forestalled repression by the oligarchic government, whose claims to legitimacy were based on the same institution and creed. Thus, by the end of the nineteenth century, the gap between the government leaders and their opponents, including the ultranationalists, had narrowed considerably. Another historian, Herbert Norman, has noted that the ultranationalist societies, such as the Genyōsha and Kokuryūkai and their numerous offshoots, were the advance guard of Japanese imperialism and served as the cement which held together the whole edifice of Japanese aggression. The truth is elusive. The major policymakers denounced and suppressed their critics when they posed inconveniences but exploited their zeal and knowledge when it was expedient to do so.

The question of timing needs careful discussion—not only the familiar argument about when to implement imperialistic policies but the issue of how long a proposal must be under consideration or in preparation before it may be viewed as "planned." Should the time period be a year, five years, a decade, two decades? One begins to realize how difficult it is to define planned and unplanned. Moreover, the familiar debate on timing that was supposed to have arisen on the occasion of the famous *seikanron* (Conquer Korea) argument challenges whether there was indeed a fundamental difference between the supporters and opponents of the great debate.

The final question to be asked is how *specific* a scheme must be before it may be considered a plan. May one construe the general intention to make Korea a part of the Japanese empire a plan? Or must that general intention be spelled out to make the peninsula a Japanese sphere of influence, protectorate, or colony? May not Meiji's general territorial intentions be considered a plan although the specific policies for operationalizing those intentions in a given situation might not be particularized in advance? Thus Marlene Mayo, a historian, points out: "If there were no fixed ideologies, no master plans, or well-considered policies, then certainly principles of some sort, broad purposes, ambitions, or attitudes must have guided Japan's actions in times of crisis."

One final point is seldom discussed in this connection: the nature and structure of Meiji leadership. At the highest level, the leadership consisted of a small number of individuals known first as an oligarchy and later as genro. The leaders were interdependent members; they were not dominated by one group. As Nakane Chie, a Tokyo University anthropologist, pointed out in characterizing Japanese leaders, they were seldom Napoleonic and their freedom was limited. As powerful members of a group with decision-making responsibility, they considered it important to maintain harmony. Furthermore, for those who had won out in power struggles, successful personal and group performance was a requirement. Thus it was natural that a member of the oligarchy could neither insist on his own view nor implement it. The result is an appearance of harmony and unanimity of opinion which historians are now discovering to be the consequence only of long deliberation and a series of compromises. The end product of this group leadership was therefore flexibility in response to a situation regardless of the basic goals.

Although I would like to discuss in detail every major foreign policy crisis of Meiji Japan, such an ambitious undertaking would be beyond the scope of this essay. A clear pattern would emerge, however, demonstrating that each foreign policy crisis was absorbed into the wider goal of strengthening the country. One would discover, moreover, that in addition to all-embracing nationalistic goals, realistic policies were implemented to suit each situation. In lieu of a general discussion, then, I wish to concentrate on one specific case: Japan's Korea policy.

The modern Japanese state under the leadership of the restored Meiji emperor was established with the mandate of *jōi*—expelling the barbarians. However, the leaders of the restoration had realized even before the success of the movement that the barbarians could not be expelled without first "Enriching the Nation and Strengthening the Army," *Fukoku Kyōhei,* which became the motto and long-range goal of the new government. The immediate national security problem, therefore, was to strengthen the country so that Japan could conduct her diplomatic relations on a basis of equality with the Western powers.

The consolidation of Japan's territory was one obvious way to strengthen the country. Immediate attention was paid to settling the sparsely populated northern island of Ezo (Hokkaido) and to extending jurisdiction over the islands strung out south and north in the Japanese archipelago: the Ryukyus, the Kurils, and Sakhalin. Although the Japanese ambition to acquire at least the southern half of Sakhalin Island was thwarted despite long negotiations with the Russians, the new government did gain Russia's reconfirmation of Japanese jurisdiction over the Kurils by treaty in 1875. Japan was to wait thirty years to wrest the southern half of the island from Russia. In this case it may be construed that the long-range purpose of Japan was to acquire the southern half of the island; yet Japan did not risk war with Russia to obtain the territory by force.

In the case of the Ryukyus, the Meiji government was more determined to implement its general goal of territorial acquisition than in the Kuril–Sakhalin negotiations. The Japanese claim on the islands was based on close historical ties, allegedly dating back to the twelfth century and continuing through modern times, although the rulers paid homage to China as well. Then, in 1871, the murder of shipwrecked Ryukyuans by Taiwanese aboriginals provided an opportunity for Japan to implement this general goal. Through a combination of skillful diplomacy and military expedition, which is often interpreted as nothing more than a measure to placate jobless samurai, the Meiji government won the de facto recognition of its sovereignty over the islands not only from China but from the Western powers as well. In 1879 the islands were incorporated legally into the Japanese state as Okinawa prefecture.

Much more important than these islands, in terms of Japan's national security, was Korea. All past contact with the Asiatic continent, including invasions, had been made either from or through the peninsula; thus Korea was regarded as a dagger pointed at Japan's heart. Korea was perceived to be especially dangerous for Japan's security at the end of the nineteenth century for it remained weakened, dominated by a third power. Korea was becoming a hotbed of international rivalry. The dagger in the hands of a hostile power would indeed become a lethal weapon. Thus, from 1885, the first instance when Japan's foreign policy decision was affected by a professional military estimate, the independence of Korea had provided the starting premise for army policy. This meant, of course, a Korea independent of any foreign influence except that of Japan. For Korean "independence" Japan should be prepared to fight China if necessary—so recommended the army's German advisor, and Yamagata Aritomo, architect of the modern Japanese army, concurred. Since Japan had prepared carefully between 1885 and 1894, she was thus ready to respond unhesitatingly to the "various unexpected happenings" in Korea early in 1894.

The Sino-Japanese War of 1894–1895 was fought mainly for the long-range goal of securing Korean independence. The battle was also fought to acquire the Liaotung Peninsula, the territory adjacent to Korea lying between China and Korea, as a means of guaranteeing it. However, the entry of Russia into Korean politics and the Triple Intervention wrested from Japan the immediate fruits of her victory. Yet there were other rewards. In addition to the staggering amount of indemnity, Japan also won Taiwan and the Pescadores, demands on which, according to a recent study by Edward I-te Chen, were not premeditated. Even if the acquisition of the islands was not part of the long-range planning, Chen should have at least recognized that the Japanese navy's aspiration for domination of East Asian waters had a long history.

In the meantime, antagonism between Russia and Japan increased. The problem was caused by Russia's leasing from China the very territory that was denied to Japan and Russia's procrastination in withdrawing troops from southern Manchuria in the wake of the Boxer Rebellion. By early 1902 Japan, armed with an alliance with Britain, Russia's traditional foe, concluded that Korea should be made part of the Japanese empire in long-range plans. The alliance indicated the extent of Japan's determination in dealing with Korea.

What form Korea should assume as Japan's dependency—a sphere of influence, a protectorate, a colony—was not yet clear. Important to this discussion, however, is the fact that Japan's long-range planning remained constant. After another major victory in war, this time against Russia, Japan fulfilled most of the goals of Meiji foreign policy. The southern half of Sakhalin was won, the Liaotung Peninsula was recaptured, entensive leasehold and economic privileges were obtained in southern Manchuria. Finally Korea became a de facto protectorate of Japan. Most of these accomplishments were achieved with either the blessings or the acquiescence of the Western powers. Another noted historian and contributor to this section, Hilary Conroy, denies the existence of a plot to annex Korea following the Russo-Japanese War, citing differing opinions within the Japanese government. This argument, however, is beside the point because both a protectorate and an annexed colony are the result of imperialism.

It is inconceivable, then, that Japan became an empire and a world power in forty-four years without long-range goals and plans. Also inconceivable is the idea that the able Meiji leaders pursued these goals ruthlessly and relentlessly. The Meiji leaders, working as a group of dedicated patriots, had goals and plans for national strength and international equality but carried them out with characteristic flexibility and realism as each situation demanded.

Meiji Imperialism: "Not Based on Preordained Design"

Ann M. Harrington

The Meiji Restoration marked a major turning point in Japanese history. This is not the place to debate the complex conditions within and outside Japan which brought about the fall of the Tokugawa *bakufu*, but there was clearly a crisis of confidence in the shogunal leadership evidenced in growing dissatisfaction in various sectors of Japanese society and intense unrest with the *bakufu*'s policies toward the West. The Meiji leaders, legitimized by their promise to restore imperial rule, were faced with enormous tasks: creating national unity, establishing a workable government, maintaining the integrity of the Japanese homeland against Western imperialism, to name but a few. As the leaders gradually came to understand the modern world of nation-states, they set about the task of transforming Japan to ensure her survival.

Convinced that Japan had the potential to become a strong, rich country, the early Meiji statesmen forced themselves (with some help from Westerners) to take a realistic look at Japan and at the world outside Japan. The Iwakura mission to the West (1871–1873) proved a sobering experience. It discouraged its members from pursuing a policy of imperial expansion and focused their attention instead on creating a strong, stable nation.

The nineteenth-century world forced Japan to maintain an intimate relationship between her self-strengthening and her foreign policy. Foreign powers, winners of unequal treaties under the *bakufu* government, resided in Japan. Neighboring China, having suffered such a fate first, was subjected to spheres of Western influence in its cherished Middle Kingdom. As Korea continued to acknowledge the suzerainty of the Chinese empire, Japanese leaders believed it was vital to Japan's national security to establish Korea's independence for fear that either the West or a traditionalist Chinese rule would dominate the Korean kingdom. For this reason the issue of Korea and Korean independence dominated Meiji foreign policy. Because Meiji expansionism ended with the annexation of Korea, it is tempting to argue that Japan achieved in 1910 what she had set out to do in the early years of Meiji. A brief review of several policy decisions made during the Meiji period will demonstrate, however, that the Japanese empire grew primarily for two reasons. One was the internal pressure exerted by expansionists within and outside the government when they thought Japan's prestige or security was threatened; the other was Japan's desire to enhance her position with the Western powers. That the empire's growth was not based on a preordained design to spin a web which would ultimately ensnare all East Asia will become clear as we examine Japanese–Korean relations during the Meiji period.

Meiji Japan's initial overture to Korea was a formal announcement in 1868 of the new regime. It expressed hope for friendly relations between the two countries and contained plans to initiate new diplomatic relations. By 1869, however, it was evident that the Koreans were not going to acknowledge the Meiji government. This set the stage for the crisis of 1871–1873.

It has been argued that the invasion was rejected only because Japan was not yet ready for a show of force; it was just a matter of waiting. This notion indeed seems to be supported in a summation statement made by Iwakura to the emperor in 1873. Iwakura says in part:

> We must well in advance of any action build warships, prepare to supply provisions for our forces, arrange funds and decide on procedure and objectives to the extent of tightening up a hundred aspects of our internal administration. Even if our mission to Korea is delayed a while by this, it will still not be too late.

When one considers the deep divisions caused by this question, Iwakura's statement can also be read as an effort to temper the rejection by leaving an opening at least for future discussion. It did not necessarily imply that Japan was planning one day to invade Korea. This was borne out by the next twenty years of Japan's foreign policy toward Korea, a policy which was consistent in its attempts to open Korea for trade and to safeguard its independence.

Coincident with the Korean crisis, there was intense debate over what steps to take against Taiwan for murdering fifty-four Ryukyuans shipwrecked near Taiwan's coast in 1871. In 1874, Ōkubo and Iwakura finally authorized an expedition to Taiwan. As Marleen Mayo points out, the government was faced with severe internal unrest and the expedition was one way to diffuse some of the tensions. The encounter ended with Japan receiving an indemnity and asserting a stronger hold over the Ryukyus while China laid claim to Taiwan.

The status of Korea proved to be a more difficult issue to settle. Using the gunboat approach, in 1876 Japan pushed Korea into establishing diplomatic relations and opening three ports to Japanese trade. At the same time, Japan declared Korea an independent state. China, however, was reluctant to give up the suzerainty she had traditionally held over Korea. The Koreans themselves were divided over the issue: the traditionalists leaned toward China while a reform-minded element of the population sought Japanese help. Both countries sent in troops in 1882 to put down a riot against foreigners, and both became increasingly involved in Korea's modernization. As tensions mounted, a compromise was reached in 1885 whereby both countries agreed to withdraw their troops from Korea and not to send them back without alerting the other party.

Hostilities eventually broke out in 1894 when Korea called in Chinese troops to put down the Tonghak Rebellion. Japan retaliated by declaring war on China, claiming China had violated the 1885 agreement. The war was fought, from Japan's point of view, to ensure the independence of Korea. The prime aim of the peace, therefore, was an assurance of this independence by demanding the cession of the Liaotung Peninsula to prevent further Chinese interference. Why then did Japan ask for Taiwan in the peace talks? Does not such a peace term indicate plotting to get what Japan had failed to acquire in 1874? Edward I-te Chen indicates that it was only after the war had begun and Japan was clearly winning that the idea of demanding Taiwan entered into the discussion. Since there was some concern that the Western powers might balk if Japan sought territory on the continent, Taiwan served as a safeguard against Japan's leaving the peace negotiations empty-handed. At the war's end, a severely defeated China agreed to peace terms which included the cession of both the Liaotung Peninsula and Taiwan. Chen believes that Japan pressed the issue of Taiwan for four reasons: the chance to expand Japan's empire and placate somewhat the demands of the expansionists; the fact that Japanese naval leaders thought it would strengthen Japan's position in the Pacific; the belief that Taiwan would pose the least threat to

Western spheres of influence in China; and, finally, the opportunity to enhance Japan's status with the West.

The prize of the peace was lost, however, when Russia, Germany, and France put pressure on Japan to relinquish the Liaotung Peninsula. The Japanese public was outraged but their leaders were helpless. Japan's ability to keep Korea independent remained in question. Furthermore, the Japanese learned the bitter truth that they were not considered equal to the Western imperialist powers. The insult was intensified in 1897–1898 when Russia, Germany, France, and Britain widened their spheres of influence in China. The real threat and ultimate insult was leveled by the Russians in 1898 when they leased the Liaotung Peninsula for twenty-five years and, in addition, won the right to build an arm of the South Manchurian Railway down to the cities of Port Arthur and Dairen.

The loss of the peninsula became a serious issue after the Boxer Rebellion when the Russians were reluctant to withdraw their troops from Manchuria. Britain, also uneasy over Russia's increasing penetration into Manchuria and China and threatened by the growing naval powers in East Asia, concluded the Anglo-Japanese Alliance in 1902. Some Japanese statesmen by this time were certain that war with Russia could not be avoided, and the alliance protected them against the intervention of a third power if war should ensue. It also moved Japan a step closer to her desired position of equality with the West.

Tensions between Russia and Japan intensified as the Russians made advances into North Korea. Negotiations between Russia and Japan over Korea and Manchuria began in the summer of 1903 and continued until February of 1904. Although Russia agreed to recognize Japan's interests in Korea, Manchuria was not considered to be within the Japanese sphere of influence. Negotiations broke down and Japan was once more at war to secure Korean independence.

Japan's surprise naval attack on the Russian fleet in the Straits of Tsushima in May 1905 brought both countries to the peace table. Japan won the peace on the following terms: recognition of her paramount interests in Korea; the lease on the Liaotung Peninsula along with control of the railway as far north as Chang-chun; the cession of the southern half of the island of Sakhalin; and return of Manchuria to China's control.

Thus, by 1905, Japan had achieved the primary goals of Meiji foreign policy. She was regarded as one of the major powers; Korean independence was guaranteed with Japan's special interests recognized;

and Japan's foothold on the continent served as a buffer zone for Korea's borders. At home Japan was progressing rapidly as a stable nation-state with a growing sense of national unity. How then does one explain the Meiji government's decision to annex Korea in 1910? Was this really Japan's goal all along?

Hilary Conroy spells out clearly the differing government views over the question of the annexation of Korea, and it is evident that annexation was not a foregone conclusion at the end of the Russo-Japanese War. Itō Hirobumi was appointed resident-general in Korea and there was government agreement to let him carry out his plan to

> establish a sort of triangular balance, Residency General, Korean court, and Korean reform ministry, through which Japanese-Korean cooperation could obtain to produce reform and modernization of Korea and which would render Japan secure from any possible threat launched via Korea. Of the two objectives, the second, Japanese security, was the overriding one.

By the time Itō resigned his post in 1909, many government leaders thought that the plan was inadequate for keeping peace in Korea. When Itō was assassinated by a Korean patriot that same year, the move toward annexation met little resistance from within the Japanese government and no protest at all from the Western powers.

It is clear that there was a great deal of expansionist sentiment in Japan. This feeling was partially responsible for the acquisition of the Ryukyu Islands, Taiwan, and southern Sakhalin. There was also fear for Japan's national security as Western powers penetrated further into China. Unless she achieved equal status with the Western powers, Japan thought she would be unable to maintain her independence. These fears were partially responsible for the acquisition of Korea and the control of the Liaotung Peninsula. A combination of opportunity and capability spun these hopes and fears into the web we know as Meiji imperialism. Whatever design we might see in hindsight was either not available to the spinners of the web or else they succeeded well in hiding their pattern.

Meiji Imperialism: "Mostly Ad Hoc"

Hilary Conroy

When I took up the study of Meiji imperialism in the late 1940s, it was in the shadow of Pearl Harbor and the Pacific War. Japan had become a militaristic, aggressive nation in the 1930s and the question posed for me as a young historian interested in Japan was this: What were the roots of this aggression and how far back did those roots go?

Since Hawaii was literally in the path of the Pacific War and had received its first blows, the search started there. Had Japan hoped to seize Hawaii in the nineteenth century and then, frustrated by the American annexation, bided her time until another chance arrived—Pearl Harbor? The answer my research produced to this simplistic question was a resounding NO. Japan's Meiji government handled the Hawaiian question with the greatest circumspection and reserve. The initiative for Japanese immigration to the Hawaiian Islands came from Hawaii, largely from Americans there who needed labor for the developing sugar plantations, and the push factor from Japan was nothing but poverty. This caused poor drifters to Yokohama and Tokyo and even poorer sons of farmers in the Hiroshima, Kumamoto, Yamaguchi, and Fukuoka areas to respond to blandishments emanating from the Hawaiian consulate in Japan (which was manned by Americans, first Eugene Van Reed and then for many years by Robert W. Irwin) to come to the Pacific Paradise and try to earn money toward a happier future in Japan.

Proof of Japan's deference to the United States regarding Hawaii is contained in the historical record—not only in Japanese documents but in documents housed in the Archives of Hawaii. For example, an invitation from the Hawaiian king, Kalakaua, to the Japanese emperor asking him to establish an Asiatic federation including Hawaii so that Eastern nations could "maintain their footing against those powerful nations of Europe and America" was *declined* by Japan in January 1882. Between that time and the American annexation in 1898 Japan several times backed away from opportunities for political meddling in Hawaii. And finally, even at annexation time, though vexed by the highhanded American actions accompanying that episode, the Japanese government emphasized that it had no desire "to embarrass the United States" and allowed its consul general in Hawaii to accept "with pleasure" the invitation to attend the ceremonies of Annexation Day, 12 August 1898.

With regard to Korea, which was my next test case on Meiji imperialism, the evidence was more contradictory. Indeed, it required a book of over five hundred pages to work through various imperialist versus anti-imperialist strands that played upon the Korean theme between 1873, when *seikanron* emerged and almost ruptured the Meiji government, to 1910 when annexation of Korea took place. "Conquering Korea" was rejected in 1873, but the fact that annexation took place thirty-seven years later had led most students of the subject to conclude that it was only a question of timing *(jiki no mondai)*.

My conclusion was that, at least as far as the central core of the Japanese government was concerned, it was *not* merely a question of timing. Even though certain antigovernment elements on the Japanese political scene had long and consistently advocated seizing Korea for one reason or another, the Japanese government, in particular the dominant Itō (civilian) faction, had fought hard to avoid this, not as immoral but as unrealistic and dangerous, almost to the moment of Itō's death in 1909. (Ironically Itō's death, by assassination at the hands of a Korean patriot, provided the final proannexation argument.) What Meiji Japan had planned, it seemed to me, was not the seizure of Korea but the development of a modern nation-state able to hold its own in the international competition of the times, and the Korean question was always kept subordinate to problems of international relations in general.

My conclusions on the Korean question, published in 1960, were, I should candidly admit, roundly denounced in Seoul, where Korean scholarship, only recently freed from the fetters of Japanese colonialism, was not yet ready to accept anything short of blanket condemnation of Japan for her Korean role. A subsequent wide-ranging discussion held under the auspices of the University Seminar on Modern Japan at Columbia University cleared the way for a more general acceptance of the "revisionist" interpretation my Korean study had proposed and for further analysis of the sort attempted therein by Korean and Japanese scholars.

Of course, even if one accepts my thesis that Hawaiian interference and Korean annexation were unplanned, at least in any long-range sense, there are other examples of Meiji imperialism to be considered: the Liu-ch'iu (Ryukyu) Islands, Taiwan, the attempted grab of Liaotung after the Sino-Japanese War, and the taking over of Russia's southern Manchurian holdings after the Russo-Japanese War. The first three of these, I would argue, were unplanned. The last may mark a turning point toward planned imperialism.

There *was* a conspiracy for Japanese seizure of Formosa as early as 1872, but its instigators were Americans rather than Japanese. In fact, the whole Liu-ch'iu Taiwan syndrome, which resulted in Japan's annexation of the entire island chain, was so permeated with Western influence that, given the early Meiji government's nervous sensitivity to Western advice, Japan may be depicted as doing only what she was given Western permission to do by way of empire building.

The Taiwan scheme emerged from the shirt-sleeves diplomacy of the U.S. minister at Tokyo, Charles E. DeLong, whose principal objective was to prevent the Sino-Japanese Treaty of 1871 from becoming an Oriental alliance against Western states, a prospect he regarded as "calamitous." His approach was to encourage Japanese Foreign Minister Soejima Taneomi in a program of expansionism against China, for which purpose he recommended and secured the employment at the Japanese Foreign Office of the recently recalled American consul at Amoy, General Charles LeGendre, a Taiwan "expert." LeGendre was employed, not only as a counselor in the Japanese Foreign Office, but with the presumption that he would eventually lead a Japanese army to conquer Taiwan.

The scheme did not immediately materialize because of the split in the Japanese government over conquering Korea (which DeLong and LeGendre also advocated) in 1873, a split that resulted in the ouster of Soejima. LeGendre remained as counselor, however, and when the smoke had cleared from the Korean argument he reminded the new (Ōkubo–Terashima) foreign policy leadership of Japan's right and duty to punish Taiwan aborigines who had murdered Japanese subjects (Liu-ch'iu Islanders) shipwrecked there in 1871. Ōkubo and Terashima, smarting under criticism for squashing the great samurai Korean conquest scheme, lent willing ears, especially when LeGendre promised, and arranged, American assistance in the form of two military officers, an American ship, the *New York,* and LeGendre himself as advisor to the expedition.

Unfortunately for LeGendre, however, his old friend DeLong had been replaced as minister by Judge John A. Bingham, a man of far more cautious temperament. Bingham alerted the U.S. State Department, which ordered cancellation of all American participation, and Ōkubo, now nervous about the whole thing, diminished the project to "punitive measures" which were less than successful. Nevertheless, LeGendre next turned up in Beijing where he assisted the Japanese delegation in settling the resulting dispute with China—not only to save face but to gain an indemnity for the cost of the expedition and to register the point that the wronged Liu-ch'iu Islanders were subjects of Japan. In time and with the probably innocent assistance of another American, ex-President Ulysses S. Grant, who visited Japan in 1879, Japan established her sovereignty over the Liu-ch'ius.

In 1895, when Japan did annex Taiwan by the Shimonoseki Treaty with China, her plan was very much a contingent one linked with the abortive effort to establish a foothold in the Liaotung Peninsula at Port Arthur (Dairen), which the Triple Intervention prevented. None of the Western powers objected to her taking Taiwan, just as, indeed, none had objected to her going to war with China over the Korean issue in the summer of 1894. There had been no precise plan for war; rather, as Foreign Minister Mutsu put it, "various unexpected happenings" were the cause.

The "Liaotung first, Taiwan second" plan seems to have been formulated by Mutsu in response to a British request for a statement of Japan's war aims presented in October 1894, some ten weeks after the outbreak of hostilities on 25 July with the sinking of the *Kowshing,* a British ship carrying Chinese troops to Korea. The proposed terms, which included Chinese recognition of the independence of Korea and payment of war expense and reparations, as well as the Liaotung–Taiwan territorial cession, were surprisingly modest in view of the victorious war fever that was by that time gripping Japan. Clearly they were being thought of in terms of acceptability to the Western Powers. On the advice of Premier Itō, Mutsu did not state the details immediately in his reply to the British government, but they became the basis for the eventual settlement the following spring when, after the Triple Intervention, it became clear that the cession of Taiwan, but not Liaotung, was acceptable to the West.

The Russo-Japanese War has been described elsewhere as a turning point; in the sense of planning imperialism, particularly in reference to southern Manchuria, it may indeed have been that. Going to war with Russia was, to Japan, a defensive measure caused by Russian intransigence over Korea and encouraged by the British alliance and

Theodore Roosevelt's admiration for "plucky little Japan." But having defeated Russia, Japanese policymakers became emboldened. Itō was still not willing to annex Korea, but his rivals in the Tokyo government, Katsura and especially Komura, began behaving like self-confident imperialists. The tip-off on this, in my opinion, was their refusal to go through with the Harriman plan for joint financing of the South Manchurian Railroad, which was badly in need of repair and money. According to Richard T. Chang the decision to rebuff Harriman and go it alone in Manchuria was indicative of a new, careless attitude about international balances in East Asia. Indeed Komura, then foreign minister, subsequently made it clear that the basis of his thinking was that Japan "must always maintain a dominant position in China."

We can say, then, that the tensions of the Dollar Diplomacy era in Manchuria were not all caused by Taft and Knox. There was, indeed, a new intransigence in Japanese diplomacy after 1905.

Before concluding, I should add a few words about the Marxist interpretation, once widely held in Japanese intellectual circles, that Japanese imperialism proceeded automatically from the economic-political conditions of Meiji Japan. In a chapter entitled "Some Economic Matters" in my *Japanese Seizure of Korea* (1960) I showed that economic motivation was not the cause, but in the preface to the 1974 paperback edition I admit that the view of American revisionist historians that "unconscious" imperialism proceeds from trade may have merit when applied to Japan's case.

In conclusion, Meiji imperialism was ad hoc rather than planned until 1905, remaining so in the case of Korea until the passing of Itō. But a new more ominous imperialism got its start in Manchuria in the post-1905 days of Meiji. Japan became less cautious, more confident, and a victim of the pathology of imperialism; the more Japan expanded the more insecure she became, and the more compelling became the logic that additional territory was needed to protect the latest gains.

Meiji Imperialism: Pacific Emigration or Continental Expansionism?

Shumpei Okamoto

$\mathbf{A}$s superbly discussed in Akira Iriye's *Pacific Estrangement: Japanese American Expansion, 1897–1911*, the causal relationship between Japanese emigration across the Pacific and Japanese expansionism to the Asian continent has fascinated historians. Recently Etō Jun, a noted Japanese literary critic, joined them when he stated:

> However, with the outbreak of the anti-Japanese movement in America, disenchantment with that country grew rapidly among the Japanese. In the place of America, the Asian continent, particularly China and Manchuria, came to be strongly projected upon the consciousness of the Japanese. Then, with the closing of the door across the Pacific, the Japanese turned to the Asian continent to seek their lifeline. This fact also strongly influenced in the long term various Japanese government policies which led to the Second World War.

This short essay attempts to participate in the intriguing controversy through an analysis of the mind of a Japanese policymaker in the 1911 negotiations for a revised treaty with the United States.

The series of revised treaties concluded with the Western powers, beginning in 1894 and put into effect in 1899, abolished the extraterritoriality under which Japan had suffered since the last days of Tokugawa. These treaties, however, retained several elements of inequality. Therefore, when the expiration of the treaties in 1911 provided an opportunity for new treaty negotiations with thirteen Western nations, it was the objective of Foreign Minister Komura Jutarō of the second Katsura cabinet to eradicate these elements of inequality. The most serious problem in the Japanese–American negotiation which resulted in the Treaty of Commerce and Navigation of 21 February 1911 was the immigration issue. Komura's attitude toward Japanese emigration to the United States had, therefore, a significant influence on the negotiations and their conclusions.

The 1894 United States–Japan Treaty of Commerce and Navigation stipulated in Article 1 that "the subjects or citizens of the two High Contracting Parties shall have full liberty to enter, travel or reside in any part of the territories of the other Contracting Party, and shall enjoy full and perfect protection for their persons and property." The effect of this broad statement was, however, greatly curtailed by a reservation clause in Article 2 which stipulated that Article 1 did "not in any way affect the laws, ordinances and regulations with regard to trade, the immigration of laborers, police and public security which are in force or may hereafter be enacted in either of the two countries."

The Japanese government at the time was anxious to conclude a treaty eliminating extraterritoriality without delay. Faced with the United States' uncompromising stand on immigration control, the Japanese government accepted the reservation clause. The year was 1894 and immigration was yet to become a feverish issue between the two Pacific nations. In succeeding years, however, as Japanese aspirations for emigration grew and the immigration issue flared up on the West Coast, the reservation clause came to be regarded by the Japanese as a major stumbling block.

More significantly, after the wars with China and Russia, the Japanese, with greater self-confidence, pride, and national power, found increasingly insulting the reservation clause which allowed the United States to single out the Japanese immigrants for its restrictive measures and thus to treat them as inferior to immigrants of other nationalities. This concern with the harmful effect of the reservation clause on the prestige and honor of Imperial Japan provided the primary motivation for Komura's demand that the United States agree to the deletion of the reservation clause from a new treaty. He was not interested in promoting greater Japanese emigration to the United States. In February 1909, Komura delivered a foreign policy speech at the Imperial Diet. Regarding emigration, he stated that as a result of the war with Russia, Japan's world position had completely changed. Areas that Japan must control and manage had so expanded that it became imperative for her to concentrate Japanese nationals in these areas instead of having them scattered in distant foreign lands. Japan's vital concern overseas, Komura stressed, was the development of commerce and industry. Factors detrimental to the steady improvement of Japan's overseas commercial and industrial activities should therefore be eliminated. In consideration of these facts, Komura concluded, Japan would continue to observe the restrictive policy regarding Japanese emigration to Canada and the United States.

Komura's emigration policy was widely debated as the "Komura doctrine for concentrating Japanese emigration to Manchuria and Korea" or even as his "anti-emigration doctrine." Although Komura emphatically denied that he was advocating an antiemigration policy, there is considerable evidence that he held a negative view on Japanese emigration to the United States.

The official policy to restrict emigration to the United States was of course not new. The Japanese government had for some time engaged in voluntary restriction. Furthermore, Komura's emigration policy had the full support of Genrō Yamagata Aritomo and Itō Hirobumi. By that time Yamagata was advocating a speedy entrenchment of Japanese control in Manchuria and urging greater Japanese emigration into the region. On the other hand, Genrō Itō, while disagreeing with the Komura–Yamagata expansionism over Manchuria, endorsed Komura's restriction on emigration to the United States. As early as November 1907, Itō had advised the Foreign Ministry to solve the immigration issue with the United States—even if it required replacing the Japanese ambassador in Washington, who Itō believed was insensitive to the problem.

Komura's policy, reflecting a deeply pessimistic view of Japanese emigration to America, seems to have derived from his many years' experience with emigration issues themselves and his firsthand knowledge of the situation in the United States. Once, recalling his student days in the mid-1870s, where he studied in Boston and New York for some five years, Komura is said to have praised the Americans he had encountered for their fair and respectful attitude toward him. "Though I was so small, even for a Japanese, the professors loved me. The students not only did not slight me but respected me," Komura said. "The American spirit is the true samurai spirit. They love the underdog. Their spirit is filled with a sense of honor and justice."

Komura's enthusiasm for the American spirit seems to have abated in later years, however, particularly during the two years from June 1896 to September 1898, when it was his duty as vice–foreign minister under Ōkuma Shigenobu to handle the perpetual emigration problems. By the time Komura became minister to Washington in

October 1898, he seems to have totally despaired of the future of Japanese emigration to the West Coast of the United States. The year-and-a-half stay in Washington only confirmed this despair. On 11 April 1900, Komura reported his views on emigration to Foreign Minister Aoki Shūzō. Komura stated that the influx of unskilled lower-class Japanese laborers fostered inevitable clashes with their American counterparts, and he recommended the suspension of Japanese emigration for two primary reasons. First, the presence of those Japanese in the United States was detrimental to the prestige of Japan because America would judge the entire Japanese nation on the basis of this group. Second, the development of overseas commerce was adversely affected by the political issues originating in the presence of these Japanese immigrants in the United States.

Thus Komura was opposed to Japanese emigration to the United States for reasons beyond the immediate political expedience of avoiding friction with West Coast Americans. He was opposed to it for reasons of national prestige and commercial development. There is no evidence that his conviction, that emigration was secondary to national honor and commercial expansion, ever weakened. In fact, in handling emigration issues as foreign minister in the first Katsura cabinet and in observing the post–Russian war immigration crises between Japan and the United States, Komura's conviction seems only to have hardened.

Meanwhile another factor arose which influenced Komura's emigration policy: Japan's acquisition of new areas for emigration, namely Manchuria and Korea. It was only natural for Komura, whose life-long aspiration was the promotion of Japan's continental expansion, to find a solution for the emigration problem by seeking to limit it to the Asian continent. Determined thus to push his idea of concentrating emigration to the Asian continent, Komura even prohibited a Japanese envoy to Brazil home on leave from making speeches among rural Japanese encouraging their emigration to that country. In November 1908, Komura told the American ambassador in Tokyo that there was ample territory under the jurisdiction of Japan where people could find employment; that it would be in the interest of the country to develop its own resources and not to allow its most ambitious, capable, and adventurous young people to go elsewhere; and that Japan had no interest in populating the United States and desired only to continue and to increase international trade.

Thus the views Komura expounded in his comprehensive foreign policy position paper, which was adopted by the Katsura cabinet on 25 September 1908, represented the culmination of his previous thoughts on emigration and continental expansion. In this document Komura stressed that Japan must maintain her position of dominance in Manchuria; in order to extend her influence over China, Japan should seek substance rather than form. Reiterating his emigration policy, Komura noted that the Russo-Japanese War had drastically altered Japan's world position. As an empire with possessions on the Asian continent sharing borders with the two major powers, China and Russia, Imperial Japan must devise a hundred-year plan which would prepare her for any eventuality. In order to cope with these two powers on the continent, Japan had to concentrate her energy on East Asia. Moreover, since she desired the expansion of overseas commercial and industrial activities, Japan must promote friendly political relations (and eliminate elements causing friction) with the United States, her greatest trade partner. She should, therefore, refrain from sending immigrants to such Anglo-Saxon countries as America, Canada, and Australia in order to avoid arousing anti-Japanese feelings which would have harmful effects not only on Japan's political relations but also on her commercial and industrial expansion in these countries. Thus, for Komura, restriction of Japanese emigration to the United States was not merely a political tactic for facilitating the treaty revision with that country. It was his deeply rooted conviction that emigration was secondary to economic expansion and that Manchuria and Korea were the areas in which Japan should concentrate her national energy.

Consequently, when Komura demanded that the United States delete the reservation clause from a new treaty he was concerned primarily with national prestige and honor. Here, in contrast to his approach to China, he was seeking form rather than substance. It was therefore ironic that immigration constituted the major issue in the negotiations. Well aware of the difficulties of the negotiations, Komura nevertheless was prepared from the beginning to accept a compromise solution, even if it nullified the effect of the treaty provisions on immigration, so long as the distasteful and insulting clause did not appear in the text of the treaty.

We need not repeat here the details of the negotiations carried on between Ambassador Uchida and Secretary Knox in Washington from October 1910 to February 1911. Faced by the United States' unwillingness to remove unconditionally the reservation clause from the new treaty, Komura immediately suggested a compromise. He proposed that should the United States, because of domestic difficulties over immigration, desire to terminate the treaty at any time, Japan would be willing to do so on six months' notice. The United States was not completely satisfied with this compromise alone and suggested that the phrase "limited only by the present arrangement" be inserted at the beginning of Article I, which was to stipulate the right of immigration. When Komura rejected this suggestion, negotiations shifted to seeking a solution through a diplomatic arrangement which would assure that Japan would not alter her policy restricting emigration after the new treaty was signed. Komura was amenable to such an agreement.

Consequently, after some exchanges over exact wording, Komura agreed to declare on the day the new treaty was to be signed that the Japanese government would "maintain with equal effectiveness the limitation and control which it has exercised for the past three years in regard to the emigration of laborers to the United States." The so-called gentlemen's agreement, A. Whitney Griswold commented, thus passed into its third, and final, stage of development:

> It had originated as an expeditious Japanese practice during the early immigration troubles of the nineties. In 1907 it had been elevated to the status of a formal understanding, resting on an exchange of notes. In 1911 it was recognized in a specific declaration as the condition precedent to a treaty. Such it remained until the enactment of the immigration law of 1924.

The treaty was signed on 21 February 1911. The United States Senate, however, resolved to advise ratification only with the understanding that it should not be deemed to repeal or affect any provisions of the Immigration Act of 20 February 1907. It seems astonishing that Komura should have readily accepted the United States' explanation that the law applied to the immigration of aliens from all countries and made no discrimination against any country. Not only did he raise no objection, but he used the same explanation in his letter to Prime Minister Katsura in which he sought the emperor's ratification of the treaty. No doubt Komura knew that the 1907 act included the Root Amendment which, as the secretary of state himself explained, empowered the president to stop the flow of Japanese immigrants from Hawaii to the mainland. This, accordingly, allowed President Theodore Roosevelt to issue on 15 March 1907 an executive order directing that Japanese or Korean laborers who had received passports to Mexico, Hawaii, or Canada be refused entry to the continental territory of the United States. In accepting such an exception to the new treaty, therefore, Komura afforded the United States the opportunity to take measures which discriminated against the Japanese. Komura's action could be explained only through his primary motive: he was seeking form, not substance.

It is true that the 1911 United States–Japan Treaty of Commerce and Navigation eliminated the reservation clauses. On paper Japan achieved a treaty of equality with the United States. Closer examination, however, reveals that it was a treaty of equality with reservations and defects. The declaration continued the gentlemen's agreement. The senatorial understanding seriously compromised Japan's position of international equality. Furthermore, the treaty left the matter of landownership so indefinite that it failed to provide full legal protection against later discriminatory alien land laws.

Even the first article of the treaty proved so ambiguous as to permit two diametrically opposing interpretations. Early in the negotiations Komura presented a draft treaty prepared by the Foreign Ministry legal adviser, Henry W. Denison. Article I of the draft treaty stated: "The subjects or citizens of each of the High Contracting Parties shall have full liberty, with their families, to enter and sojourn in all parts of the territories of the other." Thus it sought unconditional liberty for the Japanese to enter the United States with their families. During the negotiations, the United States redrafted the article, as it claimed, "in the form adopted in the great majority of treaties" and revised it to read: "The citizens or subjects of the High Contracting Parties shall have liberty to travel and sojourn in the states and territories of the other to carry on trade." To this Komura raised no substantive objection, but he asked that "travel and sojourn" be changed to "enter, travel and reside." Thus Article I of the 1911 Treaty in the final version read: "The subjects or citizens of each of the High Contracting Parties shall have liberty to enter, travel and reside in the territories of the other to carry on trade."

In later years, the United States asserted that it interpreted the passage to mean that the Japanese had liberty to enter the United States only in order to carry on trade. The ambiguity left in the article by Komura thus weakened Japan's position in ensuing immigration law controversies. It is impossible to know exactly how Komura himself interpreted the article. When compared with the first articles of the 1911 treaties with Great Britain, Germany, and France, each of which basically followed the Denison draft treaty, the contrast is so clear that it is difficult to assume that Komura failed to note the ambiguity in the treaty article with the United States. Consequently one might suspect that Komura suppressed a demand for further clarification of the article in order to effect a speedy conclusion of the treaty.

The ambiguity which Komura manifested in his treaty negotiations with the United Staes suggests that form, not substance, was his primary concern. More significantly, however, it was the existence of Korea and Manchuria, as the places where he sought, conversely, substance, not form, which fundamentally influenced Komura's objectives and posture in the treaty negotiations. By this time Komura had compelled China to accept new agreements on Manchuria, and he had played a major role in the annexation of Korea. Thus possibilities for expansion into Korea and Manchuria and even beyond constituted the background of Komura's negotiations. In this sense, his was a perfect example of Meiji Japan diplomacy, in which, as Fukuzawa Yukichi put it, Japan sought from her Eastern neighbors what she lost to her Western neighbors.

PART VI

The Russo-Japanese War: Turning Point in Japanese History?

IN THE MODERN HISTORY of Japan two major events are indisputably noted as turning points: the Meiji Restoration and the Second World War. Strictly speaking even these two events were products of causes that extended backward in time a decade, and in the case of the Meiji Restoration more than a century in the view of some scholars. Still, an argument can be validly made that Japan after both these events was never the same country again in values, attitudes, and orientation. It is in just such a sense that some students of modern Japan have selected other periods to argue a "turning point" in the course of the nation's history: 1890–1895, 1905–1912, and the Taishō period (1912 –1926), for example.

In this part of the book three essays deal with the question of whether it is legitimate to maintain that the period 1905 to 1912— between the end of the Russo-Japanese War (1904–1905) and the end of the Meiji era (1912)—was a major turning point in Japanese history. The argument is more than an academic debate. The answers to it reflect upon how successful the Meiji leaders were in creating an orderly, harmonious, integrated Japan and how much the 1930s were an abberration in Japanese history. If the answer is that the 1905–1912 period did result in an altered direction and emphasis by the late Meiji leaders, the student of Japan may then be led to reexamine and reevaluate two major issues:

1. How successful the Meiji leaders were: Were they men who may have succeeded too well in building a strong, wealthy nation but in the process unwittingly created institutions and values by late Meiji which they could no longer control? Were they men whose limited vision of the needs of the state led them to create less than satisfactory institutions and to ignore the needs of the masses of Japanese society? Did these failings live on to plague the Japan of the 1930s?
2. The Taishō period and the 1930s: Were the limits of Taishō democracy and liberalism conditioned by the mood and actions of the late Meiji leaders? Were the 1930s an outgrowth of solutions or lack of solutions to problems of late Meiji times?

To answer in the affirmative is not to maintain that Taishō and Shōwa leaders' actions were determined by the past but rather to recognize that their ability to shape their destiny was limited by Meiji precedent, values, and institutions. Refocusing the perspective and the inquiry also results in further illumination and richer interpretations—steps toward winning that jealous mistress, truth.

I believe that after the Russo-Japanese War the Meiji elite made a concerted effort to revitalize old values and create an ideal of 90 million Japanese living in harmony as one blood-related family which denied individual and corporate self-interest but also denied socioeconomic change. They allowed tensions to accumulate, and eventually the leaders and the masses were seduced after 1905 by simplistic propaganda centering on the *kokutai*. This new orthodoxy was taught everywhere. I have found it to be well documented in the nation's elementary schools and textbooks after 1910. Elsewhere in this book Richard Smethurst's essay argues a similar thesis from a different focus and other data.

In the first essay of this part Peter Duus concludes that a turning point did occur between 1905 and 1912, and he examines foreign affairs and foreign investment to support his conclusion. Duus contends that Japan's victory over Russia in 1905 was the takeoff point of Japanese imperialism. In making this judgment he joins those essayists in Part V who contend that Japan did not engage in planned imperialism before 1905 nor secure a conclusive hegemony in East Asian international politics by the Sino-Japanese War of 1894–1895. With the gains of Korea and Manchuria, however, "the maintenance and enhancement by this sphere of influence became the central goal of Japanese foreign policy over the next four decades. After the Russo-Japanese War Japan became a peer of other imperialist powers. Japanese business interests, motivated by the myth of great trading and investment opportunities (that had motivated and misled Westerners since the 1800s), emigrated, developed holdings, and demanded from the home government protection of their lives and investments. Further, Duus argues that holdings on the continent created an inflated sense of Japan's strategic military needs, a pervasive popular imperialism linked to a strong nationalism, and put Japan squarely on a collision course with the goals of Chinese nationalism.

Byron Marshall's essay concerns itself with domestic affairs and argues that at the turn of the century there was much concern within Japan that the results of modernization were threatening Japanese cultural identity and social integration. As a result, Marshall says, a general debate occurred over how to counter industrial conflict, to "cushion the shock waves of economic progress on the agrarian communities of rural Japan," and to preserve social harmony and economic justice. This debate constituted as important a turning point as Japanese imperialism after the victory over Russia.

In the concluding essay Banno Junji examines both domestic and foreign affairs to ask whether Japan underwent a turning point in late

Meiji times. In foreign affairs, Banno comes down squarely in agreement with Duus that victory over Russia launched Japan on a new track. The acquisition of special military and economic prerogatives in Chinese territory created an irrevocable and fundamental conflict with China because it violated Chinese territorial integrity and sovereignty. Of interest is his view that the bitter disagreement within the leadership by 1900 over advancing into southern Manchuria proves that a turning point was made when one faction won out and Japan went to war with Russia; thenceforth there was no turning back.

Banno's argument in domestic affairs is more subtle, complex, and cautious. He maintains that a turning point occurred there in only a limited sense because historians have overemphasized the growth of the Seiyūkai (the dominant political party), the activation of urban popular movements, and the increased political participation of the army and navy. It should be observed that these three essays have a significant bearing on two other topics in this volume—"How Democratic Was Taishō Democracy?" and "The 1930s: Aberration or Logical Outcome?"

—HARRY WRAY

The Takeoff Point of Japanese Imperialism

Peter Duus

Was the Russo-Japanese War a turning point in the development of Japanese imperialism? Some would argue that it was not. Japan's emergence as an imperialist power, they contend, was an unbroken chain of events stretching back to the Japanese opening of Korea in 1874, and perhaps beyond that to the expansionist dreams of late Tokugawa pamphleteers. There were no turning points because, once in motion, Japanese imperialism was carried inevitably forward by the pressure of events and precedent until the empire collapsed in 1945.

This argument is not very convincing, particularly if one does not accept the notion of historical inevitability. Moreover all the evidence suggests that the decision to build an empire came fairly late in the Meiji period. The foreign policy decisions of the oligarchs in the 1870s and 1880s display a grave reluctance to expand rather than a powerful urge to do so, and even the decision to fight China in 1894 was taken with considerable trepidation. There was nothing inevitable or inexorable about Japanese expansion. The nation's leaders could have arrested or accelerated its pace at any moment had they wished to.

A more persuasive argument is that the Sino-Japanese War of 1894 –1895 marked an important turning point, perhaps the beginning of modern Japanese imperialism. After all, as a result of the war Japan acquired her first overseas colonial possessions, Taiwan and the Pescadore Islands. But one can still ask whether the results of the Sino-Japanese War were as significant as those of the Russo-Japanese War. The central impulse behind Japanese imperialism was to secure hegemony in East Asian international politics. In this regard, the Sino-Japanese War ended rather inconclusively and far less decisively than the war with Russia. The victory over China did not enable the Japanese to dominate Korea, and the Triple Intervention deprived Japan of a foothold on the Liaotung Peninsula. At the end of the Sino-Japanese War, Japan remained an offshore island empire with virtu-ally no influence on affairs in China and facing heavy competition from the Russians for influence in Korea. Had the Russo-Japanese War ended in defeat for Japan, or been fought to a draw, Japan might have lost even this marginal position.

In fact, however, Japan did win the war with Russia, and her posi-tion in the Far East was substantially altered as a result. The peace set-tlement and the international agreements that followed secured for Japan a new sphere of influence in Korea and southern Manchuria. The maintenance and enhancement of this sphere of influence be-came the central goal of Japanese foreign policy over the next four decades. In this sense the Russo-Japanese War marked the takeoff point of Japanese imperialism—the historical moment when a posi-tion on the Asian mainland and hegemony in East Asia became a fun-damental national commitment. At any subsequent moment, critical decisions might have moved Japanese foreign policy in a different direction, but the Russo-Japanese War did create conditions that re-duced the likelihood of a nonimperialist foreign policy.

First and foremost, the victory over Russia established Japan as the peer of the other imperialist powers in East Asia. This had not been the case after the victory over China. In 1895 Japan had only just be-gun to negotiate an end to the "unequal treaties," and she had no al-lies among the Western nations. The leaders of the country, well aware of their modest international stature, had been fearful of for-eign intervention throughout the months of diplomatic maneuvering that led up to the Sino-Japanese War, and the Triple Intervention proved that their anxieties had not been without foundation. The powers had not divided China among themselves, and they were not willing to let the upstart Japanese make the first slice.

The situation in 1905 was entirely different. Instead of being forced by a coalition of Western nations to give up their wartime gains, the Japanese secured formal recognition of their new sphere of influence. By a series of bilateral agreements with the Russians, the British, the Americans, and the French, the Japanese in effect promised not to in-fringe on the colonies and enclaves of the other imperialists if they were left alone in Korea and Manchuria. Western assent to the new Japanese position on the Asian mainland reflected a mixture of self-interest, indifference, and helplessness. By the standards of the day, as long as the Japanese did not infringe on the rights and privileges of the other powers (excepting the defeated Russians) their gains were legitimate. A new status quo had been established by the Japanese victory, and there was nothing to be gained by upsetting it. None of the powers, not even the perennially idealistic Americans, was willing to risk war to challenge the Japanese. Neither did any of the powers heed the appeals of the Korean court to protect them from Japanese domination. By 1910 the Japanese were sufficiently confident of their position to annex the country formally as a colony. In imperialist politics the strong make friends, and the Japanese had proved their strength to the Western nations by driving the Russian armies into central Manchuria and by demolishing the Russian fleet.

The establishment of a sphere of influence recognized by the other powers had other consequences that locked Japan ever more firmly into an imperialist foreign policy. The first of these was the emergence of new business interest in economic expansion. To be sure, expanding domestic markets continued to provide the main motor for Japanese business and economic growth, but in the immediate postwar years business journals and magazines touted optimistic visions of future economic gains in Korea, Manchuria, and China. A small army of traders, speculators, and businessmen began to migrate to the continent to take advantage of the new opportunities. The economic possibilities of the empire attracted not only the big capitalists and financiers but also provincial investors prompted as much by national pride as by profit. When the quasi-governmental South Manchurian Railway Company was charted in 1906, bids came in for 109,643,000 shares even though only 99,000 were offered for sale. Nothing similar had happened in the wake of the Sino-Japanese War when many overseas business promotions had gone wanting for capital. The difference lay in the new confidence businessmen had in the ability of the Japanese government to protect their economic interests in the Far East. Indeed, protecting Japanese lives and property became a frequent reason for later forays on the continent.

A second consequence of Japan's new position was an inflated sense of Japan's strategic military needs. The politics of imperialism were uncertain, and neither diplomatic guarantees nor recognition as an equal by the Western nations was a sufficient guarantee for an empire of the kind Japan now possessed. The victory over Russia, far from reducing Japan's defense requirements, had vastly expanded them. No sooner had the war ended than the army and the navy began to press for increased armaments. In 1907 a new national defense plan was formulated on the assumption that Russia, the United States, and France would be the country's principal hypothetical enemies. All were formally on good terms with Japan, but all had substantial interests in East Asia and the Pacific, and as such all were potentially threatening to the Japanese sphere of influence. The military establishment urged arms expansion to meet this potential threat. Imperialism did not satisfy a craving for strategic security; it created new needs that clamored ravenously to be met.

The postwar settlement also enhanced the influence of the military establishment in domestic politics. The prestige of the military had already been raised by the defeat of the Russians, even though the margin of victory had been narrow. To this prestige was now added the urgent need to defend the imperial perimeter, a need that gave the military a powerful claim on the nation's economic resources. The army in particular was not reluctant to use its constitutional power to secure that claim. Many civilian leaders objected to the new arms expansion program in a way they had not objected to raising war appropriations in 1904–1905. They were reluctant to prepare for future wars when the most recent one still had to be paid for. In 1911, when the civilian-dominated Saionji cabinet attempted to postpone the expansion of the army by two more divisions, the army brought it down by refusing to provide a war minister. The resulting constitutional crisis brought a change in the procedure for selecting war ministers, an apparent setback for the army, but in fact its formal power and influence remained strong. The army buttressed that influence by the organization of the National Reservists Association, a network of local veterans' organizations devoted to spreading the "military spirit" among the general population and providing a powerful popular constituency for the army leaders. An element of civilian-military conflict, largely absent before the victory over Russia, now became endemic in Japanese domestic politics.

A final consequence of the victory over Russia and the postwar settlement was to create a pervasive popular imperialism. In the final analysis, an empire is as much a state of mind as a question of political boundaries. The formal colonial empire of Japan did not expand much between 1905 and 1931, but the psychological commitment of the populace to imperialism grew in intensity. Manchuria, site of the land victory over Russia, was not simply an area of "special rights and interests" in the diplomatic sense but an extension of the homeland "bought by the blood of one hundred thousand valiant souls and two thousand million from the national purse." The sacrifices the population had made during the war required justification, and the maintenance of the Japanese sphere of influence served that purpose. To question the legitimacy of the Japanese economic and political activities on the Asian mainland was to invite public criticism, if not outright accusations of treason. The Russo-Japanese War, at the deepest level, had made imperialists of all Japanese, even those as yet unborn, who were to learn of the glory of the Japanese victory from their primary school textbooks.

In the long run this may have been the most important consequence of the Russo-Japanese War for it committed Japanese popular nationalism to imperialism. Such need not have been the case. Many Japanese intellectuals, and not a few Asian nationalists, heralded the victory over Russia as an opportunity for Japan to champion the interests of other Asian peoples against the continuing exploitation by the European colonial powers. But the acquisition of an imperialist sphere of influence forestalled this historical possibility. The Japanese increasingly identified their interests with those of the exploiters rather than the exploited, and though many continued to proclaim Japan's identity as an Asian have-not nation, the government pursued policies that continually widened the gap between Japan and her neighbors. Most significant of all, Japan's new sphere of influence put the country on a collision course with new nationalist currents in China.

To be sure, Chinese nationalism took as its enemy all the imperialists and, for a time, mainly the Western imperialists. But in contrast to the Western nations, Japan was close to China and her intrusions into Chinese politics in defense of her sphere of influence made her a more tangible and immediate threat to the integrity of China than the distant machinations of the British, the French, the Russians, or the Americans. Had the Japanese gone down to defeat in 1905, confrontation between a popular imperialist Japanese nationalism and a popular anti-imperialist Chinese nationalism might never have occurred and ultimately the East Asian crisis might have been avoided. In this sense, the Russo-Japanese War was a turning point not only in the history of Japanese imperialism but in the history of the world in the twentieth-century.

The Late
Meiji Debate
over Social Policy

Byron K. Marshall

There is always a strong temptation for historians to organize their
narratives around major wars and see victories or defeats as pivotal
events in the life of a society. Certainly the Russo-Japanese War was a
turning point for the emergence of Japan as an imperialist power in
the international arena. Yet it can be argued that a no less crucial domestic struggle was taking place within Japan during these same years
—the late Meiji debate over social problems and social policy.

The emergence at the turn of the twentieth century of "social problems" *(shakai mondai)* and "social policy" *(shakai seisaku)* as the primary focus for political controversy was in one sense a reformulation
of the central issue of the mid-nineteenth-century debates over the
Tokugawa tradition of isolation. Then the question had been whether
to modernize Japan—that is, should she borrow from the barbarian to
protect her political autonomy? That question as originally formulated had been resolved by the Meiji reforms of the 1870s and 1880s, and
Japan had been preserved as a political entity. The issue now became whither modern Japan. Now that the ship of state had set forth
to achieve national strength through Western technology, what precise course should it follow?

Was modernity simply to be equated with Western institutions and
values? Was the historical tradition of a Japanese cultural identity—a
tradition that had been instrumental in overcoming the disintegrat-
ing forces of feudal *han* regionalism and hereditary class divisions—
now to become washed away in the tide of westernization?

Although the question had been raised throughout the early decades of the Meiji period, it was at the turn of the century that the debate became more sharply focused as the political implications became more concrete and the need for decisions more pressing. A

sophisticated reading of the experience of the industrial West no longer offered assurances of smooth progress even for those who were convinced that westernization was essential to Japan's future. That course now held out the frightening prospect of Japan sailing into the whirlpools of industrial class conflict which might destroy agrarian community life, trap the laboring classes in urban ghettos, and polarize the nation into warring camps of a privileged rich and a permanent poor. One ominous portent of the political strife such a future would bring was seen in the appearance of a socialist movement within Japan. Alienated from the political compromises of the Diet parties and inspired by a variety of Western radical ideologies, several tiny but determined groups attacked the capitalist base of the Meiji state and sought to organize the working classes into a political and economic force capable of creating a just society.

Although these socialists proved to have little appeal in the 1900s, the movement did have a direct impact on a set of actors who were in a position to have greater influence on government policy—the circle of academic intellectuals and career bureaucrats connected with the Association for the Study of Social Policy (Shakai Seisaku Gakkai). This circle included a majority of the young professors of political economics and public administration at Tokyo Imperial University, the major institution for training the Japanese elite. Among their allies were a growing number of rising civil servants who held strategic posts within the Home Ministry, which controlled the national police and supervised local government, and the Ministry of Agriculture and Commerce. For these men the appearance within Japan of socialist agitators was clear evidence that decisive measures must be taken to safeguard the country from the storm of social evils that awaited along the route of industrialization. Their central argument was that having imported Western technology to propel Japan into the future, there was now no choice but to adopt the most sophisticated of Western social legislation in order to preserve social harmony and economy justice between urban labor and capitalist management as well as to cushion the shock waves of economic progress on the agrarian communities of rural Japan.

There was little opposition to the latter aim, which entailed a series of bureaucratically sponsored measures to consolidate local administration, create agricultural cooperatives, and reorganize youth and other groups that might promote social cohesion at the village level. The proposals for regulating labor–management relations in the industrial sector, however, touched off a controversy which was to con-

tinue well into the twentieth century. The focal point of this controversy in the late Meiji period was a plan to introduce new labor laws
designed to prohibit the employment of young children, limit the
hours of women workers, and improve safety conditions in Japan's
manufacturing industries. Behind the actual provisions of the various
versions of factory legislation proposed between the 1890s and 1911
was a well-defined view of Japan's future course. Western liberal
values of individual self-interest as well as the socialist concept of class
struggle must be kept from weakening the Japanese ship of state.
This task required, on the one hand, firm central control to restrain
capitalism from the excesses witnessed in the West and, on the other
hand, granting concessions to ensure minimal welfare benefits to
keep the workers docile. Only by rejecting the laissez faire approach
and social Darwinish philosophy of England and America, these social policy advocates insisted, could the perils of industrial strife be
avoided. As a more appropriate Western model they held up Bis-
marckian Germany where the threat of radicalism had been turned
back by government intervention into labor–management relations.

The threat of government intervention was resisted with great determination by the modern business community of late Meiji Japan.
Leading industrial bankers, managers of such new giants as Mitusi
and Mitsubishi, and members of the various chambers of commerce
were united in their rebuttals of the views of the social policy advocates and deployed a wide variety of arguments to deny both the
necessity and the desirability for government regulation of the industrial workplace. Two major themes, however, were to form the core of
the case for the defense. First, since Japan was still far from entering
the area where the advanced Western nations had encountered the
storms of class conflict, it was much too early for government measures that would retard or even block continued industrial progress.
And second, Western methods of coping with the crosscurrents of social strife were not appropriate to Japan's cultural system.

It was the second of these two themes that was potentially the more
crucial for it denied the fundamental premise that the Western social
experience was directly relevant to Japan. Granted that the technology had been borrowed from the West, it was nevertheless claimed
that the values and institutions of Japanese capitalism were in fact *sui
generis*, owing little if anything of essential importance to Western in-
spiration. Thus whatever the need for German-style social legislation
in Europe and America, Japan was an entirely different case. Indeed,
social legislation based upon Western concepts of law and interper-

sonal relations would weaken rather than strengthen the vessel of Japanese society for it would severely erode the traditional bonds of mutual concern and respect for authority that made possible the cooperation that was beneficial to both management and workers. Foreign notions of legal rights were in fact the major threat to Japan's cultural heritage since their spread would lead to the very conditions and radical responses that the advocates of the social policy school themselves feared.

It was this antireform camp that prevailed in the Meiji debate over factory legislation. The business community and its allies within government blocked new labor legislation until the passage of the Factory Law of 1911. Moreover, the provisions of that law regarding minimum age (twelve years), maximum workday (twelve hours), and prohibition of night work for females and minors were not only strikingly weak in view of the exceptions permitted but were not even to become mandatory until a waiting period of five years (fifteen in case of limitations on night work). More significant for the future of Japanese industrial relations, however, were the new directions taken by private management to reinforce the attitudes of submission to authority which they considered traditional. They adopted a wide variety of paternalistic devices—including wage scales rewarding seniority, on-the-job training programs, insurance, and other fringe benefits—intended to enhance loyalty to a single company and make interfirm mobility more costly to the worker. Although these practices spread slowly and it was two decades before they could be said to characterize even the most profitable large-scale Japanese enterprises, it was during the 1900s that what came later to be called a "uniquely Japanese style" of labor management originated. Late Meiji capitalists thus invented a tradition to shore up their rhetorical claims about a uniquely Japanese cultural heritage.

Before concluding, I wish to pay closer attention to the different sets of participants in late Meiji debate over social legislation, for this focus reveals a far more pluralistic political scene than the previous decades of Meiji oligarchic decision-making. The issue of government intervention into industrial relations signaled the emergence of a modern Japanese business elite capable of playing a role much more independent than in the earlier pattern of subordination of business to government. Modern Japanese business history would continue to the present to be marked by close cooperation between the political elite and corporate managers, but it was in the 1900s that business leaders demonstrated their ability to unite on critical issues and reject government initiatives. Within the government itself, the debates brought to the fore a new type of career civil bureaucrat. These men were the direct heirs of the samurai administrators who launched the reforms of the Meiji Restoration but, trained in the new schools and recruited through a formal examination system, they owed authority to their mastery of bureaucratic techniques rather than participation in the upheavals that had toppled the old regime. As advocates of systematic government coordination of social change, these activists were temporarily frustrated by the failure to pass rigorous factory legislation but their views on the regulative role of government would by the 1930s be dominant within bureaucratic circles.

The debates also marked a watershed for modern Japanese intellectuals. The consensus attained within the Association for the Study of Social Policy in the 1900s could not be sustained in the period after the First World War. While the majority of the academic elite at Tokyo and the other imperial universities remained committed to bureaucratic solutions to the problems of industrial society, an increasing number gave their support to left-wing groups advocating the organization of mass movements. Here the legacy of the pioneer socialists of the late Meiji took on new meaning. Although the abortive movement of the 1900s had failed to gather sufficient support to steer Japan leftward and most of its leadership were jailed or driven underground by government suppression, by 1911 it had provided heroes and legends of considerable significance for the later development of a more potent socialist movement in the 1920s.

In closing, then, it can be argued that the late Meiji debate over social policy constituted a turning point at least as important as the victory in the war with Russia. While Japanese industrial leaders and the bureaucratic elite continued to disagree on whether government regulations or company policies were the most effective in keeping the workers politically passive, the two cooperated in charting a course that rejected ultimately both the liberal values and the socialist theories of the West. It was a heading that was to result, nevertheless, in considerable political turbulence over the following half century.

External and Internal Problems After the War

Banno Junji

Since modern Japanese history is a short period of only one hundred years, it is not easy to find commonly acceptable "turning points" that can be ranked in magnitude with the Meiji Restoration and the defeat of the Second World War. Nevertheless, historians specializing in a certain period are apt to find turning points which are supposed to mark major chronological divisions in modern Japanese history. This essay on the Russo-Japanese War as a turning point does not go beyond this specialist sense of periodization.

In a previous article on the political history of modern Japan between the end of the Russo-Japanese War and the outbreak of the First World War, I argued as follows. In the nine years between the end of the Russo-Japanese War in September 1905 and the outbreak of the First World War in July 1914, we find three significant phenomena in Japan's domestic politics. They are, first, the growth of the Seiyūkai, second, the activation of urban popular movements, and third, an increase in political participation of the army and navy, which until then had been a relatively amenable part of the bureaucratic clique.

With slight oversimplification, the argument follows that Japan's political structure hinged on these three aspects after the Russo-Japanese War. The end of the war was a turning point in only a limited sense, however, because these three changes in Japanese politics were generated by gradual processes begun before the Russo-Japanese War and because they did not fade out even after the Taishō political crisis of 1912–1913.

Before discussing these three aspects of Japan's political development and their interrelationships, let us first examine an aspect of modern Japanese history of this period that is more worthy of the term "turning point." In the area of foreign relations, particularly those with China, the Russo-Japanese War was clearly a turning point, the significance of which is second only to the Meiji Restoration or to Japan's defeat in the Second World War. Only after the Russo-Japanese War did Japan acquire special military and economic prerogatives in China or, more precisely, Southern Manchuria. Although tensions existed between China, Japan, and Russia in East Asia prior to the Sino-Japanese War of 1894–1895 and the Russo-Japanese War of 1904–1905, these tensions and both these wars were initiated over the issue of control over Korea and had no direct bearing on the independence or sovereignty of China or Russia. In consequence, China and Russia were ready to acknowledge Japan's control over Korea in peace treaties after they found the battlefield had become unfavorable for them.

In contrast, the special interests in southern Manchuria which Japan acquired as a result of the Russo-Japanese War had a much greater influence on the territorial integrity and sovereignty of China. In the course of the political and military developments in subsequent years China's quest to regain southern Manchuria intensified. Hence, as long as Japan refused to return the special interests in southern Manchuria to China, Sino-Japanese relations were fundamentally in conflict and incompatible. Japan's foreign relations in East Asia after the Russo-Japanese War were therefore centered on the issue of Manchuria. In this sense, then, we can safely say that the Russo-Japanese War was a turning point in foreign relations.

Although recent Japanese historians, including the Marxist school, do not seem to be concerned with exact periodization for the beginning of Japanese imperialism, the consideration outlined above strongly supports the conventional view that it was firmly established around the year 1900. The actual advance into southern Manchuria did not start until 1905, but strong opinions urging this move began to appear in 1900 within the government and foreign policy circles. That year was the time of the Boxer Rebellion in China, and foreign policy leaders were bitterly divided on this issue. The conflict between prowar and antiwar camps was reflected in the vacillation among such prominent leaders as Itō Hirobumi and Yamagata Aritomo. The withdrawal of Tani Kanjo, a hard-line foreign policy advocate, from the prowar circle further indicates the extent of the dissonance.

Such discord is a typical characteristic of a historical turning point. In this respect it should be remembered that there was no discord at the time of the Sino-Japanese War. Even though the conflict over supremacy in Korea was at its height, there had been discussion of this issue within the Japanese government since 1873 and a consensus on the matter had been reached long before the actual beginning of the war. On the basis of this long-established consensus, the Japanese government was able to give substance to the slogan of national unity: *Kyōkoku Itchi*. The Sino-Japanese and Russo-Japanese wars tend to be given equal weight in the course of Japanese expansion, but their significance is, in reality, not comparable.

The Limitation of Seiyūkai Power

Since the appearance of two prominent works by Mitani Taichirō and Tetsuo Najita on the development of the Seiyūkai, there seems to be general acceptance of their thesis that this political party achieved supremacy over the bureaucratic faction during late Meiji and early Taishō times. Despite my respect for the value of these pioneering works of a decade ago, I must point out certain shortcomings in the Mitani–Najita thesis.

First, both Mitani and Najita overestimate the strength of the Seiyūkai and, moreover, that of Hara Kei's leadership within the party. Prior to the period of the Yamamoto cabinet (February 1913–March 1914) the Seiyūkai position vis-à-vis the bureaucratic faction under Yamagato and Katsura Taro was not as strong as these writers maintained. Nor was Hara Kei's leadership within the party as strong as they indicated.

Second, both books underestimate the severity of the financial problems of the period 1906–1913. Because of them the increase in the Seiyūkai's political power cannot possibly be attributed to pork barrel politics supposedly induced by its "positive fiscal policy." Contrary to Mitani and Najita's claims, expenditure of government funds on local public works was quite limited indeed.

Third, as a result of their focus on Seiyūkai development, both works underestimated the role played by non-Seiyūkai cabinets such as the second Ōkuma cabinet (March 1914–October 1916) and the Terauchi cabinet (October 1916–September 1918). For the same reason, both works neglect the growth of anti-Seiyūkai groups.

Among these three misinterpretations for the growth in the Seiyūkai power, the second is the most serious. After coming to power in 1906 through cooperation with the Yamagata faction, the Seiyūkai, according to the Mitani–Najita thesis, expended government funds on the local level to expand its political base. However, a closer examination reveals that, except for 1907, the Seiyūkai cabinet did not have an opportunity to make such expenditures—that is, to realize its widely proclaimed "positive fiscal policy"—due to the financial condition of the nation. The 1906 budget having already been prepared by the former cabinet, the first Seiyūkai cabinet of Saionji was not able to realize its policy throughout that year. Faced with the problem of a postwar depression, this cabinet postponed its spending policy in the preparation of the government's 1908 budget. When the Seiyūkai returned to power with the second Saionji cabinet in 1911, financial and economic conditions were even worse. Because of the accumulation of foreign loans and interest payments, and the considerable excess of imports over exports, deficits in the balance of payments were very serious. Accordingly the second Saionji cabinet again unwillingly adopted a retrenchment policy from the start. These qualifications leave only the year 1907, of the six years that followed the Russo-Japanese War, for the Seiyūkai to have implemented its positive policy in finance.

Dissension in Urban Popular Movements

Emphasis on urban popular movements against the coalition between the bureaucratic faction and the Seiyūkai is also prevalent among historians of Taishō democracy. Recent works by Matsuo Takayoshi, Eguchi Keiichi, and Miyachi Masato are representative of this school. Undoubtedly the role played by the left-wing faction of the Kenseihontō party, the Yūko-kai (later Yūshin-kai) circle, and the Association of Chambers of Commerce and Industry was important, and so was their support of urban popular movements on both political and taxation issues. As these scholars emphasize, the politics of this period cannot be fully understood without reference to these popular movements and their supporters.

Here again, however, we can detect some exaggeration in their arguments as to the extent to which these antiestablishment political forces were united in their struggle against the bureaucratic forces. Matsuo, for example, emphasizes the importance of the anti-tax movement in 1908 as the starting point of the Taishō political crisis. He does not pay much attention, however, to the rapid decline of this movement in the same year. This decline corresponds exactly with the fall of the Seiyūkai cabinet and the establishment of the second Katsura cabinet. In fact, one of the most important groups in this movement, the Kenseihontō, tried to form a coalition with the bureaucratic faction after their failure to obtain a majority in the 1908 general election. The Association of Chambers of Commerce and Industry, on the other hand, withdrew their support from the urban popular movements by discarding their demand for the abolition of the three consumption taxes and began to support the bureaucratic government in order to seek a reduction of the business tax.

Moreover, there were quite a few left-wing leaders of popular movements, notably those of the Yūshin-kai, who actually hoped to form a coalition with the Daidō Kurabu, the party representing the bureaucratic faction. Their purpose was to break up the rule of the Seiyūkai. In short, the opposition groups, while fiercely attacking the corruption of the Seiyūkai, were at the same time striving to form beneficial relationships with the bureaucratic clique as the only other effective political force. To miss this tendency on the part of the anti-establishment groups is to misunderstand the political dynamics of the period altogether. Indeed, after a series of popular meetings and demonstrations—the so-called Taishō political crisis of 1912–1913—the second Ōkuma cabinet was formed on the basis of an anti-Seiyūkai coalition. Ironically it was this cabinet which emerged out of the antiarmament movements. Yet, in the end, the Ōkuma cabinet increased the army by the two divisions the latter had sought in 1912.

Conflict Between Army and Navy

The third misunderstanding is based on an exaggeration of the cohesiveness of the bureaucratic faction and the consistency of its hostility to party politics. The one-sided and simplistic image of a single bureaucratic faction derives from face-value acceptance that the entire bureaucracy adhered to *Fukoku Kyōhei* principles as the absolute policy orientation. In fact there had never been consensus or consistency within the bureaucratic faction regarding enlargement of the military.

Unlike the aftermath of the Sino-Japanese War, Japan did not gain reparations after the Russo-Japanese War. Therefore the postwar government was faced not only with the repayment of the interest and loans it had borrowed from overseas during the Russo-Japanese War but also with the financial drain caused by trade imbalance. These were the main causes for the steadily worsening state of the international balance of payments. Because of these fiscal problems, the Finance Ministry was able to support neither the Seiyūkai's positive fiscal policy nor the enlargement of the military. Under these conditions, there was not even a choice between the positive policy of the

Seiyūkai, which justified their policy in the name of the national slogan: *Fukoku Kyōhei*. In fact, the problem was so serious that the conflict between army and navy intensified over the question of priority in the use of available funds.

The interservice struggle over limited budgets for armament was one of the most significant causes of the Taishō crisis. To survive in this competition, the navy succeeded in forming a close political alliance with the Seiyūkai. Tsunoda Jun delineated this connection between the navy and the Seiyūkai and its impact on the Taishō crisis, but his valuable insight has not received sufficient attention in subsequent research.

Yet the result of the alliance of the navy and the Seiyūkai did not end with the successful ousting of the third Katsura cabinet as Tsunoda maintained. The navy–Seiyūkai alliance induced a similar alliance between the army and the anti-Seiyūkai parties. It was this latter alliance which enabled Ōkuma Shigenobu to form his second cabinet immediately after the Yamamoto cabinet in April 1914. Under the second Ōkuma government the twelfth general election was held; the opposition party, the Seiyūkai, was defeated by a landslide and the anti-Seiyūkai–army coalition increased the army by two divisions.

The Key to the Taishō Crisis

This essay has tried to demonstrate that the positive fiscal policy of the Seiyūkai has been overestimated, that the antigovernment nature of popular movements and their supporters has been exaggerated, and that the image of the bureaucratic faction implementing *Fukoku Kyōhei* ideology into policies has been oversimplified. Combined these three mistakes have become a great obstacle to understanding the essence of the Taishō crisis. Now I want to add a few more words by way of conclusion.

Tokutomi Sohō, in his book *Taishō Seikyoku Shiron* of 1916, rightly says that the period 1905–1914 contains three important elements of conflict and cooperation: military power, financial power, and popular power. Research into various aspects of this period has greatly increased since his statement, but no one has matched his insight concerning the essence of the Taishō crisis in terms of the interrelationships of these three elements. Each element ought to be further divided into two opposing elements, though. The military interest was in fact divided between army and navy. Financial circles were split in their support of "sound financial policy" by the Finance Ministry and "positive fiscal policy" by the Bank of Japan. The once-united popular power was fractured into Seiyūkai supporters and anti-Seiyū-kai sympathizers. The conflict and cooperation and the fission and fusion that occurred within each political element and among the three political forces are the key to understanding the political dynamics of the Taishō crisis. Once the political dynamics of modern Japanese history have been clarified, there will no longer be any question of periodization or turning points.

PART VII

How Democratic
Was Taishō Democracy?

ONE OF THE LEAST studied and least understood periods of modern Japanese history has been the Taishō period (1912–1936). Much more glamorous were the 1930s. Here one could find answers for major questions such as why Japan embarked on a policy of expansion that led to the Pacific War and why Japan became more militaristic, authoritarian, and ultranationalistic. The more extensive the research carried out on the period, however, the more compelling has become the need to find explanations for the 1930s in earlier times. Consequently, in the past decade the relative neglect of the Taishō period has been corrected and a greater understanding of the period is unfolding.

One of the central questions of the Taishō period is how liberal and democratic it was. The tendency twenty or thirty years ago among American scholars was to portray the period as quite democratic and liberal. From such a point of view Taishō democracy seemed a continuation, even a significant acceleration, of liberal trends in the Meiji period. It also seemed to explain to earlier interpreters of modern Japanese history why so many reforms of the Allied Occupation (1945–1952) were accepted by the Japanese people. Such an interpretation, however, made the 1930s puzzling. How could that period be explained? The answer given by the proponents of this view was that the 1930s should be seen as an aberration from the trend of Japanese history. Hence the explanation for the 1930s had to be found in Chinese nationalism, the world depression, or an alliance of hot-headed young military officers and ultranationalists who carried out government by assassination. This older interpretation is not dead; it has more than a little logic and a great deal of historical fact to recommend it.

Recently scholars have become less satisfied with the foregoing interpretation. The more they examine the nature of Taishō democracy, the more shallow they find it to be. Peter Duus, Tetsuo Najita, and Arthur Tiedemann at first, and recently Gordon Berger, have found the political parties of Taishō opportunistic, self-centered, and limited in their conception of democracy and allegiance to its principles. Examination of many intellectuals in the Taishō period, with a few exceptions, has revealed their liberalism to be either the classic nineteenth-century variety or an apolitical search for private autonomy or meaning in asceticism. Apparently very few liberals were willing to challenge the position of the emperor above the constitution or to extend their conception of democracy to social and economic justice for the peasants and the growing proletariat. Nor did the political parties or liberals work for structural changes which would strengthen their position vis-à-vis the state and opponents of a liberal and democratic Japan.

This latter interpretation of the Taishō period obviously entails new thinking about the 1930s. If the Taishō period were less liberal and democratic than previously thought, the 1930s seem more understandable as a logical consequence of preceding Japanese history. But such a conclusion would be hard to reconcile with an interpretation that Japanese society had become democratized after the Second World War. For if one's view of postwar Japan is that occupation reforms succeeded and made Japan a participatory democracy, the interpreter must explain *why* democratization was so successful. If the scholar does not explain that success by arguing that Japan's defeat was so traumatic that it resulted in a nationwide conversion to democratic values, he or she must look for prewar roots that allowed democracy in postwar Japan to flourish. Likewise the interpreter would seem to be led to a criticism of the recent research deemphasizing the extent of Taishō democracy.

If, however, one views the success of the occupation reforms and their Japanese reception more caustically and considers contemporary Japan to be characterized by institutional rather than participatory democracy, the recent research deemphasizing Taishō democracy and liberalism seems validated.

In the essays that follow three contributors make their assessments of how liberal and democratic Taishō democracy was. All three scholars have been engaged in research on the Taishō period and bring fresh insights and persuasive arguments to bear on the topic. In the first essay Stephen Large expresses grave reservations about the depth of Taishō democracy. Large finds that the two middle class parties were not liberal, dedicated to principles, or democratic in their suppression of the proletarian parties. But the proletarian parties, themselves, did not advance the cause of democracy much. The right wing socialists compromised themselves and their ideology by sacrificing many of their principles in order to be acceptable to the two liberal parties and other elite groups. The more radical anarchists and communists failed to develop a real base among the proletarians, to be pragmatic, or to tone down radical theories of revolution and imperialism which alienated Japanese public opinion.

David Titus argues that the political parties were democratic. Their failing was that of obtaining and using political power. In his view five criticisms leveled at the political parties in the Taishō period are not valid arguments for showing that they were undemocratic. They are "nonissues" that becloud our judgment, namely, corruption, aggressive nationalism, bureaucratism, imperial sovereignty, and loyalty.

In his essay Henry Smith II maintains that liberalism as we know it in nineteenth century England never took root in Japan. There were very few liberals devoted to freedom of the individual in either political or economic areas. In fact, he finds four serious limits to Taishō liberalism that help us understand much of what happened in the 1930s. His essay seems at direct loggerheads with the one written by David Titus.

—HARRY WRAY

The Patterns of Taishō Democracy

Stephen S. Large

"Taishō democracy" refers to a diverse set of unrealized potentials for the democratic transformation of Imperial Japan. Although the phrase rightly implies that these potentials were strongest during the reign of the Taishō monarch (1912–1926), the social and political forces of Taishō democracy overlapped the Taishō period at both ends, extending back into Meiji times and forward into the early Shōwa period. This essay surveys the history of Taishō democracy—especially the complex interaction, within their shared context of nationalism, of the two levels comprising Taishō democracy: *liberal democracy,* closely tied to capitalism, served the interests of the middle class; *proletarian democracy,* representing the *musan kaikyū* (propertyless classes), found political expression in anarchism, communism, and socialism.

The idea and institutions of both levels crystallized significantly in the First World War period, the so-called dawn *(reimei)* of Taishō democracy. In those years, the victory of the democracies in the war, the corresponding popularity of Western liberal ideas, and the gathering strength of the two Japanese liberal parties, as disclosed by the formation of the Hara cabinet in 1918, which was a breakthrough for the parties in challenging the power of the genro, inspired proponents of liberalism such as Yoshino Sakuzō to believe that trends at home and abroad augured well for the evolution of political liberalism in Japan.

Quite different expectations for the future among Japanese who interpreted democracy in proletarian terms were nurtured by other contemporary events in Japan and abroad. For some, the 1917 Russian Revolution, coupled with the upsurge in wartime Japan of popular protest manifested in an unprecedented wave of labor and agrarian disputes and the Rice Riots of 1918, indicated that the *musan kaikyū* could soon achieve liberation *(kaihō)* from capitalism and a repressive emperor system through revolutionary class struggle. Hence Ōsugi Sakae's anarchist appeals for militant direct action and violent confrontation with the existing order received support in sections of the emergent labor union movement during the war. Later, after the formation of the Japanese Communist Party in 1922, the revolutionary impulse of anarchism was largely displaced by that of communism as the new party, led by Yamakawa Hitoshi and Arahata Kanson, sought to apply Marxist-Leninist concepts of class struggle to the task of overthrowing the capitalist system and imperial order in Japan.

A more pragmatic approach to redistributing wealth and power in favor of the *musan kaikyū* characterized still other Japanese who were active in the social movements of early Taishō. Embracing a nebulous mixture of Fabian socialism and a Marxist concept of historical process shorn of Marx's emphasis on the revolutionary outcome of class struggle, they envisaged a democratic reconstruction *(kaizō)* of Japan through strictly legal, peaceful, and evolutionary tactics to be implemented from within the established order. Accordingly they attacked the deprivations of the *musan kaikyū* under capitalism and advocated higher wages and better conditions for factory workers, lower rents for tenant farmers, welfare legislation for the poor, the legalization of labor and agrarian unions, and universal suffrage. Representative of this reformist impulse in Taishō democracy were the Christian socialist Kagawa Toyohiko, many progressive intellectuals in the Shinjinkai (New Man Society), and workers like Nishio Suehiro who had helped build up the labor movement in early Taishō.

The vitality of these liberal and proletarian perceptions of democracy in early Taishō at once reflected and stimulated the rapid process of social class differentiation and political change attending Japan's industrialization and national development as an Asian power. The prospects for achieving democracy, however, no matter how it was interpreted in terms of ends and means, were disastrously undercut by ruinous civil wars within Taishō democracy itself. At the proletarian level, anarchist, communist, and socialist organizations fought each other to influence the *musan kaikyū*. Their mutual antagonism was no less intense than that between all these groups and liberalism and capitalism, which they opposed in different ways.

Meanwhile the liberal parties and their principal supporters, the *zaibatsu* and rural landlord class, tried to contain and control proletarian democracy lest it jeopardize social stability and threaten the *kokutai*. This policy of containment and control arose from a loose historical nexus among liberalism, capitalism, and nationalism that had been forged before the Taishō period when the liberal parties and big business had sought to gain legitimacy in society by demonstrating their patriotic service to the national drive for wealth and power that had begun in the Meiji era. The liberal party governments of 1918–1921 and 1924–1932 were in most respects liberal in name only. They concentrated on preserving their power through the politics of compromise with other more conservative elites (genro, bureaucracy, peers, the military) which resisted them. Progressives like Yoshino had never intended their liberal ideas to justify repression of organizations that endeavored to speak and act for the *musan kaikyū*, but repression nonetheless occurred.

Containment and control of proletarian democracy took many forms which can only be summarized here. The spread of organized social protest movements among the *musan kaikyū* was limited by denying them a legal right to exist and by undermining their horizontal thrust as mass-based, class-oriented, organizations. An example of this policy can be found in the institutions and practices associated with industrial paternalism in many large modern factories. There employers, often with government encouragement to stimulate industrial rationalization, brought the skilled workers who comprised the core of the labor movement into a vertical relationship with the enterprise in which their loyalty to the firm superseded their loyalty to the unions. This was done by catering to the workers' aspirations for security through such devices as permanent employment for loyal workers, wages based on seniority, and welfare programs provided by the company. Such strategies left the unions, which never exceeded an organizational rate of more than 8 percent of the work force at their peak (in 1931), a weak foundation for political action in the cause of either reform or revolution.

Containment and control were also achieved politically by the state in applying the whip of repression against movements whose revolutionary doctrines made them subversive while extending the candy of concessions to those which were more moderate politically. Thus anarchist and communist organizations were crushed by the police while reformist socialist organizations were lulled into believing that Japanese social democracy would evolve through cooperation with the state by granting them piecemeal welfare legislation and by permitting them to function as long as they remained politically moderate. The most important concession in this regard was the promulgation of universal male suffrage during the liberal Katō Komei administration in 1925. In allowing socialist parties to represent the *musan kaikyū* in the Diet, the government sought to make reformist socialism a buffer against revolutionary radicalism in proletarian democracy. The same administration sponsored the Peace Preservation Law to ensure this outcome.

Not all of the socialists wanted to assume this buffer role. Some feared that participation in parliamentary politics would obscure the identity of the socialist movement. They insisted on a narrow definition of class in which action on behalf of the factory workers, the "genuine proletariat," would be the main priority. Extralegal as well as legal tactics and occasional cooperation with the communists in class struggle typified their reaction to the government's whip and candy. Others, however, claimed that for socialism to gain traction it would have to voice the grievances of the petty bourgeoisie in addition to those of the *musan kaikyū* and, moreover, that any emphasis upon other than legal parliamentary politics or any association, however loose, with communism would provoke the police.

These disagreements soon threw socialist labor into disarray and prevented the socialists from achieving a united political front after the enactment of universal male suffrage, as three socialist parties, each with its own labor and agrarian base, emerged in 1926. Their competition for proletarian votes in an expanded franchise contributed to their gaining only a handful of Diet seats in the late 1920s, a situation that did not improve significantly thereafter. The 1920s ended with most of the socialists having arisen initially in reaction to anarchism and communism as well as liberalism, playing the very buffer role against leftist radicalism expected of them by the state. They never did resolve the acute dilemma which their co-optation into the established order had imposed upon them: how to be progressively socialist and nationalist at the same time.

This brief discussion suggests two general observations about Taishō democracy as of the late 1920s. First, the advent of liberal party rule fostered a political environment beneficial to both the liberal parties and the more moderate (socialist) elements of proletarian democracy. The liberal parties, however, imposed decisive limits on their own concept of political purpose and also on proletarian democracy, the revolutionary impulse of which was destroyed and the reformist impulse of which was skewed in the direction of conformity to the existing political and social system.

Second, both levels of Taishō democracy remained weak in relation to their shared external context. The liberal parties, despite holding

power for much of the 1920s, still faced opposition from more conservative political centers. The *zaibatsu,* influential in party affairs,
never overcame their basic insecurity in the economic muddle of the
1920s, a time of slow, uneven growth. The many instances of corruption involving the parties and the *zaibatsu* soiled their mutual reputation and any association with democracy they had in the public mind.
For their part, the agencies of proletarian democracy were weaker still,
overwhelmingly so. Branded as dangerous, the anarchists, communists, and socialists were easy targets for whip and candy manipulation. Worse yet, due to apathy or submissive respect for the authority
of emperor and state, only a few of the *musan kaikyū* joined their organizations.

Clearly, then, the potentials inherent in Taishō democracy during
the First World War were foreclosed by the late 1920s. To be sure, as
institutions the liberal parties survived the political crisis of rightist
terrorism, the economic crisis of the depression, and Japan's plunge
into war and confrontation with the West in the 1930s, although liberal party government itself was destroyed (in 1932) by these upheavals. On the proletarian level of Taishō democracy little remained
in the 1930s of the anarchist and communist movements, but the socialists sufficiently closed ranks into new united political party, labor,
and agrarian fronts to maintain an organized presence on the scene,
albeit a fragile one. In 1940, however, when the liberal parties and all
remaining socialist organizations were voluntarily dissolved into the
authoritarian New Order, even the institutional story of liberal and
proletarian democracy came to an end.

In conclusion, the eclipse of Taishō democracy occurred not in 1940
but much earlier—sometime in the late 1920s not very long after
the dawn of Taishō democracy. Certainly external factors pressing
in heavily upon Taishō democracy were an important cause: the
constraints posed by the Meiji constitutional framework, opposition
from antidemocratic elites, the corrosive impact of uneven economic
growth, crises in Japan's international relations, and others. But the
inner history of Taishō democracy, with its persistent civil wars in this
deleterious context, also explains why the potentials of Taishō democracy were so short-lived.

Significantly, all parties to these conflicts failed to reach a balance
between ideology and action in advancing democracy as they perceived it. The anarchists and communists were too preoccupied with
radical theories of revolution to see the futility of revolution given the
power of the Japanese state. Nor did they give sufficient attention to

developing their strength in organizations among the *musan kaikyū*. Thus they never broke out of political limbo. The liberals, and to a much lesser extent the socialists, did more to build up their organizations with support from the middle class and the *musan kaikyū*, respectively. However, most of them were not ideological enough in pursuing pragmatic policies designed almost exclusively to maintain these organizations as an end in itself. Impoverished in their ability to project a compelling vision of what democracy might mean in Imperial Japan, they demonstrated that liberal organizations without truly liberal ideals and socialist organizations without progressive socialist ideals were little better than no liberalism and no socialism at all.

Political Parties and Nonissues in Taishō Democracy

David A. Titus

> *I do not see history as a pageant but as a motley procession with some bright banners but many dingy emblems, marching out of step, and not very certain of its destination.*
>
> —Sir George Sansom

In contrast to the heroic purposiveness and successes of the Meiji period (1868–1912), the Taishō era (1912–1926) witnessed a pluralism of motley processions, very much out of step and not at all certain of their destinations. Japan's victory over Imperial Russia in 1905 signaled the achievement of Japan's national purpose during the Meiji period: to stand tall in the world as one of the Great Powers by building "a Rich Nation and a Strong Military" *(Fukoku Kyōhei)*. Once this modernizing purpose had been largely achieved, as many conceded in 1905, Japan faced three major sets of problems.

First, where was the nation to go now? What was to be the new national purpose? Into the void of national purpose left by the very success of Meiji modernization rushed every conceivable social and political theory—from Japanist reactionism to revolutionary Marxism, from Shinto obscurantism to Christian internationalism, from bureaucratic statism to liberal democracy.

Second, how were the new social forces unleashed by Japan's modern transformation, and those traditional forces affected by Japan's modernization, to be integrated into the political system? This problem became especially acute with Japan's enormous industrial expansion during the First World War, which spurred forward a modern labor movement, intensified dislocations in agriculture and village life, and greatly accelerated the pace of urbanization. Japan had become a land of societal pluralism and conflict, of strikes and tenant disputes, of urban demonstrations and even riots.

And third, what was Japan to do about the extensive rivalry among government institutions that by 1920 exercised the emperor's governing prerogatives under the Meiji Constitution of 1889? The military chiefs of staff, for example, exercise the emperor's prerogative of supreme command. The Home Ministry exercised the emperor's prerogative to maintain public peace and order. The Imperial Diet exercised the emperor's prerogative of legislation. The Foreign Ministry, with the Privy Council, exercised the emperor's prerogative to make and ratify treaties. But who was to mediate the institutional disputes that inevitably arose when a policy involved two or more of the emperor's prerogatives and consequently two or more institutions of government? This institutional rivalry was intensified by the fact that most governmental institutions were manned and led by careerists whose lives and loyalty were primarily confined to "their" institution of imperial prerogative.

At the center of these intellectual, social, and governmental pluralisms were the established political parties. Based in the elected House of Representatives of the Imperial Diet, the political parties had managed by 1912 to mount a powerful challenge to the other institutions and groups of imperial prerogative—the "domain cliques" that had wielded power during the Meiji period and whose ultimate sanctuary was the imperial palace, the civil and military bureaucracies, the aristocratic and appointive House of Peers. The political parties became established during the first decade or so of the twentieth century because the cooperation of political parties came to be considered essential, if not desirable, to government effectiveness by most of Japan's political leaders. Leading civil and even military bureaucrats increasingly joined political parties and assumed leadership positions. So successful were the parties that by 1927 they appeared destined to unify and control Japanese politics. But ten years later this reasonably safe assumption turned into a chimera, and in 1940 the established political parties voluntarily dissolved into the amorphous Imperial Rule Assistance Association in submission to bureaucratic fascism at home and militarism abroad.

Despite their failure to achieve complete political power and their subsequent submission to bureaucratic fascism, Japan's prewar political parties, it will be argued here, were indeed democratic. They sim-

ply failed to integrate the intellectual, social, and governmental pluralisms that engulfed Taishō Japan. This was a failure of their political
power, not their democracy.

Samuel Huntington has argued persuasively that economic modernization creates acute social change that more often than not causes
acute political instability. The political decay occurs when governments fail to institutionalize—to develop autonomous, complex, coherent, and adaptable structures able to respond to the forces, new
and old, brought forth by economic modernization and social mobilization. Political modernization means the creation of political institutions that can expand political participation, so that the government
is literally able to reach everyone in the nation. Huntington maintains, "the principal means for organizing the expansion of political
participation are political parties and the party system." If this is so,
then the capacity of Japan's prewar political parties to integrate the
social forces and groups demanding participation into the political
system would be of crucial importance to Japan's political *modernization* in the prewar period. And if Japan's political parties were able to
accomplish this task by noncoercive mobilization of voters at each successive stage in the expansion of political participation (suffrage), by
voluntary and open recruitment of party leaders and party workers,
and by persuading both elites and nonelites of the virtues and necessity of party government, then Japan would achieve the essentials of
political *democratization* as well.

In defending my argument about the essentially democratic nature
of the prewar political parties and of Taishō democracy in general, I
want to focus on various alleged impediments to the development of
parliamentary democracy and party government in prewar Japan.
These alleged impediments, frequently cited to explain the failure of
the prewar political parties, involve the so-called undemocratic nature
of the political parties. But I prefer to call them nonissues in Taishō
democracy. Suppose we examine these nonissues one by one.

Loyalty

Loyalty to the emperor and imperial institutions was the primary
political value articulated by the government and inculcated in the
people. Many scholars and commentators, primarily Japanese but
also foreign, have argued that absolute loyalty to the emperor meant
submission to the authoritarian will of an absolutist government. If

political parties professed such loyalty, they were ipso facto undemocratic.

The logical weakness of the loyalty argument is apparent when one asks: Must political parties be *disloyal* to be democratic? If the vast majority of the English people and British party leaders have great respect for the queen of England, does this mean that England is undemocratic? Political party leaders as well as leading theorists in prewar Japan argued that loyalty to the emperor was most perfectly expressed in the union between emperor and people. Because the party leaders were the representatives of the people, they epitomized that union and therefore the loyalty that bound people and emperor. Prewar Japan's leading constitutional theorist during the Taishō and early Shōwa (1926–   ) periods, Minobe Tatsukichi (1873–1948), argued that the emperor was sovereign under law and always acted in the best interests of the people. Were not elected representatives of the people best able to advise the emperor on the welfare of the people? In short, loyalty was used by Minobe, other democratic theorists, and the party leaders themselves to rationalize and *strengthen* democratization in prewar Japan.

Imperial Sovereignty

The loyalty nonissue might appear to be a real issue because of imperial sovereignty. Popular sovereignty has long been linked with democracy. Japan's prewar political system rested on imperial sovereignty. Therefore prewar Japan's political system was not only undemocratic; it could be nothing other than undemocratic. And loyalty to such a political system would only reinforce its undemocratic and authoritarian nature.

History and logic run contrary to such a sweeping generalization. British democracy evolved from monarchial sovereignty. Today the queen is still formally sovereign, the queen in Parliament is conventional or legal sovereign, and the electorate is political sovereign. Nevertheless one does not question the reality of democracy in England.

In Japan the theoretical and logical way to parliamentary democracy was cleared by Taishō democracy's leading political theorist, Yoshino Sakuzō (1878–1933), and by Taishō democracy's leading constitutional theorist, Minobe Tatsukichi. Yoshino argued that legal sovereignty was distinct from political sovereignty and that parliamentary democracy in Japan should evolve *politically* within the legal theory of imperial sovereignty. Minobe's theory, as we have just seen, had the same effect as Yoshino's in rationalizing parliamentary democracy under imperial sovereignty.

Finally, the emperor was to transcend politics—the concrete process of governing. His authority was not to be tarnished by open involvement in partisan politics. If the emperor appointed a disastrous prime minister and cabinet on his own personal initiative, for example, he could be held responsible for that disaster. Party leaders, and even Japan's last elder statesman, Prince Saionji Kimmochi (1848–1940), believed that the transfer of political power from one major party to the other when a cabinet fell would detach the emperor from visible involvement in the political conflicts that raged in the midst of Taishō pluralism. Ironically, party government was here being advocated to *preserve* the transcendental authority of the emperor and therefore imperial sovereignty itself.

Aggressive Nationalism

Like loyalty, aggressive nationalism is not the exclusive preserve of authoritarian or totalitarian political systems. Historically nationalism and democracy have emerged together with the rise of the modern nation-state. Moreover, British imperialism in the late nineteenth and early twentieth centuries was rationalized by a host of British liberals and utilitarians as a civilizing mission—the white man's burden, in Kipling's now embarrassing phrase. And are not Manifest Destiny and the 1898 Spanish-American War two examples of aggressive nationalism on the part of the United States? To argue that aggressive nationalism in all its manifestations is undemocratic, or the product only of authoritarian regimes, flies in the face of historical fact.

Japan's quest for domination in East Asia was explicitly rationalized by some leaders as Japan's version of the Monroe Doctrine, which was designed to keep Latin America free from all external influences (except that of the United States). Japan's political party leaders concurred with the vast majority of other prewar leaders in Japan's quest for domination. The issue was not domination but *how* that domination was to be achieved and by *whom*—diplomacy and economic penetration managed by the Foreign Ministry, political parties, and business leaders or military conquest managed by the military establishment, especially the army? Although we like to think that virulent militarism and aggression are functions of authoritarian (especially fascist) regimes, this does not mean that democratic regimes and democratic political parties are necessarily immune to patriotic rhetoric. Patriotism, like loyalty, is not inherently undemocratic.

Corruption

Prewar Japanese parties were censured for their corruption by democratic idealists and authoritarian bureaucrats alike. Corruption is condemned as undemocratic because it interferes with the freely expressed will of the people: votes are bought, not won on the merits. Corruption is undemocratic because party leaders are bought off by special interests against the "welfare of the people." Bad money drives out good morality. Corruption undermines public trust in the political parties and democratic processes.

But corruption may be a question of viewpoint rather than a political reality. Emerging democratic parties may be seen as corrupt precisely because they solicit public support. In contrast to hidden bureaucratic or authoritarian decision-making, vote-getting is a more or less public process. Some critics, both idealists and traditionalists, who watched politicians pander to the public for support regarded the very process of electioneering as inherently corrupt. The same could be said for party finances. Elections and party politics cost money. Like electioneering, the efforts of parties to obtain financial support, and their subsequent close ties with business, were seen by many military and civil bureaucrats, a hypercritical press, and philistine intellectuals as inherently corrupt. Political parties in prewar Japan were often faced by hostile forces unsympathetic to the seemingly undisciplined forum of democratic politics and unaccepting of open political processes—and by government leaders whose political values and bases of political power made them all too willing to condemn party politics as corrupt on sight.

More important, however, is the fact that emerging political parties in potential democracies must build political power, a process that involves capturing political power at the top and political support from below. If this is to be done by nonrevolutionary means, parties will be obliged to win over nondemocratic elites by compromise and use various devices including liberal use of money to attract public support. But if corruption is used judiciously as a means toward democratic goals, then corruption may indeed be functional to democratic development. Japan's first true party prime minister, Hara Kei, built his party from 1900 by compromise with nondemocratic elites, patronage, the pork barrel, favors, and ingenious vote-gathering methods. He amassed no personal fortune thereby, but his party amassed enough political power to make him prime minister in 1918 and to create a cabinet whose ministers were all party members—with the critically important exception of the army and navy ministers.

Bureaucratization, Elitism, and "Undemocratic" Organization

The organization of the prewar political parties has been criticized as undemocratic. Quite possibly the most severe criticism of party organization was the alleged bureaucratization of party leadership: Japan's prewar parties became established by forming alliances with (and co-opting their very leadership from) nonparty elites such as the elder statesmen, civil bureaucrats, and even military bureaucrats. Such alliances, compromises, and co-optations meant that the parties were more often than not led by nondemocratic elites that undermined their democratic nature and goals.

If, however, democratic political parties in emerging democracies are to fulfill their mission of democratic integration they must be able to bring most leadership groups into the marketplace of democratic politics. To do so requires compromise, bargaining, and pragmatic power manipulations. The crucial question is not whether the parties compromised and bargained but what their compromises and bargains achieved. Given the record of co-opted bureaucratic leaders, most notably the enactment of universal male suffrage under Katō Komei in 1925, it might be argued that the parties were not bureaucratized but that the bureaucrats were "partyized." It was precisely because the parties won over such leaders that they were able to challenge so successfully the nondemocratic institutions, elites, and social forces arrayed against them. Were one to insist that co-opting such leaders, especially military elites, made the political parties, and the entire system, undemocratic, then one would have to conclude that the selection and election of Generals Ulysses Grant and Dwight Eisenhower (to name but two military figures) as presidents of the United States made American political parties and the government itself undemocratic. It is what political leaders do, not where they come from, that is important.

Internally, moreover, prewar Japan's political parties were far from authoritarian. Party unity was maintained by persuasion, rewards, and compromise. Communication between the party leaders and the rank and file, especially under Hara Kei's leadership of the Seiyūkai, was close and constant. As Najita notes: "Major party decisions in the Seiyūkai were made by the executive staff and were then discussed by the board of councillors. About twenty, or two-thirds, of this board were elected by the eight regional groups; the rest were appointed by the president." The elected representatives of the party's regional organization outnumbered the central appointees on the board. In 1913 the rank and file of the Seiyūkai rejected an imperial command to withdraw a motion of no confidence against the government, despite efforts of the party leaders to the contrary, and the party leaders ultimately accepted the decision of the rank and file. One critical result of this action was that never again would a prime minister use the political prerogative of the emperor against a party in the Lower House. It is untenable to argue that Japan's prewar political parties were undemocratic in their internal organization and decision-making.

But what of their alleged unresponsiveness to the masses and the welfare of the people? Because the parties did not respond to every Suzuki in the street and rice paddy does not mean that the parties were undemocratic. Given the social and intellectual pluralism of Taishō Japan, such complete responsiveness was an impossibility. Moreover, should the parties have been responsive to authoritarian demands from both the radical right and the revolutionary left? If the parties acted to suppress "dangerous thought," as they did in 1925, does that mean they were ipso facto undemocratic? Is it undemocratic to suppress political thought that advocates the suppression of parties, party government, and parliamentary democracy and is backed by a terrorist organization and action? Do not *democratic* governments have the right to defend themselves from internal subversion by authoritarian political movements? Granted that the prewar parties, and certainly the bureaucracy, were unduly alarmist about the left but not the right, this does not mean that suppression is per se undemocratic. This depends on who or what is suppressed—and how.

Finally, were the parties responsive to the *democratic* forces that demanded political participation in prewar Japan? The development of democratic parties, as in England, often begins with factions that emerge in a parliament. Their initial efforts are directed at gaining control over the executive—the prerogatives of the monarch. As political modernization proceeds, these factions develop into parties in response to the expansion of political participation. This means the development of an organization capable of mobilizing new voters into politics. If democracy is to evolve, in other words, parliamentary factions must develop into institutionalized political parties responsive to each new social force that demands political participation.

Japan's prewar political parties did achieve universal male suffrage in 1925. The prewar parties did respond to demands for political participation. The question is not whether they responded so much as whether their responses were timely and effective. And here there is considerable agreement that the parties responded with too little, too late, and did not take adequate organizational measures to integrate the newly enfranchised voters before and after 1925.

The Key to Failure

In this discussion of loyalty, imperial sovereignty, aggressive nationalism, corruption, and undemocratic organization as nonissues in Taishō democracy I have attempted, in an exaggerated if not perverse fashion, to underscore the essentially democratic nature of Japan's prewar political parties and of Taishō democracy in general. But when all is said and done Japan did fall victim to bureaucratic fascism in the 1930s. The parties failed.

Taishō democracy and the political parties which held the key to democratization did not fail because they were undemocratic, however. Their failure was a failure of the *political power* of democratic parties—the ultimate inability of the parties to gain unquestioned ascendancy over the plural institutions of government in prewar Japan, most notably the military establishment and its allies in both government and society. Unable to bring unity to the pluralism of government institutions, Taishō political parties were unable to serve as the sole channel for mobilizing new and traditional social forces into politics. The military establishment was never forced to relinquish its control over the cabinet appointments of the army and navy ministers. Consequently the parties were unable to gain complete control over the cabinet, the key executive policymaking institution.

When a powerful segment of the military establishment was able to forge alliances with like-minded comrades in the other plural institutions of government, including even members of the House of Representatives, and then link itself to the right-wing movement that had emerged as a powerful force in Japanese society after 1918, "bureaucratic fascism" was able to overpower parliamentary democracy. The emergence of bureaucratic fascism was marked by conspiracy and assassination: in the 1930s party prime ministers and several of their sympathizers in the palace and elsewhere were simply murdered. And the magnitude of the bureaucratic-fascist alliance, with its attendant terrorism, that was brought to bear against the political parties of Taishō democracy indicates how powerful the parties and parliamentary democracy had become.

There was nothing inevitable about the failure of Japan's prewar political parties and the death of Taishō democracy. The intellectual, social, and governmental pluralisms that constituted the "motley processions" of Taishō were not the stuff of which historical determinism is made. If Taishō democracy led to bureaucratic fascism at home and militarism abroad in the 1930s, it also bequeathed a democratic tradition that is basic to the successful functioning of parliamentary democracy and party government in today's Japan.

The Nonliberal Roots of Taishō Democracy

Henry D. Smith II

Taishō society was increasingly democratic but not especially liberal. Let me first distinguish between democracy as a type of social and political structure and Democracy as a set of beliefs and prescriptions. It was for the most part in the structural rather than the attitudinal sense that Japan was becoming more and more democratic in the early twentieth century. This change was to some extent the result of deliberately engineered institutional reforms (such as an expanding electorate), but for the most part it followed willy-nilly in the wake of modern economic and technological development. Vastly expanded transportation and communications, higher levels of education, increasing social mobility, rising economic expectations: all these trends created a society more effectively "democratic"—that is, a society in which everyone had a growing ability and will to influence his (and even her) political and economic destiny. But democracy did not lead necessarily to Democracy; on the contrary, the very rapidity and seeming inevitability of these changes was often unsettling, even terrifying, thus encouraging attitudes that were commonly anti-Democratic.

A parallel distinction may be made between liberal and Liberal. In this case liberal may be regarded as a general political temperament favoring gradual change away from the bonds of the past in the direction of some ideal society at once more moral and "free" than the present; Liberal, on the other hand, may be regarded a historical political ideology derived from the English middle class and fundamentally committed to an individual freedom of economic and political activity. Originally Liberalism was liberal, but by the twentieth century, under changing perceptions of the past, it could as often be conservative.

It is my general argument that while there were doubtless many temperamental liberals in Taishō Japan (although no more, surely, than in the eras before or after), there were very few ideological Liberals: neither freedom nor the individual has ever been an overriding political ideal in Japan and the Taishō period is no exception. On the contrary, Taishō society was conspicuous for a variety of non-Liberal trends.

Four Limits to Taishō Liberalism

Limit 1

The Liberal character of the party movement has been exaggerated. This is not a particularly original assertion: it follows logically from the complementary studies by Tetsuo Najita (*Hara Kei in the Politics of Compromise, 1905–1915;* 1967) and Peter Duus (*Party Rivalry and Political Change in Taishō Japan;* 1968), both of whom suggest that Taishō party politics was rooted in a realistic quest for power rather than in an idealistic pursuit of ideological goals. Important structural reforms were made along democratic lines, but typically as a result of interparty and intraparty rivalries rather than from public pressure or grand Democratic ideals. Much as in the debate over the constitution in the 1870s, the issue was less the desirability of a more democratic form of government than the timing of the necessary reforms. In both cases, desirability was judged as much by adherence to contemporary Western practices as by an ultimate conception of Democracy. Universal male suffrage was accepted in the 1920s, as the Lower House of the Diet had been in the 1880s, as much because it was the universal trend of the times as for its ideological merits.

Limit 2

Taishō Liberalism as a significant political movement was very short-lived. It was only in the autumn of 1918—almost halfway through the Taishō period—that a coherent Liberal-Democratic movement began, inspired largely by wartime Allied propaganda but given considerable domestic impetus by the Rice Riots and growing labor unrest. Whatever the causes, this movement peaked in 1919 and rapidly waned. In domestic politics, Liberalism was laid to rest by the Kanto earthquake of 1923, a much-neglected turning point in modern Japanese cultural and political history. Even before the earthquake, Liberalism had been largely supplanted by socialism among the middle-class intellectuals and labor leaders who had been its major advocates.

Limit 3

The most Liberal thing about the Taishō period was the international rather than the domestic political environment. The wartime and postwar ideologizing by the Anglo-American victors of 1918, particularly Woodrow Wilson, inspired a brief but heady mood of internationalist Liberalism throughout the world; Japan was no exception, and the cries for domestic "Democracy!" can be understood only in this global context. The struggle to devise a new peaceful multilateral world order in the 1920s in East Asia has been detailed by Akira Iriye in *After Imperialism* (1965). I think it fair to suggest that Japan's commitment to this experiment was as much pragmatic as idealistic, scarcely surprising for a nation increasingly dependent on unrestricted world trade. A further limit to this internationalist Liberalism was its strict confinement to an imperialist frame of reference: even among the most dedicated of Taishō Democrats—Yoshino Sakuzō was the exception that proves the rule—Japanese colonialism was rarely called into question. Whatever the level of Japan's commitment, the experiment had failed by the end of the decade, and it would be difficult to assign Japan any more than a modest share of the blame.

Limit 4

True Liberals did exist in Taishō Japan, but their numbers were few and their influence limited. Classic Anglo-American Liberalism has never been much more than a marginal political ideology in modern Japan, and even such textbook spokesmen as Fukuzawa Yukichi and Yoshino Sakuzō have been singled out for certain un-Liberal qualities. It is rather the continental European tradition of Democracy, with its statist emphasis, that has proved far more hospitable to Japanese political ideologues of both left and right. Nevertheless there *were* true Liberals in Taishō Japan—men like philosopher Kawai Eijirō, economic journalist Ishibashi Tanzan, educator Nitobe Inazō, and party politician Ozaki Yukio. Some, like Nitobe, were temperamentally quite conservative and came in time to be known by the patronizing tag of "Old Liberals" *(orudo riberaru)*. As a whole, the true Liberals were isolated and in no way typical of the Taishō period in general. More numerous were a variety of individualistic artists, no-

tably the members of the Shirakaba-ha, who are often called bourgeois liberals. Yet politically they were more Romantics than Liberals,
as suggested by their drift to cultural nationalism in the 1930s.

Four Varieties of Taishō Non-Liberalism

Bureaucratic Non-Liberalism

As E. Herbert Norman first stressed and Kenneth Pyle recently reem-
phasized, the bureaucracy is the most important and least understood
area of modern Japanese political life. Certainly the bureaucracy was
vastly more important in Taishō politics than the Diet—and yet almost all scholarly attention has focused on the party movement. This
Democratic bias in favor of nonbureaucratic politics has blinded us to
what was certainly the most influential form of Taishō Non-Liberalism: the bureaucracy. This powerful bureaucratism was characterized
above all by its hostility to politics in the Liberal sense of open conflict
and competition among diverse interest groups. Bureaucratism espouses instead reliance on elite technical expertise to solve social and
economic problems; as a totalistic conception of society, it does not
recognize privatized interests. Like any working political ideology,
bureaucratism harbors a range of political temperaments. One thus
finds Taishō bureaucrats who were temperamental liberals espousing
extensive government efforts on behalf of the poor and oppressed.
These liberals were distinctly non-Liberal, of course, in their totalistic
conception of politics and basic distrust of such Democratic devices as
local autonomy and party rule. Yet they were in a sense democratic in
their tolerance and accommodation to the structural changes of an industrializing society. In formally terming this ideology "Non-Liberalism," I hope to convey the idea that bureaucratism worked not in direct opposition to Liberalism but rather within a wholly different
political world view.

I should interject at this point a caveat: we must not forget that
Taishō Japan was a capitalist nation and that private enterprise was
not only tolerated but positively supported by the state. Bureaucratism, in short, admitted a distinction between public and private;
it did not, however, admit of a firm and litigable distinction. It is this
blurring of public versus private that has led to the contemporary concept of Japan Incorporated—a perfect description of bureaucratist ideology and a term of abuse only when pronounced with a Liberal ac-
cent. I suspect that the Taishō period is in fact the place to search for

the origins of Japan Inc. and, moreover, that future research will un-
earth the emergence of bureaucratist Non-Liberalism in big business
as much as in government.

Socialist Post-Liberalism

The true bourgeois liberals—that is, middle-class advocates of progressive social change—in Taishō Japan were to be found in the socialist movement rather than among the advocates of the established
parties that are conventionally labeled bourgeois by Japanese historians. In its communist wing to the left, the socialist movement of the
late Taishō period also harbored many temperamental radicals hoping
for abrupt rather than gradual change. But whatever their political
temperament, all Taishō socialists shared one crucial form of non-
Liberal sentiment: they believed in more government rather than
less, and they looked in particular to a strong central state as the
means of achieving their ideals. The emphasis was, in other words, far
more on egalitarian goals than on libertarian ones, an emphasis confirmed in the course of the Taishō period by the total victory of the
Bolshevist over the anarchist wing of the left-wing movement. (Given
the obvious vulnerability of libertarian anarchism in a nation with
such strong statist traditions, it is surprising that Taishō anarchists
were as prominent as they were; perhaps it is time we paid closer attention to these anomalous radicals.)

The general appeal of socialism over Liberalism among Taishō
Democrats is explained not only by the strongly statist and collectivist
emphasis of traditional Japanese political thought but also by Japan's
position as a latecomer to modernization. As sociologist Robert Bellah
has proposed, radical socialism (along with romantic nationalism) has
emerged with particular strength in such latecomer nations as Japan
and Germany as counterideologies to the firstcomers' Liberal Democracy, the "primary ideology of modernization." It is in this broader
sense that Taishō socialism was a form of Post-Liberalism—sharing the
progressive and modernizing stance of classic Liberalism yet seeking
to avoid the obvious pitfalls to which an excess of liberty had led.

Grass-Roots Il-Liberalism

This is a controversial issue in Japan these days. On the one hand,
some Japanese scholars (notably Matsuo Takayoshi) have argued that
Liberalism was strong in provincial Japan. I tend to support this view

with respect to certain local politicians, journalists, and intellectuals; but I consider these figures as mere extensions of Liberalism in the metropolitan centers and subject to the same four limits outlined above. The grass roots I have in mind correspond rather to what Kano Masanao and other Japanese historians call the *minshū*, translatable perhaps as "the common people."

I consider the Taishō period to be notable for the widespread growth of local voluntary organizations at all levels of Japanese society. By their voluntary and often communal nature, such groups were structurally democratic. Yet in political temperament and ideology, they tended to be conservative and "il-Liberal"—that is, espousing values at odds with those of both liberals and Liberals. Although they varied widely, such groups were typically formed for the purpose of *fraternity*—after liberty and equality the third and most neglected ideal of the democratic revolution in the West—in the face of growing alienation and uncertainty in a rapidly industrializing society. Typical of these groups were urban neighborhood associations *(chōnaikai)*, rural youth groups *(seinendan)*, school alumni organizations *(dōsō-kai)*, student governments *(gakuyūkai)*, labor and tenant unions, urban prefectural clubs *(kenjinkai)*, village religious unions *(kō)*, new religions—and many more. In virtually all these groups, solidarity rather than freedom was the ideal and political attitudes tended to be conservative, nationalistic, and supportive of the state. One can doubtless find progressive and even Liberal exceptions, but they would be a minority.

Nationalist Anti-Liberalism

Of all the forms of Taishō Non-Liberalism, nationalism was the most explicitly and belligerently opposed to Liberalism—hence Anti-Liberalism. Nationalist groups thrived in the Taishō period, although the generally Liberal international climate of the First World War and its aftermath made them less conspicuous and popular than they would be in the 1930s. Still, there was a fair amount of right-wing nationalist activism in these years and it deserves more attention. Remember, for example, that Kita Ikki wrote his *Outline Plan for the Reorganization of Japan* in 1919 and that Prime Minister Hara Kei in 1920 and *zaibatsu* leader Yasuda Zenjirō in 1922 were both assassinated by right-wing nationalists. In the nationalist mind, Liberalism was identified with a world order dominated by white Anglo-Saxon interests and dedicated to the oppression of the Asian races and the destruction of Japan's non-Liberal cultural traditions. The very popularity of internationalist Liberalism in the mid-Taishō period helps explain the virulence of the nationalist reaction. One might finally suggest that many Taishō nationalists were in a sense Democratic by virtue of their professed concern for the welfare of the Japanese common people and their emphasis on the equality of all Japanese under the emperor. It was a highly anti-Liberal conception of Democracy.

Making Sense of the 1930s

The study of Taishō political life has been dominated for three decades now by the hopeful search for Liberal Democracy. Despite differences in the ideological climate within which they work, both Japanese and American scholars have pursued this search with equal vigor, the former tending to view it as a necessary stage on the way to socialism and the latter as a healthy foundation for the reforms of the occupation. Although I would grant a degree of truth to both interpretations, I offer the following refinements.

To Japanese Marxist scholars in search of bourgeois Liberal Democracy, I would suggest that Japan was able, indeed compelled, to *skip* the stage of classic Liberalism for two important reasons. First, as Ronald Dore has pointed out, the modern Japanese middle class was the product and not the cause of political revolution; hence it maintained a spirit of un-Liberal obligation to the state. Second, Japan as a latecomer believed it possible to avoid the obvious mistakes of nineteenth-century England by reliance on the close engineering of political and economic life rather than leaving things to the laissez-faire economics and local autonomy politics of classic Liberalism.

To American scholars (like myself) I would make two points. First, we have greatly overemphasized Taishō Liberalism and need to turn our attention to the forms of Non-Liberalism outlined above. Second, it is not necessary to give up our genuine commitment to Democracy and its survival in Japan by admitting that there are viable forms of non-Liberal Democracy. Indeed I would suggest that contemporary American Democracy, despite the obvious persistence of strongly rooted Liberal (in the American variant, highly libertarian) sentiment, is bearing an increasing de facto resemblance to the amalgam of bureaucratist Non-Liberalism and socialist Post-Liberalism which flourishes in Japan today.

Let me finally emphasize that to focus on Taishō non-Liberal trends is by no means to paint a bleak picture of the era. It is true that such an approach makes more sense of the 1930s. But it makes even more sense of the 1970s. The simple point is that Taishō political life was complex, contradictory, and multivalent, leading no more surely to fascism than to communism or to social democracy. The great imponderable in assessing both Taishō and contemporary politics in Japan remains the specter of a new wave of nationalist Anti-Liberalism, both in Japan and in the world at large.

PART VIII

Japanese Colonialism: Enlightened or Barbaric?

WHEN THE SECOND World War ended, the modern world's only non-Western colonial power lost all its overseas possessions. Yet between 1895 when Japan gained her first colony and 1945 when her entire empire disintegrated, Japan's experience as a colonizer was wide-ranging and variegated. Taiwan, the first acquisition, ceded to Japan after the Sino-Japanese War of 1894–1895, had hitherto been a relatively untamed area on the periphery of the great Chinese empire. By contrast, the densely populated peninsula of Korea, made a protectorate in 1905 and annexed in 1910, was a fiercely independent kingdom with a history even more ancient than Japan's own. Gained about the same time, Sakhalin was a barren, almost unoccupied landmass in the sea north of the Japanese islands. In 1905 Japan also took over the lease of the Kwantung territory in the southernmost tip of Manchuria, which Russia had wrested from a weak China seven years earlier. The Micronesian islands in the South Seas were seized by the Japanese navy from an embattled Germany in 1914, and in 1919 at Versailles the Allied Powers confirmed Japan's claim to them. Although never formally a colony, Manchuria was so in all but name, and control tightened after Manchuria became the Japanese puppet state of Manchukuo in 1932; Japan's ambassador to Manchukuo was simultaneously the governor-general of the Kwantung territory and commander-in-chief of the Japanese Kwantung Army.

The first essay in this part provides a chronological overview of Japanese colonialism that traces the history of each of the colonies. It evaluates Japanese successes and failures as a colonial ruler in terms of Japan's own goals as a colonizing power. The second contribution reminds us that times and intellectual currents have a great deal to do with how we perceive a phenomenon like colonialism. It presents a profile of Japanese colonialism in a framework which compares Japan's record as a ruler with those of the Western imperialist powers. Focusing on the Taiwanese colonial experience, the third essay asks questions about the damaging psychological legacy of colonialism and the unequal distribution of the rewards of colonial development. The fourth analyzes the meaning of Japanese rule for the country and people of Korea. Thoughtfully it discusses different scholarly approaches to Japanese colonialism in what was Japan's largest and most important outside territory. The final essay takes a different tack altogether. Set in Manchuria, it is a portrait of the changing attitudes of a group of Japanese colonists who are subtly but markedly altered by their overseas experience.

—E. PATRICIA TSURUMI

Japanese Colonialism: An Overview

Edward I-te Chen

Japan was the only non-Western colonial empire before it was terminated in 1945 as a result of her defeat in the Second World War. Her colonies included Korea, Taiwan (also known as Formosa), the southern half of Sakhalin Island (Karafuto), the Kwantung Peninsula (Kantoshu), and the South Sea Islands, totaling some 155,000 square miles or more than three-quarters the size of Japan herself. Manchuria, a colony in all but name after it became a Japanese puppet state in 1932, added another 300,000 square miles.

The five colonies—Manchuria's status was formally not that of a colony—shared two common denominators. First, they were all acquired as a result of victories Japan won in the three wars fought between 1894 and 1914: the Sino-Japanese War, the Russo-Japanese War, and the First World War. Second, they were classified as *gaichi* or "outer territory" (dependency) as opposed to *naichi* or "inner territory" (metropolitan Japan). A *gaichi* was a territory where the constitution and the Diet-enacted laws were not, as a rule, enforced, and where its inhabitants with customs and traditions different from those of the Japanese were regulated by special ordinances of the colonial governor.

The Five Colonies

Korea was by far the most important colony of Japan because of its size, geographic proximity, and long historical ties. Its uniqueness lay in the fact that it was annexed not as a result of military conquest but because of a treaty agreement. In the Treaty of Annexation concluded in 1910 the Japanese government pledged, however superficially, to provide "equal treatment" for Koreans. As a result of this pledge an unusually large number of Koreans were employed in the colonial

government at all levels, even the police force. In vivid contrast, virtually all officials in other colonies—from governor to county clerks—
were Japanese. Unique also for Korea was the fact that the Koreans
possessed a strong cultural identity fostered by more than two thousand years of history as an independent nation. Once annexed, this
cultural identity manifested itself in a strong nationalist movement
with an open demand for restoration of the lost independence. The
only other colony in which a nationalist movement was organized was
Taiwan. There, however, the nature of the movement was reformist,
demanding only a greater degree of home rule within the confines of
Japanese laws.

Taiwan, the first colony acquired, brought Japan into the coveted
position of colonial power. Annexed in 1895, a full ten years before
Sakhalin and the Kwantung Peninsula and fifteen years before Korea, the island became a training ground for numerous colonial officials whose experience proved to be very valuable for the administration of other colonies. After being successfully implemented in
Taiwan, such programs as land survey, population census, government monopolies, and investigation of native customs and traditions
set examples for other colonies to follow. But more important the island was the most profitable colony within the Japanese empire. Like
Korea it shipped to Japan annually one-half of the rice it produced.
Moreover, Taiwan's sugar industry enabled Japan to become the
fourth largest cane sugar industry producer of the world, converting
the island into a lucrative place for investment of Japanese private
capital. Within seven years of annexation, the colonial administration
of Taiwan achieved the goal of financial self-sufficiency. It took Sakhalin twenty-eight years, the Kwantung Peninsula thirty years, and even
the much smaller South Sea Islands ten years to accomplish the same
goal. The Korean administration had to be subsidized from Tokyo
throughout the thirty-five years of Japanese rule.

Sakhalin was acquired under the provision of the Portsmouth Treaty concluded at the end of the Russo-Japanese War in 1905. Unlike
Korea and Taiwan, it was a colony of settlement where virtually all the
inhabitants were Japanese. In 1941 the native population (mostly
Ainu) numbered only 1,697 and was declining. As a colony of settlement, Sakhalin was more integrated with Japan in many aspects than
other colonies. After 1907 the colonial judiciary became part of the
Japanese judiciary, directly supervised by the Ministry of Justice in Tokyo. Colonial education was essentially for Japanese children and was
heavily subsidized by the central government, relieving the colonial

government of the heavy burden that sapped the energy and financial resources of the governments of the other colonies. Military rule was terminated in 1907 in Sakhalin well ahead of other colonies, and in 1943 the colony was given the status of *naichi*.

The Kwantung Peninsula was first ceded to Japan in 1895 but was retroceded to China as a result of the Triple Intervention. Later it was leased to Russia. When Japan defeated Russia in 1905 the lease was transferred to her together with the right to control the South Manchurian Railway and a narrow stretch of land on both sides of it. The peninsula, therefore, was unique in two aspects. First, it was a leased territory; Japan had no exclusive sovereignty over it. Second, the colonial government of the peninsula was entrusted with the administration of the railway, paving the way for the expansion of the Kwantung Army deep into the heartland of Manchuria. In 1934, after the creation of Manchukuo, Japan initiated a peculiar system of appointing her ambassador to this puppet kingdom concurrently as the governor-general of the peninsula. He governed it from his office situated in Mukden.

The South Sea Islands, also known as Nan'yo and Micronesia, consisted of more than 1,400 tiny volcanic islands scattered in the South Pacific north of the equator (Guam excepted). Long controlled by the Spaniards who "discovered" them in the early sixteenth century, the islands were purchased by Germany in 1899 after the Spanish defeat at the hands of the United States. Shortly after the outbreak of the First World War in 1914, these islands were seized by the Japanese navy. At the peace conference, the South Sea Islands were declared to be a Class C Territory of the League of Nations, which in turn awarded Japan the mandate to rule them as part of the empire. Japan retained control of the islands even after her withdrawal from the league in 1933. Technically, therefore, the South Sea Islands were a mandated territory over which, like the Kwantung Peninsula, Japan held no exclusive sovereignty. The native population of the islands was very small and rapidly became outnumbered by Japanese settlers. Like Sakhalin, the South Sea Islands should be regarded as a colony of settlement.

Colonial Institutions

How were the five colonies governed? There was in each a colonial government headed by a colonial governor. Entrusted with a broad range of political, legislative, and judicial powers, he ruled his colony as a virtual sovereign. Except for such matters as defense and foreign affairs which were explicitly reserved for the jurisdiction of the central government, it was he, not the central government, who formulated and implemented colonial policies. He was authorized to issue special ordinances to enact laws as binding on the people as the laws of Japan. (Governors of the Kwantung Peninsula and the South Sea Islands did not have this power.) Except in Sakhalin where the judicial system was integrated with that of Japan, he could appoint and dismiss judges at will and regulate, through the use of his special ordinances, the functions and organization of colonial law courts at all levels. To implement his orders at the grass roots he relied on a large number of trained local officials who, in turn, were supported by efficient police. He received his ultimate support from the colonial garrison of which, prior to 1919, he was concurrently commander-in-chief.

Despite the overall similarity, the power of the five colonial governors depended on local conditions, the degree of integration achieved, and the importance with which the Japanese government regarded the colonies. In the more significant but less integrated colonies of Korea, Taiwan, and the Kwantung Peninsula, the emperor personally appointed the governor-general; in contrast, the chief colonial officer of Sakhalin and the South Sea Islands was known merely as *cho kan* or chief administrator. Even among the governors-general of Korea, Taiwan, and the Kwantung Peninsula, the governor-general of Korea was considered the most powerful of the three. His prominence was matched only by that of the prime minister. Thus he was the only colonial chief having the privilege of being responsible directly to the emperor (until 1919) and to the prime minister (until 1942); all others were required to accept the supervision of relevant cabinet-level colonial officers (ministers of colonial affairs, home affairs, foreign affairs, and the like).

Prior to 1919 all colonial governors were military officers in active service and were, ex officio, commanders of the colonial garrison. In 1919, in line with trends of Taishō democracy in Japan proper, civilian rule was introduced to all five colonies, establishing a system of separation between civil and military authorities. The civilian governor, however, was authorized to "request" the use of military force from the garrison commander. It is significant that in Korea, where the celebrated March First Uprising had just been suppressed, military officers (in civilian clothes) continued to hold the post of governor-general, reform notwithstanding.

At the national level the colonial institution underwent three stages of evolution. From 1895 to 1929 all colonial affairs were handled by a bureau attached to the office of the prime minister or by a department of colonial affairs within the Ministry of Home Affairs with its functions limited to coordinating and data-gathering. In June 1929 the Ministry of Colonial Affairs was created to provide uniform supervision and the second stage began. But the power to formulate colonial policies remained in the hands of colonial governors. In December 1934, upon the creation of Manchukuo, the Bureau of Manchurian Affairs was established within the office of the prime minister and the practice of appointing the ambassador to Manchukuo as the governor-general of the Kwantung Peninsula was introduced.

The third stage began in November 1942 when the Ministry of Greater East Asian Affairs was created to replace the Bureau of Manchurian Affairs and the Ministry of Colonial Affairs. It was charged with the responsibility to supervise the Kwantung Peninsula, South Sea Islands, Manchukuo, and other areas under Japanese occupation, whereas the Ministry of Home Affairs was made the central institution for Korea, Taiwan, and Sakhalin. In addition, all ministries in the central government were authorized to direct the governments of the three colonies in the fields related to their respective functions (colonial education by the Ministry of Education, for example). The move apparently was designed to achieve political integration and material and psychological unity between the colonies and metropolitan Japan.

A Balance Sheet

How successful was Japanese colonialism? The question evokes emotional controversy between opponents and supporters. One objective way of determining its success or failure is first to ascertain the goals advocated (explicitly or by implication) by the Japanese government and to measure how well these goals were met. Among these goals four were paramount: military strategy, emigration, economic development, and political integration.

Military Strategy

Japan's intention was to convert the colonies into defense outposts of the empire as well as springboards for expansion. The war in China and the Pacific War conclusively demonstrated that she was quite successful in attaining this aim. Earlier in her history, moreover, Japan had aspired to be a world power equal in prestige with the Western nations. Her debut as a colonial power was indeed an essential factor that helped her attain such an end.

Emigration

Japan wanted to make the colonies absorb some of her excess population. The results of emigration efforts were mixed. Emigration was successful in Sakhalin and to a lesser degree in the South Sea Islands. In Korea, Taiwan, and the Kwantung Peninsula, which were heavily populated by native inhabitants, emigration was a dismal failure. Japanese residents in those colonies were largely officials, business employees, and their families whose presence caused frequent racial friction. Despite repeated efforts and generous subsidies, the three colonies did not attract a significant number of agricultural settlers.

Economic Development

Japan hoped to develop an integrated economy in which she would provide the colonies with capital and technology in return for supplies of foodstuff, raw materials, and lucrative opportunites for investment. All available economic data clearly indicate that Japan succeeded in interlocking the economy of the five colonies with that of her own.

It should be emphasized that economic development was carried out with the welfare of Japan, not the colonies, in mind and that economic success was often achieved at great expense to the native population. Furthermore, one can raise a legitimate question as to whether Korea, the only colony with a native government before the annexation, could have achieved the same degree of economic success without Japanese colonialism.

Political Integration

To make Korea, Taiwan, and Sakhalin parts of metropolitan Japan by assimilating the native population through education and acculturation was regarded as the ultimate goal of Japanese colonialism. Japan envisioned an empire where the colonized people would learn to speak Japanese and accept the Japanese way of life and where the Japanese constitution and laws would be applied to all equally. In this Japan can claim success only in Sakhalin, where the native population was insignificantly small. In Korea integration efforts failed. In 1943, for example, after more than thirty years of colonial rule, still a mere 20 percent of Koreans were recorded as being able to comprehend the Japanese language. Nothing the Japanese did in Korea, including education and the introduction of home rule more generous than that adopted in other colonies, seemed to discourage Korean aspirations for independence.

In Taiwan the policy of integration produced better results. The 1943 record shows that 62 percent of Taiwanese could speak Japanese and the percentage was fast rising. More than half the laws enforced on the islands originated in Japan, and the governor-general could issue legislative ordinances only if he could find no comparable Japanese laws. Above all, education, reinforced by improved living conditions (and an adequate amount of police repression), persuaded the Taiwanese to keep their political movements within the limits of the law. All this, nevertheless, does not mean that Taiwan had become an integrated colony and that the Taiwanese had been converted into loyal subjects of the emperor. Far from it. It does permit us to speculate, however, that Japan might have achieved the goal of integration in Taiwan had her colonial rule not been so abruptly terminated by war in 1945.

We may say that Japan's colonial record is a mixed one. The smaller the colonial possession and the less developed its political institutions the greater the success of Japan in administering and assimilating it. In addition, Japan may have been more successful in the economic than the political area. Even in Korea an infrastructure was developed which benefitted the country after it achieved independence. Viewed from hindsight it may safely be said that Japan's poorest record was in Korea. Few Koreans thought Japanese rule was enlightened; most thought it was destructive and barbaric.

Japanese Colonialism: Discarding the Stereotypes

Mark R. Peattie

Few disciplines, ultimately, lend themselves so poorly to the stark alternatives of either/or as does history. Each epoch in the human past, initially infused with bold judgments by human pride and passion, once coolly examined, blurs into a series of shadings and qualification, compromises and contradictions. This has proved no less true of the study of colonialism than it has of any other great force in world history. In the late nineteenth and early twentieth centuries the positive contributions of colonialism to the order and progress of the human race in general and subject colonial peoples in particular seemed readily apparent to European nations who administered much of the rest of the world. National pride, racial and cultural arrogance, material self-interest, noble intention—all had much to do with maintaining the colonial ethos and the white man's burden.

By mid-century, however, after two destructive global confrontations had shattered both the prestige and the confidence of all colonial powers, colonialists as a breed stood condemned before the court of world opinion, now largely composed of their former subject peoples. Colonialism was stridently called to task for most of the ills of the globe and for the humiliation of colored races by those with white skins. Within the past decade, however, certain analysts of European colonialism, particularly in its African manifestation, have commenced a careful study of the complex origins, workings, and legacy of colonialism. In so doing, they have begun to contribute to a cautious reappraisal of the role of the colonialist which draws attention to the constructive legacy in material and even cultural terms which a good many European powers left their former charges after the colonial bonds dissolved.

The day seems at hand when it may be possible to make a similarly careful reappraisal of modern history's only non-Western overseas imperium. Of all the colonial systems in this century none came to earn a more malodorous reputation for repression than that of the Japanese colonial empire. By the beginning of the Second World War, in the minds of most Americans, its outlines were blurred with the image of ceaseless aggression in East Asia and the dragooning of support from the conquered peoples of Japan's Greater East Asia Coprosperity Sphere for further Japanese military expansion. In the years since 1945 the understandable and long pent up bitterness of many of its former subjects, especially those in Korea, has deeply etched the picture of the Japanese as the worst of all the world's colonial masters. For their part, the Japanese have been too guilt-ridden by their record in Asia to have attempted to refute even the most exaggerated of these assertions.

Yet with more than three decades elapsed since the liquidation of Japan's colonies, with a wealth of written record to draw upon, and with the techniques of comparative history and modern social science analysis to employ, it should be possible for others, at least, to take a fresh look at the record of Japanese colonialism in its entirety, seeking less to justify or condemn than to understand. In doing so it is probably that a number of stereotypes of the Japanese as colonialists may have to be discarded. The balanced picture which should emerge once historians get a grip on its complexities is impossible to paint in these short pages. Indeed, while my own remarks are affirmative, the reader should understand that in making them I am fully aware of the darker landscape of Japanese rule over some 20 million people.

I leave others in this volume to debate whether or not Japan's successive overseas acquisitions fit into some predetermined plan of Asian conquest. I find it more useful to recognize that the Japanese colonial empire was pieced together between 1895 and 1914 in the high noon of imperialism around the globe with methods—military force, political pressure, and alliances with imperial powers defining respective interests—which were accepted means of imperial expansion at the time. These facts help to explain the general tolerance and even approval with which Westerners noted Japan's initial efforts at the turn of the century in her first colonial acquisition: Taiwan.

A number of postwar studies of Japanese colonial development in Taiwan, particularly in the economic sphere, have tended to confirm these earlier Western impressions of Japan's initial colonial policies as reasonably enlightened. These studies have described the significant economic progress of Taiwan at the outset of the twentieth century, brought about by an enterprising colonial bureaucracy nominally headed by Governor-General Kodama Gentarō but guided largely by the urbane and imaginative Gotō Shimpei, civil administrator, who was assisted by honest and skilled young subordinates dedicated to bringing order and security to the island, improving its road and communications systems, modernizing its cities, reducing disease, and above all transforming the island's economy—particularly its agricultural and industrial base—which made the colony economically self-sufficient within a decade. In view of the fact that those responsible for these undertakings had had little background or experience in colonial development, the reward they achieved stands equal to that of most contemporary and far older Western colonial regimes.

Given the methods by which Japan gradually obliterated the independence of Korea and the ruthless suppression by the Japanese administration, once established, of any resistance to its rule, it is admittedly more difficult to make a case for Japanese enlightenment on the peninsula. Yet a recent study by David Brudnoy, generally critical of Japan's experiment in Korea, noted that:

> During its forty year rule in Korea, Japan took a backward nation with one of the world's least efficient, most corrupt governments, and brought important elements of modernization to her. In place of the capricious rule of the House of Yi and the large parasite yangban class, Japan established a government efficient in accomplishing certain material aims, one in the long run probably less arbitrary than that which existed before. Japan created a rationalized tax structure, telegraph and telephone systems, undertook steps to increase agricultural yield, and gave a start to technology.

The reader has a right to ask, of course, whether this cornucopia of civilized blessings did not in fact benefit Japanese colonial masters in far greater measure than it did Taiwanese and Koreans, neither of whom had welcomed Japan's rule. The response to this query must be twofold. First, far greater benefit did indeed accrue to the Japanese ruling elite than to Japan's colonial regimes. Second, even in Korea, Japanese improvements in the economic, administrative, and educational infrastructure provided indirect benefits to Koreans in terms of higher wages, better health, quicker and easier travel, and so on. The crux of the problem is whether, for Japan's colonial peoples, the ratio of humiliation and misery in relation to the receipt of these modest benefits was greater or lesser than that for the subject peoples of other colonial empires. For it is against other colonial situations, not against some theoretical utopia, that Japan's colonial efforts should be judged. While a precise answer to this question must await intensive and wide-ranging study, it can be argued, I believe, that Japanese rule in Korea was every bit as generous in the material benefits it provided to its subjects as, for example, were the French in Indochina or the Belgians in the Congo.

In pondering the degree to which Japanese colonial rule may have made a positive contribution to the development of their subject peoples, a unique aspect of the Japanese imperium deserves mention. With the exception of its mandate in Micronesia, Japan's colonial empire was entirely East Asian in extent and character and thus its most populous entities—Korea, Taiwan, Manchuria, and the Kwantung Leased Territory—were, along with Japan, the legatees of the great traditions of Chinese civilization, of which the most important element was the written language. This cultural commonality was two-directional in its effect on the empire.

On the one hand, it meant that in Japan's Asian territories a common knowledge of *kanbun* (Chinese-style writing), a relatively high literacy rate (in relation to other non-Western areas of the globe), and a general interest in East Asian history and traditions helped to facilitate and diffuse Japanese education, technology, and rhetoric through most levels of colonial society. It enabled, for example, Japanese colonial administrators in Taiwan and Korea to transmit improved agricultural technology to Korean and Taiwanese farmers—landowners and tenants alike—through various publications and from experimental farms established in various centers in the colonies.

On the other hand, it also meant that Japanese colonial administrations had an uncommon interest in the history and cultural traditions of the territories in their charge. Indeed, with the possible exception of the work of the French École d'Extreme d'Orient in Indochina no other colonial agencies over the years actively manifested as much interest in the cultural heritage of their colonies in terms of research, publication, and historic preservation. The countless heavy volumes in ponderous and formal Japanese writing which crowd the shelves of the larger Japanese collections in American libraries on East Asia give ample testimony to the mountainous results of these efforts—ranging from multivolume histories, numerous biographical dictionaries, and gazetteers to huge compendia of the fauna and flora of places as remote as the Marshall Islands. Nor were the Japanese content merely to publish. A doctoral dissertation by Edwin Gragert shows that various Korean cultural sites were saved from total decay by the efforts of the government-general.

I have spoken so far only of Japanese colonial rulers. But this perspective leads to the image of a homogeneous Japanese colonial elite, a stereotype which is neither accurate nor enlightening. What is often overlooked is that a sizable proportion of Japanese in nearly all Japan's colonies were not high officials, compradors, or great landowners but shopkeepers, farmers, fishermen of very modest means. Indeed, southern Korea at the beginning of this century saw the influx of great numbers of poor farmers, laborers, peddlers, and tinkers from Kyushu who emigrated to find a new start but whose economic and social status was below that of the indigenous population into whose midst they intruded. Two-thirds of all Japanese engaged in agriculture at the time of Japan's annexation of the colony worked as laborers and tenants on land owned by Japanese *and* Korean landlords; similar patterns held true for Japanese in other occupations.

Finally, in assaying whatever positive contributions Japanese colonialism may have made, one might consider the historical events in Japan and the rest of Asia which created and eventually warped it. During the period of its formation, 1895 to 1914, the Japanese colonial empire was, in impetus, rhetoric, and character, not widely dissimilar to a number of Western empires. It was run in this period as a highly regimented, authoritarian system, largely for the economic and strategic benefit of the metropolitan homeland, a system in which not even lip service was paid to the concept of self-government for its subject peoples—a description which could fit a number of contemporary Western colonial regimes.

Yet during the 1920s a more liberal, less regimented colonial policy, moved by the high tide of post–First World War liberalism around the globe, washed over much of the empire. This new wave was most perceptible in Taiwan, noticeable in Japan's formal acceptance of the responsibilities of a League of Nations mandate power in Micronesia, and even feebly projected in Korea, the most regimented of Japan's colonies. The meager administrative, economic, and social reforms that comprised this more liberal policy could hardly have earned the gratitude of Korean and Taiwanese patriots, but their official approval by Japanese colonial authorities was at least a step in the right direction. Had events not impelled Japan in the 1930s upon the tragically mistaken course of expansion beyond her old formal empire, this brief period of liberalization might have continued and might even have been strengthened by international example.

On the other hand, many Koreans who were either part of the late Yi dynasty, or who had recently attained wealth and position, can be clearly identified as part of the colonial elite. Recent studies, moreover, tend to confirm that there was a Korean white-collar class with access to responsible bureaucratic and business positions during the colonial period and that the harm done to Koreans by Japanese discrimination in assigning position, while a reality, appears to have been greatly exaggerated. All this is not to say that the Japanese in Korea did not occupy a distinctly privileged position under Japanese rule, but merely that the roles of exploiter were filled by both nationalities, not just by a Japanese colonial elite.

These realities of the Korean situation highlight a problem in our understanding of Japanese colonialists when we ask whether they were enlightened or barbaric. The Japanese in their colonies were not a faceless elite of hideous oppressors; nor were they all marble men of noble vision and public virtue. They were administrators and speculators, wealthy landlords and tenant farmers, ruffians and policemen, adventurers and doctors—who collectively embodied Japanese visions and prejudices, plans and passions, knowledge and ignorance, altruism and greed. When contemporary scholarship begins to populate the Japanese colonial landscape with living creatures, Japanese colonialism will at last take on a humanity, if not a humaneness, which it does not yet possess.

By the mid-1930s, however, the imperatives of quasi-wartime and then wartime conditions stifled whatever prospects there may have been for Japan's voluntary loosening of its grip on its colonial territories. Most of these latter were now run by military commanders whose task was to dragoon from the colonial peoples economic, political, and ideological support for the home country which increasingly perceived itself as embattled. Then, as Japanese armies poured through Manchuria, China, and eventually Southeast Asia, the perception abroad of Japan as a responsible colonial power gave way to the image of an empire of the lash whose only raison d'être had been to serve as stepping stones for the reckless conquest of all Asia.

It is this last wartime stage of Japanese colonialism, inextricably linked in our minds to the horrors of China and the Pacific War, that distorts our view of the half-century of Japanese colonial development. As the passions of those conflicts recede from the historical foreground, a new interest is becoming apparent among Western scholars—not only in Japan's colonial epoch but also in the origins and workings of our Western colonial acquisitions. Soon it may become possible to ask not whether Japan's colonial experiment was either enlightened or barbaric but how it affected the modernization of Japan and how it relates to the overall pattern of colonialism in modern world history.

Colonizer and Colonized in Taiwan

E. Patricia Tsurumi

Japan's career as a colonial power began when China ceded the island of Taiwan to Japan after the Sino-Japanese War of 1894–1895. Before the ink was dry on the Treaty of Shimonoseki, which authorized the cession, debate on principles and structures for ruling Taiwan was raging in Japanese government circles. Japanese politicians disagreed on the suitability of ruling the new possession directly or indirectly, the wisdom of applying Japanese laws to it, the advisability of assimilating the island's inhabitants. Yet everyone in the Japanese government agreed that, as the first non-Western nation to enter the hitherto exclusive ranks of the nineteenth-century imperialists' club, their country was in a particularly sensitive position. Japanese leaders were certain their conduct in their first colony would be closely watched and compared to European colonial rule in other parts of the globe. This sense of embarking upon a colonial career from the inside of a fishbowl was indeed realistic in 1895. As a Canadian missionary in Taiwan recalled, "When Formosa was ceded to Japan, the eyes of the world were on the Japanese government. The Western nations wondered how she would succeed in her new experiment of subjugating and colonizing alien races."

As soon as the Treaty of Shimonoseki was ratified in April 1895, the Japanese government commissioned studies of major European colonial policies and sought advice from Western legal experts in the service of Japan. This interest in other nations' colonies continued throughout the fifty years of Japanese rule in Taiwan. Successive governors-general of the colony ordered inquiries into conditions in domains under Western flags and arranged for works like Charles Prestwood Lucas' many-volumed *Historical Geography of the British Colonies* to be translated into Japanese. Not infrequently, specialists in the government-general of Taiwan visited other territories to study how other rulers had handled specific colonial problems. In 1907, for example, Mochiji Rokusaburō, chief of the colonial education bureau, made an extensive tour of educational facilities in the American Philippines, Dutch Java, and British India.

As often as not, the comparative colonial research of the administrators of Taiwan made these men aware of aspects of Western colonialism which they thought Taiwan could do without. Mochiji's findings in 1907, stressing as they did the undesirable attributes of educational planning in the colonies he visited, are a case in point. Ever conscious of the Western yardsticks of colonial success, the Japanese in Taiwan by no means slavishly copied Western models of colonial government. Between 1898 and 1906 when the fourth governor-general, Kodama Gentarō, and his key administrator, Gotō Shimpei, were energetically laying the foundations for Japanese rule on the island, both insisted that Japan must challenge and outstrip, not mindlessly imitate, the Western nations in Western-style achievement.

By the 1920s Taiwan was a highly successful colony by contemporary Western standards. European visitors to Taiwan were often lavish in their praise; and even those with little sympathy for the Japanese were usually grudgingly impressed. What the Americans Alice and Harold Foght wrote in 1928 after a stay in Taiwan was fairly typical:

> The changes that have come about in the island within the thirty-three years of Japanese possession speak well for Japan's greatness as a colonizing people. What Japan has done for Formosa is the exact counterpart of what the United States has done in the Philippine Islands, in Cuba, and in Porto Rico. Both nations have instituted much needed legal reforms, have built highways and railways, have reorganized all their institutions of life in harmony with scientific principles.

Even Westerners who sympathized with the people over whom the Japanese in Taiwan ruled acknowledged "remarkable material advancement" including "law and order, economic prosperity, elevated standards of living, widespread education." And years before the 1920s the Japanese themselves were proudly writing about their colonial showpiece.

To all Japanese but leftists and a few liberal critics of imperialism, success always meant success for the ruling country. Generally Western observers thought in similar terms. During the 1920s an occasional

European visitor to Taiwan might voice concern for the welfare of the island's native population—for the condition of the Taiwanese, those inhabitants of Chinese descent who made up about 96 percent of the colonized, or for the state of the aborigines of Polynesian descent who comprised the rest of the indigenous populace, or for both. Yet, on the whole, for Westerner as well as for Japanese, success meant profit, power, and prestige for Japan.

Economic prosperity was overwhelmingly for the benefit of the home islands and for the Japanese in the colony; elevated standards of living were enjoyed mainly by the island's Japanese residents. Law and order in Taiwan demonstrated the imperialist's effective manipulation of its first subject people and—although the military was less conspicuous than in Korea—its capacity to wage modern warfare against unarmed populations. Even the widespread education was first and foremost for the advantage of the Japanese colonists. As H. A. Wyndham, a British author of a comparative study of colonial education in Asian territories, noted in 1933 about schooling in Taiwan, the privileged position of the Japanese was much like that enjoyed by the nationals of other colonial powers in their overseas holdings:

> Here [in Taiwan's secondary schools] again the disproportionate number of Japanese pupils is natural. No English child is uneducated in Ceylon, nor Dutch child in Java, nor French child in Indochina. All colonial powers made the education of the children of their colonial nationals a first consideration and afterwards do all that the colony's finances will permit for the education of natives. To allow the descendants of the former to degenerate through lack of education would be a retrograde step and a negation of the trusteeship which is the justification of empire building.

Thus rings the rhetoric of the most liberal of imperialist mentalities before the end of the Second World War. (This comparative study was highly critical of Japanese rule in Taiwan because it concluded that no clear provision was being made for future participation by native islanders in significant economic and political decision-making.) Hemmed in behind electric fences in rapidly thinning forests or isolated on barren mountaintops, the aborigines witnessed Japanese bombing of their poverty-stricken villages. Subject to constant surveillance and harassment by increasingly efficient policemen, in dwindling numbers they eked out a precarious existence in such a

wretched state that no one yet has seriously suggested that they bene-
fited in any way from Japanese government. Even so it could be argued that the Taiwanese gained from the spillover effects of colonial
government. Certainly the largest profits of economic exploitation in
Taiwan went to the home islands. Certainly wage and salary differen-
tials—Japanese usually were paid at least twice as much as Taiwanese
for performing the same jobs and in some cases many times more—
reserved major economic rewards for Japanese residents. Yet, even at
the bottom of the heap, did not Taiwanese also benefit as the pile
grew higher?

Indeed *some* Taiwanese did. Over the years a new native elite of
Japanese-trained Taiwanese emerged to fill important middle-level
slots in the expanding economy. They did so by seizing educational
and employment experience offered by conquerors eager to make basic economic and social changes and to acquire local instruments of
control over their new subjects. The most fortunate of those who responded to such opportunites in the early days became physicians.
Others became clerks or trained as teachers for the Japanese-run
schools. Later others became engineers and technicians. By 1920 another layer was forming beneath the top rank of this elite as a broad
range of paraprofessionals were learning new trades to go with the agricultural experimental stations, hospitals, railroads, telegraph lines,
and mines which had become part of island life. For such Taiwanese,
then, economic life did improve. But grow as it did, this elite never
included more than a small fraction of Taiwan's subject population—
perhaps at its largest it amounted to between 5 and 8 percent of that
population.

Most members of the Taiwanese population were from poor peasant families. Streamlined agricultural production, transport, and
marketing brought about by the investment of Japanese capital and
the expertise of collaborating Taiwanese entrepreneurs meant little
enrichment for their lives. In fact, for such people "development" often meant increased struggle against poverty. From about 1923 the
development stimulated by large agricultural corporations—usually
Japanese-owned or Japanese-managed—and the government-general
began to threaten the livelihood of numerous poor farmers. In 1924
and 1925 proposed sales of bamboo forests to the Mitsubishi Corpora-
tion, which intended to use the trees for pulp, brought forth desperate protests from peasants who had always used the bamboo to supplement their meager farm incomes.

About the same time, the governor-general sold "public lands" at giveaway prices to retiring Japanese administrators although these lands had been reclaimed by Taiwanese farmers who lived on them, worked them, and considered them their own. Corporations which collected and processed such important crops as sugar forced poor farmers to deliver cane to company mills on monopoly conditions and at monopoly prices. They also made the sharecropping peasants bear the heaviest burdens of weather risks and dictated such important details as how the cane was to be weighed and what types of fertilizer were to be used. The beginning of a mining industry was part of the colony's development, but for the thousands of Taiwanese who labored in the mines—many of them women—this source of "material prosperity" meant incredible suffering.

Most of the "remarkable material advancement" occurred in the cities and larger towns where the Japanese and Japanese-trained Taiwanese professionals lived. Little of the comfort and convenience-bearing infrastructure of economic development reached the country-side residences of the vast majority of the Taiwanese populace.

A central pillar of control and development from the earliest years, the colonial education system which by 1945 took in large numbers of islanders, was often singled out as an indicator of progress. After a cautious beginning, the system began turning out impressive numbers of Taiwanese elementary, secondary, and eventually tertiary school graduates of institutions run by the regime and staffed with Japanese and Japanese-trained native teachers. Although in terms of the total populace the number of islanders who received an education in the home islands was always a small minority, thousands more did so. And by 1944 some 80 percent of the young boys in the colony (and 60 percent of the girls) were enrolled in Japanese schools. Fifty years previously, only a privileged handful of the offspring of gentry or merchant families, almost all of them male, received any schooling.

Yet the *quality* of this widespread Japanese education varied immensely. Although Japanese residents and a small percentage of the Taiwanese had access to fine schools, the vast majority of the school-going population was taught only the rudiments of Japanese language and arithmetic as well as some lessons regarding basic hygiene and sanitation and perhaps agriculture or commerce. In addition, they were fed large doses of a morality aimed at fashioning loyal, obedient and industrious subjects who would know their proper places within the hierarchical empire of Japan.

Not surprisingly, the crudest schools of all were the "education centers" provided and staffed by the police for aborigine children. Late in getting started, these centers could be found in most aborigine villages by 1940. Periodically village children were rounded up and herded into them to be taught—sometimes forcibly—a little Japanese. Aborigines who experienced such "education" in the 1930s and 1940s remember their policemen-teachers as terrifying disciplinarians who "didn't even teach one to read or write."

As in the ruling country, educational opportunity largely determined employment opportunity and therefore well-educated Taiwanese reaped economic and social rewards—at least up to a certain point. Even Taiwanese with the most prestigious of Japanese educations—graduates of Tokyo Imperial University, for example—were barred from top economic and social ranks in the colony and were unhappy about their lack of political power. Yet, in contrast to most of their fellow Taiwanese, they did indeed enjoy the "material advancement" which Japan had brought to their island.

The native elite paid an enormous price for this enjoyment, however. It was not only that, as the elite's articulate leaders were fond of pointing out, Taiwanese taxes and skills supported the luxury of Japanese residents. It was not only that the interests of the ruling country were always put before those of Taiwan. In life-style and attitude Taiwanese physicians, lawyers, clerks, journalists, technicians, businessmen, and urban schoolteachers appeared much closer to their Japanese rulers than to the poor Taiwanese in country villages. Hundreds entered the ranks of Japanese professional and intellectual life, in Tokyo as well as in Taihoku, the colonial capital, becoming almost indistinguishable from their mentors. But no matter how close they came to the original, they remained no more than clever forgeries. They became good imitation Japanese, but never quite the real thing. While in Japanese eyes even assimilated Taiwanese remained more or less natives, assimilated Taiwanese, like native elites in other colonial settings, lost their footing in the traditional community without gaining full-fledged acceptance in the new world they entered. Albert Memmi's poignant sketch of the dilemma of the colonized comes from his Tunisian experience under French rule, but what he depicts was also the lot of "assimilated" subjects in Japanese-held Taiwan:

> But if the colonizer does not always openly discourage these candidates to develop that resemblance, he never permits them to attain it either. Thus they live in painful and constant ambiguity. Rejected by the colonizer, they share in part the physical conditions of the colonized and have a

communion of interest with him; on the other hand, they reject the values of the colonized as belonging to a decayed world from which they eventually hope to escape.

Even the relatively few Taiwanese beneficiaries of Japanese colonialism fell victim to what Syed Hussein Alatas has called "the captive mind." They learned so well from their captors that they sometimes forgot who they were, although the former never did.

In its most critical mood, during the heyday of the Taiwanese anticolonial movement against Japanese rule which peaked in the late 1920s, the Japanese-trained elite still displayed attributes of its captive mind. Although a segment of this anticolonial movement did fight against Japan's whole capitalist development of a forcibly held Taiwan, the mainstream of the Taiwanese anticolonial movement pursued reformist attacks on Japanese rule which never stepped outside the boundaries set by the legal framework of Japanese imperialism.

The energies of the leaders of the mainstream went predominantly into such activity as the tireless campaigns which, from 1921 to 1934, resulted in the presentation to the Japanese Diet of fifteen petitions requesting home rule for Taiwan. Reformist leaders agitated against de facto as well as de jure restrictions upon Taiwanese participation in political, economic, and social life. They sought Taiwanese access to high positions in the colonial administration, relaxation of Japanese monopoly of the mass media, a halt to Japanese domination of post–elementary school facilities, institution of compulsory Japanese schooling for all island children, and an end to the onerous system of mutual responsibility and forced labor applied only to Taiwanese inhabitants of the colony.

Since the government-general always moved swiftly against open resistance to Japanese rule, Taiwanese leaders of the home rule movement might have chosen other channels of protest had the colonial government been less repressive. The ultimate end of the home rule movement may well have been Taiwan's independence from Japan. Yet the methods pursued on behalf of this goal are revealing. The movement's leaders publicized their cause exhaustively through Japanese media and attempted as well to win Taiwanese support in the colony. In totally Japanese fashion, they cemented personal relationships with politicians and opinion-makers in Japan. Most of all they sought out those with power and influence. Yet they were willing to approach any individual or group of almost any respectable political color—from the prime minister down to a labor union alliance. Year after year, humbly submitting their petitions to the Japanese Diet, they appeared astonishingly willing to wait patiently until Japanese institutions and leaders implemented change.

Even more symptomatic of their captive minds is the nature of the Taiwan they intended to govern once they had succeeded in gaining independence. Police repression certainly helped keep the anticolonial movement in legal channels, but a large proportion of the discontented among the Japanese-trained elite appears to have been genuinely more interested in acquiring bigger economic, political, and social rewards than in disturbing the status quo. And in seeking to do so they paid a heavy price in terms of their cultural identity.

The psychological consequences of colonialism are difficult to delineate, but they are nonetheless of enormous importance. Investigators figuring "balance sheets" for colonial regimes in different parts of the globe might do well to pay more attention to the effect of colonialism on the minds of subject peoples. Intellectual and emotional factors play crucial roles in "development" and "material progress": attitudes among the masses are vitally important and so is the mentality of their leaders. Railway mileage, quarantine stations, harbors, electric power plants, and the like are only part of the picture. Standards of living, distribution of income, and economic exploitation add to the portrait but do not complete it. As Taiwan's fifty years as a Japanese possession illustrate, colonialism is not only political, economic, and military domination. It is a state of mind too.

Japanese Colonialism in Korea

Han-Kyo Kim

Japan ruled Korea for forty years, first as a protectorate (1905–1910) and later as an annexed territory (1910–1945). It was during these years that Japan rose as the predominant regional power in East Asia and Korea provided a crucial base for Japan's further advances into the Asian continent. Viewed from the Korean perspective, this alien rule was degrading and oppressive but it left, for better or worse, lasting legacies for the future independent Korea.

In 1905, the Japanese victory over Russia finally cleared the field for unchallenged Japanese control of Korea. Backed by a powerful Japanese army of occupation—which was not to leave Korea until 1945—Itō Hirobumi extracted an agreement from a weak Korean government that entrusted Japan with the power to conduct Korea's external relations. To fulfill her role as protector of Korea, Japan established an administrative structure headed by a resident-general *(tōkan)*. Itō became the first *tōkan* and his successors relentlessly consolidated Japan's control in Korean domestic as well as foreign affairs. When disbanded Korean soldiers and other dissidents resisted Japanese advances, a reinforced Japanese army, especially its gendarmerie, ruthlessly crushed these "Righteous Army" organizations. By 1910 Korea's independence had become an empty pretense, and a treaty of annexation formally ended five centuries of Yi dynasty rule in Korea.

So ended the initial phase of Japanese rule, a period in which the establishment of military hegemony was a primary concern. The subsequent thirty-five years may be divided into three periods: 1910–1919, a period of institution-building and consolidation; 1919–1936, a period of adjustment and economic development; and 1936–1945, a period of increasing totalitarian control and Japanization.

The years 1910–1919 witnessed creation of a full-fledged colonial administration in Korea (now renamed Chōsen) headed by a governor-general *(sōtoku)* who was to be selected from among army generals or navy admirals. The governor-general was to be a quasi-sovereign in the colony enjoying legislative and judicial as well as executive powers; he was to report directly to the Japanese emperor through the prime minister, thereby bypassing ministerial supervision by the cabinet in Tokyo. To the colonial subjects all modes of political expression were denied.

An important measure undertaken by the first governor-general, Terauchi Masatake (minister of war at the time of appointment), was an extensive land survey which purported to establish a modern system of landownership and registry but which had the effect of taking the land away from many Korean farmers, especially those in the lower classes. Terauchi, a man not known for political skills or subtlety, helped project the image of the colonial regime as something to be feared. All public officials including elementary school teachers wore uniforms and sabers. This and other measures designed to awe the Koreans into submission justified the general description of this period as an era of military rule *(budan seiji)*.

The famous March First Movement of 1919 was an outburst of popular discontent against harsh colonial rule. Impressed by the apparent triumph of Western democratic ideals in the postwar world, particularly by the Wilsonian endorsement of the right to national self-determination, massive waves of peaceful demonstrations demanding immediate independence swept through Korea on 1 March and during the following months. The colonial administration struck back and bloody encounters and mass arrests ensued. The magnitude of the Korean protest and the brutality of the Japanese countermeasures evoked considerable criticism among the nations of the West—particularly in the United States, which furnished the greatest number of foreign missionaries working in Korea.

In the aftermath of the March First Movement, Japanese leaders announced modification of their policies in Korea, thereby beginning a new phase of colonial rule (1919–1936). Admiral Saitō Minoru became the new governor-general, the only nonarmy man ever to hold the position, and he popularized the slogan "Cultural Policy" *(Bunka Seiji)* to highlight his intention to grant limited concessions to Korean demands for self-expression. Civil officials including schoolteachers took off their uniforms and sabers. Publication of a few Korean-language newspapers and magazines was permitted. Steps were also taken to institute limited political roles for elected local assemblies that included a minority of Koreans.

More substantive than these concessions were a series of economic measures designed to promote production. In particular, a campaign to boost rice production was launched with considerable fanfare by Saitō and his immediate successor, General Ugaki Kazushige. At the same time, as Japan began to gear up for large-scale military activities after the Manchurian Incident of 1931, much emphasis came to be focused on industrial development, especially heavy and chemical industries in northern Korea.

Ugaki's successor in 1936 was General Minami Jirō, whose administration marks the beginning of the last period under study (1936–1945). Japan's involvement in protracted warfare in China and later against the Allied Powers led naturally to imposition of wartime controls and totalitarian mobilization of all resources. Recruitment of Korean youth into the Japanese armed forces began in 1938 on a limited volunteer basis, but it was changed to a mandatory conscription system in 1943. A far greater number of Korean labor conscripts, numbering in the millions, were forced to work in war-related construction sites, factories, and mines in Korea and elsewhere across the entire map of the Greater East Asia Coprosperity Sphere.

The colonial officials in Chōsen sought to maximize the cooperation of the Koreans not by promising greater concessions to Koreans but by intensifying the Japanization campaign. Assimilation had always been one of Japan's announced goals in Korea. The Japanization campaign that Minami launched, however, was far more fanatical, hasty, and ill-advised than mere assimilation. Use of the Korean language was discouraged and, wherever possible, prohibited. Much pressure was exerted to urge Koreans to adopt Japanese names—both family and personal names. "Patriotic Neighborhood" groups were organized. Worship of the Japanese emperor as a demigod and frequent pilgrimages to Shinto shrines were made mandatory and enforced more rigorously in Korea than in Japan itself. Few Koreans willingly complied but all had to submit.

In summary, we can say that Japan's objectives progressed from the establishment of military hegemony to the creation of efficient machinery for political and administrative control, to economic development and mobilization, and lastly to Japanization. How well did the Japanese succeed?

Japan's military domination over Korea was not difficult to establish. Except for the early years (prior to 1912), armed resistance against the Japanese garrison forces in Korea was simply impractical, if not altogether impossible. Similarly, the Japanese were successful in

creating efficient political and administrative machinery with only token participation by Koreans except at the lowest levels. Supported
by a strong military force and an effective police, the government-
general was an authoritarian regime that exercised its powers virtually
without formal restraint. Unlike Taiwan, but much like Manchuria,
the management of the Korean colony was largely the responsibility
of the Japanese army. Even before 1931, therefore, Korea was essentially a military outpost and a state within a state.

In terms of economic modernization and development, Japanese
achievements in Korea were readily observable and substantial. Modern business organizations and practices, official protection of private
property rights, and other legal and institutional preconditions for a
modern economy were introduced, as well as the more obvious inflow
of capital, machinery, and technical knowhow. Economic growth received much attention from successive governors-general while many
Japanese officials at lower levels were task-oriented technocrats primarily concerned with efficient management and greater productivity. Indeed, official statistics tell a story of impressive gains: the land
area under cultivation increased by 83 percent in 1910–1933, and
farm productivity per unit of land rose by 27 percent in 1910–1934. A
sevenfold increase in mine output in 1910–1933, a sixfold increase in
railroad mileage in 1910–1943, and, most impressive of all, a sixteen-
fold jump in industrial production in 1911–1936 are substantial by
any standard, even allowing for the low production figures in the base
period.

It should be noted, however, that it was not Korea as such, but
rather the Japanese colony of Chōsen, that was being developed to fill
Japanese needs. The Korean economy was made a complementary
part of the larger economic system of Japan; the benefit for Koreans,
either short-term or long-term, was at best incidental. Increased production of rice, for example, was encouraged when Japan proper
needed Korean rice, but the Grow More Rice campaign was discon-
tinued in 1934 when the price of rice fell too low in Japan. To take
another set of figures, the proportion of tenant farmers among all
farm households in Korea rose from 35 to 52 percent in 1914–1933
while those of owner-cultivators and part-owner/part-tenants declined from 22 and 41 percent to 18 and 24 percent respectively in the
same period.

Japanization of Koreans, the fourth and the last objective of Japanese rule, was least successful. From the very outset of her dominion
over Korea, Japan stressed the racial and cultural affinity between the

two nations and the impartial benevolence of their emperor toward all his subjects *(isshi dōjin)*. Education in Korea was for the purpose of inculcating loyalty to the emperor—and to his agents. Japanese official propaganda endeavored to set the case of Chōsen apart from other cases of colonialism, particularly as practiced by the Western nations. The final act of seizure of Korea in 1910 was carefully designated as *heigō* ("annexation") rather than *gappei* ("merger") or *gappō* ("merger of nations") in order to emphasize the uniqueness of this act and also to avoid the overtone of outright conquest. The term *shokuminchi* ("colony") was extremely rare in Japanese references to Chōsen, which was also referred to as *gaichi* ("the outer land" in contrast to the "inner land" or Japan proper) or simply as *hantō* ("the peninsula").

Despite these efforts to represent their colonial rule in Korea (which came to be publicized as *naisen ittai:* "the union of the inner land and Chōsen into one body"), the reality of Japanese behavior, public or private, fell far short of the goal of assimilation. Koreans were separate and unequal. Discrimination by law, by administrative actions, or in personal relations was rampant, and the Koreans suffered from political disability, economic handicaps, and, above all, personal abuse and indignity that were meted out by Japanese officials and private individuals alike. When Japanization or *kōkoku shinminka* ("transformation into a loyal subject of the emperor") was shrilly advocated in the final phase of the Chōsen period, it did not and could not go beyond imposition of ritualistic outward trappings of obeisance. Incongruence of stated goals and actual deeds was nowhere more flagrant than in this juxtaposition of assimilation and discrimination.

What, then, does this mixed record of Japanese achievement mean to the Korean nation after liberation in 1945? Japanese rule undermined the *ancien régime* in Korea. The demise of the old order was poignantly manifest in the growing impotency and eventual atrophy of the traditional ruling class, the *yangban*. The loss of political power eroded the economic and social positions of the *yangban* class and, by 1945, its preeminence as a class in Korean society was preserved only in memory.

Colonial rule helped arouse Korean nationalism, albeit inadvertently. Koreans had long had a sense of national identity even before the advent of modern changes, perhaps because of the frequent incursions into their territory by northern tribes and occasional invasions by Chinese or Japanese. Japanese colonial rule in the twentieth century was more systematic and effective then any previous experience; by the same token, however, it helped bring forth a more virulent and more widely shared sense of nationality among Koreans. Racial discrimination fed the fire of nationalism among the discriminated. Throughout the colonial period Koreans doggedly carried on, in Korea and abroad, political agitation and activities of armed resistance against Japanese rule. Unlike the case in Taiwan, Korean nationalists never entertained the thought of demanding greater local autonomy under Japanese rule; nothing short of complete independence was their goal. After Japan's withdrawal, anti-Japanese nationalism was to become an important principle of political legitimacy.

The Japanese introduced many modern changes in Korea's social, economic, and cultural life. The complex changes that took place in Korea as opportunities for modern education expanded, industrialization and urbanization progressed, and more Koreans came to be exposed to the modern way of life can best be summarized as modernization. Intentionally or not, the Japanese did nothing to prepare the Koreans for self-rule. The basic premise of the Japanese administration was to deny Korea's separate nationhood. By denying Koreans significant political participation, by monopolizing the decision-making roles in major public organizations for Japanese only, Japan left Korea in 1945 leaderless and without experienced personnel to manage a modern society.

More than three decades after Japan's departure from Korea, the topic of Japanese colonialism still arouses keen interest among Koreans. A large number of publications, mostly in the Korean language, have appeared in Korea, both south and north. They vary a great deal in scholarly quality but tend to have one common feature: strident denunciation of Japanese colonialism. Certainly a tendency to dwell on heroic tales of anti-Japanese activists or on the repressive aspects of colonial rule marked these publications in the early years after the liberation. This pattern of denunciation has yielded in recent years to a more sober analysis of the Japanese performance, however, especially in such areas as economic change. A great deal of painstaking work is still needed to examine relevant documentary data that are available but scattered and largely unexamined.

In contrast, most Japanese today are uninformed and uninterested regarding this topic. A prime minister is said to have publicly confessed his ignorance of what transpired in Korea under Japanese rule. A study of high school history textbooks shows virtual silence on the former colony of Chōsen. If conscious or subconscious avoidance of an embarrassing topic is the prevalent attitude of most Japanese, there is, nevertheless, an extremely small number of scholars and publicists who write on the subject. Most of these authors fall into two polarized categories: those who defend the colonial rule and those who denounce it. The former group includes ex-colonial officials and right-wing political leaders who emphasize Japan's benevolent, if not altruistic, intentions even when they concede the harmful impact of specific policies upon the Koreans. The second group includes ideologues who apply Marxist-Leninist concepts to the Korean case in largely inflexible doctrinaire fashion. It appears, therefore, that further systematic study of Japanese rule in Korea is highly desirable. It would be valuable not only for those interested primarily in Korea's modern history but also for those engaged in the study of colonialism in Asia and elsewhere.

Pan-Asianism in
Action and Reaction

David G. Egler

Japanese have always had a certain fascination with Manchuria. Since archaeological theories indicate that many of their forebears migrated to the Japanese archipelago from there, one might almost imagine that their interest represents a kind of mass subconscious seeking for original roots. More likely there was a passion for economic security which continental resources promised. Like the lure of the China market in United States history which prompted Americans to extend themselves to the Far East, the possibility of unexploited fuels, food, or metals would have exerted quite a pull on a people bereft of those resources. Finally, the fascination with Manchuria was the longing of a physically and psychologically cramped people for a frontier wherein their energies and talents could have scope to move and shake. In Japan everything was stratified and rigidified—jobs, schooling, etiquette—and forced into a mold. On the continent, in Manchuria, there was no mold.

Although clearly recognized by most foreign powers as under Chinese sovereignty, Manchuria through the last decade of the nineteenth and first third of the twentieth century was the very nexus of international rivalry. This sense of incomplete sovereignty was enhanced by the existence in Manchuria of substantial non-Chinese ethnic minorities. Although ethnic Chinese comprised 75 to 80 percent of the population, there were also Manchus and Mongols, Koreans (who had emigrated in substantial numbers across the Yalu border in search of better agricultural opportunities in Manchuria), smaller numbers of Moslem Tartars, and a tight-knit community of White Russian émigrés. Finally, there were the Japanese residents of Manchuria, numbering about 200,000 by the 1920s, whose impact far outstripped their numbers.

The core of the Japanese presence was the South Manchurian Railway Company. The original trunk line stretched from the icefree ports on the Liaotung Peninsula in the south to the Chinese Eastern Line controlled by the Russians in the north. Since acquisition of the lease in 1906, various additional leases had been acquired and branch lines built into a major network. This semigovernmental firm was also involved in mining, manufacturing, and a host of social services—schools, hospitals, commissaries, libraries—and an estimable research facility. Taken together, it was a multifaceted organization going far beyond the term "conglomerate"; perhaps its only modern counterpart would be the Panama Canal Company. All told, it was probably the largest capital enterprise in the world at the time.

Within the railway and Kwantung leased zones there grew up alongside the South Manchurian Railway Company installations a sizable private commercial and service establishment. All of this, including the company itself, encouraged a large number of Japanese to immigrate over the years. These so-called Manchurian Japanese possessed a natural pride in the mother country but had a strong sense of local identification. The children of the first generation of immigrants had, by the 1920s, grown up, been educated, and become adults in the colonial milieu. The Manchurian Japanese enjoyed a higher standard of living then their counterparts in Japan. Moreover, there seemed to be a greater opportunity to apply talent and energy to creating change.

These Manchurian Japanese did not, for the most part, regard themselves as birds of passage. Given a reasonable degree of acquiescence on the part of the rest of the Manchurian population, most looked forward to spending their lives there. They were very much a part of the continent, planted in alien soil but determined to grow. It was inevitable that they should, first, come to some general conclusions about the nature of the majority Chinese society and, second, formulate some theoretical framework for their action as colonialists—that is, something we can call an "ideology" for lack of a better term.

Tachibana Boku, the Manchurian Japanese scholar, social critic, and journalist, has suggested that Chinese peasant society is composed of a durable set of natural local groupings—either bloodtied or geographical—which are principally self-centered and have little to do with the modern concept of nation or state. After the revolution of 1911, however, the Chinese government, in its effort to create a state through political and economic centralization, not only failed to deal with the problem of local indifference to the state but also managed to undercut traditional props to the old natural units. Warlord regimes which divided China into regional factions following the revolution of 1911 represented the worst of both worlds—neither national integration to oppose foreign domination nor the traditional laissez faire gap between ruler and ruled. According to Tachibana the way for the Japanese to achieve mass unification was by first working *with* the natural units in finding some common consensus, material or otherwise, which would bring them together; subsequently, a greater effort could be made to move to a more general society.

This proposal assumes that it was possible for outsiders like the Japanese to work in a context like Manchuria in which one could appeal to the self-interest of self-sufficient units without having to cope with undue nationalistic opposition. The relationship between the Japanese and the rest, known as "cultural dominion," summarized the philosophical outlook of Gotō Shimpei, first president of the South Manchurian Railway Company, and was reiterated in various forms through the 1920s. It was at once Darwinian and Confucian. Under modern conditions, so the Darwinian line went, Japanese culture had proved itself fittest by virtue of its remarkable achievements since the Meiji Restoration. It would therefore prevail by a natural process of acceptance by those who would benefit by the replacement of the corrupt and inefficient Chinese organs, which had failed to exploit Manchuria riches and bring security to the common people, by a modern bureaucracy, and by modern industry.

Since prosperity and security already reigned among the Japanese in the leased areas, so the Confucian line went, they would serve as models to be emulated by the bulk of Manchuria's inhabitants. It would be all the more plausible for other ethnic groups to acquiesce in cultural dominion because of their local affinities and the weakness of Chinese nationalism. The prospects of security, prosperity, and mitigation of the evils and capriciousness of warlord government would promote self-interest and gain legitimacy for the Japanese presence by default.

The major flaw in the reasoning behind cultural dominion was in the assumption that Chinese nationalist feeling in Manchuria would remain quiescent. The Japanese diplomatic position, for the record, had always asserted that Manchuria and neighboring Inner Mongolia were not necessarily integral parts of China. Perhaps they began to believe that assertion to the extent of assuming that Manchuria could somehow be kept isolated from the political riptides of China Proper. South of the Great Wall, the great civil struggles of the 1920s indicated chaos and division to contemporary foreigners. But the great process of politicizing the articulate elements in China—which began with the May Fourth Movement in 1919, continued with the joining and splitting of Kuomintang and communist movements, and culminated with the Northern Expedition of 1926–1928—generated a nationalist and antiforeign sentiment that could not be kept within artificial boundaries.

Although the Manchurian Japanese had posed warlord government as a *bête noir* to enhance the allure of a "progressive" Japanese presence, it was ironic that the warlord ruler of Manchuria through the 1920s, Chang Tso-lin, was one of the forces pushing for Manchurian separation. His separatist policy was largely to the taste of many in Manchuria apart from the Japanese, since embroilments in the south seemed of little practical advantage. There were powerful groups in Manchuria who developed a separatist position summed up in the slogan *Pao Ching An Min*—"Maintain the Borders, Pacify the People"— implying that only by keeping out of Chinese affairs could the people of Manchuria remain at peace. It was a conservative and rather parochial stance based on self-interest, one which dovetailed nicely with Manchurian Japanese notions of cultural dominion.

Unfortunately from the standpoint of the Manchurian Japanese, Chang Tso-lin did not follow this separatist policy consistently but tended rather to use Manchuria as a secure and affluent base from which to press his ambitions in China. During the early and mid-1920s he became embroiled in a series of major conflicts with other warlord combinations in an effort to win a leadership position. Thus regular taxes in Manchuria went up, unofficial exactions became more capricious and burdensome, and the currency depreciated. It was the familiar warlord syndrome.

To achieve greater Japanese influence in Manchuria, conspirators in the Japanese Kwangtung Army assassinated Chang Tso-lin in June 1928. He was succeeded by his son Chang Hsueh-liang. Hsueh-liang, whether out of revenge or because he wanted to use the Nationalist government to counterbalance Japanese power in Manchuria, began a steady process of rapprochement with the government of Chiang Kai-shek. The Japanese in Manchuria, living among the Chinese and therefore on the front line of any confrontation, perceived the dangers of Chinese nationalism very clearly.

Reflecting this concern, the Manchurian Young Men's League (Manshu Seinen Renmei), which played a key role in articulating Manchurian Japanese opinions and formulating ideology, was formed in November 1928. Their opening proclamation began: "Since Manchuria–Mongolia is a region of residence for both Chinese and Japanese, it is the great task of our state to promote culture, open up natural resources for the use of all, and maintain eternal peace in the Orient." They began with ninety members, including one Korean, and within six months had organized nineteen branches with some three thousand members from most ethnic groups but overwhelmingly Japanese leadership. This core, mostly from the South Manchurian Railway Company, was middle class and in their mid-thirties. Somewhat articulate but, even more, remarkably energetic, they were comparable in character and background to those who formed the core of right-wing movements in Japan of the 1930s. Their discussions, pronouncements, and actions over the period 1929–1931 give us an idea of their perceptions and ideological responses to the challenge posed to their world by Chinese nationalism.

In 1928 there was still optimism in the Young Men's League regarding cultural dominion—if the Japanese could merge with the majority population. Their meetings reflect a great deal of effort at overcoming the natural insularity of Japanese, promoting intercultural goodwill in various forms, and learning the Chinese language. The slogans "Sino-Japanese Amity" *(Nikka Wago)* and "Live Together, Prosper Together" *(Kyōson Kyōei)* sum up their line. In China, the Tsinan Incident, anti-Japanese boycotts, and a call for abrogation of unequal treaties ("rights recovery"), coupled with a dissatisfaction with Japanese government response, led the Manchurian Young Men's League to advocate a homegrown autonomy movement. As long as it achieved some popular support, it would pose few problems with the powers and it might keep the source of nationalist agitation (still seen as China Proper) behind a cordon sanitaire. At that time it was still believed by a majority of the league that anti-Japanese agitation was induced by the Chinese leadership and was not spontaneous among the masses. Hence the natural process of cultural dominion would still work if it could be isolated by nonmilitary means.

Through 1930 and into 1931, however, there was increased desperation and cynicism among the Manchurian Japanese engendered by pressures from the Chang regime *within* Manchuria—individual harassment by officials, widespread anti-Japanese agitation, Chinese-backed competitive railroad-building, and the feared call for rights recovery in Manchuria. Even if the Japanese could have held out behind their military garrisons or punitive expeditions (as at Tsinan), they now faced ultimate stagnation and an end to their utopian dream.

Moreover, the effects of world depression and the ill-timed effect of the Hamaguchi cabinet's return to the gold standard and resultant retrenchment began to be felt in Manchuria. The South Manchurian Railway Company began cutbacks, and the government decided to back the building of a major installation of the Shōwa Steel Works in Korea rather than Manchuria. The Young Men's League now cried for the still-considerable profits of the South Manchurian Railway Company to be reinvested in Manchuria rather than sent home—often in the form of political contributions. They also wanted more industrial activity rather than less.

This retrenchment in the face of world depression by the home government brought forcefully home to them that the great potential of Manchuria might somehow provide the antidote to these and other "outside-connected" ills if only it were not frittered away. The Manchurian Japanese had no Diet representation in Japan, and their interests, they thought, were treated cavalierly. The Seiyūkai, a major political party at home in Japan, often called for a more activist policy in Manchuria, but this call was seen as empty party politics with no commitment behind it. The Manchurian Young Men's League dispatched a series of propaganda-lobbyist teams to Japan to press its point on all possible fronts. From politicians and bureaucrats they got polite but noncommittal responses. Although there was a more enthusiastic reception from right-wing and proletarian political groups, the lobbyists' mission was put down as a failure.

The Manchurian Japanese, vocalized by league spokesmen, now began to see themselves as simply one more minority in Manchuria, orphaned by indifference. If Manchuria were drawn into the Nationalist vortex, the prospects looked extremely dim. There was even some retroemigration back to Japan. The bitter feeling among those left behind was that they could return to Japan only as outsiders and misfits. With a subtle shift in rhetoric they began to abandon cultural dominion as a dead letter. Autonomy began to be viewed as autonomy from *Japan* as well as from China. They were coming to feel they had little to lose—in the face of indifference from home—and something to gain in making common cause with other minorities in Manchuria, who had little to gain from full amalgamation with China. (There was no love lost between Koreans and Chinese in any case, and the Nationalist government's record of treatment of minorities had not been impressive.)

Politically the Manchurian Japanese were aware of strong anti-Nationalist sentiment, particularly among the monarchist Ch'ing loyalists and *Pao Ching An Min* advocates. There were even proposals for giving up Japanese citizenship, proposals which raised objections but gained reluctant support in the Manchurian Young Men's League. The ideological element which emerged was expressed in the slogan "Harmony Among Races" *(Minzoku Kyōwa)*. At the same time, the league began to support separation by military force. There was, moreover, a growing cooperation between the league and certain Kwangtung Army staff conspirators who had, independently, been laying plans for a lightning campaign against Chang Hsueh-liang's Fengtien Army in order to create an independent entity administered largely by the army.

The call for independence from Japan may well have been ideological bluster designed to shake a complacent government in the home islands. The *independent* elements of this "Harmony Among Races" ideology was its ostensible willingness to take a practical step toward making common cause with other Asians.

During the Manchurian Incident of September–October 1931, most of the league's members acted as paramilitary auxiliaries handling most of the transport, communication, translation, and mounting ideological warfare to win popular support for the new state of Manchukuo and undercut opposition to it. They became closely involved with local government guidance as advisors and "Harmony Among Races," rudimentary perhaps as an ideology, provided a ready cloak for collaborators. The Manchurian Young Men's League dissolved itself shortly after the incident and formed the nucleus of the Kyōwatō (Harmony Party) in an effort to create a single mass party to cement local units in the new state, units which Tachibana had seen the foundation of nation-building.

Ever since the Meiji Restoration there had been many Pan-Asian writers and thinkers—both Japanese and Chinese—saying essentially that it would be a good thing if Japanese and continental Asians cooperated for a brighter future (especially against the West). The Japanese, in the context of Manchuria, were the first to translate this notion into action by researching the stark conclusion that Pan-Asianism, in the form of "Harmony Among Races," was an integral working relationship, not just a stance vis-à-vis the outside world. Without it there could be no progress into the advanced realms of industrially based self-sufficiency. Relatively cosmopolitan, it ran directly counter to the forces of nationalism by favoring a kind of counternationalism. This is not to beg the question of whether Manchukuo was or was not a puppet state. The strings were there and they were pulled, though not so often by the Japanese home government as might be supposed. "Harmony Among Races" was not idealism but an ideology used for Japanese ends. Had the conception been maintained on a more ideal basis—that is, equal partnership, the hope of a number of Manchurian Young Men's League veterans—the history of Sino-Japanese relations of the 1930s and 1940s might have been different.

PART IX

The 1930s: Aberration or Logical Outcome?

THE 1931–1945 DECADE and a half has been condemned before a world tribunal as a series of internationally criminal acts inasmuch as Japanese military forces plundered China, provoked border clashes with the Soviet Union, overran Southeast Asia, and plunged into war with the United States and Western Europe. The Japanese also see it as such because it led to widespread sacrifice and suffering within Japan and to the defeat of the country.

What went wrong? Were these actions by Japan an aberration of her development as a peace-loving nation or were they a logical outcome of imperialist trends either emerging from her own history or learned from the West? Were there other alternatives? If so, what were they and when were they viable? Will similar trends arise again? What is the significance of Japan's experience for her own people and for other countries? These are questions often asked.

The answers are varied. They vary with time, of course, because the interpretation of history is always colored by the present. Interpretation also varies from scholar to scholar depending upon one's philosophy of life. Obviously differences may also arise from the scholar's degree of knowledge: no one can know *everything* about even one decade in as large and dynamic a country as Japan.

In this part of the book we have five different answers. Each contributor perceived the question somewhat differently according to the focus of his own expertise. The most straightforward historical account is presented by the only Japanese author, Kisaka Junichirō. He rejects the thesis that this period is an aberration in an otherwise successful march toward modernization and democracy. He likewise rejects the view that Japan's foreign aggression was essentially a war of liberation for the colonial and semicolonial peoples of Asia. Instead he traces the origins of the trend that led Japan into an ever-deepening fifteen years of war to the Meiji leaders' policies identified by the slogans "Rich Country, Strong Military" and "Increase Production, Promote Industry." Although he does indicate various alternative foreign and domestic policies, he notes that the alternatives narrowed as the war spread and internal suppression increased.

While agreeing on Japan's aggression abroad and suppression at home, Robert M. Spaulding considers these phenomena as an aberration in Japan's history, sandwiched between an incipient democracy in the 1920s and a sturdier variety after the Second World War. He sees the war in China not as a conspiracy but as a campaign motivated by good intentions. The Japanese met unexpected resistance in China, however, and reaped the opposite from the intended results.

In my own essay I agree that the 1930s was a "dark valley" or worse. In focusing on the political parties I note that their loss of control over the cabinet followed the takeover of Manchuria and that the dissolution of parties preceded Pearl Harbor. But I warn that one cannot conclude from this that the parties favored democracy and renounced the use of force. There were differences between the established parties and the social democrats, differences that have continued into the postwar period. I see the 1930s as already set on a course that stifled freedom to such a degree that defeat became liberation, allowing an induced revolution to take place; but in terms of world history I consider the 1930s as an aberration of ideals proclaimed during the First World War and as an experience that should have warned the United States not to get involved in Vietnam.

While not arguing that war was inevitable, Richard J. Smethurst implicitly endorses the thesis that it was a logical outcome by showing that well before 1930 the military, together with the Home and Education Ministries, had penetrated the hamlet *(buraku)*, the lowest traditional grouping above the family. Not only were military veterans organized from that level up but also those eligible for service and youths. These massive forces could be, and often were, mobilized for what we would define as political action on behalf of army policies or national positions endorsed by the military. They spread the military's views through the rest of the population. The biggest stumbling block consisted of those who had higher education and had been taught to think for themselves.

Harry Wray extends the search for causes for the 1930s to the Japanese school system by a content analysis of textbooks. In content that espouses a pluralistic democratic, peaceful, and internationally-oriented Japan from 1903 and 1920 textbooks that is at opposite poles from the stridently nationalistic content of textbooks of the 1930s, he finds evidence for the aberration thesis. On the other hand, in the 1930 textbooks he finds a number of ideas that go back to the earliest textbooks promoting Japanese chauvinism and emperor worship, notions which provided precedents for Japanese attitudes condoning expansion in the 1930s. Wray thus argues for both theses but believes that continuity outweighed change in prewar Japan.

—George O. Totten III

The 1930s:
A Logical Outcome
of Meiji Policy

Kisaka Junichirō

How the 1930s should be handled in interpreting modern Japanese history is an intriguing question. For over a decade now this has been a focus of controversy among Japanese scholars. The main points of view may be summarized as follows.

The first position can be represented by Edwin O. Reischauer's evaluation of the modernization of Japan:

> The most important period in world history is the last ninety years of Japanese history. The reason is that it contains the only example of a country that has with great success speeded up the process of modernization, using the Western model. While there are several difficult questions regarding this interpretation, such as the militarism that appeared, Japan's modernization generally speaking has been a great success. It should be considered a "model" for developing countries to follow today.

This interpretation, however, by considering the 1930s as an aberration of a successful process of modernization, praises Japan's modernization too highly and falls into the trap of either belittling or ignoring "several difficult questions," such as Japanese militarism.

The second position can be represented by the work of Hayashi Fusao. In his *Affirmative Evaluation of the Greater Asia War* (in Japanese), Hayashi contends that ever since the opening of Japan the Japanese have been fighting for "the liberation of the peoples of Asia" from the grip of the Western Powers. "The Greater East Asia War," he claims, "seemed in appearance to be a war of aggression, but in essence it was a war of liberation." From this viewpoint open praise is given to Japan's wars of expansion on the Asian continent (since the Meiji period) as wars to free the Asian people from the oppression of the Western powers. Hence Hayashi sees the 1930s as a logical consequence of events in modern Japanese history.

The third position is that of Ueyama Shunpei:

> The course of modern [Japanese] history since the opening of the country almost of necessity proceeds logically, comprehensively speaking, from the abolition of feudalism to the industrial revolution to aggression against more backward countries to a conflict with the advanced nations. . . . During the course of history from the end of the Tokugawa shogunate to the Greater East Asia War, if a nation [such as Japan] had been without military forces, that would have been tantamount to denying its own status as a nation-state and would have meant its becoming a colony. Therefore, under conditions in which no effective international organ existed, there was no other way than to appeal to force for any country which [like Japan] undertook to arm itself, to establish itself as a sovereign state, to carry out an industrial revolution, and to defend its interests against those of other advanced capitalist nations.

According to this view, all the possible choices found in modern Japanese history were discarded as conceptual possibilities and the whole course from the opening of the country to the Greater East Asia War was discussed in terms of "logical necessity." This fatalistic interpretation means that the 1930s was the only logical outcome that would have resulted from the opening of the country.

I myself am opposed to all these interpretations. To place the 1930s correctly in the framework of modern Japanese history, I shall first have to delineate the objective situation in which Japan found herself both internally and externally. And, secondly, I shall strive to analyze the behavior of classes, strata, groups, and individuals in their struggle to find other alternatives that existed within the objective conditions. From this vantage point I shall then summarize the characteristics of the historical developments of modern Japan. Finally I shall attempt to draw forth an answer to the theme of this part by explaining the general characteristics of the 1930s.

After the Meiji Restoration, Japan, under the state control of the emperor system, pursued the policies of "Rich Country, Strong Military" and "Increase Production, Promote Industry" and, as the only imperialist country in Asia, succeeded in being accepted by the European powers and the United States as one of their number.

The economic system that enabled Japan to develop to this degree was a special type of capitalism based on low wages in industry and tightly tied in with a parasitic landlord system that guaranteed a high rate of rent from the tenant farmers. Consequently the workers, tenants, and others lived lives of great poverty—the most pressing reason for the severity of the labor and tenant farmer disputes that ensued. The very narrowness of the domestic market, dominated as it was by the parasitic landlords, sharpened the external aggression which resulted from the ruling class's attempts to extend Japan's sphere of influence into Korea and China.

The Japanese political system was regulated by the Imperial Constitution of Great Japan promulgated in February 1889. This constitution, which was drawn up under the concept that sovereignty is lodged in the emperor, was characterized by an outward constitutional facade which made a mockery of the principles of modern constitutionalism. More specifically, it had six basic characteristics. First was the dominance of the military and the bureaucracy whose top personnel acted in the name of the emperor. Second was the primacy of the executive over the Imperial Diet. Third was the lack of guarantees for basic human rights as well as a set of strong controls to be operated by police enforcement. Fourth was local self-government institutions that were nothing more than the lower levels of the dominant bureaucracy, as embodied in the practice of appointment of prefectural governors. Fifth was the existence of the genro (elder statesmen), who were not even mentioned in the constitution, as well as the independence of the military from cabinet control. Sixth, the people were indoctrinated through the schools with a nationalistic ideology that placed the emperor at the center of the value system and severely limited the spread of ideas concerning democracy and socialism among the people.

The success of aggressive war in 1894–1895, 1904–1905, and 1914–1918 served as a springboard for the development of modern Japan, enabling her to increase her spheres of influence in Asia and gain colonies. In other words, domestically Japan built her militarism on the poverty of the workers and farmers and externally moved toward erecting an imperialist state at the expense of the Korean, Chinese, and other Asian peoples. The "modernization" that Reischauer extols was carried out within this economic and political framework.

Although the two democratic manifestations of the Freedom and People's Rights Movement (1874–1886) and Taishō democracy (1905–1925) did occur, they both collapsed through their own internal political and ideological immaturity and the policies of forceful suppression and cunning division instigated by the government. Just as earlier the setting up of the authoritarian Meiji Constitution was made possible by the collapse of the Freedom and People's Rights Movement, in the same way a reorganization of the emperor system took place from above after successfully resisting Taishō democracy from below. The establishment of the Katō Kōmei (Takaaki) cabinet, composed of a three-party coalition for the preservation of the constitution, ushered in party government in 1924. The following year, however, both the law for universal male suffrage and the public Peace Preservation Law were passed. Thus "party government" was basically undemocratic and did not change the fundamental principles of the constitution.

Turning to the world scene after the First World War, we see a new international order led by Great Britain and the United States. It was first known as the Versailles Treaty system in 1919 and later, after 1922, as the Washington Treaty system. Already the Soviet Union had come into existence and began developing on its own after 1917. Not unconnected with these events, nationalist movements against the dominant imperialisms arose here and there throughout the world. Specifically anti-Japanese movements reached a new high in 1919 in the March First Movement in Korea for independence from Japan and the May Fourth Movement in China, touched off by Japan's claim to the former German territories in China. In 1926 Chiang Kai-shek began the Northern Expedition and the Chinese Revolution got under way.

Japan had to respond to these changes in the world situation. She did so with the development of the so-called Shidehara diplomacy. That is, most cabinets from 1924 to 1931 employed Shidehara Kijūrō as foreign minister. These cabinets were all based on the Kenseikai, a political party which changed its name to the Minseitō in June 1927. This policy of diplomacy consisted of international cooperation along the lines of the Versailles Treaty first and then the Washington Treaty —particularly with the United States and Great Britain but also making accommodations with the Soviet Union. With regard to China, the policy consisted of nonintervention in the Chinese civil war as long as Japanese interests were not directly affected. To counter this, the military, the Seiyūkai, and right-wing groups attacked the Shidehara foreign policy as weak. The Tanaka cabinet (1927–1929), based on the Seiyūkai, pushed forward the policy of detaching Manchuria and Mongolia from China. It also dispatched troops into Shantung three times between 1927 and 1928. But this Tanaka policy ended in failure, and with the formation of the Hamaguchi cabinet in 1929 Shidehara diplomacy was resurrected. Such was the situation at the advent of the year 1930.

In that year the waves of the worldwide Great Depression reached Japan and severely affected the livelihood of the masses. The increased poverty of the people stimulated existing labor and agrarian movements. But the Hamaguchi cabinet's policies for dealing with the depression gave priority to the interests of big finance capital. Because the cabinet did not have the strength to clean up the political corruption exposed by new cases one after the other in both the Seiyūkai and the Minseitō, an aversion to political parties and to big business grew up among the masses. They began to look for some kind of breakthrough in the status quo.

On the international plane, the London Naval Arms Limitation Conference began in January 1930. With the support of a public opinion that greatly favored arms reduction in the conditions of the world depression, the Hamaguchi cabinet was able to override the objections of the Naval General Staff and the Privy Council and signed the Naval Arms Limitation Treaty. Certain rightist military officers and politically right-wing elements, however, criticized the action of the government as an "encroachment on the supreme command." Some members of the House of Peers and even of the Seiyūkai agreed and attacked Shidehara diplomacy.

Again anti-Japanese nationalist movements sprang up in Korea, Taiwan, and China, and Soviet influence penetrated the nationalist movements in Korea and Manchuria. Moreover the South Manchurian Railway Company and other Japanese enterprises were severely affected by the Great Depression.

The ruling circles in Japan called the depression a "national economic disaster." They labeled the increasingly militant labor and agrarian movements in Japan and the increasingly fervent anti-Japanese nationalist movements abroad as manifestations of an "ideological crisis." Conditions in Manchuria were characterized as the "Manchuria–Mongolia crisis." In this atmosphere of crisis psychosis certain militarists and right-wingers initiated a movement for "national renovation."

Given these external and domestic conditions, there were five directions in which Japan might proceed. First was the choice of carrying out a national renovation as advocated by the military extremists and the right wing. This move would involve the overthrow of party government through a coup d'etat and the establishment of a military dictatorship. At the same time, it would involve a military solution to the Manchuria–Mongolia problem—that is, a military occupation of Manchuria.

The second choice was that of following the line advocated by the Seiyūkai. Although a few were willing to go along with the army extremists, by and large the party members advocated positive financial policies for getting through the depression while still maintaining party government. As for a China policy, they called for detaching Manchuria and Mongolia from China.

The third choice was that of following the line of the Minseitō and the Hamaguchi cabinet. In terms of domestic policy, this meant strongly supporting party government, encouraging the formation of cartels as a means of dealing with the depression, and strengthening the international competitive ability of Japanese capital by financial retrenchment, rationalization of industry, and lifting the ban on gold shipments. In terms of foreign policy, this meant pushing forward Shidehara diplomacy. This line was strongly supported by the *jushin* (senior statesmen) and financial circles and the dominant ruling class.

Still there were two more choices. The fourth possibility was the line of the legal (noncommunist) proletarian parties—Japan's social democrats. This line was supported by the labor unions and the tenant farmer unions. While opinions ranged from the anticommunist social-democratic right wing to the procommunist left, they all advocated the democratization of politics and the economy through legal (constitutional) means and opposed an imperialistic foreign policy of resorting to force. And, finally, the fifth alternative was the line of the (illegal) Japanese Communist Party. Having a good deal of influence in certain labor unions and tenant farmer organizations, the party had worked out a detailed program for a thorough democratic revolution, including the overthrow of the emperor system, an end to the parasitic landlords, a restructuring of monopoly capitalism, and the abolition of imperialism.

In reality, however, the outbreak of the Manchurian Incident stacked the cards in favor of the first choice—national renovation— thus overwhelming and superseding the mainstream third choice. The Manchurian Incident began on 18 September (Japan time) 1931 when the Japanese Kwantung Army itself blew up a section of the South Manchurian Railway at Liu-t'iao-kou located in the outskirts of Mukden and falsely accused the Chinese of the act.

The second Wakatsuki cabinet announced a policy of containing the affair, but the military ignored this pronouncement and went on to occupy all Manchuria. The Japanese government ratified this action and Shidehara diplomacy collapsed. The Inukai cabinet, based on the Seiyūkai, was set up in December of the same year. It attempted to readjust all the foreign and domestic policies and went along to a degree with the strong policies of the military. The military in January 1932 provoked the Shanghai Affair and thus diverted the attention of the Western powers from Manchuria to Central China. Meanwhile they set up the puppet Manchukuo government in Manchuria. This fighting stimulated the national renovation movement and provided the atmosphere for the assassination of Premier Inukai on 15 May. The succeeding Saitō cabinet was set up as a national unity cabinet on the basis of an understanding among the *jushin* and the elites, thus bringing an end to the eight years of political party government.

Even before the Manchurian Incident, the mass media had begun to picture China as an enemy. Following the outbreak of hostilities, the media began to agitate for victory. Chauvinist feelings directed against China increased. Many of the common people who were suffering under the Great Depression came to expect a breakthrough in the situation by the use of force. Ultimately they supported the war. Even the right wing among the social democratic parties came to construe Japan's actions in the Manchurian Incident as defensive. In contrast, some liberals, the left wing of the social democrats, and the Japanese Communist Party denounced the war, but these people were labeled as "un-Japanese" by the government and by war supporters and became isolated from the great majority. These forces were by their very nature the ones that should have been working together for the realization of democracy and to oppose war, but they failed to effect a united front. The main reason for their failure can be found in the increased suppression carried out under a broad interpretation of the Peace Preservation Law. Another reason was the infighting among the social democratic party leaders as well as policy mistakes by the Communist party leadership. As a result, the fourth and fifth choices explained above were precluded.

Not only did the Manchurian Incident usher in the so-called fifteen years of war (the Manchurian Incident, the China War, and the Pacific War); it also constituted Japan's open defiance of the Versailles–Washington world order and eventually led to the conflagration of the Second World War. Japan bolted the League of Nations in March 1933 and in December 1934 informed the United States of her denunciation of the Washington Naval Arms Limitation Treaty. In January 1936 Japan withdrew from the London Naval Arms Limitation talks. Thus Japan chose to secede from the Versailles–Washington Treaty system, to deepen her confrontation with the United States and Great Britain, and to isolate herself on the world stage. Japan signed the Anti-Comintern Pact with Germany in November 1936 and was joined by Italy in November 1937. Now the fascist camp opposed not only the Soviet Union but also the Western democracies.

From the time of the Manchurian Incident political fascism in Japan marched forward to the cadence of shouts that Japan faced a "period of emergency." The government not only obliterated the Communist Party; it stamped out liberalism through the Takigawa Affair of 1933 and the Minobe or "Organ Theory" Affair of 1935. In the midst of such ideological oppression, a number of former communists and left-wingers converted to ultranationalism (or emperor worship), school textbooks were revised, and in the name of "thought guidance" *(shisō zendō)* education was used to indoctrinate ultranationalism. In the country side from 1932 on the government promoted a campaign for the revitalization of the economy of the agricultural, mountain, and fishing villages and tightened its control over the farming population. Again, after the assassination of 15 May 1932, the cleavage between the Tōseiha (Control Faction) and the Kōdōha (Imperial Way Faction) widened. Young officers of the Kōdōha initiated the uprising of 26 February 1936. The failure of this attempted coup d'etat, however, enabled members of the Tōseiha gradually to gain power after mending their own fences with the bureaucracy and the financial circles. A reorganization took place just as the existing national structure was about to crumble, and the fascistization of Japanese politics from above proceeded apace.

Facing an impasse in its administration of Manchuria and in order to get a greater area of North China under its sphere of influence, the Japanese government adopted the strategy of splitting off North China from the rest of China. In response to this and specifically as a result of the Sian Incident of December 1936 (in which Chiang Kaishek was seized by his own troops and persuaded to change his priorities), the Nationalists (Kuomintang) and the Chinese Communists provisionally ended their civil war. Anti-Japanese activity intensified throughout China. It was under these conditions that the Marco Polo Bridge Incident of 7 July 1937 occurred and war broke out between China and Japan.

At the beginning of hostilities, Japan could choose from three possible lines of action: (1) the line of full-scale war in China under the military, led by the Tōseiha and involving the establishment of a fascistic total mobilization of the country for war; (2) the line of a limited military involvement in China under the anti-Tōseiha groups in the army in alliance with the cabinet of Konoe Fumimaro; and (3) the line of opposing the war as advocated by certain social democrats under the leadership of the left wing. Options for Japan now were considerably fewer than on the eve of the Manchurian Incident. The opposition between the first and the second lines of action disappeared when the Konoe cabinet, which had at first taken the position of not extending the war, gave its approval in the middle of August to the policy of enlarging the conflict. As for the choice of the third line, it disappeared when the Japanese Proletarian Party and others were outlawed at the time of the government's breakup of the Popular Front in December 1937. The Peace Preservation Law was broadened to include certain religious leaders and those advocating independence for Korea; organized resistance to the trend toward war was impossible. In January 1938 the Konoe cabinet, by declaring that Japan "refuses to deal with the National government" of China, torpedoed any chance for a negotiated peace, and in November of the same year it announced its plan for building a New Order in East Asia. After October 1938 the China front bogged down and the conflict took on the aspect of a long war of attrition.

In the context of the mass media's stirring up a victory fervor among the people after the outbreak of the China Incident and the people's response to this media campaign, the Konoe cabinet began mobilizing popular morale by organizing the people more fully under governmental direction. Simultaneously the economy was placed under semiwartime controls by the National General Mobilization Law of April 1938. Though not immediately invoked, this law eventually became the vehicle for the government to extend its controls to every aspect of people's daily lives.

With regard to Japanese-Soviet relations, disputes along the Russian-Manchurian border took place in July 1938 at Chang-ku-feng and along the border with Outer Mongolia in May 1938 at Nomonhan. Because the Japanese forces were badly beaten the army abandoned plans to move north against the Soviet Union and instead directed its attention to the invasion of Southeast Asia.

When the Second World War broke out in Europe in September 1939, the Japanese government announced policies of nonintervention and a quick settlement of the war in China. The victories of the Nazi forces greatly inspired the Japanese ruling class, however, especially the military, and consequently in July 1940 the military brought down the Yonai cabinet which favored continuing the status quo and opposed an Axis Pact. The second Konoe cabinet with the support of the military originated new foreign and domestic policies and made public the concept of the Greater East Asia Coprosperity Sphere. To secure such strategic materials as oil and rubber and to cut the supply route to China through French Indochina (Vietnam), the Japanese government decided on a policy of armed expansion into Southeast Asia. In September of the same year, it signed a Three-Power Pact among Germany, Italy, and Japan. This pact was an anticommunist, aggressive, military alliance among the three fascist powers, whose aim was to divide up the world militarily in order to secure Lebensraum. Since Great Britain and the United States were the targets of this treaty as well, Japan's relations with them took a turn for the worse.

While these events were taking place, the movement in Japan for a New Order unfolded under the direction of the Konoe cabinet. After all the political parties had dissolved themselves, the Imperial Rule Assistance Association was set up the same year (October 1940) to aid the administration; its purpose was "to convey the will and ideas of those who govern to those who are governed" *(Joi gadatsu)*. Premier Konoe became its president. The IRAA was organized at every level down to fascistic neighborhood groups which had as their function the promotion of the aggressive war implied by the Three-Power Pact. Labor and farmers unions were disbanded. In their place, national movement bodies were organized and directed by the government. Through these groups the fascist system was consolidated under the leadership of the military and the bureaucracy. After Japan secured her northern flank by signing the Japan-Soviet Neutrality Pact in April 1941, she embarked on a southward advance into French Indochina that made confrontation with the United States and Great Britain decisive. On 8 December (Japan time) 1941 Japan provoked the Pacific War.

Looking at these events in this way, it seems that modern Japan threw away quite a few alternatives. Instead she created an imperialist state and chose a road leading to fifteen years of war. We can thus say that the decade of the 1930s was not an aberration for Japan but the natural outcome of the "Rich Country, Strong Military" and "Increase Production, Promote Industry" Meiji policies chosen by successive Japanese governments.

As we have seen, the 1930s can be described as a period of war and fascistization. Why did Japan in the 1930s embark on such a reckless adventure? We have already found at least six explanations. It was, in my opinion, the fact that the Japanese people were unable to clear away these six obstacles to democratic development that made the fifteen years of war inevitable.

[Translated by GEORGE O. TOTTEN III]

Detour Through
A Dark Valley

Robert M. Spaulding

In the 1930s, the central events of Japanese history were repression at home, aggression abroad. To ask whether these were aberrations or logical consequences of Japan's past is to ask whether they are likely to recur. The answer from history is that they resulted from unique circumstances which no longer exist and are unlikely to exist again. They reveal not a conspiracy but a series of improvised policies often based on miscalculation.

Japan's domestic and foreign policies in the 1930s were dominated by a new ideology so different from traditional nationalism that it merits the label of ultranationalism. Historically, Japanese nationalism had been concerned chiefly with preserving Japan's uniqueness while selectively borrowing and adapting from other cultures. Internally, it preferred that decisions be made collectively by consensus. Externally, it produced either peaceful contacts or isolation, not imperialist aggression. Wars of conquest were characteristic of Chinese history, not Japanese. Before the modern era, Japan's only foreign war was Hideyoshi's sixteenth-century invasion of Korea. It is no coincidence that this campaign was launched by the only Japanese ruler who truly approximated the Chinese model of an autocrat and, moreover, that it was stopped as soon as he died.

Roots of ultranationalism can be found in the 1890 Imperial Rescript on Education ("offer yourselves courageously to the state") and in the wars of the Meiji period. But unlike the British and French wars against China, Japan's first wars with China and Russia were at least partly defensive moves to prevent hostile control of Japan's close neighbor Korea. And in seizing more distant Taiwan and Liaotung, Japan was not yet asserting a claim to hegemony in East Asia but merely imitating her European competitors in an age of imperialism.

Even the sonorous phrases of the Education Rescript remained little more than rhetoric until after the First World War, when they were made the centerpiece of a new ideology designed to restore a fading consensus. The Meiji leaders' success in modernizing Japan rested on their skill in building national unity and directing it toward creative effort. But in trying to combine German authoritarianism with the Japanese tradition of collective decision-making, they had created a political system of multiple semiautonomous elites. This system worked well as long as they survived. By the 1920s the able and homogeneous leaders of the Meiji period were gone, and the consensus they had held together for half a century was falling apart. The causes included intractable social and economic problems, rising expectations for better living standards and wider political participation at home, and misgivings about the practicality of an idealistic new international order based on restraint and cooperation.

The ultranationalist ideology of State Shinto helped restore a national consensus and thus made the suppression of civil liberties less extreme in Japan than in Germany, whose Nazi ideology stressed a divisive racism and forcible recovery of lost territories. On the other hand, State Shinto's vagueness could be used to justify almost any policy a government might adopt at home or abroad. It was most adroitly exploited by the military service. Though they were never able to govern alone or without compromise, their ability to act with impunity outside Japan (as in Manchuria in 1931) enabled them to shape national policy to a greater degree than any other elite. This flaw in the political system, combined with fear induced by ultranationalist terrorism, stifled effective resistance as Japan strode into the dark valley of the 1930s.

The first step, creation of the puppet state of Manchukuo, is usually misunderstood as merely a drive for territory and economic gain. It was much more than that. Japanese army officers saw Manchukuo as a laboratory classroom in which they could demonstrate the efficiency, the organizational innovations, and the ideological purity which they found lacking in their own country. At least initially, they saw Manchukuo as a stepping stone not to control of China but to reform of Japan.

Accurately perceiving that some of Japan's problems stemmed from diffusion of power among rival elites, the army created a much more monolithic system in Manchukuo. Japanese diplomats and consuls were brought under army control by three measures. The Kwantung Army commander was made ex officio Japanese ambassador to

254 • THE 1930S: ABERRATION OR LOGICAL OUTCOME?

Manchukuo. The army minister in Tokyo was made ex officio chief of the cabinet-level Manchurian Affairs Bureau. Manchukuo's own ministry of foreign affairs was demoted to the status of a cabinet bureau. The Japanese army saw Manchukuo as an efficient working model for rebuilding and purifying Japan itself.

On the other hand, the Japanese army's efforts after 1937 to reorganize China Proper reflect a different and more complex reason for Japanese aggression. In simplest terms, this was a growing Japanese resentment of the appalling mismanagement that had characterized China since 1800. This resentment was by no means confined to the army. Before 1931, its most dramatic manifestation had been the grandiose Twenty-one Demands on China in 1915, drafted by civilians considered liberal and friendly to China.

It is unrealistic to argue that mismanagement in China, however bad, was none of Japan's business. The Japanese argument in the 1930s that "propinquity" (an undeniable fact of geography) justified a special Japanese concern with events in China is used today by China to justify a special Chinese concern with events in Japan, Korea, and Vietnam. But the multiple causes of Japan's concern in the 1930s involve much more than mere closeness to China.

At least five separate lines of Japanese thought came to be intertwined in policy toward China in the 1930s. Probably first in time was the idea of repaying a cultural debt. As China had been model and teacher for seventh-century Japan, so Japan could be model and teacher for twentieth-century China.

Second, the Japanese thought that China's inept management of its vast natural resources was needlessly injuring Japan as well as China. Japan, although woefully deficient or totally lacking in nearly all the natural resources needed for industry, had achieved far more than richly endowed China. It was galling, as well as wasteful, for Japan to have to import raw materials from great distance while living next door to one of the world's largest hoards of undeveloped resources. To Japan, the Chinese looked like egregious examples of Aesop's dog in the manger, depriving others of what they themselves could not or would not use.

Third, Japanese pride in their own achievements after 1868 convinced them—regardless of any cultural debt or need for Chinese resources—that they were infinitely more capable than Chinese in governing, improving, and developing any area in sight. By many standards they had proved that by 1930 in Taiwan and Korea, and they soon proved it in Manchuria as well. What they failed to understand was that even the most tactful efficiency experts are likely to be feared and resented, and Japanese in other Asian countries were seldom noted for tact. Most Japanese seem to have been genuinely puzzled by Chinese and Southeast Asian resentment of the Japanese presence and by their resistance to measures which Japan thought beneficial. Eager to share the French "civilizing mission" and the British "white man's burden," the Japanese should have read the rest of Kipling: "Take up the white man's burden—and reap his old reward: the blame of those ye better, the hate of those ye guard."

Fourth, the Japanese felt a regional shame or vicarious humiliation in the fact that no other Asian country had managed to remain genuinely independent of Western domination. China's long and costly procrastination in modernizing was due chiefly to Chinese refusal, even after losing three wars, to admit their technological backwardness and do something about it. But while becoming more and more impatient with China's inability to put her own house in order, Japan recognized that the Western presence made China's task more difficult. The Japanese slogan of "Asia for the Asians" was therefore not as cynically self-serving as is usually assumed. Like Hercules cleansing the Augean stables by sending a river through them, Japan thought it had a mission, which no one else could fulfill, to purge Asia of Western colonialism.

Finally, the specter of communism in China added a critical urgency to the four other concerns felt by Japan. China's inability to modernize reflected a lack of national unity. In the 1880s, the Japanese had used Sakuma Shōzan's formula of "Eastern ethics, Western science" to preserve their own heritage while modernizing according to an alien model. Though later distorted by ultranationalist ideology, this formula gave the Japanese a basis for national unity that was lacking in China. The Chinese, facing the same dilemma as the Japanese at the same time, managed only to discredit and discard their old ideology without agreeing on a new one. Japan had good reason to fear the consequence if this ideological vacuum were filled by a militant communist party controlling China's territory and immense resources.

The *Bōkyō* ("Resist Communism") slogan of Japan's intervention in China was therefore sincerely and deeply felt. Unfortunately for both countries, the results of intervention were the opposite of what Japan wanted. Instead we have the spectacle today of Maoist China brandishing nuclear weapons, the world's largest army, third largest navy, and a large air force, professing to fear that it will be attacked by

Japan's tiny self-defense forces. This would be merely ludicrous except for the tendency of Maoist officials, dangerously ignorant of other countries, to believe their own myths. This particular myth had asserted until recently that Japan is unchanged from the 1930s, but in fact the last forty years have changed Japan more than China.

Rebuilding after the devastation of twenty years of civil war in China and eight years of international war in the Pacific, both countries have achieved economic growth. Japan's has been spectacular, China's more modest and spasmodic, partly because Mao's bumbling political interference squandered time, labor, and resources on the absurdities of the "great leap forward" and Red Guard terrorism. In other respects, Japan and China have moved in opposite directions. Land reform brought a bloodbath in China, not a single casualty in Japan. China acquired the most absolute dictatorship in its long history, Japan one of the world's most democratic systems. In China, dissent was ruthlessly exterminated and people lost even the right to be uninterested in politics. In Japan, civil liberties were greatly expanded and protected by formidable legal and judicial safeguards.

Even in the darkest valley of the 1930s, Japan was never as totalitarian as China is today. But since the aberration of the 1930s gravely injured China and nearly destroyed Japan, the possibility of a recurrence cannot be ignored. It is disturbing that the bigotry and violence of Japan's former right-wing extremists have been matched or exceeded in recent years by left-wing Japanese extremists. Their terrorism has been seen repeatedly on the streets and campuses of Japan and even on distant foreign soil, as in the murders at an Israeli airport in 1972.

But there seems to be a major difference. The number of Japanese who either condone extremism or are intimidated by it appears to be much smaller now than in the 1930s. Thus far, at least, extremists have been less successful in postwar Japan than in postwar America, where right-wing McCarthyism in the 1950s and left-wing McCarthyism in the late 1960s and early 1970s inflicted lasting traumas and were widely condoned.

Most other signs are encouraging. The incipient Japanese democracy of the 1920s, aborted by the ultranationalist movement, was reborn in much sturdier and more mature form after the Second World War and has flourished ever since, despite predictions that it would die when the American occupation ended in 1952. The flaws in the prewar political system which permitted repression and aggression have been corrected. The arguments of the 1930s in support of aggression have been discredited and would in any case be irrelevant in today's greatly altered world. The military imbalance between Japan and China has been reversed, to say the least. The postwar pacifism which many foreigners thought was feigned looks more genuine with each passing year.

Most encouraging of all, the Japanese have demonstrated that peace can be profitable and that democracy and individual rights can coexist with the traditional Japanese emphasis on teamwork and group loyalty. These are the keys to Japan's social and economic health. And that health is powerful insurance against recurrence of the tragic errors of the 1930s.

Japan's Political Parties in Democracy, Fascism, and War

George O. Totten III

That the existence of democracy in a country is a guarantee against the adoption of imperialistic policies abroad was a widely held assumption at the time of Japan's surrender in 1945. This view is now questioned, however. If it is true, it should be qualified by saying that democracy must be based on a thoroughly enlightened public, deeply involved in a political process, who can express themselves without fear. This public must not be prone to a mystical mission to police other countries, convinced of its own superiority morally and physically. Such was not the case with Japan in the 1930s.

During that period Japan displayed few pretentions to being democratic. This despite her maintenance of political institutions often considered the essence of democracy—namely, elections in a multiple-party system until 1940. Japan was ruled by an elite coalition sometimes referred to as a "limited pluralism" consisting of five groups. The first was the political parties; they constituted the weakest group. The second was the military; they became the most powerful group, reaching their zenith with the installation of General Tōjō Hideki as premier in 1941. The third element was the civil bureaucracy. This was the backbone of government, but it was weakened by the various ministries vying among themselves for funds and split by interministry factions. Fourth was big business. This group too was divided into competing *zaibatsu* economic concentrations. They had close government connections but also warded off the government's attempts to control them even during the war, enabling them to profit handsomely.

The fifth element was the monarchy or imperial institution itself.

This group included the various advisers to the throne: the Privy Council and various extraconstitutional decision-makers, such as the court officials, the *jūshin* (senior statesmen), and the genro (elder statesmen). They worked consensually in dispensing official sanctions from the highest source of legitimacy: the emperor. They chose the premier who in turn formed his cabinet, but in order to get legislation passed the premier needed the cooperation of the Diet, which itself was divided into two houses: the Peers and the Representatives. It was in the Lower House that the political parties were lodged. Their ace card was their power to approve the budget. This right, however, was restricted because the premier had a lesser countervailing right to make expenditures, in case the budget was not passed, at least to the level of the previous year's budget. Beside their budgetary role, the political parties, over the years, had won grudging acceptance from the other elite groups for playing a mediatory role, or acting as a broker, among them. This was not an absolutely necessary function. Yet it was usually helpful in making the political process work better. More face-saving was possible if the various factions in the four other elite groups did not have to deal with each other directly.

The very existence of the parties, however, had always been under attack. At first, in the late Meiji period from 1890 to 1918, the opposition came from groups of oligarchs still in control. Later, as modernization produced more of a mass society by the late 1920s, true believers in direct rule by the emperor appeared. In their eyes the political parties, because of their ties with the venal *zaibatsu*—the Seiyūkai with Mitsui and the Minseitō with Mitsubishi—were less able to put the national interest first than, say, the military. The parties were at the height of their influence in 1932 when the premier, a party man, was assassinated by such a true believer on 15 May. That a nonparty premier was chosen to succeed him was at first considered a temporary situation. But loss of power fed on itself. Eight years later, in 1940, all the political parties were pressured into self-dissolution to make way for a single organization that, although not a political party, was supposed somehow to transcend partisanship in total support for a united nation. On the face of it this organization looked like the Fascist or Nazi parties, but in actuality the same Diet members elected under their former party labels continued to hold their seats and even maintained their former party ties informally.

All this happened during a period of Japanese aggression abroad and suppression of ever more loosely defined "dangerous thought" at home. In postwar Japan this period has been often labeled "fascist" and the period preceding it romanticized as one of "Taishō democracy." Because of this stereotyped periodization, it has widely been assumed that the political parties opposed war and supported democracy. This was hardly the case, however. If it had been so, it would be easier to argue for a general trend toward democracy prior to the 1930s. One could point to the increase in the size of the electorate from 1 percent of the population in 1890 to the passage of universal male suffrage in 1925. One could show that, with one exception, party government existed between 1918 and 1932, during which period Japan evinced a generally cooperative approach to world order. The fall of the parties could then be equated with the end of liberalism and democracy. And one could add that Japan attacked Pearl Harbor in December 1941, significantly after the disbandment of parties. The period from about 1930 to the autumn of 1945 could then be seen as an aberration of this general liberal trend.

This argument, however, overlooks a number of facts. The established political parties, best known as the Seiyūkai and the Minseitō (although the latter, particularly, changed names), differed only in tactics, not in principle, from the other elite groups on the questions of the need to use force in China, the advisability of limiting the freedoms of speech, assembly, or organization, and the importance of keeping sovereignty in the hands of the emperor. Apart from these increasingly pervasive commitments, all the elite groups were characterized by variations of opinion, factionalism, infighting, and temporary alliances. Party factions sought common cause with sections of the military against one or more government ministries at one time and switched partners later. But the parties' lack of expertise on both foreign affairs and domestic questions in a period perceived as a "crisis" lowered their stature in the view of the other elites, who claimed greater professional competence. In this sense the eclipse of party cabinets was due more to practical than to ideological reasons.

Nevertheless, while competing among themselves in this limited pluralism, all the elites abided by a basic ground rule. That rule was not necessarily respect for law. Bribery, intimidation, and even assassination cast a pall over the entire Japanese political process. The ground rule was none other than reverence for the emperor (abroad often called "emperor worship"), summed up in the theory of the kokutai, which held that Japan was unique in being ruled by an unbroken line of good emperors from time immemorial.

Actually the emperor institution was recent in Japan, compared to China where succession was often manipulated, and during the long shogunates emperors frequently languished in obscurity and neglect.

After the restoration of 1868 the Meiji emperor at first did help make decisions in the 1870s and 1880s, but thereafter the emperor institution was elevated "above the clouds." The last of the genro (Saionji Kimmochi, who lived till 1940) devoted his life to protecting the "unseen" emperor from political involvement. Saionji did this even though he deplored the trend toward war and even though he knew the emperor might have been able to prevent war at some points. Ironically it was the ultrarightists, the true believers, who professed they wanted direct imperial rule (which would have involved the emperor politically) to clean up big business corruption and give more power to the "unsullied" military, not knowing of the Shōwa emperor's concealed proclivities for big business and disdain for some of the military.

Political party leaders often tried to outdo one another in supporting—or attacking others for not supporting—the overawing sanctity of the emperor. Their stake was in the inviolability of the Meiji Constitution because it had been bestowed on the people by the emperor. It provided for a house of representatives (the home of the political parties), and this could not be altered (despite attacks by ultrarightist elements) except by consent of the emperor. While political parties were not mentioned in the constitution, parliamentary groups (whether factions or parties) proved necessary for operating the Lower House and for carrying out elections. In the election of 1942, when all Diet members belonged to the Imperial Rule Assistance Association (supposedly nonpolitical), the candidates' support networks (jiban) in reality functioned much as before. In fact the election even helped get some former party leaders into the succeeding cabinet for the first time since 1932. While often overlooked, this fact helps to explain the revival of parties after the war.

Before the war, since policy decisions were often made outside of parliament, the parties' function of representing the will of the voters was less important than their role of giving consent to the collective decisions reached through compromise among the five elite groups. According to democratic political theory, parliaments should be representative of the interests, classes, and other attributes of the whole population. But in Japan representation was skewed to a high degree. The House of Peers was specifically designed to represent only the tiny percentage of the population made up of the nobility, big business, and top bureaucrats, with some successful intellectuals thrown in to add prestige. "Popular representation" in the Lower House too represented in fact only a minority of the population. By the suffrage law of 1925 the restrictions which limited the right to vote to certain categories of male taxpayers were dropped, but the vote then was only extended to males twenty-five years old or older who met residence and other requirements (which in effect discriminated against workers, unemployed, and youth). There were only some 13 million eligible voters out of a population of about 65 million.

Also according to democratic theory, the people should take part in the political process in some significant way. But in Japan a number of factors led to political apathy on the part of the masses. The established parties built up local bases of support *(jiban)* through personal connections with local notables *(meibōka)* or men of influence *(yūryokusha)* in the community—usually landlords in the countryside and businessmen or professionals in the cities. These people could deliver the vote through various forms of social and economic pressures in return for local patronage by the Diet candidate mediating with the bureaucracy. The political parties had no party organization on the local level (and the politicians did not want their own parties to interfere in their own bailiwicks). We may say that because the parties lacked grass roots, they were Diet-centered. The masses voted because of a web of obligations rather than from a sense of involvement in the political system.

The exceptions to this pattern were the leftist or labor parties that in Japan were called proletarian and in Europe would be classed as social democratic. Formed in 1926–1928, they managed to unite in 1932 to form the Socialist Masses Party (Shakai Taishūtō) or SMP. Their original divisions had arisen over the question of the degree to which they separated themselves from the illegal Communist Party that was a special concern of the police and the object of rightist intimidation and violence. That party was the only one which challenged the emperor system directly and called for a republic. To do that was considered worse than advocating socialism in the economy. To strive for their aims the small band of communists could only be effective as members of mass organizations, such as labor and tenant farmer unions and the proletarian parties.

These legal social democratic parties, though small, were mass parties in the sense that they had at least skeletal nationwide organization. Thus they enabled common people (of the types that made up the overwhelming majority of the Japanese people) to take part in the political process directly in their own interest instead of through parties controlled by former bureaucrats in alliance with politicians tied to giant financial combines. In this sense, then, the social democratic proletarian party supporters were consciously fighting against the system and in favor of democratic rights. Although these parties had grown out of organizations of workers and tenant farmers, the communist issue had split and weakened the labor federations, allowing the government, through the police, to destroy the most militant unions and drive others underground. While the legal social democratic parties and unions did not on the surface attack the Meiji emperor-centered constitution, they clearly called for legal recognition of labor unions and the right to strike. They were never able to secure these basic rights in presurrender Japan.

When the Socialist Masses Party was formed in July 1932 as an amalgam of earlier social democratic parties now shorn of their leftist elements, they had begun compromising their previous domestic and foreign policies. In the 1928 general elections, for instance, they had opposed Japanese imperialism and Japan's resort to force in international relations and called for recognition of Chinese nationalism. But after the Japanese army overran China's northeastern provinces in 1931, they came to accept the creation of a new puppet state they called Manchukuo. As if to salve their consciences, however, they demanded that the Japanese army, which wielded effective power in Manchukuo behind the scenes, turn it into a socialist state. By that they meant excluding the influence of the Japanese bourgeoisie, specifically the giant Mitsui, Mitsubishi, and other *zaibatsu* conglomerations, which they feared would profit at the expense of Japanese workers back home. Surprisingly this demand was echoed by a number of young officers in the military, who, because of their belief in direct rule by the emperor, were often classified as radical rightists.

Even before the formation of the SMP, some social democrats, stimulated both by the excitement of Japanese military advances in Manchuria and by the worldwide depression, threw over their social democratic and pacifist tenets and formed a national socialist party. To a degree, they were influenced by the Fascists who had ruled Italy for some time and the Nazis who had not yet achieved power. They argued that the interests of Japan's proletariat were more tied in with the rest of the Japanese as a nation or race than allied with the proletarians of other nations as a class. In other words, the interests of the working classes of rich nations clashed with those of poor nations. Therefore Japanese workers and farmers should help defend Japanese interests abroad even by force.

While some of the leaders who remained with the SMP developed contacts with factions in the military, the party still had about it an aura of resistance to the trend toward war even during the April 1937 election when it achieved its largest presurrender vote and became the third largest party in the Diet. This enabled it for the first time to have a voice in day-to-day procedures in the House of Representatives. The party received almost a million votes then, about one-tenth of the total, and 37 seats out of the 466 total.

To the left of the SMP, the Japan Proletarian Party, which fruitlessly appealed to the SMP for a popular front against war and fascism in Japan, elected its leader, Katō Kanjū, to the Imperial Diet. On the right the national socialist groups, also opposing the established parties, got eleven seats, which showed they had little mass support.

With the outbreak of the China Incident on 7 July 1936, the mood in the country again changed and the Socialist Masses Party came out clearly in support of the holy war on the continent. The Japan Proletarian Party, on the other hand, was forced to disband and its Diet representative Katō was arrested. Thereafter any hint of resistance to Japan's military involvement abroad could lead to detainment by the police, not to mention social pressure, ostracism, or physical assault by self-styled patriots.

Not only the labor or proletarian parties, but also the established political parties, the Seiyūkai, Minseitō, and others, regained some strength. The increase in the voting rate and reduction in independents were interpreted as support for the party system. This counted in the premier's decision to resign.

In a curious way groups on both extremes and in the middle all thought they had found their man in the ambiguously transcendent imperial prince, Konoe Fumimaro. Having contacts in all quarters, the conservatives thought that only he had sufficient rapport with the radicals and the military to restrain them. The radicals believed that only he had sufficient standing to force through the creation of a garrison state in which private profit would be subordinated and a new spirit of national determination generated among the people.

As a result, Prince Konoe became premier in June 1937, after the election, with the support of mutually antagonistic elements in all five elite groups. He led an outwardly united Japan into war with the outbreak of the China Incident the following month. In the next year he engineered the enactment of the National General Mobilization Law which gave the government power to place Japan on a total war footing whenever necessary. The radicals had fought for this law in order to enable the government to control big business and mobilize the people behind the radicals in the army, but, disappointing them, Konoe left a loophole. The law provided that the decision to invoke a national mobilization would be participated in by the party leaders who represented big business—which this law was supposed to control.

After stepping down for a year and a half, Konoe again became premier in 1940. He then presided over the creation of the Imperial Rule Assistance Association, which, as noted, aimed at replacing the political parties. It is an irony of history that the IRAA was the result of the long struggle of the radicals to create a powerful totalitarian party, inasmuch as it turned out to be so emasculated that it had little effect on the power structure after all. Furthermore, while it more fully mobilized the people from above, the power over this stricter control was grasped by the traditionalists in the Home Ministry rather than by the army's radicals or their allies in the civil bureaucracy. Nor was the influence of the old party politicians through the local community leaders broken. Even a number of the former social democrats gained positions in it.

In that crucial year of 1940, it appeared that Konoe had the influence, conditions, and ability to turn Japan into a completely totalitarian state resembling the European fascist type. Yet instead of reasoning, like the rightist radicals, that because Japan faced a long war she had to be streamlined for that purpose, he took the opposite conservative approach of *not* tampering much with the existing power structure in the face of the continuing war in China. While wanting to end the fighting, Konoe was not willing to pay the price of getting a truce with the potentially compromising Chiang Kai-shek regime. This despite the fact that he considered at least a ceasefire was a necessary condition before Japan could turn her attention to a thorough reorganization of the political and economic structure. Thus he decided to strive for the defeat of the Chiang government by stepping up the blockade of China. He also sought to neutralize the Soviet Union. And he prepared for Japan's expansion into Southeast Asia. In underestimating the strength of Chinese nationalism and overestimating Japan's military and economic capabilities, Prince Konoe and his army minister and successor as premier, General Tōjō Hideki, and their colleagues committed Japan to a course that led to total defeat.

How can we explain this colossal miscalculation that apparently had a consensus of the leadership behind it? It can be argued that Japan was suffering a leadership crisis that traced back to the time of the First World War when the old oligarchy that had ruled Meiji Japan was fast disappearing. After 1924 only Saionji survived as a genro. The new elites were continually growing in strength and struggling with one another for power within the state. They collectively used the imperial institution to dampen or crush movements organizing the people from below and they each attempted to wield it to gain advantages for themselves or discredit their enemies, but not fully succeeding. No elite was able to dominate the rest because each had somewhat different functions and power bases. In the 1930s the snowballing war effort lent a measure of apparent unity—the Diet voted unanimously to support war measures—while struggles went on behind the scenes. Intellectual life, including politics and culture, increasingly succumbed to the pressures for demonstrating loyalty to a mystical imperial will which now directed Japan to "liberate," reorganize, and develop East Asia all the way to India in the south and at a later time to include Siberia in the north as well.

Fortunately for Japan (in contrast to Germany and Italy), sufficient rationality remained at the very center to enable the decision to surrender to be made before the destruction of Japan was complete. But the decision was so close that the emperor himself was needed to tip the scales. His voice was also needed for the final broadcast to the people.

American government opinion was so sharply divided as to whether the emperor should later be tried as a war criminal and whether the monarchy should be retained that in effect these decisions were left up to General Douglas MacArthur, Supreme Commander of the Allied Forces. He found the emperor cooperative, willing to deny his divinity, and sympathetic to Christianity. MacArthur decided to retain him on the conditions that he be "humanized," "democratized," and made merely a symbol in the new constitution.

The reevaluation of the 1930s by the Japanese people after defeat created a strong reaction against militarism and against war as a means of settling international disputes or policing other countries. That is one reason why the new constitution of 1947 with its "no war" clause (Article 9) was so readily accepted. The surprising thing is that this clause has been retained unamended in the constitution—despite the creation of full-blown military forces in literal violation of the constitution on the rationalization that defense forces do not constitute war potential.

The nightmare of the 1930s, particularly for the left, has also played a strong role in maintaining the 1947 constitution intact. That constitution, which replaced the Meiji Constitution of 1889, contains no clauses that can be used to vitiate its ample bill of rights. It provides unambiguously for freedom of speech, assembly, and organization. In order to amend it, a two-thirds vote in the Diet is necessary to launch the process and amendments must be ratified by a majority of the electorate. The voters have always returned more than a third of the Diet members as an opposition to the dominant conservative majority, even in the latter half of the 1950s, an opposition pledged to defending the constitution in toto. The conservatives called for revising the no-war clause and making the emperor the head of state rather than simply a symbol, but the left feared that any tampering with the basic law of the land could prove to be its undoing.

What this review of the 1930s tells us, however, is that the existence of a political party system is not enough to keep a country out of war and place the well-being of the people first. By and large the prewar established party leaders never compromised on the war issue, because they never committed themselves to the idea of Japan not using force when considered effective. Support for Shidehara diplomacy in the 1920s, for example, which sought to use negotiations rather than force in promoting Japan's interests in China, was not argued on the basis of principle but expediency.

The social democratic parties, however, did compromise, because in the beginning they professed internationalism and pacifism (on the basis of a tradition that went back in Japan to the Russo-Japanese War of 1904–1905 and much farther back in time in the West). Given their guilt feelings over having compromised principles, the post-1945 social democrats have shown a strong desire to make Japan a world spokesman against nuclear and conventional armament.

Japan's suppression of freedoms and increasing resort to force in the 1930s were the logical outcomes of a number of trends already clear in the 1920s. Of prime importance was the antisubversive legislation of the early Shōwa years (1925–1928). The established parties went along with passing the Peace Preservation Law of 1925 on the understanding that it would apply only to communists; moreover, its penalties were then not so severe. But as time passed, not only were they stiffened but the coverage of the law was extended by the government. A police bureaucracy developed to enforce thought control. One of its major successes was the conversion *(tenkō)* to loyalty to the emperor of two top communist leaders in 1933. Communists who did not succumb to conversion pressures (and still managed to survive with their lives and health, some after eighteen years imprisonment) were able to reap a reward of great acclaim in the immediate postwar years, which was one reason for the rapid growth of the Communist Party between 1945 and 1950.

In sharp contrast stand many of the most prominent conservative prewar politicians. Their records of active promotion of the war effort, which had brought them rewards in the 1930s, became liabilities in the immediate postwar period. The American occupation quickly instituted a purge to drive such persons out of politics and mass communications. This purge extended even to those leaders of the former Socialist Masses Party who had taken part in the Imperial Rule Assistance Association. Since the gradual blackout of freedom to criticize the trend toward war had occurred while party activity continued, one must be careful not to equate the existence of a party system with democracy. While it may be a necessary condition for a democratic polity, it is not a sufficient one.

The surrender turned out to be a liberation for the great majority of the Japanese people, just as it was a trying time of adjustment for the former military and militarists, only a few of whom, however, were actually tried in the War Crimes Tribunal. After the promulgation of the new constitution of 1947, the struggle for democracy has gone on within its broadly democratic framework.

The struggle for democracy, in my opinion, had little chance under the Meiji Constitution. It took defeat in war and a subsequent "induced revolution" to overturn the political barriers to popular rule. The bureaucratic, militarist, thought-controlled state that grew up under the aegis of the Meiji Constitution had many of the characteristics of fascism. From this point of view, the 1930s were not an aberration in terms of Japan's internal development.

Nevertheless, one can ask whether the decade was not indeed an aberration in terms of world development. Certainly the ideals of human rights for all and the abandonment of military force in international relations have been honored more in the breach than not since the setting up of the League of Nations in 1919 and the signing of the United Nations Charter in 1945. Even so, it seems to me that at least lip service to these ideals shows that they point in the direction the majority of people want the world to go. If this can be granted, Japan, while a product of her own history, turned out to be an aberration, along with Italy and Germany, in the 1930s and first half of the 1940s, in terms of world trends.

Since 1945, though she has become economically powerful, Japan can boast one of the best records in the world of honoring the democratic freedoms at home and not using force abroad. Whether she can maintain this record in the future, as the sobering experience of the 1930s recedes into the past, remains to be seen.

A Social Origin of the Second World War

Richard J. Smethurst

There is a rich literature on the origins and causes of Japan's war with China and the United States in the 1930s and 1940s. We have monographs on Japanese–American relations, army factionalism, right-wing extremists, left-wing dissidents, the thought police, the imperial house, key generals, the London Naval Conference crisis of 1930, the Manchurian Incident, the 26 February 1936 coup d'etat attempt, and even a dissertation on the impact of the world depression on the nationalistic sentiments of Tokyo blue-collar workers. Although most of these contributions are valuable, one finds two inter-related shortcomings in this scholarship: all limit their focus to the events of the 1930s, and all but one concentrate on the educated and ruling elite.

Although one must not underestimate the impact of the 1930s, the immediate prewar and wartime decade, in understanding the causes of war, scholarly overemphasis gives a one-sided view. Certainly the worldwide economic crisis, the Japanese sense of international isolation and persecution after the London Conference and Manchurian Incident, the assassinations and attempted coups d'etat between 1931 and 1936, and the machinations of various cliques within the military and civil bureaucracies and political parties played a role in leading Japan to war. No matter which of these elements was central in involving Japan in conflict and disaster, however, none could have done so without the foundations of nationalism and mobilization laid in the nineteenth century by the Home, Education, and Army Ministries. Therefore the scholar who seeks to determine the causes of the Second World War is wise to investigate the years before 1930 and the role of the nonelite—the "inarticulate" ruled—as well as that of the elite leaders in the Shōwa era. Japan's political, economic, and even intellectual authorities who made the decisions that involved Japan in war did not decide in a social and political vacuum. Rather they led Japan to war with a correct perception of popular support. This nationalistic following was born of the 1930s' sense of crisis *and* long-standing government groundwork, and it is the investigation of the latter which is my purpose here.

The social foundation on which the leaders of the 1930s operated, however, was not designed to pave the way to war; the Second World War was not inevitable. The officials who defined modern Japanese nationalism, and built the educational system to disseminate it, aimed to make Japan a unified, wealthy, and militarily powerful state in the face of severe internal and external threats. They came to their positions in the 1870s in a setting of feudal disunity, rural provincialism, economic backwardness, and potential imperialistic dismemberment by the world's powers; thus the goal of their nationalistic education was cohesion, strength, and productivity, not aggressive war. When, by the turn of the century, the world recognized Japan's equality, the new purpose became competition with the world's other powers and its accompanying empire building; the threat of war and thus the need for unity founded on nationalistic education and mobilization continued.

The ideology that these Meiji leaders and their successors propagated, which became the basic precepts of their attempts at integrated national mobilization and which in their xenophobic form carried the decade in the 1930s, was a loose amalgam of ideas that varied in importance for each believer. Among these ideals, five were prominent. First was commitment to a Puritan-like work ethic. Second was a belief in the virtue of filial piety. Third was the martial values of the premodern warrior code as reinterpreted in Field Marshal Yamagata Aritomo's "Imperial Rescript to Soldiers and Sailors" of 1882: obedience to the emperor and his officers, loyalty to emperor, nation, and law, bravery, frugality, simplicity, and the rejection of luxury. Fourth was a belief in a semidivine emperor who functioned not only as sovereign but also as national symbol descended in an unbroken line from the creating deities and founding rulers. Because of this notion of the emperor's ties to the gods, Japanese leaders propagated the idea that their monarch was unique and superior to other kings; because of their close relationship to the emperor, the Japanese people too were considered unique and superior. Fifth was an emphasis on cooperation and unity at all levels of society. The idealized patriarchal family and the rural hamlet, characterized by cooperation, conformity, hierarchy, and cohesion, were models advocated for social organizations.

Government leaders combined these ideas, many aspects of which predated even the modern era, into a coordinated if amorphous whole: it was the duty of all Japanese, under the hegemony of their semidivine ruler, to live simply, to be brave, and to work hard, cooperatively, and productively for the good of their family, village, organization, and nation.

Once the Meiji government's leaders had defined the new nationalistic synthesis to be used in building a modern state, they needed also to create organs through which to disseminate it. In the 1870–1900 period, two groups performed this function—the army and the school system. Through the conscription system, as established in 1873 by Field Marshal Yamagata, but especially as revised in 1889 by his protégé, General Katsura Tarō, thousands of young men were called to the barracks for patriotic and military training each year. After three years (and, from 1907, two years) on active duty, they returned home to the reserves and other young men replaced them. Although this indoctrination—"socialization for death," to use Tsurumi Kazuko's phrase—was effective, even at the peak of pre-1937 conscription only 15 to 20 percent of the eligibles actually served and received training.

The Meiji government's compulsory educational system brought nationalistic values to far more people (50 percent of all eligible children by 1890 and almost 100 percent at the turn of the century) but with considerably less intensity than in the army. Each student attended school, where the ideals described here became part of the curriculum, and for a required period of time learned ethical and patriotic, if not always military, lessons. But for most Japanese, at least before 1925, graduation from elementary school ended their schooling. Only 10 to 15 percent matriculated in middle school or higher. Complementary organizations were necessary to make nationalistic and military indoctrination more pervasive.

The decades around the beginning of the twentieth century brought Japan and her leaders new status, new problems, and the perception of the need for an intensified national integration. With her victories over China in 1895 and Russia a decade later, Japan received recognition as a world power and opened the way for the creation of an empire, one of the ornaments of international high status. But expanded interests and demands also required a larger army, more advanced weaponry, a higher level of technology, and greater agricultural and industrial productivity. These new needs along with the emergence of total war, a concept necessitated by new weapons and communications which in turn led to the creation of larger, "popular" armies fighting in dispersed formations, demanded national mobilization. At the beginning of this century, civil and military leaders of industrialized nations felt the need for economic, political, and spiritual integration to achieve the state's goals, and Japan's rulers, obsessed with unity, were certainly not exceptions.

New dangers as well as these new demands awakened the Japanese leaders' belief in the need for national integration. As the twentieth century began, Japan's efforts at industrialization and modernization began to result in good and bad consequences. Factories and nationalistic education brought Japan her required wealth, power, and unity; but they also produced conflict and tension. Factories created not only the tools necessary for a strong Japan but also working conditions which led to labor organization and class conflict. Between 1903 and 1907, some 107 strikes took place; by 1919, the number had burgeoned to 497; and by 1927, to 1,202. Many government and business leaders, anxious over growing labor unrest even before it was matched by rural unrest after the First World War, decided to take strong steps toward maintaining or recreating unity.

A new intellectual and political antigovernment movement, born from increasingly widespread literacy, more extensive higher education which encouraged critical thinking, and greater knowledge of Western social and political thought, shocked government leaders. In the first decade of the twentieth century, a few educated men attempted to organize laborers and gradually became more radical in their opposition to government. Their heresy of pacifism during the Russo-Japanese War led to antimonarchism and anarchy a few years later and to Comintern-led bolshevism in the 1920s. These few radical dissidents garnered most of the attention of the police, but middle-class discontent worried leaders as well. Small businessmen's opposition to the continuation of wartime taxes after 1905 grew into substantial political dissatisfaction when the government attempted to add two costly divisions to the army in 1912–1913.

In the face of these new dangers, Army, Home, and Education Ministry officials and industrial managers made great efforts to reinforce national unity and integration. Ariizumi Sadao has pointed out in his essay "The Meiji State and Mass Mobilization," in the *Iwanami Seminar History of Japan,* that between 1900 and 1910 various agencies of government established and modified various organs in an effort to combat dissidence. They expanded elementary education and revised its curriculum to educate a larger number of people with more intense nationalistic sentiments for a longer period of time. They established vocational and patriotic training centers outside the regular school system. They sponsored the Local Improvement Movement through which the Home Ministry amalgamated villages *(mura)* and merged hamlet *(buraku)* property into larger entities in order to break down long-standing loyalties and create new suprahamlet ties among farmers. They merged hamlet shrines into larger village shrines for the same purpose. They required rural residents to perform patriotic ceremonies at the elementary school or new village shrine rather than in the individual hamlets. They sponsored the formation of productive associations in each administrative village to encourage the cooperative buying of tools and fertilizer, cultivating and marketing of crops, and borrowing at the suprahamlet level. They rewrote army training manuals to introduce the idea of the family as the model for military organization. They founded or revitalized army reservist, youth, and service associations to train fourteen to forty-year-old men patriotically, morally, physically, and militarily at the local level.

Ariizumi concludes that the venture miscarried for two reasons. First, officials centered their plans on administrative towns and villages, not on hamlets where people had lived and worked together for centuries. And second, the government's efforts at building harmony around the family ignored the widening economic and social chasm between landlords and tenant farmers. (In researching the second question I find little evidence of a widening chasm.) His argument is based largely on an army report, "The Present State of the People's Conditions, Customs and Ideology in the Jurisdiction of Each Regimental Area," dated December 1913, which is housed today in the Law School of Tokyo University.

It is clear that Ariizumi is correct as far as he goes; the 1913 army document does not indicate success and for the very reason he pinpoints: failure to use the hamlet. Other evidence for later time periods reveals, however, that some government agencies, especially the army, modified their efforts at mobilization to use the cooperative and cohesive hamlet more fully and subsequently met success after 1913. In recognizing the usefulness of rural "hamlet consciousness" in mobilizing Japan, possibly a lesson learned from a reading of the military's report, the army in particular was able to train "national villagers." To understand this transformation in the thinkin, Japan's strategic planners, one must place the "People's Condition." in its historical context.

The "People's Conditions" is a seven-volume collection of reports sent in 1913 by the regimental area commanders of seventy-three of Japan's seventy-four regimental training areas to Watanabe Jōtarō, aide-de-camp to Field Marshal Yamagata and later the army's director of military education. These reports are in answer to a request by the conservative marshal, the Meiji–Taishō leader most obsessed with national unity, for information about the military preparedness and ideological state of the country; they include his underlinings and marginal comments. The documents indicate, as the following examples illustrate, that in the eyes of most officers posted at domestic area headquarters the people's spiritual preparation to serve their country was modest at best. The Kofu commander reported that farmers in Yamanashi were individualistic, unlikely to cooperate and obey, congenital rule breakers, and aggressive—traits compounded because these farmers were physically strong and mentally tough. The Toyohashi commander wrote, and Yamagata underlined, that "the wearing of purple and auburn scarves like girls is in vogue now. Not only middle-aged and old people but even youths wear them. Recently some people are even wearing scarves with patterns, and they are worn for decoration, not for warmth." Apparently these colors were too ostentatious and individualistic for the conservative leaders. The same colonel added that the youth associations in his area had not reaped a patriotic harvest because they were based on administrative, not natural, villages. The army did not think the social basis for mobilization complete in December 1913.

In the years 1913–1938 military and civilian officials, most of them long-standing associates or disciples of Yamagata who had been involved in the late Meiji ventures, modified existing organs or established new ones to use farmers' "hamlet-centric" attitudes for nationalistic purposes. Major General Tanaka Giichi is a prime example.

Tanaka, born like Yamagata a samurai in Chōshū domain but twenty-five years later, had played a key role, as a field grade officer in 1905–1910, in the introduction of familism into the army's training manuals and in the foundation of the Imperial Military Reservists' Association. Tanaka, following the lead of more orthodox army officers, had stated originally that the reservist association's major task was the preparation of ex-servicemen for wartime mobilization. The association's original list of duties emphasized military training at the administrative village level, and its membership came mostly from returned draftees. In 1910, the reservist associations' year of founding, only about 20 percent of the members were drawn from the 75 to 80 percent of eligibles who had passed the conscription physical examination but had not been called to active duty, and the army announced plans to phase them out gradually but completely.

Because of his new education experiences, a more powerful position within the army, and possibly the lessons learned from the reports gathered by his mentor, Tanaka in 1914–1915 revamped the army's system for indoctrinating fourteen to forty-year-old men. Tanaka returned from a half-year tour of Europe and the United States during which the German chief of staff, Erich von Falkenhayn, had lectured him on the benefits to national unity of local reservist organizations, and in 1915 he became a lieutenant general and vice-chief of the general staff. During the early years of the First World War, decisions were made which led to the reorganization of both the reservist and youth associations to serve the needs of patriotic education and mobilization while downgrading the local reservist branch's role in the recall of ex-soldiers to active duty.

Under Tanaka's guidance, the reservist organization fit into the existing rural framework rather than trying to change it. He and others in Tokyo central headquarters decided to use the cooperative and cohesive hamlet—and not, like their compeers in the Local Improvement Movement, attempt to submerge the hamlet and its members' local chauvinism into village-wide loyalties. Since the economic and psychological life of most rural Japanese focused on this "natural" community the army's choice seemed wise.

From this time, the reservists established hamlet subunits within their village branches and gradually broadened their duties from the village-wide patriotic and military tasks to include hamlet-level, public service functions as well. Members transplanted and harvested rice for the families of men on active duty, patrolled at the time of emergency, performed disaster aid and relief, served as volunteer firemen, carried out road, school, and irrigation canal repairs, led their community's youth association, organized and lectured to the local service club, and organized the funerals of men who died while on active duty. Then by superimposing patriotic and military educational functions at both the hamlet and village level—lectures, funerals, and ceremonies; memorial services for the war dead; movies, plays, and exhibitions; organization of activities around the annual conscription physical examination and reservists' inspection; drill and martial arts training for themselves, teenagers, and women; the greeting and comforting of servicemen—the reservist branches popularized the army and its values. Tanaka hoped that members would serve army and hamlet at the same time by carrying out both long-standing hamlet obligations and new patriotic and military activities while wearing the reservist uniform. Many local sources show that his hopes were fulfilled.

Tanaka's ideas about the selection of local reservist officials elucidate his stratagem of using hamlet custom, and the nature of the leadership in the interwar decades shows that, for the most part, he attained his goals. As Tanaka had made reservist enlistment voluntary, so too he gave local branches the right to choose their own officials. Then he proceeded to encourage villagers to elect men of high military rank *and* high local status as branch and subbranch, hamlet-level leaders. In many cases his purpose was easily achieved because the same men fulfilled both requirements; at least a middle-school education was necessary to become a reserve officer, and generally the landlord's son had the time and money to receive schooling beyond the elementary level. In other cases, however, branches chose men who did not meet both conditions. Men of high military rank were not chosen, refused to serve, or migrated to the city; and in some cases no officer lived in the village. An Army Ministry report in 1933 indicates that slightly more than half the reservist branch chiefs were not officers. But even when the branches did not select men of commissioned rank as branch officials, the local branch could fulfill the army's indoctrinal purposes by choosing men of high local status.

Tanaka, on his return from Europe in 1914, did not content himself with the mobilization of twenty- to forty-year-old men who had passed the conscription physical examination; he wanted to organize teenagers, too, and set out to do so through the unification of local youth groups. The Local Improvement Movement's effort at the indoctrination of young men ten years earlier had given the initiative for reorganization of the traditional hamlet *wakamono gumi* to the local administrative village office. In 1914 Tanaka argued for central direction and at the same time greater hamlet-level autonomy; he found Home and Education Ministry bureaucrats, some of whom were old Yamagata associates from the marshal's years as home minister, thinking similar thoughts. Their cooperation resulted in the Home and Education Ministries' publication in September 1915 of a joint order establishing the Greater Japan Youth Association with headquarters in Tokyo.

The 1915 order and the explanatory letter which followed established four basic youth guidelines: (1) the local groups were to be community service and ideologically educational organizations; (2) they were to have town or village headquarters but hamlet subdivisions; (3) they were to seek the active support of village, school, police, reservist, and religious leaders; (4) members were to have a maximum age of twenty. In 1920 the ministries raised the age limit to twenty-five to bring it in line with the hamlet custom of membership until marriage.

Although the national leadership of the youth group came from civilian ministries, and that of the reservist association from military ones (the navy played a marginal role), Tanaka helped guide both until he left the army for politics in 1925. Moreover, the branches of the two organizations were intimately interrelated at the hamlet/village level; they performed similar community service, patriotic, and military duties, often together, and the reservists provided many of the young men's leaders. They were able to do so because reservist officials and officials-to-be were the most respected twenty- to forty-year-old villagers and, further, because of the long-standing hamlet custom of young adults leading teenagers in local activities. Before the creation of the two nationally sponsored organizations, the boys and men functioned together because of the needs of hamlet cooperation; afterward they did so as youth group and reservist association members as well. A plethora of local data substantiate this conclusion about cooperation and integration.

The army achieved success in its effort at reservist-led martial training for youth within the framework of the youth associations, but local custom and bureaucratic resistance prevented a uniform system nationwide. Army hopes for total conformity, therefore, served as an impetus for the creation of a complementary organ for military and patriotic indoctrination in the closing years of the Taishō era. Army Minister Ugaki Kazushige, who was a Yamagata–Tanaka follower, Education Minister Okada Ryōhei, who had been instrumental in the establishment of the service associations under the Local Improvement Movement and was like Tanaka a national youth association adviser, and the heads of the two major political parties, one of whom was Tanaka in 1925–1926, cooperated to establish and fund a nationally uniform system of Youth Training Centers. These centers, which opened their gates for 900,000 teenage boys in July 1926, provided their students with 800 hours of extraschool education over four years: 400 hours of drill training under reservist direction and 400 hours of ethical, patriotic, physical, and academic courses taught by the elementary school's teachers. Although the centers were organized by village-wide school districts, here too it was hamlet pressure which enforced enrollment.

When the Shōwa era began in 1926, over 6 million young men were enrolled in the three organs of the Army, Education, and Home Ministries' indoctrinal system; 80 to 90 percent were villagers. With the merger of the training centers with the vocational schools and the creation of the National Defense Women's Association in the 1930s, the three ministries, especially the army, more than doubled their clientele. The military and civil efforts to create national integration by using the hamlet and then superimposing national values on local custom seems to have borne fruit between 1913 and the crises of the 1930s.

The political activities of reservists and youth group members, especially after 1930, and the obedience and fighting capacity of rural recruits during the Second World War indicate the extent of military-civil success at inculcating patriotic and military values. The reservist association became the largest and most powerful political pressure group for military and patriotic policies in the interwar decades. As early as the end of the First World War, the reservist association became involved in what can be termed political action when members helped suppress the Rice Riots in August 1918; they also helped break strikes at the Muroran Steel Plant in Hokkaido in 1917 and the Yawata Iron Works in Kyushu in 1920. Reservist activity at the time of the 15 March Incident in 1928 again reveals the organization's involvement in what outsiders must certainly have interpreted as politics. After Prime Minister Tanaka's government arrested hundreds of Communist Party members because of an alleged plot on the emperor's life, local branches met all over Japan. Tokyo area units gathered at the Yoyogi parade grounds and publicly pledged to suppress any ideology which rejected the preeminence of the emperor or threatened the national polity.

After 1930, reservist political activity became increasingly oriented toward influencing government policy. Between the London Naval Conference furor of that year and the coup d'etat attempt of February 1936, reservist members and their leaders at both the branch and the central levels made vigorous efforts to coerce the prime minister and his cabinet officers to adopt stiff defense and foreign policies. Confidential police reports catalog hundreds of meetings and thousands of participants in political pressure activities. Reservists gathered to protest the Hamaguchi cabinet's naval disarmament policy in 1930, to urge the consolidation of the Manchurian conquests and the establishment of the puppet state of Manchukuo, to "encourage" the ambassadors to the Geneva Disarmament Conference in 1931–1932, to advocate withdrawal from the League of Nations, to force the courts to give light sentences to the "sincere" assassins of Prime Minister Inukai in 1933, and to purify Japan of Professor Minobe's blasphemous thesis that the emperor was only an organ of the state and was contained within rather than being above the state. In each case local and central meetings were organized, often with both the people to be influenced and the heroes of the right in attendance; resolutions were passed and then presented to officials by letter, telegram, petition, delegation, or leader's visit. One such occurrence, a series of gatherings to influence the delegates to the abortive Geneva Disarmament Conference in December 1931, illustrates the reservists' political pressure activities.

On 10 December 1931, the head of the reservist association General Suzuki Sōroku, who had served as chief of the Army General Staff during the Tanaka cabinet, convened a conference to inspire the Geneva Conference delegates to defend Japan's national defense interests. After small groups of reservists heard lectures on Japan's national defense from officers of the two general staffs, twelve thousand reservists from all over the Japanese empire gathered at the shrine dedicated to the war dead to "stimulate" the delegates. The meeting was attended not only by the reservists and delegates but also by such luminaries as the home minister, army minister, navy minister, speakers of both houses of parliament, and the governor and mayor of Tokyo. Chairman Suzuki's speech, the climax of the meeting, was broadcast nationwide. In it he called for reservists to arouse the general public to support policies aimed at building a more powerful military establishment and eliminating any possibility of compromise at the Geneva Conference; he also added a call for a solution of the Manchurian problem along lines advocated by the Japanese army.

The Japanese representatives, thus stimulated, sailed for Europe several days later, but General Suzuki did not end his pressure, and it is here that regional reservist branches came into play. On 18 December, when the ship bearing the delegation docked at Moji, the last Japanese port of call, thousands of reservists, youth group members, and schoolchildren assembled to greet them. A large group of local reservist and military leaders then boarded the ship to remind the delegates that they must not compromise Japan's national defense and to convince them that if they failed, the Japanese people would not accept the results as they had after the London Conference the year before. The military's unwillingness to compromise meant that Japan's delegation could do little to save the conference from the impasse into which it fell in the spring of 1932 as a result of the intense rivalries and mutual fears of the European powers involved.

Another example, that of the annual celebration on Imperial Founding Day, attests to youth association members and youth training center students' participation in nationwide patriotic and political events. In 1926, superpatriot Akao Bin suggested that reservists and teenage males from the two youth groups join to commemorate 11 February, when the first emperor allegedly descended from heaven to establish imperial rule. By 1934, some 59,000 reservists, youth association members, and training center students participated in the festival in Tokyo alone. Each year they paraded from Yasukuni Shrine to the imperial palace after hearing patriotic speeches from military and civil bureaucrats and party politicians. Since the oratory was broadcast by radio nationwide, local celebrants in every city, town, and village in Japan could share in the sentiments expressed from the Tokyo podium.

This political activity seems to have had an impact. Both prime ministers between 1932 and 1936, Admirals Saitō Makoto and Okada Keisuke, commented on the frightening power of the reservists. But even if the influence of the reservists and young men did not alter national policy drastically, one fact is indisputable: by the 1930s, the Army, Home, and Education Ministries were able to mobilize thousands of young men in support of their nationalistic and military programs. The extent to which individual youths actively advocated these policies is difficult to determine—evidence drawn from interviews and questionnaires seems to indicate that they did. But whether fourteen- to forty-year-old males were fervently patriotic or simply manipulated by their leaders, it is clear that the army and its naval and civilian collaborators in the 1930s perceived a solid basis of support.

Japan's Second World War experience underlines the army–civilian success at indoctrination: most Japanese soldiers showed remarkable commitment to duty, obedience to superiors, acceptance of discipline, and bravery. Rural recruits were the best soldiers. Tsurumi Kazuko's content analysis of letters by fifty peasant soldiers and seventy-seven student soldiers, most of whom were drafted out of higher schools and universities, reveals clearly the attitudes of rural recruits. They rarely complained about their army experience and often found it as good or better than civilian life; they did not reveal doubts about the war, the legitimacy of authority, or Japan's ultimate victory; and they did not show reluctance to die. Conversely, student-soldiers were critical of all these values. Since both types of recruits went through the same coercive basic training it is clear that their varying attitudes developed before they entered the army. Differences in their home community, in their social class origin, and in their schooling must have played a role in this contrast; but the impact of indoctrination by the reservist and youth associations and youth training centers cannot be ignored. The rural recruits, subjected to more intensive patriotic and military education before conscription, served the army well; the student draftees, educated in a system which encouraged critical thinking, did not.

The Lesson
of the Textbooks

Harry Wray

In what follows I have chosen to use elementary textbooks written between 1903 and 1945 as instruments to shed light on our topic. My analysis of the government-authored history, geography, moral education, and national language textbooks issued in 1903, 1910, 1918–1922, 1933–1938, 1941, as well as the history and geography books issued in 1943–1944, has led me to conclude that the "aberration" thesis and the "logical consequence" thesis are both validated. The textbooks are indeed a mixed bag. But, simultaneously, the continuity to be found in those textbook messages, rather than their responses to transitory national and world trends, compels me to accept the stronger argument that the 1930s were in fact a logical result of the past.

Let us first use the textbooks to substantiate the view that the 1930s were an aberration. If we delete discussion of the 1910 textbook edition which does not substantiate the aberration thesis, an examination of the 1903 and 1918–1922 editions shows them to be characterized by confidence, a sense of optimism, restrained nationalism, open friendliness to the West, a cautious attitude toward militarism, and a mission of developing a great civilization.

Some examples demonstrate these qualities. A passage in the 1903 textbook expressed both admiration and a feeling of inferiority before the West:

> When we compare our conditions with the various countries of Europe and America there are still many fields in which we do not equal them. We must think about this fact and work to undertake the completion of national power.

The 1903 moral education and national language textbooks presented thirteen and three Western heroes respectively. These heroes include Lincoln, Washington, Socrates, Franklin, D'Agesseau (an eighteenth-century philosopher), and Nightingale. The four chapters on Franklin described his inquisitive and innovative spirit, orderliness, thrift, and public consciousness. Students were urged to emulate him; society and the nation would benefit indirectly. A lesson on Lincoln spoke vigorously on behalf of liberty and his Emancipation Proclamation: "Because it is evil to sell or trade human bodies and restrict their liberty, we should never forget his attitude in regard to people." The 1903 textbooks expressed liberal views regarding the constitution which seem to be a reflection of Minobe Tatsukichi's organ theory. The editors concluded one essay:

> The Constitution became the fundamental law of the country and from the Emperor above to the people below we are expected to obey it. . . . At this time the goal of deciding things by public debate was for the first time completely realized and our country became the first in Asia to have constitutional law.

Ignoring the 1910 textbook editions, we find that the 1903 and 1918–1922 textbooks do not substantiate the commonly held view that from the promulgation of the Imperial Rescript on Education of 1890 there was a straight line of textbooks inculcating the students in narrow nationalism, militarism, and shibboleths which proclaimed Japan's superiority and right to expand. Quite the contrary, the 1918–1922 national language textbooks promoted internationalism through a running theme in all the texts of "Make a Companion of the World." A lesson on "Diplomacy" in the morals textbook emphasized the need to cooperate with the League of Nations and the achievements of the Meiji and Taishō emperors in "attaining international amity and world peace." Japan's indebtedness to China, Korea, and India in the premodern period and later to the West was freely acknowledged. A final essay in the sixth-grade reader titled "The Weak and Strong Points of the Japanese Character" even criticized eight weaknesses in the Japanese mentality including a military outlook inherited from the past and a lack of international orientation. Among the defects was

> a tendency—as a result of the long isolation of the country—for Japanese to extinguish the spirit of developing abroad and foolishly to think our small country an ideal paradise.

This essay showed too that militarism was no stronger in the 1918–1922 textbooks than it was in the 1903 edition. Merchants, scholars, and others were also expressing patriotism and loyalty by advancing the technology and civilization of the country. Karasawa Tomitaro's analysis concluded that military materials were reduced to the lowest point ever in this edition of the national language textbook. In sum, then, the foregoing analysis does not seem to demonstrate a legacy of educational content promoting ultranationalism and expansion. Rather one is left incredulous that the Japan of the 1930s could be so different from the 1918–1930 period and is thereby led cozily to embrace the view that the 1930s were indeed an aberration.

Further, my content analysis of the 1933–1938 textbooks shows them to be markedly different in mood and in certain messages. Reflective of change were the essays that appeared in every moral education textbook on the obligations and expectations of "A Good Japanese." Children should:

1. Respect the national anthem.
2. Follow the example of Crown Prince Yoshihisa, who willingly gave his life in Taiwan for his country; the Emperor Meiji, who continually sacrificed his own personal pleasure for the good of the country; and those honored at the Yasukuni Shrine, who had given their lives from loyalty to the Emperor.
3. Work diligently at patriotism and loyalty in times of trouble to the country.
4. Work hard at making inventions useful to the country.
5. Be composed.

A fifth-grade textbook added that "a good Japanese" realized the importance of furthering the development of national power.

Psychological conditioning of students was promoted in the textbooks of the 1933–1938 period. Death-defying bravery was lauded. In stirring verse "The Army Flag" sang of soldiers advancing the emperor's banner "straight ahead" despite bullets which left it in tatters. The first three pages of the national language reader (published in 1933) spoke of cherry trees in blossom and used the words *"saita, saita, sakura ga saita"* (they blossomed, they blossomed, the cherry trees have blossomed). The next two pages showed pictures of toy soldiers lined up for military drill and the words "advance, advance, soldiers advance." Throughout the first three readers, pictures of cherry blossoms, the Japanese sword, and military symbols were conspicuous. An essay, "The Enlistment of Elder Brother," told the story of an entire community headed by the mayor, the school principal, the highest military representative, and a youth drill group assembling to say banzai to a departing hero off to the battlefront.

The textbooks emphasized spartan values and heroic action. Many lessons glorified military heroes (such as General Nogi Maresuke), denial of self, and ignoring of pain—the old Bushido ethic. Each citizen was told to sacrifice willingly not only to pay taxes for the military and improvement of industry but to be prepared for a real military emergency in the future when "bombs may drop like rain." An essay on "The People's Duties" taught that modern wars are total wars

> between countries, and for this reason one cannot win a victory unless the entire people fight with one mind. Consequently, the people back home have as important a job to do as the soldiers who fight at the front line. . . . In times of war, when we must accomplish the object of national defense, we must mobilize all our natural resources to defend the country.

The textbooks of 1933–1938 proclaimed a more assertive, exclusive, and totalitarian nationalism. Japan would pursue an independent policy, create a self-sufficient empire, and develop East Asia to achieve coprosperity and international peace. For the materialistic and disruptive individualism of the West she would substitute in East Asia a synthesis of a purified Western culture and the old and new cultures of East Asia. The Japanese were now a "great people" and a world power that exported manufactured goods to almost every country in the world. Her national honor had never been stained by foreign occupation.

Now State Shinto and ultranationalism were promoted. The words "god-country" appeared frequently in the textbooks. There were now eight lessons on mythology, rather than three, in the history textbook; stories on the national holidays, flag, anthem, and the greatness of the imperial family underscored Japan's uniqueness. Emphasis on Japan's past resulted in a marked increase in lessons devoted to Japan's ancient literary classics, heroes, and historic places.

A striking change in direction had developed in the textbooks of the 1930s; the aberration thesis thus seems substantiated. But a historian must not allow interpretations to force facts. At least an equally good argument can be made from the content of the textbooks that the Japan of the 1930s was also a logical outcome of what had preceded that anguished decade. Although I have maintained to this point that all textbook messages did not proceed in a straight line from 1868 or 1903 to the 1930s, further analysis indicates there may be more continuity than change in their messages, messages which had a bearing on what occurred in the 1930s.

The 1930s were to some extent a product of long-range psychological conditioning of children from at least the time of the Imperial Rescript of Education of 1890. Although I have argued here and elsewhere that the rescript was a fairly bland document interpreted loosely and with little intensity until the 1910 textbook editions, I have to disagree with Robert M. Spaulding that it was only utilized in the late 1920s and 1930s. Especially from the time of the 1910 textbook editions of the Ministry of Education, authors steadily expanded State Shinto and its vague glittering slogans, such as "Purifying the *Kokutai*." More important, from 1910 onward textbook lessons from the first through the sixth grade taught that loyalty to the emperor and filial piety were one and the same and that the ancestral will was obedience to imperial will. The individual was nothing; the will of the emperor and the *kokutai* were everything.

A lesson in a 1910 sixth-grade textbook, utilizing the emperor's rescript to the military in 1882, clearly tried to inculcate the view that each subject was a soldier:

> We look up to the emperor as the generalissimo. The citizens of this period are all soldiers and should have the intention to be a soldier. In 1882 the Imperial Rescript to the military was decreed and it is a document we cannot ignore for even a moment.
>
> The five articles [the military rescript of 1882] should become part of our everyday living and not be observed for the first time when we become a member of the military.

Another example from the same 1910 textbook is an extremely jingoistic poem, "A Soldier at the Front," in which every member of the family had a word of farewell for the young man leaving for the battlefront. The soldier replied:

> Goodbye, goodbye! Mother and father goodbye. . . .
> I will give my life bravely
> and attack the enemy of my country.
>
> Gallantly, bravely, the soldier leaves home,
> The whole house encouraging him.

The spirit of courage goes with him and others remain behind—
A separation of courage, tenderness, and manliness.

The textbooks of 1918–1922 present a paradox. While promoting international cooperation they intensified the message of complete loyalty and sacrifice to emperor, nation, and the *kokutai*. A story on the Forty-seven Rōnin quoted the leader Oishi Yoshio as saying: "Obligations to one's lord are heavier than ten thousand mountains; one's life is lighter than a hair." The history textbook was the boldest in promoting the kamikaze mentality. The following account tells of the effort of Taira no Shigemori (1138–1179) to dissuade his father from treating the Imperial House in a shameful manner:

> Now, if we forget our obligations and make light of imperial authority, divine punishment will be directed upon us immediately and our family shortly will be destroyed. If you do not take notice, father, I shall lead an army and protect the retired emperor ruling from the cloister; however, I cannot bear to oppose my father. Consequently, if you are determined to carry out your plan, first cut off my head.

The textbooks taught the myth of Japan's divine origins and the historical relationship between the imperial line and the Japanese subjects as facts. The early period of Japanese history was for the first time entitled "The Age of the Gods," and stories of mythical names and events not included before were now presented. Motoori Norinaga, a Tokugawa scholar, was praised because his research "tried to make clear that our *kokutai* raised our country above all other countries." A divine wind *(kamikaze)* was credited for having saved Japan from the Mongol invasions of the thirteenth century. A poem, "Great Japan," boasted:

> We seventy million Japanese revere the Emperor as a God
> And serve him as a parent.
> Great Japan,
> We have never once been defeated,
> And with the passage of time
> The glory of the country shines ever more.

A fourteen-line essay on "Yasukuni Jinja" repeated the phrase "for the emperor and the country" three times. Three brothers who died and a fourth who was eager to give his life during the Russo-Japanese War were praised.

The ideal expressed in the textbook edition from 1910 was not only that of unflagging loyalty but the notion that self-interest, whether individual or corporate, was not permissible. Self-interest was equated with disloyalty. The ideal taught now was of all 90 million Japanese living together in harmony under a benevolent father-emperor—the family state. The Japanese people should promote the *kokutai* and imperial will by denying self-interest and performing unflinching filial obedience to the emperor.

This concept, taught not only in the nation's schools but also in the mass media on an increasing scale from 1890, achieved three objectives. First, it created a populace that by the 1930s believed the ideal; some of them would become the nation's kamikazes. After all, 83 percent of Japanese subjects before the war only had a sixth-grade education and the mass media provided few countervailing messages. Second, the teaching of the *kokutai* ideal created a climate in which the masses, perhaps to some extent even the elites, became the victims of their own propaganda. They came to accept the view of the ultranationalists and the militarists that the political parties, *zaibatsu*, radical parties, and labor unions were interested only in self-interest. Since they were not true to the spirit of the *kokutai*, their suppression was considered acceptable. In contrast, as Spaulding writes, the military services were viewed as "above self-interest." As they were pure and loyal instruments of the emperor their influence in the government seemed perfectly acceptable. Third, the increasing emphasis of each textbook edition on the greatness and uniqueness of Japan created a psychology which assumed Japan's superiority over other Asian nations and demanded the autonomy of imperial will abroad as well as within the country. In these senses, Japan in the 1930s was definitely a logical outcome of what had preceded.

There is another area of textbook content where the expansion of the 1930s was indebted to the previous forty years. I am speaking here of the textbooks proclaiming an ever-widening mission in East Asia. Beginning with the 1910 textbooks, Japan's mission was to accomplish in East Asia what she had already achieved at home. Merchants were encouraged to look to China as a market where they could fulfill their duty "to develop foreign trade and increase their nation's wealth." Other countries and regions in East Asia were mentioned with increasing frequency.

Through a condescending interpretation of conditions and events in Taiwan, Korea, Manchuria, Sakhalin, and China the textbooks promoted an atmosphere conducive to future citizens' acceptance of a

Japanese mission to civilize East Asia. A letter from a settler in Sakhalin encouraged future settlement in both Taiwan and Karafuto (Sakhalin) for the "enlightenment and civilization" of those areas. A poem entitled "Fifty Million Countrymen" contained these stanzas:

> The God-given mission of peace in East Asia rests on the shoulders of such a people as we.
> Japan has a heavy responsibility in advancing the civilization of the East.

The "peace of East Asia," "historical intimacy," and "geographic propinquity" were phrases often used by the Japanese government to justify its actions in the 1930s. But the Ministry of Education's Editorial Division had been using such arguments since 1910 for Korea and Manchuria. Korea, Manchuria, and China's geographic propinquity necessitated Japan's interest; Japan had an obligation to preserve peace in East Asia. The textbooks complained that the Chinese failed to recognize Japan's peaceful intentions. The Chinese were smug, insincere, guileful in their diplomacy, and "ignominious in their military affairs."

Despite Japan's general attitude of international cooperation and devotion to multilateral diplomacy in the 1920s her attitude with respect to China and East Asia differed. This divergence is reflected even in the 1918–1922 textbooks which, in turn, inherited the message of the 1910 textbooks that Japan had special interests and special responsibilities in East Asia. The former now taught attitudes regarding Korea and Manchuria that could easily be utilized in the 1930s to justify Japanese goals in China Proper. Korea's failure to carry out real reforms had created a power vacuum; hence her annexation by Japan not only improved internal conditions in Korea and made the base of peace in East Asia more secure but was an action with which the Korean people and emperor allegedly concurred. Japan's growing interest in Manchuria was expressed by extensive treatment in the textbooks. Japanese emigration and technical and economic assistance had contributed to a high level of development of Manchuria. The Manchurian and Japanese economies were mutually beneficial and close ties had developed between the two. Japan's long historical relationship with China and Chinese cooperation had allowed Japanese bases in the Kwantung Peninsula and their operation of the South Manchurian Railway and other enterprises.

As Japan's interests in China and her concern about what was happening intensified, the 1918–1922 textbooks increasingly advanced her claims. The authors advocated a cooperative policy which involved keeping out the West, China's acquiescing to programs promoting greater Sino-Japanese trade, and Japanese development of China. The more nationalistic history textbook criticized China for her policy and behavior in Korea before 1894, her poor military showing in the Sino-Japanese war, and her insincerity and weakness as a nation. Little by little the textbooks were advancing a "Monroe Doctrine for East Asia"—a doctrine which the generation studying the 1918–1922 textbooks would feel justified in supporting by the 1930s. To preserve peace in East Asia Japan had joined an alliance with England, had fought Russia in 1904–1905, and during the First World War had joined the conflict because "German ships threatened peace in the Far East." Japan could not allow any other nation to endanger China's integrity or Japan's interests.

Thus we see that this essay has turned full circle. At first the striking differences between the textbook content of the 1903 and 1918–1922 editions and those of the 1930s seemed to demonstrate that the 1930s were in fact an aberration. Yet I have retreated from this conclusion by noting that an examination of the same textbooks, along with the 1910 edition, ferrets out two strong trends that lead to an opposite conclusion—namely, that the direction traveled in the 1930s resulted from attitudes, values, objectives, and roles taught from at least 1910.

I believe that future historians examining the 1930s will arrive at similarly divided conclusions. Their conclusions, like mine, will depend not only on the phenomenon examined but also on their philosophy of history. Perhaps no other nation is more receptive to outside influences and trends than Japan. But is it too much to suggest that the student of modern Japan who concentrates on trends may very likely conclude that the 1930s were an aberration while the student who concentrates on the core and continuity of Japan will conclude that the 1930s were a logical consequence of preceding Japanese history? History may be given a shove, but it rarely suffers from avalanches.

PART X

Japan's Foreign Policy in the 1930s: Search for Autonomy or Naked Aggression?

THE FOLLOWING ESSAYS continue the analysis of Japan in the 1930s with special reference to foreign policy intentions and results, which may not have been the same thing. To have obtained the broadest possible range of views on this subject we should perhaps have included those of David Bergamini, who saw the whole epoch as an "imperial conspiracy" for world domination fomented by Emperor Hirohito and a clique of villains (see *Japan's Imperial Conspiracy*), and those of James Crowley who saw the central theme as a "quest for autonomy" (see *Japan's Quest for Autonomy*). The contributors to this section are well aware of the views expressed in these opposing presentations, however, and they attempt here to reconsider the scene with more light and less heat than was generated by the controversies surrounding these two works in the early 1970s.

Various Japanese problems and perspectives are considered against the backdrop of international events of the 1930s. Among them are Japan's drive for self-sufficiency, disillusionment with the post-Versailles international system, and internal politics in which factionalism became endemic. The possibility that Japanese leadership, especially in Southeast Asia, had a positive side is also considered.

—HILARY CONROY

Japan's Drive
to Autarky

Michael A. Barnhart

The question posed in this part of the book can be answered in
two ways. Subjects of the Japanese empire would have seen their
country's foreign policy as an attempt to attain the requisites for its
survival. Most Americans observing the course of that policy bluntly
called it aggression. To discover why two peoples viewed the events of
the 1930s in such different terms, it is necessary to find out what sort
of perceptual filters they were using while observing those events. I
contend that the lessons of the First World War—and the international environment created by that war—led directly to a second conflict in Asia as well as in Europe. Further, the lessons learned by Japanese policymakers were radically different from those learned by the
leaders of the West.

The First World War convinced most Westerners that modern war
had become unthinkable. Much of Europe lay ravaged. Revolutions
rocked the already disturbed societies of Russia and Germany. Even
for the victors of the war, the cost in money and men had been staggering. The result was a peace movement of unprecedented breadth
and intensity. At base, this movement had three components. All
three had to be embraced by the great powers if a new order of international relations was to be created. First, the powers had to dis-
arm, for the very possession of weapons led to the temptation to use
them. Second, the powers had to forswear the use of force itself as an
instrument of foreign policy. Third, the nations of the world had to
avoid any interference in the development and domestic affairs of
their neighbors, since little would be gained if intrigue merely replaced the use of force.

In the years after the First World War, the United States joined actively in this movement's pursuit of peace. It convened a naval arms

limitation conference at Washington in 1921 that led to agreements sharply reducing the competition in armaments among Britain, Japan, and the United States. That same conference saw nations with an interest in Asia sign the Nine-Power Treaty pledging respect for China's right to develop itself without molestation. Later in the decade, American Secretary of State Frank Kellogg played a central role in inviting all powers to sign the Pact of Paris to outlaw war itself—except in self-defense.

While the conflict of 1914–1918 contributed to a strong peace movement in the West, it inspired great alarm among Japanese leaders, especially in the military. In all Asia, only Japan had managed to escape colonial or semicolonial status at the hands of the expanding West. She had succeeded in maintaining her independence.

The lessons of the First World War, however, indicated that perhaps the Meiji oligarchs had erred. The Imperial Army had been modeled after the land forces of Germany, since those oligarchs had judged Germany's to be the best army in all Europe. Why, then, had Germany lost the war? Feverish research and long consideration produced a disturbing answer. The German army had not been defeated by Allied military prowess on the field of battle. Instead, the German nation had succumbed to the slow strangulation of the Allied naval blockade. Deprived of food, fuel, and other resources of modern war, the mighty German military machine had come to a creaking halt.

The implications for Tokyo were clear. Japan was even less self-sufficient in the resources needed for warfare in 1920 than Germany had been in 1914. If Japan was to maintain her great power status, perhaps even her independence, won at such great cost since the Meiji Restoration, Japanese self-sufficiency was imperative. This goal could be achieved by two means. Japan had to acquire control over the resources of territories outside her pre-1920 empire. And that empire needed to reorder its own economic structure so that those resources could be used with greatest efficiency.

These two differing views of the lessons of the First World War initially collided in September 1931 when elements of Japan's Kwantung Army began to occupy Manchuria. Publicly, Japanese spokesmen claimed that the occupation was forced by China's inability to maintain peace and order in the region. Privately, many Japanese leaders welcomed the occupation as a step toward autarky and the continuation of their country's survival as a power.

Japan's explanations failed to convince many Americans, including Secretary of State Henry Stimson. To them it was clear that Japan had resorted to the use of force in interfering with China's peaceful domestic development. When private citizens began to call for economic sanctions against Japanese aggression, Stimson was inclined to agree, at least to the bluff of sanctions in the hope that Tokyo would retreat, but President Herbert Hoover refused, arguing that sanctions could lead to war. Blocked on this front, Stimson instead announced that his government would refuse to recognize any territorial changes made as a result of the application of force. America might not have been ready to prevent Japanese wrongdoing, but neither would Washington assent to it.

In the years after the occupation of Manchuria, the Japanese consolidated their hold on that region, developed its resources, and began to extend their influence into the provinces of North China. The United States looked on with dismay—dismay that briefly turned to alarm in 1934 after a spokesman for the Japanese Foreign Office, Amau Eiji, announced that Japan alone would be responsible for maintaining stability and peace in East Asia. Western newsmen quickly dispatched stories of the new Asian Monroe Doctrine, an analogy that deeply angered Secretary of State Cordell Hull. No one could quarrel with peace and stability, Hull maintained, but it seemed odd that Japan had resorted to bluster, threat, and intrigue in China to achieve these worthy aims.

During the mid-thirties, the second element of the attempt to achieve self-sufficiency gained momentum in Japan. Under the guiding hand of Ishiwara Kanji, an army officer who had been instrumental in the seizure of Manchuria, a group of officers and civilians drafted a five-year plan to expand Japan's productive—hence war-making—capacity. Ishiwara's radical plan called for nearly complete governmental control over all major industries. It was too radical for some. Even the army minister found it overly bold and suggested amendments. When Prince Konoe Fumimaro became prime minister in June 1937, his new cabinet faced a decision. Should either plan be adopted? Should the cabinet call a special session of the Diet for immediate approval or wait? Konoe, after some hesitation, elected to ask for a session in late July. In the meantime his finance minister, Ikeda Seihin, cooperated with Ishiwara and the army minister to work out a proposal acceptable to military and industrial circles alike.

The delay was fatal to Ishiwara's hopes. On 7 July 1937, Japanese forces exchanged fire with Chinese troops near the Marco Polo Bridge at the outskirts of Beijing. Despite Ishiwara's fierce opposition, the government authorized the mobilization of the empire's military forces. As Japan geared for war, battlefield successes mounted. Chiang Kai-shek's capital city of Nanking fell on 13 December. But Chiang's regime did not. Vowing to fight to the death, the Chinese Nationalist leader had drawn Japan into a Vietnam-like quagmire just as Ishiwara had feared. After that summer, Japan's precious resources would go to the fields of China rather than to the infant factories and mills in Japan. Her dependence on the United States and other Western nations for the sinews of modern warfare increased rather than declined. Any realization of autarky seemed doomed.

In America, Japan's actions only confirmed her image as a barbaric nation bent on conquering all Asia. Sentiment rapidly grew among the public for utilizing the United States' superior economic position to constrain Japanese plans. By the end of August, newspapers such as the *Washington Post* were running front page headlines which read "American Scrap Iron Plays Grim Role in Far Eastern War." Henry Stimson, in 1937 a private but still influential citizen, penned a letter to the *New York Times* in October urging his countrymen to end their nation's trade in war materials with Japan. One month later, the State Department under Secretary Cordell Hull sent representatives to an international conference in Brussels called under the Nine-Power Treaty. There economic sanctions against Japan were discussed, but too many Westerners believed that Japan would attack Dutch, British, and perhaps American possessions in East Asia if pressure were applied. No action was taken.

There was plenty of action on Capitol Hill in Washington, however. By the middle of 1939, no fewer than four resolutions were before Congress proposing embargoes of war-related exports to nations violating the Nine-Power Treaty. A vocal "American Committee for Non-Participation in Japanese Aggression," formed in August 1938, conducted a vigorous press, letter, and petition campaign to force President Roosevelt to cut off shipments of supplies to Tokyo. Even inside the normally cautious State Department, studies of Japan's economic vulnerability began to proliferate.

Under such unremitting pressure, Hull began to adopt a more punitive policy toward Japan—a policy advocated by hardliners in the State Department. By July 1938 the State Department had announced a "moral embargo" on the export of airplanes or aeronautical equipment. Not wishing to condone the bombing of innocent Chinese civilians, State later acted to ensure that no technical rights or patents for processing aviation gasoline fell into Japanese hands. But these restrictions were insubstantial. In July 1939 Hull opened the way for sanctions on a significant scale by proclaiming his government's intent to abrogate the American-Japanese Treaty of Commerce and Navigation. Decisive action was deferred until a year later when Congress passed the National Defense Act. Roosevelt, now legally empowered to ban the export of any material deemed necessary for America's defense, began a long series of increasing restrictions on shipments to Japan.

The Japanese reacted to these policies with a mixture of dismay and anger. As the conflict with China escalated, the Diet rapidly approved mobilization measures of wide scope and great power. A National General Mobilization Law pointed the way to a controlled national economy. Yet all of this was too late. Members of the Cabinet Planning Board, the agency charged with developing the means to realize autarky, believed as early as the spring of 1938 that the China War was causing the breakdown of their five-year plan to expand productive power. They knew that Japan's quest for economic independence grew increasingly impossible every day that the war with Chiang continued. But negotiations to end the conflict were out of the question after Konoe's public declaration of the end of Sino-Japanese talks on 16 January 1938. The Nationalists had to be forced to capitulate.

When Japanese planners considered this thorny problem, they came face-to-face with a dilemma. To them, it seemed that Chiang only wanted to survive until increasing Anglo-American aid (and eventual participation in the fighting) rescued him. If this were true, then Japan should isolate Chiang from the West. But to do so entailed increasing the pressure on Chiang and hence enlarging the scope of the war. This in turn might bring the Western powers into open conflict with Tokyo, just as Chiang hoped.

These deliberations resulted in a decision to seek stronger ties with Germany to deter further Western aid to China. Konoe, after a final abortive attempt to make peace with the Nationalists, resigned in January 1939. Even before, in August 1938, the Five Ministers Conference, an "inner" cabinet, had resolved to strengthen the German-Japanese Anti-Comintern Pact signed in 1936. Under Konoe's successor, Baron Hiranuma, negotiations with the Germans proceeded. They did not get very far. Hitler desired an alliance directed against Britain and France. Japan wanted only the Soviet Union in the category of potential enemies. The Imperial Navy, acutely aware of its need for American iron and oil for its building plans and daily operations, refused to accept any terms which might have led to an Anglo-American combination against Japan. Hiranuma concurred. The talks were summarily ended in August 1939 when Germany stunned Japan by signing a nonaggression pact with the Soviet Union.

After war broke out in Europe in September, Britain was no longer in a position to aid Chiang significantly. When Hitler's armies overran Belgium, Holland, and France in a spring 1940 offensive, Japan's position in the Orient seemed stronger than ever. French Indochina could look to no mother country for support; nor could the far greater prize of the oil-rich Netherlands East Indies. Perhaps Japan's dreams of becoming truly self-sufficient could be realized. Only the United States remained to prevent Japan from completely isolating Chiang, defeating him, and resuming her quest for final economic security.

The result of Japan's new position was reflected in the decisions of a conference held in July 1940 to mark Konoe's return to power. These decisions, which were quite detailed, revealed in remarkably blunt terms Japan's need to seize the moment to render herself independent of foreign nations. They directed Japanese policy increasingly toward the "Southward Advance" idea officially broached by the navy four years earlier. This advance did not have to be warlike. Already in May the Japanese Foreign Ministry had commenced negotiations with the East Indies' authorities to secure shipments of oil, tin, rubber, and other strategic materials. By September the imperial government had signed a military convention with Vichy French authorities in Indochina enabling the Japanese army to occupy the northern half of that colony. The cabinet, encouraged, resolved to secure the Netherlands East Indies' recognition of Tokyo's political and economic predominance over East and Southeast Asia. It also resolved to again seek ties with Germany in order to cow America and keep her out of the European and Chinese wars.

The government's decision to recommence alliance talks led to renewed discussion over the advantages of an agreement with Germany. After the accord had been reached, Japan's privy councillors had to ratify it. During the ensuing debates, these senior statesmen questioned whether the pact would give the United States an opportunity to redouble its increasing economic pressure. Supporters of the alliance in the Foreign Ministry assuaged these fears by arguing that it would ensure the empire's control over the plentiful resources of the Netherlands East Indies with full German acquiescence. Afterwards the United States would not dare to challenge the rest of Japan's bid for economic independence. On 27 September 1940, Japan formally joined the Axis Powers.

This move severely strained America's relations with Japan, which had deteriorated further by the following July. On the second of that month, an imperial conference decreed that Japan would invade southern Indochina even if this meant war with Britain and the United States. When imperial forces executed this directive, American proponents of total economic sanctions against Japan finally gained the upper hand. Stimson, back in government as secretary of war, and Henry Morgenthau, secretary of the treasury, pressed hard for the freezing of Japanese assets in the United States. The move would cut off Japanese trade with America. Roosevelt acceded by the end of the month. America now subjected Japan to the full pressure of economic warfare.

After July, matters came to a head rapidly. Japanese leaders no longer were able to rely on American shipments of badly needed raw materials. They had to make a final bid for autarky or else submit to American terms. Viewed from Tokyo, these terms were harsh indeed. The Americans demanded prompt and complete evacuation of China by all Japanese armed forces; even Tokyo's position in Manchuria could not be guaranteed. Japan asked for a gradual and incomplete pullout. Washington was adamant: until the last Japanese soldier left Chinese soil, America would not resume commercial contact with the empire.

Konoe desperately wanted to avoid a showdown. He suggested a conference between Roosevelt and himself. The American president was initially interested, but Hull and his advisors were not. Roosevelt declined and Konoe resigned. In mid-October General Tojo Hideki took the reins of government. Soon after, Navy Minister Nagano noted his service's ever decreasing stockpiles of petroleum. A decision for war or for what amounted to surrender had to be made quickly. The cabinet, after much debate, agreed to submit two final proposals to Washington. Neither promised prompt or total evacuation of China.

When Hull rejected these offers brusquely on 26 November, the Tojo government gave final authorization for the navy's attack on Pearl Harbor. Five American battleships were sent to the bottom to protect the flow of oil and other resources through Japan's Greater East Asia Coprosperity Sphere. Four years later, that sphere was an empty dream and Japan a nation in ruins.

It is possible, then, to interpret Japan's expansion onto the continent of Asia as a rational search for order and independence or, alternatively, as stark aggression. Readers may judge for themselves. My own verdict is that Japan, by the close of the First World War, lacked the resources which were increasingly essential to achieve or retain great power status. She had little oil and few iron deposits; nor was she blessed with other necessary resources in copious or even adequate amounts. To her military leaders, and to enough civilians to matter, the situation was intolerable. It had to be remedied. Rather than accommodate themselves to the new realities of power in the world after Versailles, these Japanese leaders chose to alter those realities and secure the needed resources and industrial base for their country. They pursued this course by means of expansion abroad and a reordering of the economic structure at home. The expansionist policy required that Japan violate many of the treaties which the war-weary nations had drawn up to spare themselves further suffering. It caused Japan to be called an aggressor nation. Economic reforms made Japan appear to Western observers as a nation on the verge of totalitarianism, fit company for Hitler. Rather than yield up China to Japanese "aggression," America chose to resist by invoking her economic power of the interwar years and applying sanctions of vast scope against Japan.

Some may contend that no Japanese leader could have advocated submitting to such blatant American pressure and still survive politically. In 1940 and 1941 this was no doubt true. But twenty or even ten years earlier, Japanese leaders could have committed their country to a course of adjusting to the new economic environment, accepting Japan's dependence on the West, and altering her foreign policies accordingly. Instead Japan followed a policy of autarky which led her to Pearl Harbor. Since 1945, Japan has accepted these realities of economic power. If her leaders had done the same after the First World War, perhaps the specters of Hiroshima and Nagasaki would not still haunt us all today.

The Great Divorce: Japan and Universalism Between the World Wars

Thomas W. Burkman

In 1919 a June wedding took place. In the Hall of Mirrors Uncle Sam, with all the dignity of a Presbyterian cleric, intoned the marriage covenant. In the company of forty other states Japan was enjoined to the League of Nations.

It was an arranged marriage beset by conflict from the first encounter. Japan was unhappy with the nuptial contract and had threatened to break the engagement a few weeks before the ceremony. Though most Japanese were proud of the status achieved by tying into a prominent family, others had to bite their tongues when the minister asked any who objected to the union to show cause. One neighbor, the Soviet Union, was not invited to the wedding and another, China, canceled out at the last minute. Most disconcerting of all, shortly after administering the vows the minister left the faith.

The war years preceding Versailles had brought Japan immense material benefits. With minimal sacrifice Japanese forces had dislodged German troops from the Kiaochow leased territory in China's Shandong province and captured the Marshall, Caroline, and Mariana Islands from the kaiser's Pacific squadron. With skillful diplomatic maneuvering Japan had gained the secret commitment of the European allies as well as China itself to support Japanese acquisition of these areas when the spoils were divided after the war. A wartime economic boom ensued as Japan provided war matériel for the Russian czar and consumer goods for East Asian markets formerly supplied by the British, French, and Germans. Far removed from the suffering of the major warfronts, the Japanese paid no attention to the statesmen and peace societies in Europe and North American campaigning for the creation of permanent international peacekeeping machinery. The press took scant notice of American President Woodrow Wilson's Fourteen Points calling for open diplomacy, the territorial integrity of states, disarmament, and the establishment of a society of nations. The Foreign Ministry approached the postwar peace conference with an eye to gaining formal international confirmation of Japan's wartime acquisitions and elevated status.

In the final weeks before the opening of the Paris Peace Conference Japan came to the realization that the talk about a League of Nations was not mere wartime propaganda. Some optimistic intellectuals of the "Taishō democracy" school openly heralded the coming league as the touchstone of human progress and urged the government to fall in step. Western-influenced diplomats in the Foreign Ministry as well as trade-hungry business figures promoted Japanese participation as a means to assure cooperative relations with the Anglo-American powers.

Most Japanese, however, had grave misgivings about the League of Nations as an international framework within which Japan could pursue her national interests. They realistically viewed the League Covenant as an instrument designed to ensure the perpetuation of the territorial status quo delineated by the allied victors. National boundaries were to be sacrosanct; aggression was to be interdicted by economic and military sanctions to restrain guilty parties. Moreover, league-sponsored disarmament programs would assure that national armaments remained below the level of aggressive war capability. Japanese diplomats outwardly applauded these arrangements. But at the same time they perceived Japan's position relative to the major Western powers as that of a have-not nation for which the status quo meant perpetual disadvantage and second-class ranking. Even those Japanese leaders who espoused a cooperative internationalism regarded as just and proper Japan's policy to expand her economic opportunity and political influence on the Asian mainland, albeit by peaceful means. A young Home Ministry bureaucrat named Konoe Fumimaro voiced in a nationalistic magazine his apprehension that the Anglo-Saxon nations, under the guise of the league and disarmament, were moving to impose a status quo order simply to perpetuate their own predominance. He warned that unless the peace conference recognized racial equality and opened all colonies to free trade, Japan might someday be compelled like Imperial Germany to break loose from her confinement. Konoe, along with virtually all Japanese, believed than any world order based on justice would end racial discrimination between states and recognize Japan's special interests in Manchuria. His complaints were reinforced when the principle of racial equality which Japan sought to inject into the League Covenant was rejected by the powers at the peace conference.

If the Japanese were so uneasy about the league, why did Japan submit to membership and its disciplines? After all, another power with regional proclivities, the United States, exercised its option to remain aloof from the organization during the entire two and a half decades of its existence. The key to Japan's submission lies in her leaders' realistic perception of Japan's subordinate position as a secondary power. Though Japan had formally entered the ranks of major powerhood at the turn of the century, she could not exercise her might on a global scale as could Great Britain and the United States. Astute senior statesmen and their protégés who had guided Japanese foreign policy since the Meiji era shared with the Hara Kei cabinet the conviction that the worst danger for Japan was diplomatic isolation from the Western monoliths. This pragmatic approach was rooted in a broader principle known as *taisei junnō*, or "conformity to the world situation." The League of Nations as it existed on paper in the spring of 1919 mirrored the prevailing power structure to a degree unsurpassed by an international organization since. In addition the peace conference at an early point decided that former German colonies, including the Pacific islands, would be entrusted to league members as mandates. Thus the securing of Japan's wartime gains presumably required cooperation in the global order.

Japan's decision after the First World War to conform to the peace program of the major powers bears a normative relationship to her generally conciliatory role in the world community during the 1920s. This stance might appropriately be termed "international accommodationism." Soon after Versailles the Army and Navy Ministries began internal studies on the degree of disarmament the services could bear and the government adhered to a general naval disarmament program at the Washington Conference of 1921–1922. The public in general supported league-instituted disarmament efforts until 1930. Japan cooperated sincerely in efforts such as the Geneva Protocol to strengthen the league's peacekeeping machinery. The Foreign Ministry sent its ablest diplomats—like Ishii Kikujirō—to the sessions of the League Council and Assembly and helped staff the Secretariat with such talent as Nitobe Inazō. It even provided financial backing to the ostensibly private Japan League of Nations Association to disseminate knowledge of the league among the Japanese public at large. In 1928–1929 Japan joined other members and the United States in signing and ratifying the Kellogg–Briand Pact renouncing war as an instrument of national policy.

In the spirit of international accommodationism Japan in the 1920s avoided military adventurism while vigorously promoting economic expansion on the mainland, particularly in Manchuria. Japan agreed to the abolition of the Anglo-Japanese Alliance and accepted in its place the multilateral Four-Power and Nine-Power Treaties at the Washington Conference. She relied upon Western countries for military and industrial technology and capital for Manchurian investments. Economic growth was substantial, free trade policies paid off, and the United States was Japan's largest trading partner. The international features of the Japanese economy provided a healthy base for a cosmopolitan world view.

Even while Japan was acting as a conscientious member of the global community doubts persisted concerning the viability of universal order. The stubborn refusal of the United States Senate to ratify the covenant, coupled with the nonmembership of Germany (until 1926) and the Soviet Union (until 1934), made it obvious that the League of Nations was not universal in scope. Reference to the league as a European club was common in the Japanese press. In the sensitive area of race relations, American league advocates in the League to Enforce Peace flatly rejected the Japan League of Nations Association's proposal that the two peace societies conduct a joint inquiry into the troublesome immigration problem. Anti-Japanese discrimination in California, capped by the exclusion of Orientals by the 1924 U.S. Immigration Act, confirmed the Japanese suspicion that universal morality was a myth. Concrete political arrangements such as the Washington treaties seemed much more dependable than covenants based on vague and untested concepts of justice.

Events in the West in the 1920s convinced realistic Japanese thinkers that even in Europe the powers were prone to circumvent the league in matters of vital self-interest. The 1923 Corfu Incident involving league members Italy and Greece was settled by a conference of ambassadors rather than league machinery because Italy refused to accept the league's jurisdiction in the case. In 1925 a set of significant political, military, and territorial accommodations with Germany was concluded by Britain, France, Italy, and Belgium at the Locarno Conference. Though elaborate efforts were made to incorporate the Locarno Pacts into the league system, it was obvious that the European powers were presenting the league with a *fait accompli* and using it as window dressing for understandings forged elsewhere. The league was clearly secondary in the European power game.

The conclusion of the Locarno Pacts gave Japan occasion to assess the effectiveness of existing mechanisms for world peace and order. When the press compared the league to Locarno, the Versailles order invariably came up wanting. The *Osaka Mainichi* proclaimed Locarno "the greatest historical event since the downfall of the great Napoleon." The *Hochi* called it "an epoch-making diplomatic document far more forceful than the treaty of peace." The model of Locarno seemed preferable to the league order because it was political rather than moralistic, concrete rather than idealistic, and regional rather than universalistic.

The late 1920s brought new challenges to Japanese security and vital interests, challenges which the League of Nations was unwilling or unable to face. China was awakening to modern nationalism. This movement culminated in Chiang Kai-shek's successful Northern Expedition in 1927–1928 which united the fragmented republic. Patriotic feelings were increasingly expressed through anti-Japanese propaganda and economic boycotts. The Soviet Union was growing in military strength and Japan feared communist ideological influence upon the Chinese nationalist movement. In 1929 the U.S. dollar collapsed, silk exports to the United States declined precipitously, and the economic props supporting international accommodationism were irrevocably weakened.

In response to these threats frightened voices in Japan called for an autonomous diplomacy to secure reliable markets, dependable sources of raw materials, and a defensible regional order amenable to Japanese leadership. Japan's military action in Manchuria in 1931 and subsequent establishment of the puppet state of Manchukuo brought Japan for the first time into direct confrontation with the league. The Assembly on 24 February 1933 condemned Japanese aggression by a vote of forty-two to one. The Japanese delegation walked out, never to return to Geneva. Japan's thirteen-year marriage to the league order ended in a dramatic divorce.

Few tears were shed in public for the dissolved union. The Japanese press uniformly placed the onus for the rupture on the league, which, it asserted, had capitulated to Chinese propaganda and the pressures of smaller states. The league had failed, journalists claimed, to deal objectively with the unique realities of the Japan–Manchukuo relationship. The government correctly calculated that the league would stop short of applying economic and military sanctions against Japan. By the time Japan's withdrawal became effective two years later, a "Manchuria boom" had stimulated an economic recovery while other industrialized nations remained in the torpor of depression. Japan's combined trade with China and Manchukuo surpassed that with the United States. A lessened sense of economic dependence on the West underlay a strident Japanese attitude at the abortive London Naval Conference in 1935. Liberal intellectuals by and large adjusted pragmatically to the new environment and wrote off the league as an anachronism and universalism as a corpse.

Universalism in the mid-1930s was impracticable at best. Germany too bolted the league seven months after Japan, bringing to naught the Geneva Disarmament Conference. To William E. Borah Japan's departure was an act of realism. "Japan withdrew," said the outspoken senator from Idaho, "because she was more candid in this matter than some other nations which still remain in the league but pay no attention to the obligations." The powers abandoned free trade and in its place erected tariff barriers and bloc economies to insulate themselves from outside competition.

Still conscious of the dangers of diplomatic isolation, Japanese intellectuals and policymakers sought the creation of an East Asian political understanding to replace the defunct Versailles and Washington orders in the Orient. Several models were given serious thought. Scholar-diplomat and later prime minister Ashida Hitoshi proposed a "Locarno Treaty for the Far East" in which Japan, China, Manchukuo, and the Soviet Union would pledge themselves to nonaggression and arbitration. Members of the former League of Nations Association discussed the viability of an East Asian League separate from Geneva. Diehard Anglophiles in the Foreign Ministry groped for a resuscitation of the Anglo-Japanese Alliance. Tokyo University Professor Kamikawa Hikomatsu and other nationalistic legal scholars called for world acceptance of an Asiatic Monroe Doctrine which would rationalize Japanese predominance in East Asia. These schemes never got beyond the rhetoric stage. The distrust created by armed aggression and Japan's dramatic exit from the league made it impossible to convince China and the United States—necessary parties to any effective Pacific power understanding—of Japan's benign intentions. As Japan's military involvement spread to North China after 1937, the attitude of the United States hardened and the viability of regional accommodation evaporated.

By the time Prime Minister Konoe Fumimaro proclaimed the New Order in East Asia on 3 November 1938, regionalism had degenerated into a one-sided imposition of the Japanese will upon Manchukuo and China. It is noteworthy that Konoe's proclamation was made just twenty-four hours after his government severed all remaining ties to League of Nations cultural and humanitarian organizations. The prime minister's radio message to the Japanese people made it clear that the East Asian order he envisioned was designed to replace the Versailles system in Asia. "It is well known," he said, "that international agreements such as the League of Nations Covenant have lost their dignity because of irrational principles. There must be brought about a new peace system based on reality."

As a consequence of embarkation on a program of militaristic expansion in the early 1930s, Japan cut her ties to the universal order which she had reluctantly embraced in 1919. A status quo system was discarded because it precluded the acquisition of territorial requisites to leadership and security. For spurning the principles of the League Covenant, the Nine-Power Treaty, and the Kellogg–Briand Pact Japan stood rightly condemned.

Her culpability notwithstanding, Japan's infidelity must be reassessed in light of the fact that the world had made universalism an undesirable nuptial partner. Long before the Kwantung Army went on the march the major Western powers had demonstrated their unwillingness to entrust their own security to the League of Nations. The United States, Japan's Pacific neighbor, had cooperated with the league only when to do so was in her self-interest. The league had showed no appetite for dealing with the problem of immigration which so vexed the Japanese. Japan's departure from the Versailles order was a symptom and not the cause of universalism's demise.

Principles of universalism have flourished anew in the post–Second World War era as evidenced in the United Nations Charter and the Declaration of Human Rights. The universalistic mode is particularly appealing to Americans in an era when global ascendency allows the United States to define the terms of universalism in accordance with her own values and interests. The positing of universalism as an ethical norm inevitably colors historical treatments of Japan's international behavior between the world wars. Objectivity demands a more serious consideration of Japanese misgivings and Japan's alternative concepts for peace and international order in that unstable period. While it is regrettable that Japan abandoned the ideal of universalism and left the league in 1933, it is equally regrettable that the United States rigidly persisted in measuring Japan's actions against the hollow standards of a moribund universalism, a universalism which America herself had jilted in 1919.

From Mukden to Pearl Harbor

Hata Ikuhiko

The new order of international politics that was formulated at the Washington Naval Arms Reduction Conference and the Versailles Peace Conference by the victorious allied nations, after the gunsmoke of the First World War had thinned and the commotion of revolution and depression subsided, is commonly called the Versailles–Washington system. This new international order was formulated mainly for the benefit of Great Britain and the United States, however. It suppressed the discontent of many countries such as defeated Germany, which was already suffering under a heavy burden of reparations, and both Italy and Japan which, even though they had sided with the victors, did not benefit much from the war. All three countries were to emerge as fascist countries at a later date. Outside this international order was the powerful Soviet Union, which succeeded in establishing the world's first socialist country despite persistent intervention from the imperialist countries. Subsequently she promoted international communism through the Comintern and supported nationalist movements in various colonial areas.

The precarious balance that existed among these three major blocs —the United States and Great Britain; disgruntled Germany, Italy, and Japan; and the Soviet Union, which was forging ahead to establish a socialist order—broke down with the stormy Great Depression of 1929, and international politics started gyrating toward the crisis of another world war. This movement was triggered by the fascist countries' efforts to break the status quo. Japan, inadvertently, was to become the vanguard of this movement because of her involvement in the Manchurian Incident.

Japan's Rebellion Against the System

Shidehara Kijūrō's diplomacy from the Washington Conference to the Manchurian Incident, with the exception of a two-year period of a different character known as Tanaka diplomacy, may be summarized as a tripartite policy of international cooperation, economy-oriented diplomacy, and nonintervention in Chinese affairs.

His policy of international cooperation is generally believed to have been a League of Nations–centered diplomacy, but in reality it was a policy of Japanese cooperation with Great Britain and the United States. The policy of economy-oriented diplomacy was one of promoting peaceful economic expansion abroad rather than through heavy-handed militaristic moves such as the Siberian Expedition (1918–1922) and the Twenty-one Demands (1915) toward China. Such militaristic approaches were thought ineffective and counterproductive among the colonial peoples striving for self-determination. This policy of economic expansion was formulated in response to the demands of industrial capitalism which grew rapidly during the war. In fact, trade volume with China and other countries showed a definite upswing under Shidehara diplomacy.

The most important aspect of Shidehara diplomacy, the policy of nonintervention in China's domestic affairs, showed understanding and a sympathetic attitude toward her nationalistic demands, such as tariff autonomy and abolition of extraterritoriality, and was to recognize the unification of Mainland China by Chiang Kai-shek. During 1930–1931, however, this moderate diplomatic policy of the Shidehara period collapsed as a result of the London Naval Power Limitation Treaty and resistance in Manchuria from the Chang Hsueh-liang regime.

Certain naval officers, unhappy with the successive restrictions on naval power imposed by the London treaty, joined forces with right-wingers and young army officers to develop a powerful opposition movement. Politicians from the opposition party supported it also. This was the starting point of the military-fascist movement which characterized Japan during the 1930s.

Chief protagonists of the Manchurian problem were Japan's Kwantung Army and some of the Japanese colonists in Manchuria. They felt that if the Chang Hsueh-liang regime in Manchuria and the nationalist movement of the Kuomintang were left unchecked, Japanese interests in Manchuria gained through the Russo-Japanese War would be lost; hence they advocated a counterattack—with military force if necessary. Japanese who felt threatened by unemployment and starvation were disillusioned by the corruption of party politics and were attracted by the slogan of "Shōwa Restoration" advocated by the military-fascists. Although the meaning of the slogan was not very clear to the masses, they perceived it as a combined policy of domestic reform and international expansion. Thus prior to Hitler's accession to power Japan took her first step toward the Second World War by an open rebellion against the Versailles–Washington system.

The Manchurian Incident

During the night of 18 September 1931, the Kwantung Army dynamited the tracks of the South Manchurian Railway in a Mukden suburb. Under the pretext that the bombing was the work of the Chinese army, the Kwantung Army attacked Chang Hsueh-liang's army and occupied Mukden. This move was a plot deliberately planned by Lt. Col. Ishiwara Kanji and staff officers of the Kwantung Army. Some members of the Army Chief of Staff (in Tokyo) and officers of the army stationed in Korea also took part in the plot.

What is important here is not the dynamiting incident itself. In order for the Kwantung Army to occupy all of Manchuria it was necessary to go beyond the zones of each side of the South Manchurian Railway which were recognized by the treaty as the area of Japanese interest. On 22 September, Colonel Ishiwara and others made a request to General Honjō, commander of the Kwantung Army, that troops be dispatched to protect the security of Japanese people in Kirin.

Honjō, who did not take part in the plot, knew by this time what his staff was planning. Under the military criminal code, movement of troops by the local commander stationed in a foreign country was punishable by death unless authorized by the emperor. Honjō's staff persuaded the reluctant commander through the night and by daybreak he acquiesced. A dramatic touch was added when the army stationed in Korea dispatched "relief" troops to Manchuria also without the permission of the central authorities.

Thereafter the Kwantung Army ignored every directive from the Tokyo headquarters. Tokyo reluctantly followed the nonexpansion policy of the Wakatsuki cabinet and its foreign minister, Shidehara. Some officers of the chief of staff then planned an abortive coup d'etat called the October Incident and circulated the rumor that the Kwantung Army planned to separate itself from the Japanese army. Four months after the Mukden Incident, the Wakatsuki cabinet collapsed and the government recognized the occupation of Manchuria as a *fait accompli*.

The power to prevent these arbitrary actions lay in international pressure exerted by the world major powers. These powers, however, themselves anguishing under economic difficulties, remained more or less bystanders. The weak solitary challenge of the "nonrecognition doctrine" advanced by Secretary of State Stimson was ignored by Japan. Likewise Japan withdrew from the League of Nations in 1933 and chose "honorable isolation" rather than accept the unfavorable findings of the Lytton Commission regarding the Manchurian Incident.

On the surface, the international policy taken by Japan in the early 1930s and the internal turmoil which gave birth to it resemble closely those of Germany and Italy. There was one significant difference, however. In Japan there was no dictatorial leader comparable to Hitler or Mussolini. Indeed, the structure of power politics in Japan during the thirties is an intriguing topic and no persuasive conclusion has yet been advanced. Postwar social scientists refer to this period vaguely as the period of *Tennōsei*-fascism or military-fascism—in an effort to separate it from the two fascist regimes in Europe. The former term expresses the fact that all reforms and military expeditions were accomplished under the name and authority of the *Tennō* (the emperor), although the *Tennō* himself was forced into a constrained private life. The latter term, military fascism, is the label chosen to emphasize that the military after the Manchurian Incident, especially after the mutiny of 26 February 1936, came to assume almost dictatorial political power.

Still, most cabinet positions after 1931 were occupied not by military officers on active service but by aging elder statesman or generals and admirals on reserve duty. Moreover, there were many politicians, bureaucrats, and businessmen who flirted with the military in their quest for a place in the sun. The only surviving senior elder statesman (genro), Prince Saionji, and other aides to the *Tennō* were still influential. Suppression of socialists and communists by the Special Political Police was harsh, but once these radicals announced their conversion and regained "the soul of the Japanese," the military gladly appointed them administrators of occupied areas or members of the wartime control organizations. In essence, Japan of the thirties was like an omnibus with various political powers aboard but no responsible driver.

The China Affair

Was Japan's foreign invasion, from the Manchurian Incident through the China War to the Second World War, an uncontrolled chain of aggression? Or was it a "quest for autonomy" in the face of a world economy fast dividing itself into blocs after the Great Depression?

The role of the Manchurian Incident in Japan's economy was akin to that of Roosevelt's New Deal in America. Escalating military expenditure and expanding war industry revived the stagnating Japanese economy. General Ludendorff's theory of total war was introduced in Japan at this time. The military was advocating the establishment of a national defense state. Relations with the United States and the Soviet Union were strained as a result of the Japanese occupation of Manchuria.

It was well known abroad that Japan was suffering from overpopulation and scarcity of natural resources. Therefore occupation of Manchuria (China's sovereignty over which was historically not altogether clear) was considered even by many Chinese to be something of a psychological loss to be tolerated. In fact, for Chiang Kai-shek a more urgent objective was to defeat Mao Tse-tung's Chinese Red Army. Under these circumstances, during the period from 1932 to 1935, it appeared as if a friendly relationship with China might be reestablished with a tacit recognition of the *fait accompli*. Foreign Minister Hirota Kōki requested that China agree to his Three Principles: discontinuation of anti-Japanese activities, recognition of Manchukuo, and joint action against communism.

But the success of the Manchurian Incident had whetted the army's appetite, especially the officers of the Kwantung Army and China hands, by 1935. Major General Ishiwara, now an important officer of the chief of staff, did not favor uncontrolled, rapid expansion. He insisted that Japan should concentrate on developing the resources of Manchuria and solidify her own national strength so that she might be able to take advantage of the world's changing situation. But Ishiwara's own past radicalism made it difficult for him to control adventurous younger officers.

In fact Japan, before fully devouring the natural resources of Manchuria, rushed to Mainland China in search of even easier gain. The mutiny of 26 February 1936 had brought to an end a bloody internal struggle for the control of leadership within the army. Through a victory of the Control faction *(Tōseiha)* over the Imperial faction *(Kōdō-ha)* there was a shift of emphasis from domestic reform to foreign invasion. Viewing these facts, it becomes clear that Japan's acts of invasion from the China Affair to the Pacific War are *not* of such a passive nature as may be termed a "quest for autonomy."

It has become popular in recent years, among Japanese historians, to call Japan's aggressive actions which lasted from the Manchurian Incident to 1945 the "Fifteen-Year War." What this term means is that the Manchurian Incident, the China War, and the Pacific War should not be viewed separately but should be regarded as one continuous conflict. To be sure, the only declaration of war under international law was made in December 1941; but from 1931 on, for almost fourteen years, there was hardly a day when guns were silent in Japanese-occupied areas.

It is doubtful, however, that these actions were carried out systematically as the result of a well-planned conspiracy by the Class A war criminals designated by the allied prosecutor at the Far East War Crimes trial. There was always a minority opinion which sought to halt these aggressive actions and to change the direction Japan was taking. It foresaw the catastrophic outcome of the continuous war. In other words, we must not forget that there was a constant struggle between the expansionists and nonexpansionists, though admittedly the freedom of choice became increasingly narrow as the years wore on. That the nonexpansionists failed to gain control was in some measure because of a not undeserved attitude of mistrust toward Japan on the part of various foreign countries. (Japan did violate official pledges often.) China, the United States, Great Britain, and others came to believe that Japan was untrustworthy, that compromises and negotiations were futile, and that the only solution was by military sanction.

In July 1937, a minor skirmish at a Beijing suburb triggered all-out war between Japan and China. At that point, China was torn by civil war and not inclined to become involved in a foreign war. Japanese military leaders, too, soon realized that large-scale war with China could become a protracted affair; hence they were willing to negotiate peace under appropriate conditions. Peace negotiations failed, however, because China judged Japan to be untrustworthy; it was not considered likely that Japan would honor a cease-fire or peace agreement.

Consequently Japan abandoned hope for a peaceful settlement and tried to solve the problem by establishing the puppet regime of Wang Ching-wei, Chiang Kai-shek's rival. But Japan's overextended battle lines were constantly harassed by the guerrilla attacks of Chiang Kai-shek's army or the Red Chinese Army. Moreover, it soon became apparent that Wang's regime could not survive without the strong support of the Japanese military forces.

For many years the Japanese army had made war plans and trained its troops with the USSR as its "most probable enemy." Following the Manchurian Incident the Kwantung Army and the Soviet Army came face to face at the Amur River. There the supposedly mighty and proud Kwantung Army was defeated by a Soviet force with modern equipment at several border disputes such as the Nomonhan Incident.

At a time when the situation in Europe was fast accelerating toward the Second World War, Japan's position was becoming increasingly uncertain. She sought a solution to this uncertainty in a military alliance with Germany and Italy.

The Road to the Pacific War

Was the Pacific War inevitable for Japan? Historians, both Americans and Japanese, have advanced various theories on the subject of who started the war. So far they do not seem to have reached a conclusion. The Japanese government sought justification for the war in the Hull Note which demanded that Japan retreat to her position in pre–Manchurian Incident days. On the very day the Hull Note was received, however, a Japanese task force left its secret base in the Kurile Islands for its surprise attack on Pearl Harbor. Inasmuch as most wars are started as the culmination of a gradually deteriorating crisis, it is useless to look for the turning point between war and peace a few days before the outbreak of war.

In this writer's opinion, the point of no return on the road to the Pacific War was the formation of the Tripartite Alliance in the fall of 1940. Foreign Minister Matsuoka Yōsuke, who promoted the idea of the alliance, had a grand illusion of global strategy. It was to add the USSR to the Tripartite Alliance. By doing so, he reasoned, the balance of power could be restored through the formation of a dichotomy between the Eurasian continent and the American continent. However, the realization of his illusion went no further than the signing of a neutrality pact between Japan and the USSR.

By "shaking hands with the satan" of Nazism through the Tripartite Alliance, Japan became unequivocally an enemy of the United States. China, which was at the brink of disintegration, resolved to continue her fight against Japan. The USSR was driven into the American camp by Germany's incomprehensible attack on Soviet Russia. Confrontation of the Axis powers and the anti-Axis powers turned into that of the have nations and the have-not nations. For a war in which material wealth and technology were to become decisive, the outcome was self-evident from the beginning.

When he made his decision to plunge into war, Prime Minister Tōjō was in a desperate state of mind exemplified by his quoting the Japanese saying that it is sometimes necessary to "jump from the high terrace of Kiyomizu temple *(Kiyomizu no butai kara tobioriru)*" to justify his policies. He was given the unfortunate role of reaping the harvest of the seeds of mistrust which Japan had sowed during the ten years since the Manchurian Incident. Unless he was willing to abandon everything Japan had gained to that point—an incredible proposition—it was not possible to expect any concession from the United States, which had become determined to strike down Japan on the day the Tripartite Alliance was formed.

[Translated by TAEKO WELLINGTON]

Fogbound in Tokyo: Domestic Politics in Japan's Foreign Policymaking

Mark C. Michelson

"**A** survey of the world as a whole today," Foreign Minister Hirota Kōki told the Japanese Diet in 1934, "reveals a sorry situation in which economic disorder, political unrest and confusion, and a conflict of ideas threaten to destroy international equilibrium at any moment, while mutual confidence of nations in one another appears to have wilted." Hirota's evaluation of the world situation was similar to that of many other Japanese civilian and military leaders in the 1930s. Many Japanese shared the perception of a crisis, a perception accompanied by an uneasy feeling of fatalism and drift. They believed that their country was isolated in a predatory world, surrounded by racist, status quo Western powers, and that political, economic, and cultural solidarity with Asia as well as limited alliances with non-Asian have-not countries were essential. There was considerable support for an Asian Monroe Doctrine and for varying degrees of expansion toward East and Southeast Asia in view of Japan's defensive and economic requirements and pressures from the West, the Soviet Union, and Chinese nationalism. Almost without exception, Japanese leaders were strongly anticommunist. They regarded the "Red Menace" as a threat to the basis of Japanese civilization and consequently believed that Japan must protect herself against the pressing dangers of the Chinese communist armies and the Soviets to the north.

Early Shōwa era officials, like their Meiji and Taishō predecessors, wanted to realize military and economic security and world recognition of Japan's "proper place" as a peer of the European and American powers. They attempted to work out foreign policies based on a pragmatic estimate of the international trend of the times. Japanese leaders did not engage in a conspiracy of aggression and national self-aggrandizement or develop policies in terms of a Pacific War. They were convinced instead that a hegemonic position for Japan in East Asia was vital to their country's survival as an independent power and to the maintenance of domestic, regional, and international stability. Manchuria and China came to be identified in numerous writings and speeches as Japan's economic and strategic lifelines and as bulwarks against communism. Using the familiar language of imperialism, Japanese diplomats actively sought the Western powers' understanding of Japan's position. Disagreements existed among Japanese elites regarding the best means to achieve these aims and the timing of certain policies, but these disputes transcended military and civilian divisions. The political scientist Rōyama Masamichi wrote in the late 1930s that the "Japanese policy of a new order in East Asia has not been a policy suddenly or accidentally conceived, but has been nationally formulated after long and serious deliberation and with a view to settling not only the present conflict but rather the age-old instability of the Far East."

Policymakers were very much concerned with the domestic ramifications of their foreign policy decisions. They recalled that during the 1920s internal socioeconomic problems had been linked in the public mind with the "elitist diplomacy" of peaceful economic expansion and cooperation with the Anglo-American powers, a policy associated with Foreign Minister Shidehara Kijūrō. By the early 1930s the methods and policies of Shidehara diplomacy contrasted sharply with the popular, nationalistic advocacy of a positive and independent Japanese leadership role on the Asian mainland, involving at times the use of military force. Right-wing activists added to the volatile atmosphere by demanding external expansion and radical internal reforms and by demonstrating that they were willing to sanction violence in order to achieve their aims. The enthusiastic public response to the 1931 Manchurian Incident and subsequent military successes was due in part to the belief that an expansionist policy would minimize the domestic effects of the world depression and the impact of Western racial and trade barriers. Control of various areas would, in this view, alleviate economic and population pressures at home and ensure Japan of a supply of raw materials and markets for her products.

Japanese leaders recognized the opportunity to promote internal unity and discipline. Dramatic foreign military adventures and diplomatic developments, buttressed by ideological rhetoric, were utilized to overcome political, social, and economic ills in Japan. Japanese officials appealed for mass support and sacrifice so that the nation could accomplish its mission of establishing peace and stability in East Asia and the world. At the height of the China War in 1938, Prime Minister Konoe Fumimaro cautioned prefectural governors that all citizens must be reminded that "the desires of individuals must be controlled for the sake of harmony of the whole" during "the present emergency." The concept of a national emergency was employed repeatedly by Japanese officials as a pretext to enhance their authority and suppress protest.

Many of Japan's diplomatic problems in this period were therefore related as much to domestic politics as to international issues. Prewar Japan had a ponderous, pluralistic political system in which policy-making responsibility was obscured. Foreign policy decisions had to be reached by means of a highly circuitous path involving numbers of key institutions and individuals. Despite generally shared perceptions and goals, policymakers had trouble achieving the necessary consensus in the midst of competition for authority and decision-making prerogatives. This power struggle was further intensified and complicated by bureaucratic sectionalism and institutional loyalties.

Who was involved in a particular foreign policy decision depended not only on the issue being considered but also on the current power of individuals and institutions. Middle and upper-level officials took part in a series of negotiating sessions during which policy proposals were debated and modified into a form acceptable to all participants. Much of this bargaining occurred during informal gatherings at homes or restaurants, through contacts with intermediaries, and during telephone conversations. By the time top officials met, a reconciliation of views among significant military and civilian representatives had usually been accomplished. While broadening participation and thereby lessening opposition to government policies, this pluralistic decision-making process blurred lines of responsibility and authority. The result was often political confusion when informed decisiveness was required.

The diffuse and intricate foreign policy decision-making process that existed in prewar Japan was caused in part by the ill-defined constitutional authority given to branches of government. Supreme authority was vested in the sacred and sovereign emperor by the Meiji Constitution. In practice, however, the emperor rarely participated directly in policy decisions. Instead ministers of state, the chief officers of the army and navy, privy councillors, Diet members, palace of-

ficials, and elder and senior statesmen were constitutionally or traditionally empowered to advise the sovereign concerning affairs of state.
They formulated the government's policy decisions for imperial ratification and then implemented the approved policies. These men were
dedicated to protecting the emperor from becoming personally involved in political issues that might threaten his transcendental position and prestige—and hence the status of the whole constitutional
structure. Each of these advisory bodies and individuals was responsible only to the emperor; all claimed overlapping jurisdictions based
on imperial prerogatives. Responsibility for decisions was dispersed
through a myriad of limitations on individual authority which guaranteed the continuation of a pluralistic decision-making system.

One of the recurring problems of the 1930s was that of determining who should represent the emperor in coordinating the disparate
institutional demands so that policy decisions could be made. This
function was previously performed by the extraconstitutional genro,
or elder statesmen, who built the Meiji state and were certified by
imperial edict. Their skill, shared experiences, and prestige usually
enabled them to achieve sufficient interinstitutional harmony, especially in regard to foreign policy matters. During the 1920s the last
surviving genro, Prince Saionji Kimmochi, expected that leading party politicians in the Lower House of the Diet would take over this
coordinating role, but legislative supremacy proved transitory.

The Manchurian Incident and its aftermath stimulated a continuing leadership struggle among military and civilian elites. As the crisis
deepened, accompanied by increasingly complex diplomatic questions, the need to reconcile these competing interests became even
more urgent. It was particularly unclear which group or groups
should have the ultimate policymaking responsibility. Throughout
the 1930s, for example, the army and Foreign Ministry argued whether China-related issues fell under the imperial prerogative of supreme
command or that of conducting diplomacy. Both sides attempted to
gain support from other institutions and individuals in order to
strengthen their negotiating position in these jurisdictional and policy disputes. All these machinations took place under the rubric of
the resilient Meiji consitutional system, which remained intact despite relocations of power among the nation's governing elites.

By the 1930s military leaders were becoming more powerful in the
Japanese government. Certainly they were aided by the weakness and
corruption of party politicians and increased terrorism by young officers and right-wing extremists. More important, the depression's ef-

fects on trade and the domestic economy, naval limitations and racial conflicts with the West, and the outbreak of fighting on the Asian mainland helped persuade many Japanese that they faced a period of national cirsis. This emergency seemed to require military and bureaucratic expertise that parliamentary government could not provide.

Military leaders moved quickly to take advantage of the general sense of malaise, the ambiguity about decision-making power, and the nationalistic reaction to crises. Using propaganda and coercion but mainly customary and legal political channels, military men, aided by sympathetic civilians, gained more authority in government. Politically active army officers claimed that it was only natural in a wartime situation that the military should take a keen interest in both politics and economics. No important policy decision in the 1930s could be made without military acquiescence, though the government sometimes refrained from approving policies which military leaders desired.

Although more unified than most elites, the military was not monolithic. Policy and personal power disputes between the army and navy and among factions in both services caused serious splits. This factionalism, together with skillful political maneuvering by civilian officials, helped prevent "political soldiers" from ever assuming complete control of the Japanese government, even during the Pacific War. Nevertheless, even those Japanese experienced in foreign affairs tended to view the world and policy choices through a narrow military lens.

Many civilian officials, however, particularly those in the Foreign Ministry, believed that foreign policy decisions should rest first with the premier and foreign minister and only secondarily with the army and navy. They strove with mixed success to surmount powerful military claims to a dominant role in determining national policies. Diplomats often found that the most effective method of counteracting military influence was to agree in principle with army and navy proposals initially. Then, using their political and diplomatic expertise, Foreign Ministry officials were sometimes able to modify original policies in small but significant ways.

Japan's decision to resign its membership in the League of Nations over the Manchurian issue in 1933 illustrated how military influence, the diffuse decision-making system, and domestic political considerations could adversely affect foreign policy. Military and civilian leaders generally agreed that their government should not accept the league's condemnation of the Kwantung Army's activities in Manchuria and the establishment of the state of Manchukuo separate from China. The government had already made a formal commitment to a nominally independent Manchukuo dominated by Japan. As an imperially sanctioned national policy, it was not really subject to compromise. There was discussion of leaving the league in extreme circumstances, but the war minister was the only unequivocal proponent among government leaders of such a drastic step.

Even so, indecision by officials who did not favor withdrawal allowed advocates of a defiant stand to exploit antileague sentiments and the perceived threat of popular agitation in Japan. Newspapers stirred up public opinion by calling for withdrawal; military reservists sent telegrams urging that their leaders remain firm against the "superior attitude" of the league majority. Criticized for his lack of policy in dealing with the league, Foreign Minister Uchida Yasuya came to support withdrawal. His decision was based at least as much on internal expediency as on implications for Japanese foreign relations. Recognizing the potency of a determined minority in the unsettled Japanese political environment as well as the benefits of bringing about the unification of the nation through vigorous, even somewhat radical views which are accompanied by action, Uchida joined with the war minister and much of the press in arguing for withdrawal. These efforts and the negative feelings many Japanese had toward the league helped persuade even Prince Saionji to submit to what he called the "inevitability" of leaving the world organization. Ironically, Saionji had headed the Japanese delegation which negotiated the covenant creating the League of Nations in 1919 during one of Uchida's previous terms as Foreign Minister.

In February 1933 Chief Delegate Matsuoka Yōsuke marched his protesting delegation out of the league assembly in Geneva. One month later the government notified the league of its intention to resign. It cited "an irreconcilable divergence of views" on the Manchurian question and accused the league majority of "attaching greater importance to inapplicable formulae than to the real task of assuring peace." Characteristically ignoring any contradictions, the imperial rescript proclaiming the withdrawal emphasized international cooperation while actually contributing to Japan's separation from the other powers. Japan's dramatic move relieved domestic tension and fortified national unity. This action appealed to many Japanese as a symbol of a break with the restrictive, outmoded diplomacy of Western nations and a sign of their country's new autonomous course in foreign affairs. Moreover, the restrained foreign response to Japan's defiance of her First World War allies seemed to vindicate the bold and resolute policies advocated by military and civilian activists.

Japan's international behavior after 1933, especially in Asia, reflected the domestic political influence of those Japanese who favored a direct, simplistic approach to solving their nation's problems, an approach distinguished by an insensitivity to foreign reactions and conditions. A cabinet and its members' political and even personal survival often depended significantly on success in foreign policy. One of the most reliable ways of satisfying this criterion in the 1930s was to pursue energetic, nationalistic policies of continental expansion and economic autarky that appeared to extend Japan's superiority over the other powers and China in the Asian sphere.

Engulfed by what one social scientist, Robert Jervis, has described as "the fog of foreign policymaking," prewar Japanese decisionmakers employed, in his words "shortcuts to rationality, often without being aware of the way they are doing so. But these shortcuts often produce systematic errors, many of which increase conflict." Lengthy and cumbersome decision-making processes, each faction protecting its own interests and status, discouraged an unrestricted exchange of information and opinions and a reasoned consideration of the broad international implications of a policy.

Japan and "Asia for Asians"

Akashi Yoji

The years under the Japanese military occupation of Southeast Asia from 1942 to 1945 comprise one of the most devastating and tragic periods of the recent history of the region. Scores of women were raped by soldiers; untold numbers of Chinese were massacred by the *kempeitai* (gendarmes). Chinese were forced to make "contributions" until they were bled white. Tens of thousands of lives were lost from hunger, exhaustion, and tropical diseases in the jungles of the Thai–Burma border and New Guinea where they served in corvée; hundreds of thousands were uprooted and displaced from city to countryside when food became scarce. Economies of indigenous peoples were ruined by spiraling inflation and their livelihood and property were irrevocably wrecked. Furthermore, social order was undermined irreparably resulting in universal distrust, communal and racial strife, particularly noticeable in Malaya, and an afflicted public morality as neighbors were pitted against one another.

These human sacrifices, personal tragedies, economic hardships, and social dislocation have been recorded and recounted by many people who lived through the period. Their accounts, understandably, accentuate the negative side of the occupation. Only in the past several years have scholars begun to reevaluate the positive impact of the Japanese military presence on postwar political, economic, and social developments in Southeast Asia.

The destructive and barbaric side of the Japanese military administration notwithstanding, I would argue that the Japanese occupation was on the whole constructive and enlightened. I disagree with those who claim that the Japanese interlude was a superficial episode that can be relegated to a preface to present-day Southeast Asia. Considering the region as a whole, the occupation was a watershed in the political development of all countries of Southeast Asia. In this short essay I argue for a positive interpretation of the interregnum and its contributions to the political development of Southeast Asia, showing why it was constructive and enlightened. Because of the brevity of this essay, I shall address myself to three points: destruction of the myth of Western superiority, growth of nationalism and national unity, and experience in military and political organizations and administration.

The most profound impact of the Japanese interregnum was the end of any claim by Western colonial authority to rule in Southeast Asia; the myth of colonial omnipotence was exposed by the defeat of Western colonial powers by the Japanese. Their ignominious surrender undermined irreparably the prestige and supremacy of the white. As one former Malayan cadet told me, he no longer considered "the white man as a superior" after he saw the British capitulation.

The humiliating defeat also bolstered incipient nationalist fervor and gave indigenous leaders self-confidence in challenging the political control of the Western nations. The Japanese slogan "Asia for the Asians" stirred up an antiwesternism which has manifested itself powerfully in the postwar years as anticolonialism. Therefore, following the Japanese surrender in August 1945 when the Western Powers tried to reassert former colonial rule, Asians vigorously opposed their attempts. Indochina and Indonesia won national independence through revolutionary war. Other nations such as Burma and India gained self-rule through transfer of power from their former colonial masters. Faced with the surging tide of postwar national self-determination, these rulers realized that they could no longer rule Asians. In the Philippines, Indochina, and Malaya national self-determination movements took a different path under communist ideology. The communists, who had fought against the Japanese throughout the war years in cooperation with the Allied Powers, emerged from the jungles and challenged Western rule. In Indochina the communist struggle succeeded after thirty years of revolutionary war; in Malaya and the Philippines the communists almost came within reach of their revolutionary aim. Whether these peoples won national independence through bloody warfare or a transfer of power, Japan's wartime slogan of "Asia for the Asians" provided a powerful stimulus for their emancipation movement. A fervor for self-determination and freedom from colonialism, stirred by Japanese propaganda, unleashed psychological, social, and political changes and upheaval even in a political backwater like Malaya.

With these developments in mind, I contend that it is no exaggeration to say that without the Japanese interlude the balance between colonialism and postwar change in contemporary Southeast Asia might still be weighed in favor of the colonial status quo or at best gradual change. This conclusion is supported by the statement of Ba Maw, former premier of Burma, that the Japanese interregnum "played an immense catalytic role in energizing and accelerating movements which otherwise [would] have remained weak and unsuccessful for many years to come." Ba Maw also said:

> No nation has done so much to liberate Asia from white domination, yet no nation has been so misunderstood by the very people whom it had helped either to liberate or to set an example to in many things. . . . No military defeat could then have robbed her of the trust and gratitude of half of Asia or even more. Even now, as things actually are, nothing can ever obliterate the role Japan has played in bringing liberation to countless colonial people.

The Japanese occupation not only set a time bomb for the demise of Western colonial rule; it also created a new class of elites who competed for influence and prestige with traditional elites. The most important of these emerging elites was without doubt the new military leadership reared by the Japanese army commands. While colonial armies had as a rule been drawn from ethnic minorities and officered by Westerners, the Japanese recruited and trained entire armies and officers' corps from among the major ethnic groups in Southeast Asia. Enthusiastic young men of common birth but without religious or Western training—hitherto the exclusive prerequisite for nonaristocratic elite status—eagerly responded to the new opportunities to gain social status.

An estimated 353,000 youths of Southeast Asia were recruited in Japanese-trained regular armies and some 180 officers were sent to military academy in Japan for further training. Possibly more young men were drafted to paramilitary units for national defense and guerrilla warfare. It is they who led postwar struggles for independence, notably in Indonesia. A significant number of Indonesians and Burmese have risen in the military establishment and have held senior posts in civil administration where they have served as agents of revolution and modernization.

The history of the Indonesian revolutionary war cannot be recounted without mentioning the role of the PETA (Army for Defenders of the Homeland) and other paramilitary units. Some 34,500 Indonesians including 2,890 officers and noncommissioned officers were recruited and drilled in the Japanese-sponsored PETA, and at least 230,000 youths were also given opportunities in paramilitary units. Numerous PETA officers later became important members of the Indonesian officer corps, and the PETA served as *pelopor* (vanguard) to unify Indonesians and guide them toward national unity. Members of the paramilitary corps later became the nuclei of irregular guerrilla units, the so-called lascars. They contributed much to the struggle for independence from 1945 to 1949. These units received military drill, and when the Allied Powers landed in Java after the Japanese surrender tens of thousands of these young men rallied to the defense of their motherland following the organizational pattern introduced by the Japanese.

Attributing the role of the Japanese to the organization of the Indonesian army, one senior officer who studied in Holland and received training from the Japanese observed, "The Dutch were better in theory, but the Japanese were more practical. We didn't learn from the Dutch how to make an army from scratch and lead it. We learned [from the Japanese] how to fight at company level, how to recruit soldiers, and how to devote yourself to your country."

Neither can the annals of the Burmese independence movement be complete without acknowledging positive contributions of the *Minami Kikan*, the "Thirty Comrades," and the Burma Independence Army (BIA) and the Burma Defense Army (BDA). Prior to and during the Japanese military operations against Burma, the *Minami Kikan* played a critical role in the creation of the BIA, officered by thirty comrades who had been drilled by the Japanese army before the outbreak of war. Recruits and officers of the 200,000-man BIA, which was to become the BDA, followed the Japanese for the liberation of Burma. The spirit of the BDA was no different from the old BIA, because the BDA was still under the command of the original Thirty Comrades. The taste for independence and revolutionary momentum gained during the wartime interlude took Burmese officers a full step toward genuine independence in the early postwar years. According to Louis Allen, a British military historian of Southeast Asian affairs, the 55,000-man Burmese National Army was "a real factor in the background of negotiations with the British after the end of the war." Aung San, founder of the Burmese independence movement, and Ne Win, head of the Burmese government, were trained by the Japanese.

The Japanese helped train Burmese officers in the Mingaladon Military Academy outside of Rangoon and drilled them further at the Japanese Military Academy in Tokyo. Most members of the present Revolutionary Council and commanders of the Burmese army graduated from the Mingaladon Military Academy during the Japanese occupation. This is true also of the Burmese diplomatic corps.

A dramatic case of the Japanese-trained army in South Asia was the Indian National Army (INA); here again Japan's contribution to an independence movement should be credited. The history of India's postwar independence struggle is not complete without giving credit to the INA, which formed a second front for India's national freedom movement. The INA was created by the *F Kikan*, a Japanese intelligence mission, of Major Fujiwara Iwaichi of the Japanese Imperial Army and led by the legendary Netaji Subhas Chandra Bose, former president of the Indian National Congress Party. The 40,000-man INA fought jointly with Japanese troops in a major operation for India's liberation: the Imphal campaign.

After the war in November 1945, the British Army held military trials charging INA officers for treason. Defendants and their defense committee, including Jawaharlal Nehru, argued that a subjugated people had the right to fight, transforming the court into a platform for an anti-British movement. The court martial added fuel to the anti-British sentiment of Indian masses who had mobilized huge nationwide demonstrations in sympathy for the former INA officers. The defendants were convicted as charged, but in the face of the mounting anti-British movement the sentence was not carried out. By this time the British realized that they could no longer ignore the overwhelming Indian sympathy for the officers. By 1947 India was free and independent. As a former INA officer observed, "There can thus be little doubt that the Indian National Army, not in its unhappy career on the battlefield, but in its thunderous disintegration, hastened the end of the British rule in India. The agitation which surrounded the trials turned the issue of independence for India into an instant, burning question once more."

Alongside the military proper we find new leaders rising from the youth groups and other organizations brought into being by the Japanese. These emerging elite groups are of more than sociological interest, for they represent a veritable revaluation of traditional social values in Southeast Asia, a concomitant of the revolutionary tide generated by occupation policies and propaganda. Politicized and often militarized during the war years, these young people rapidly developed into a clientele for political, nationalist appeals, into transmission belts between city and countryside, but also into new political leadership groups challenging older political and religious elites.

The central role of the Indonesian revolution, for example, was not played by an alienated intelligentsia, nor in the main by oppressed classes, but by the young. Young men of Indonesia in paramilitary and sociopolitical units received Japanese spiritual and physical training and an indoctrination steeped in anti-Western propaganda. The training was geared to develop their spiritual and physical strength and inculcate a burning spirit of struggle and the superiority of the spiritual over the material *(seishin)*.

The impact of the Japanese youth training program also left a positive imprint on the Malayan youth. The Japanese military administration established a *Koa Kunrenjo* for rank-and-file leadership training. Selected for their leadership potential, these youngsters between seventeen and twenty-five years old received a rigorous six-month drill emphasizing the struggle of mind and spirit over matter. The training changed the psychological outlook of young people whose way of life had been lethargic. The Japanese imparted to the trainees the assumption that the élan of the warrior was far superior to technical expertise and would enable them to overcome any obstacle. The *seishin* instilled in the Malayan youth such qualities as resilience, self-confidence, self-discipline, and self-reliance.

Thirty years later these former cadets told me that the *seishin* training they received contributed significantly to their mental outlook and the success of their professional careers: "Most students looked with favor on the strong rule [and discipline training] established by the Japanese during World War II." Even today the spirit of *seishin* training is very much alive in the national principles of Malaysia. The energetic new figures who replaced traditional and hereditary leaders stepped into a policical void created by the war. They claimed the right to lead their people in the postwar struggle for independence.

The Japanese not only implanted *seishin* in the minds of Southeast Asian youths; they also stimulated the professional pride of local administrators. Since the Japanese lacked adequate training in administering occupied Southeast Asia and knowledge of local affairs, they increasingly appointed indigenous people to administrative posts to replace Europeans. Filipinos and Burmese had the taste of self-government for two years under Japanese supervision. Though their participation in central and local administrations was limited, they acquired skills of administering government. This knowledge proved useful in postindependence years.

Another contribution of the Japanese occupation is national unification through language, particularly in Indonesia. Indonesia is a multilingual nation consisting of more than three thousand islands sprawling over three thousand square miles. Before the war there was no common language except Dutch, the lingua franca of the educated. The mass of the populace spoke in dialects and the people had no self-identity as Indonesians. During the Japanese interregnum, Indonesian became the national language due to Japanese encouragement and a ban on Dutch. Indonesian taught in government-sponsored courses, schools, and military organizations and in mass communication media spread the language even to isolated villages and discouraged provincialism. Not only did the Indonesian language reach a larger audience, but the people were brought into direct contact with national leaders insistent on the need for national unity. Sukarno and Hatta and other leaders could not have united the nation in postwar years so effectively without Japan's language policy. It aroused a desire for unity and an awareness of national identity among different linguistic groups of the archipelago.

The Japanese regime taught Indonesians and Burmese, and to a lesser extent Malaysians, the usefulness of political and national mass organizations. As a result some people in Southeast Asia became much interested in politics and became familiar with organizational techniques for leadership and discipline. Nationalists had acquired a reserve army experienced and talented in organization. Such vertical and horizontal mass organizational patterns as the Rukun Tetanga (neighborhood association), the Board of National Unity, the National Front, and celebrations of the great national holidays provided national leaders with an example of mass mobilization in postwar years.

The Japanese military administration was undoubtedly destructive and brutal in physical terms. I make no apology for it. Nevertheless, the Japanese occupation made positive contributions and proved enlightening in the historical perspective. No history can deny a page for Japan's role as catalyst in Asian nationalist movements. Japan helped Asians achieve "Asia for the Asians" and change the political map of postwar South Asia. Louis Allen, has concluded:

> Yet its impact was very great. Either as a direct result of Japanese conquest or in the dispositions which followed Japanese defeat, the pattern of history in Asia was irrevocably altered. . . . Hesitant and belated though it was, a taste of independence was given to Burma, Vietnam, Indonesia

[and the Philippines]. . . . Whatever Japan's faults as a nation between 1942 and 1945, history will restore that trust and gratitude. In the long perspective, difficult and even bitter as it may be for Europeans to recognize this, the liberation of millions of people in Asia from their colonial past is Japan's lasting achievement.

As attested by the evidence I have presented in this essay, one can scarcely disagree with this conclusion.

PART XI

The Allied Occupation: How Significant Was It?

THE ALLIED OCCUPATION of Japan fascinated observers at the time and has continued to fascinate them ever since. After a brutal and bitter war, who would have expected so amicable an occupation? Who would have expected so much genuine cooperation between victor and vanquished?

The writings of many contemporary observers reflected their astonishment. Edwin O. Reischauer, writing in 1950, began his discussion of the occupation in this way:

> The history of the American occupation of Japan will some day form one of the most fascinating and important chapters in the history of the world in modern times, telling a story which is both dramatically unique and universally significant. . . . For Japan herself, the fifth decade of the twentieth century will probably prove to be the most momentous in all her long history.

Almost thirty years later, some of the astonishment has faded and criticism of the occupation seems on the rise. Reacting in shock and outrage to the American war in Indochina, American scholars have taken a new look at American policy in postwar Asia. The general consensus had been that the American occupation was an enormous and almost unqualified success; that consensus has been shaken if not shattered.

Some scholars have examined the relation between the occupation and the cold war. What effect did American policy toward Japan have on the Soviet Union? Were American actions in Japan provocation? Or were they response? As early as 1946 Douglas MacArthur described Japan as "the westernmost outpost of our defenses," and in 1949 he gloated that "now the Pacific has become an Anglo-Saxon lake." How did thoughts like these—and the actions they led to— contribute to the development of the cold war? This argument will continue for many years; at issue is the source and the wisdom of American policy.

A related topic deserves more attention than it has received. This is the role of the occupation in *American* history. What lessons did the American public learn from the occupation—about Japan, about Asia, about the United States? In the 1950 edition of their standard textbook *The Growth of the American Republic,* Morison and Commager wrote that "within a few months after the surrender General MacArthur in cooperation with liberal elements in Japan revolutionized Japanese society and government." The ethnocentric and ideological implications of that statement are found in more explicit form in popular journalism of the period. There is a long tradition of ethnocentrism in American attitudes toward Asia, and we should be aware of the occupation's role in reinforcing that ethnocentrism.

This group of essays focuses on still another aspect of the occupation: its significance in *Japanese* history. How momentous was the occupation? In what sense and why? To what extent is Japan today the offspring of the occupation? To what extent is Japan today simply the product of trends upon which the occupation had little effect?

As befits his stature as senior statesman of American Japanists, Edwin O. Reischauer leads off. We have seen something of his 1950 assessment of the occupation. How different is his assessment today? Perhaps his biography offers clues to this question. Reischauer was born in Tokyo in 1910 to American missionary parents. Graduating from high school in Japan in 1927, he came to the United States for college (B.A., Oberlin, 1931) and graduate work (Ph.D., Harvard, 1939). Since 1939 he has been a member of the faculty of Harvard University. During the Pacific War Reischauer served in the Department of State, the War Department, and the army. Appointed ambassador to Japan by Prsesident John F. Kennedy in 1961, he served also under President Lyndon B. Johnson, resigning in 1966. How does Reischauer answer the question—how significant? And what is his attitude toward the Japan of today?

The second essay, "Reform and Reconsolidation," is by J. W. Dower. Like Reischauer, he stresses continuities: but there the similarity ends. Almost thirty years younger than Reischauer, Dower was born in 1938 in Rhode Island. Fourteen when the occupation ended, he attended Amherst College (B.A., 1959) and did his graduate work at Harvard (Ph.D., 1972). For several years after 1961 he worked in Tokyo; and upon returning to Harvard in 1965 he helped organize some of the early protests by Asian specialists against the war in Indochina. These protests led to the formation of the Committee of Concerned Asian Scholars, an organization in which Dower has been active ever since. Before 1965 a student of Japanese literature, Dower turned to the study of political history and international relations. His book on Yoshida Shigeru, prewar diplomat and post-war prime minister, develops some of the themes set forth in this essay. Perhaps this background sheds light on his arguments. What is Dower's attitude toward the Japan of today? And to what extent, in his eyes, did the occupation shape this Japan?

Although of different generations and political persuasions, Reischauer and Dower are both Americans and hence look at the occupation from outside. The authors of our third and fourth essays are Japanese scholars of the occupation. Sodei Rinjirō, author of the essay entitled "A Question of Paternity," was born in 1932 near Sendai. Thus he was twenty years old when the occupation ended. Not many years later he graduated from Waseda University, and he did graduate work at the University of California at Los Angeles. A journalist for many years, he won two national book awards for his book *Makkaasaa no nisennichi* [The two thousand days of MacArthur; 1974]. He is now professor of political science at Hōsei University in Tokyo. Recently, when asked his politics, he responded: "I once tried to be a Marxist historian but abandoned the idea when I found out that the Marxist school is seldom successful in ascertaining the role of man in history. I am a liberal thanks to my experience in America. But above all I am a realist with . . . imagination." What are the psychological ramifications of the "question of paternity"? Why should Sodei's perspective differ from Reischauer's? From Dower's?

The final essayist in this part is Takemae Eiji. Takemae was born in 1930 in Nagano prefecture in the Japanese Alps. His place or birth influenced Takemae in two ways. First, he suffered little hardship or danger during the war. Second, Americans serving in the occupation used a hotel near Takemae's home for a vacation spot. Takemae writes: "In order to test out my English, I would pack a lunch and go each Sunday to the hotel, lie in wait for Americans leaving the hotel, and practice my English conversation." He has been interested in the occupation ever since. In his opening paragraphs Takemae clarifies the terms of our debate. What are the implications of these clarifications? What is his criticism of the "modernization" school? And how does that criticism square with his concession that—viewed at least from A.D. 2052—the occupation may be insignificant? How does Takemae respond to those, like Dower, who focus on the reverse course?

"Study the historian" is an admonition honored more in the breach than in the observance. Who the historian is, when the historian writes, and why—these questions are absolutely crucial to an evaluation of what the historian says. Reading these essays without studying their authors is like placing blinders on our eyes. Only when we study the historians and see the essays in the context of their lives can we begin to grapple with our topic: "The Allied Occupation of Japan: How Significant *Was* It?"

—RICHARD H. MINEAR

The Allied Occupation: Catalyst Not Creator

Edwin O. Reischauer

The Allied Occupation of Japan—or, as it might more accurately be called, the American occupation—had a deeply significant impact on Japan in a wide variety of ways. How could it have been otherwise, when there were so many troops of radically different culture and race in Japan and the occupation authorities interfered energetically in almost all aspects of Japanese politics, economics, and society over a period of more than six years? The impact was all the greater because Japan at the time was physically exhausted by war and plunged into spiritual and intellectual confusion by defeat.

There has been a tendency, however, to attribute too much of what developed in postwar Japan to the occupation and not enough to other factors—the qualities and skills the Japanese already possessed before the occupation, the experiences they underwent before and during the war, and the general situation they faced in the postwar world. Clearly the occupation was absolutely decisive in setting certain broad parameters for Japan's postwar course. Within those parameters, however, most of what has happened in Japan during these past three decades was basically determined by these other factors. The occupation thus can be seen for the most part as merely having hastened the flow of some of these natural developments and as having given them more specific direction and shape than they otherwise might have had.

Let us first consider the general parameters set by the occupation. We can understand these best by suggesting some of the alternatives if the war had ended differently or the occupation had been of a different nature. Assuming a Japanese defeat as inevitable, it is still possible to imagine several other outcomes to the war than the one that did occur. A fight to the finish throughout Japan might have left Japan so destroyed and depopulated and feelings of animosity toward the Japanese so strong that it would have been quite impossible to restore the country to anything like its present state. A Soviet rather than American occupation might have produced something like the conditions of a satellite Poland. An occupation divided between the United States and the Soviet Union would probably have produced a situation not unlike that in Korea.

Even assuming an American or American-dominated occupation, it could have been of a different type. It might have had little interest in reform or rehabilitation and limited its activities to demilitarization and retribution. In that case Japan might not have been aided by foreign technology and capital or found world markets open to the products of her factories. Under these circumstances the postwar "economic miracle" would probably not have taken place, and Japan would still be a desperately poor and hopelessly overpopulated land. Or again, the occupation might have been unable or unwilling to maintain orderly political procedures in the early postwar years, in which case the deep distrust and animosity in Japan between left and right would probably have erupted into open conflict with uncertain results. My own guess would be that, after an initial victory of the left, there would have been a crushing reaction of the right. In either case the political system and probably social and economic conditions would have turned out quite differently from the way they have in actuality.

In steering Japan away from these various other possible outcomes of defeat and occupation, American control over the country was of course decisive. If we deny these radically different outcomes to the war as a given premise, however, I contend that much if not most of what has developed within Japan during the past three decades would have come into being in broad outline even without the interference or guidance of the occupation. The occupation obviously speeded up many of these developments and gave them a certain coloration, but the results on the whole have probably been shaped more by Japanese characteristics, skills, and past experiences and by general world conditions than by American design.

The meaning and validity of such an assertion can only be tested by examining some of the major characteristics of Japan as she exists today. We might start with Japan's economic and strategic position in the world. In prewar Japan there were sharp differences of opinion over the best way to attain security for Japan and adequate sources of raw materials to maintain her economy. Some thought this could only be done by military power and an extensive empire or zone of hegemony. Others thought it could be done through peaceful cooperation with other nations and open world trade.

After the war, the occupation threw its full weight in favor of the latter view, but that is not the chief reason why it won out overwhelmingly in Japan. World conditions made the military alternative entirely unrealistic, as the Japanese had learned full well through their own bitter experience. War had led to complete catastrophe. Rising nationalism in the less developed countries, which had contributed significantly to Japan's defeat, was becoming so strong that it made all overseas empires untenable. At the same time, Japan as a military power had become quite outclassed because of technological developments. While Japan was in military eclipse, the superpowers developed a nuclear potential that Japan, because of geographic limitations and lack of resources, could never match. Japan had no alternative but to seek security through peaceful trade. With an increased postwar population and in time a much higher standard of living than before the war, this dependence on peaceful trade became massive and global.

Thus, though shaped in detail by the occupation and continuing strong American influence, the general position of Japan in world affairs today is basically the product of Japanese experience and world conditions rather than occupation policy. It is still disputed whether Japanese or Americans first suggested Article 9 of the constitution (the article renouncing war and military forces), but in either case antimilitaristic, antiwar sentiments would, no doubt, be a major element in Japanese attitudes today. Early opposition by the occupation authorities to any Japanese military, their later sponsorship of a paramilitary force, and at times after the occupation American encouragement of limited rearmament in Japan—all have had little lasting influence on Japan's military posture. The size and role of the Self-Defense Forces, for example, and Japan's three nuclear principles— not to make, to possess, or to permit entry of nuclear weapons into Japan—have been almost completely determined by Japanese attitudes and the Japanese political process. American sponsorship and aid unquestionably hastened the Japanese development of a worldwide trade network, and American restrictions at times held back economic relations with communist countries, but Japan's current success in maximizing her trade with every part of the world is almost entirely the product of Japanese attitudes and skills, responding to worldwide economic conditions.

Only the Security Treaty is in large part an outgrowth of the occupation, though it was first suggested by the Japanese side and always had the full support of the Japanese government. It has been a major divisive issue within Japanese politics and did at one time seriously affect Japanese relations with China and other communist countries, to the great unhappiness of most Japanese. But even this legacy of the occupation is gradually losing its significance. It no longer affects Japan's relations with communist nations and actually seems to have the tacit approval of both China and the Soviet Union. It has lost most of its heat as an issue in domestic Japanese politics. And it fits quite snugly into Japan's self-chosen role in the world, making possible Japan's own small outlay for self-defense and alleviating fears of Japan's neighbors over a military resurgence in Japan.

In the realm of politics since the war, except for the possibility of a dictatorship by the right or left, the obvious alternative for most Japanese to the military leadership discredited by defeat was some form of parliamentary democracy. The occupation helped make the alternative of dictatorship less likely and worked fervently to build up a parliamentary democracy. But even without this strong occupation leadership, it seems probable that the Japanese would have gone in this direction on the basis of their own experience with such a system prior to the 1930s. Probably the movement would have been slower and less certain. There might have been a far longer period of dangerous conflict between left and right, both of which basically grew out of prewar and wartime experiences in Japan and only subsequently took on an anti-American or pro-American coloration. Very possibly there would have been no new constitution but instead a revision and reinterpretation of the old one. This might have left more unclarities and anomalies in the system. The emperor, for example, might still theoretically possess sovereignty, though his actual position would probably be what it is today. But on the whole the Japanese political system some three decades after the occupation would probably have been much the same sort of parliamentary democracy it is today, even without the strong occupation efforts to produce this result. Certainly the way the political game is played in elections and in the Diet would have been much the same, for these are clearly the natural outgrowth of political habits already well established by the 1920s, and the contemporary parties are for the most part simply the continuation of prewar political groupings.

The occupation, in intervening in Japanese politics, wisely based its efforts on the British parliamentary system, which had been the model for prewar democratic trends in Japan. Where the occupation departed from this model to inject American concepts, it efforts proved for the most part not very successful. The attempt to create a unicameral legislature was the one major point in the draft constitution prepared by the occupation authorities that the Japanese Diet rejected. A strong measure of local autonomy was another of these American concepts which failed. Except for the election of prefectural governors, the other measures designed to achieve this end, such as local control over the police and education and greatly increased powers of local taxation and legislation, withered largely away. The occupation created a separate judiciary under a supreme court with powers of constitutional review of all legislation in the American manner. The Japanese judicial system, however, has largely returned to what can be considered a natural outgrowth of the prewar system, and the supreme court exercises its review powers with great circumspection. It does protect individual rights from bureaucratic maladministration, but it attempts not to upset actions of the Diet or involve the courts in the administration of law in the American style.

In the field of economics, the initial destruction of the *zaibatsu* system by the occupation, the start it made on dissolving the great corporations, its capital levy, tax reforms, and labor legislation, all had a profound effect in breaking up Japan's prewar concentration of wealth and economic power. Subsequently occupation attitudes and actions discouraged the socialization of industry and put limits on the political power of the labor unions. Unquestionably the occupation did affect Japan's postwar economic history. But the end results, as we see them today, would probably not have been very different even without these efforts by the occupation. Japan might superficially be more or less socialistic than she is today, but the close relationship between government and business and the pattern of management–labor relations which make the Japanese economic system so unique would probably have developed anyway. These are both clearly characteristics that have emerged from Japanese skills and attitudes and were certainly not in the minds of the occupation authorities.

The occupation did set the pattern for generous American acceptance of Japan into world trade, thus making possible in time her tremendous industrial growth. In insisting on economic rationalization, despite the political and human costs of this policy, the occupation probably speeded up the recovery of the Japanese economy, and, by taking a supposedly temporary stance of strong government leadership and guidance in the industrial field, the occupation unwittingly made possible the strengthened postwar bonds between government and business. But the present Japanese economic system and its tremendous success are both overwhelmingly the product of the Japanese themselves. The American contributions should be seen as merely having helped to set the stage for these developments.

In the social field, the story is somewhat the same. Laws insisted on by the occupation authorities helped raise the status of women and worked for a general egalitarianism in society, but these trends were already present in the Japanese system and most of them would probably have come about, though more slowly, under the postwar conditions the Japanese faced. Actually Japan's highly egalitarian society is basically the product of the Japanese educational system, which had long before the war started to transform Japan from a society of inherited status to one of personally demonstrated merit through educational performance and examinations.

The occupation concentrated great efforts on reforming education in Japan and may have helped make it slightly more flexible than it otherwise might have been. On the other hand, the occupation's major education reform, which was the adoption of the American system of six years for elementary school, three for junior high school, three for senior high school, and four for college, seems to have produced nothing but temporary confusion. The really great change in postwar Japanese education is the spectacular increase in the number of high school students (to around 90 percent of the age group by the late 1970s) and of those going on for higher education (to around one-third of the age group). This astounding change, which has been a determining factor in altering Japanese society, is a clear outgrowth of prewar trends toward developing a meritocracy of education and has been made possible primarily by Japan's postwar affluence. The way postwar Japanese society has developed is probably in line with the hopes of the occupation authorities, but it has come about largely in a manner they could scarcely have imagined.

One serious prewar dilemma was the poverty of rural Japanese and the gulf that separated their experiences and attitudes from those of city people. The occupation attacked this problem by carrying out a land reform that was as thorough as possible, short of the collectivization of agriculture. But the aims and methods of this reform were not at all unfamiliar to the Japanese, who had put much thought into this problem and probably would have moved in this same direction in any case, though so drastic a reform would probably not have been possible through domestic political processes alone. Here then is probably one area in which the occupation did have a specific, lasting impact of considerable significance.

The great transformation of rural Japan we witness today, however, is probably less the result of this land reform than of the "economic miracle" and new forms of communication, both of which lay outside the scope of occupation thinking. The economic miracle reduced the rural population sharply because of the attractiveness of factory jobs and the availability of suitable farm machinery, which permitted a sudden drop in the number of workers. The quality of rural life changed because of the decline in the farm population and because of agricultural price supports that kept the farmers in line with general national prosperity. Meanwhile new forms of communication wiped out many of the cultural differences between rural and urban Japan. Telephones, television, and automobiles brought the Japanese farmer into the same cultural community as his city cousin. Thus, however significant the land reform was in the early years after the war, in the long run most of the great changes in rural Japan would probably have occurred in any case even without it.

When we come to the cultural field, the imprint of the occupation perhaps is most obvious. The presence in Japan of so many Americans and the ready Japanese acceptance for a number of years of American models for almost everything left a large residue of at least superficial Americanization in a wide variety of fields from language to sports. But the significance of this fact seemed much greater during the occupation and the early postoccupation years than it does now.

The most important feature of Japanese culture today is probably its mass character. This might be attributed in part to American influence, since the United States probably shares leadership in the world with Japan in developing a mass society and culture. But it seems more the product of Japan's egalitarian society, her extraordinary homogeneity, and her affluence.

It is also worth noting that today, more than a quarter of a century after the end of the occupation, the flow of cultural influences from the United States to Japan is as great as it ever was. Now, however, it is almost entirely the product of Japanese initiative in borrowing and is paralleled by a growing flow of influences from many other parts of the world and a reverse flow from Japan to other countries, particularly to the United States. Given a globally trading and affluent Japan inclined toward a mass form of culture, such international cultural flows are probably inevitable and would probably have produced much the same results we find today, even if there had not been the period of somewhat forced American cultural influence under the occupation. Take as a small example the blue jeans of American youth, which swept over not just Japan but most of the world, including the communist countries of Eastern Europe, many years after the end of the occupation. The torrents of cultural influence we witness today make the cultural influences of occupation days seem like mere rivulets.

In conclusion, if one views Japan's postwar development in the broadest terms, the occupation certainly set the general parameters, but within these parameters most of what developed would probably have come about in much its present form even without the efforts of the occupation authorities. When one looks at specific details, of course, one finds many points in which the actions of the occupations had a lasting effect—as in the names and nature of particular organizations, such as the PTA, or in specific areas of continuing debate, as in the field of antimonopoly legislation or labor relations. But these examples are for the most part merely details in a large picture that itself would have looked basically the same even without the occupation.

To return to our opening question—"The Allied Occupation: How Significant *Was* It?"—the answer clearly must be a mixed one. The occupation was vastly significant in some ways, particularly in helping to rule out certain possibilities that might have emerged from a different ending of the war or a different sort of occupation. It was significant in speeding up some of the changes that occurred in postwar Japan. It was significant in establishing certain detailed aspects of the Japanese system which still linger on. But it was far less significant than is often assumed in creating the generally pacifistic, world trading, affluent, egalitarian, homogeneous, culturally mass-oriented Japan we find today. This Japan is much more the result of Japanese skills and past experiences together with general world conditions than it is the product of any specific American planning during or since the occupation.

Reform and Reconsolidation

J. W. Dower

Great events capture the historical imagination, but often at the risk of creating misleading impressions of disjuncture. In the popular consciousness, the past becomes compartmentalized: pre-this and post-that. And nothing, with the exception of revolution, cuts with a sharper edge than war. Thus it is customary to separate prewar and postwar, or presurrender and postsurrender, or pre-1945 and post-1945 Japan.

In the case of Japan, this impression of a great divide has been strengthened by the unusual nature of the period between August 1945 and April 1952, when the country was subjected to alien control and a program of reform and reconstruction directed largely by the United States. Here, indeed, the terrible cataclysm of war was followed by a self-proclaimed "revolution from above." Shattering defeat thus marked a historical terminus, it is assumed, while the occupation's revolution laid the groundwork for a new Japan. In actuality, one of the striking features of postwar Japan is that so much of it is not really new at all.

Certainly Japan has experienced great changes since 1945, and many of these were accelerated and even initiated by U.S. policies during the occupation. Yet the usual Western view of these developments can easily become ethnocentric, self-applauding, and ahistorical. This perspective can be briefly suggested by dismantling the popular cliché of the occupation's "reformist legacy" and examining the several parts of this catch phrase more critically.

First, emphasis upon the *occupation's* reformist legacy tends to inflate the American role, to dwarf the activities of the Japanese, and to draw attention away from the dynamics and tensions of the presurrender society. This tendency reinforces the simplistic image of the prewar Japanese state as static, monolithic, and reactionary and the notion of the prewar populace as "one hundred million hearts beating as one."

Beyond a doubt, the presurrender state was repressive and militaristic. It was also immensely complex, however, and mobilization for war actually accelerated political, economic, and social change. The war effort promoted Japan's "second industrial revolution" in the heavy and chemical industries. Monopolistic control of the capitalistic economy was greatly strengthened. The rural hegemony of the landlord class began to erode. The bureaucracy proliferated and extended its tentacles to new areas. The status quo was challenged by "renovationist" ideologies which presented a disconcerting Janus head—as suggested in the very concepts of "right-wing radicalism" and "national socialism." Throughout the society, moreover, the traditional mechanism of indoctrination and control became strained in the very process of being tightened. As bombs devastated the cities, reduced the material disparities between the middle and lower classes, and drove millions of urban residents into the countryside, these social controls appeared to be close to the breaking point.

At war's end, Japan was a country in crisis but also in dramatic flux. And while the Japanese as a whole supported the war patriotically, or at least endured it stoically, they were far from the mindless and homogeneous tribe portrayed in propaganda. The prewar polity may have been conservative and nationalistic, but prewar society—and the wartime experience—also nourished tensions and widely divergent interests and attitudes. Even without the presence of alien reformers, these were bound to be released by defeat—although the direction they would take was uncertain. The possibilities ranged from a modified conservatism to revolutionary struggle.

In its milder guise, the potential for change was apparent in the tradition of parliamentary politics practiced from the 1890s to the early 1930s. In contrast to the Pan-Asian rhetoric and quest for autarky which characterized external policy after 1931, there also existed an earlier—and, to many, still attractive—tradition of economic and military cooperation with the West. Potentially more explosive, however, were the strains of a highly inequitable class society, which already had given rise to radicalism after the First World War: to communist and social-democratic parties, to organized protest by urban workers and tenant farmers, and to a vigorous Marxist tradition among the intelligentsia. These movements were suppressed in the 1930s, but they could not be snuffed out. Indeed, as secret wartime police reports reveal, the hardships of prolonged war raised the specter of impending radicalism among the masses as a whole. Even short of radical popular upheaval, Japan's dominant elites had proved themselves incompetent and a war-weary populace was ready for change. The occupation's more progressive reforms reflected this sentiment, and succeeded—where they did succeed—largely because of it.

The dynamics of these various trends, and the contradictions among them, profoundly influenced the direction of postwar change in Japan. The bureaucracy and big capitalists were deeply entrenched and, naturally, sought to preserve their prerogatives; they were supported by the old guard representatives associated with court circles, the Foreign Ministry, and the conservative political parties. And while most of the significant early occupation reforms were opposed by the old guard and found greatest support among the progressives and the dispossessed, in the final analysis the legacy of the occupation was a new conservative hegemony in Japan. In part this development can be attributed to revisions in U.S. occupation policy beginning around 1947 and prompted by the cold war and America's own postwar economic crisis. But it is testimony too to the weight and momentum and staying power of powerful prewar Japanese groups and institutions.

Thus it is also necessary to qualify the notion of the occupation's *reformist* legacy. When the so-called democratic revolution formally ended in 1952, Japan remained conservative and counterrevolutionary in many aspects of both domestic and foreign affairs. Certain reforms were impressive and reasonably enduring, but no less impressive was the survival of individuals and organizations, institutional structures and patterns of authority, which had not been associated with genuinely democratic practices in the prewar period.

It follows, then, that the cliché of an occupation *legacy* also can be misleading. For the occupation itself rested upon, and the Americans interacted with, a potent and complex inheritance from the past. All articulate actors in the occupation drama, whatever their ideological persuasion, had to address this past explicitly. The necessity to do this was most apparent in the immediate postsurrender period, when one's political agenda for what needed to be done in Japan required a coherent explanation of the recent disaster. At this early stage of the occupation, the fundamental U.S. position was radical insofar as it was premised upon a *structural* explanation of prewar repression and aggression.

This structural explanation was not adhered to consistently, however, for the war crimes trials and purge reflected an assumption of *individual* war responsibility. The more basic and consequential line of analysis was succinctly conveyed by Assistant Secretary of State Dean Acheson in September 1945, when he declared that "the present economic and social system in Japan which makes for a will to war will be changed so that the will to war will not continue." General Douglas MacArthur was fond of characterizing the occupation's mission as being eradication of the "feudalistic" nature of Japanese society, and early U.S. policy reflected the structural approach by postulating an inseparable relationship between overseas aggression and *institutionalized* domestic repression. This interpretation amounted to nothing less than a critique of the Meiji Restoration and the entire course of Japan's modern development, and it undergirded a policy calling for wide-ranging renovation of both state and society.

This was a victor's critique with an undeniable strain of ethnocentricity: Japan was judged to have been solely responsible for the war; the repressive and imperialistic characteristics of the prewar state were seen as being entirely dissimilar to the domestic structures and international practices of the more advanced Allied Powers. Yet at the same time the critique was bold, idealistic, subtle, and sophisticated. At a certain level it also bore striking resemblance to the orthodox Marxist view of Japan's "semifeudal" nature and the necessity for bringing about a bourgeois-democratic revolution. Occupation authorities tended to use the terms reform and revolution interchangeably, and their early mix of liberalism and radicalism gained wide support from progressive elements in Japan. The American retreat from this initial position turned these early allies into bitter critics before the occupation ended.

More moderate and conservative Japanese opposed the "excesses" of this initial agenda on several grounds. In their view, Japan's actions from the Manchurian Incident of 1931 on reflected a militarist conspiracy, an aberration, a departure from the normal and established course of Japan's postrestoration development. "Feudalism" was a fatuous label, for prior to 1931 the country was developing admirably along the path of a modernizing, bourgeois, capitalist state. Without exonerating the Japanese militarists of the 1930s, moreover, it was wrong to lay responsibility for Japan's actions solely upon the Japanese, for to do so was to ignore the global crisis which underlay Japan's fatal quest for autonomy. Thus in the view of the dominant Japanese elites there was no need for major reform and renovation in postsurrender Japan. What was required was a minor purge of the militarists, concerted attention to reconstruction, encouragement of the democratic trends already characteristic of Meiji–Taishō, and Japan's reintegration into a stable world order.

In essence the conservatives supported policies of paternalistic democracy and cooperative imperialism, and these they found ready at hand in the existing society. The former resided in the "benevolent" emperor system, in the "enlightened" bureaucratic elite, in the *zaibatsu*-dominated "free-enterprise" system, and in the tradition of "moderate" parliamentary politics. The latter was exemplified by the "traditional" policy of cooperation with the Anglo-American powers espoused by the *zaibatsu* and Foreign Ministry. By 1952 the United States was firmly allied with the Japanese spokesmen for these views, and these spokesmen were snugly back in power. Before this occurred, however, occupation authorities had sponsored reforms which were anathema to the Japanese elites—and often a cause for later regret to the Americans.

The shift of occupation priorities from democratization of a former enemy to reconstruction of a future cold-war ally was widely known as the "reverse course." The Americans did not repudiate the initial reforms wholesale, but after 1947 they proceeded as occupation overlords along a trail of broken promises and tempered ideals. Some of the original reformist policies were jettisoned, others vitiated, still others left to the mercy of conservative manipulation. As the Japanese conservatives consolidated their control and assumed de facto authority, they continued the reverse course, with general American encouragement, under the new rubric of "rectification of excesses." The process of antireformist revisionism thus extended beyond the occupation period per se. By the mid-1950s it had involved retreat in all of these critical areas: demilitarization, reparations, economic deconcentration and democratization, elevation of labor to a level of influence commensurate with that of capital, local autonomy, education, and decentralization of the police.

The reformist agenda was in fact severely hamstrung from the very outset by several critical decisions on the part of the United States. The first of these was to govern Japan indirectly through the existing Japanese administrative and bureaucratic apparatus. This decision was pragmatic and understandable, but it ensured the preservation of bureaucratic prerogative and gave the antireformist forces a powerful vehicle for subtle sabotage. There was actually a double reinforcement of centralized authority in this setup, with the Supreme Command for Allied Personnel (SCAP) itself constituting a supreme governing body with extraordinary powers of directive. While the alien overlords and indigenous administrators may have disagreed on specific policies, the nature of their dual *modus operandi* perpetuated the tradition of a strongly centralized state.

The second critical decision was to retain the emperor system and, indeed, the selfsame emperor who had just been reviewing the troops. This decision was rationalized as necessary to ensure domestic tranquility, and in the new constitution of 1947 the emperor was in fact stripped of his former political authority. Nonetheless, the throne remained as symbol of both paternalistic authority and the continuity of the prewar national polity *(kokutai)*.

A third restriction upon effective reform derived from indecisiveness more than any single explicit decision. From the outset, the United States waffled on its economic policy for occupied Japan—on both reparations and economic deconcentration—while leaving the task of economic recovery largely to the Japanese themselves until 1949. In the interim, the Japanese capitalists regrouped and played a waiting game while the economy collapsed. The disruption and crisis which resulted from this stalemate were perhaps inevitable. Although the U.S. government proclaimed support of a reformed capitalism in Japan, American policymakers were in greater unanimity on the capitalism than on the reform. The Allied Powers were at odds on reparations. And the giant industrial and financial organizations had the resources and patience and confidence to bide their time.

What this meant was that postsurrender Japan retained her emperor, her bureaucracy, and her *zaibatsu* monopoly capitalists (minus their prewar holding companies). With the exception of one floundering interlude of coalition government under a right-wing socialist premier (the Katayama cabinet of May 1947 to March 1948), the cabinet was consistently conservative. Throughout the entire course of the occupation, the conservative parties dominated the Diet. And for six and a half eventful years, the Japanese were accustomed to associate democracy with a Supreme Command and a Supreme Commander.

Thus even before the reverse course the possibility of a truly revolutionary break with the past had been foreclosed. But at the same time, even after the reverse course and after the "rectification of excesses" campaign, there did remain an important legacy from the initial reforms, most notably in four areas. First, a new constitution was promulgated which relegated the emperor to the status of symbol of the state, guaranteed a wider range of civil rights than did the U.S. Constitution, established the responsibility of the cabinet to the Diet, and ostensibly prohibited the maintenance of military forces. Second, landlordism was eradicated in the countryside and the pattern of rural tenancy was replaced by a system of petit bourgeois landowners. Third, the military establishment was dissolved—although beginning in 1950, and contrary to the constitutional prohibition, Japan was encouraged and indeed pressured by the United States to recreate a military force. And fourth, labor unionization was extensive—although the initial progressive labor laws were revised even before the occupation ended, and organized labor, contrary to the professed early objectives of the occupation, remained an articulate but subordinate and largely defensive force in the New Capitalism.

With the exception of the land reform (which removed the threat of rural upheaval, led to increased production, and did not affect the interests of the urban bourgeoisie), the conservatives lamented their inability to rectify these "excesses" as well. They desired constitutional revision, more rapid and legally untainted remilitarization, and greater restraints upon working-class activism and upon the broad guarantees of civil liberties as a whole. By the 1950s, the United States was also generally sympathetic to such concerns. These reforms, representative of the early ideals of the occupation, survived because they retained an effective constituency among the Japanese people even after they had lost the firm support of the United States.

At the beginning of the occupation, the reformers had emphasized the interrelationship between domestic and international practices. At the end of the occupation, the inseparability of internal and external policies remained conspicuous, although in altered form. The domestic reverse course and reconsolidation of a paternalistic, albeit more liberal, state paralleled Japan's integration in the global anticommunist camp. Autarky of the 1930s variety had been repudiated for Japan, but under the U.S.-Japan alliance the country had little choice but to work out its future within a new form of bloc economy: the international capitalist system dominated by the dollar. Japanese remilitarization also inevitably followed the grand blueprints of the Pentagon. Although the anticommunist mission of the new military was familiar, its total integration into U.S. strategy was a departure from the past. Insofar as this strategy involved the continued presence of U.S. forces in sovereign Japan, it contributed to a galling sense of continued occupation conveyed in the pejorative phrase "military-base Japan."

In gross economic terms, Japan derived great benefits from this policy. The country's subsequent economic boom reflected maturation of presurrender trends in technology and capital concentration, but it also rested upon the rewards for faithful partisanship in the cold war. In return for her participation in counterrevolution and containment, Japan gained access to U.S. technology and received Washington's good offices in matters pertaining to international aid and trade. More crudely, the country profited immensely from America's "little wars" in Asia—Korea in the 1950s and Indochina in the 1960s. America's military-related procurements were absolutely crucial to the development of the postwar economy.

These were gains at a price yet to be calculated. "Economy" and "efficiency" were the guiding slogans in the reverse course and rectification campaign, and it was declared frankly that these goals must take precedence over democracy. A favorite phrase of the conservatives was that democracy had to be "adapted to the actual conditions of our country." This "adaptation" resulted not merely in an attack upon genuine democratic practice but also in a disregard of social well-being. By the 1970s Japan had become a showcase of environmental abuse. Moreover, the material benefits of firm allegiance to U.S. cold-war policy were obtained at a considerable psychological cost. They locked Japan into a status of junior partner and prevented the country from exercising real autonomy in international affairs. Even the conservatives chafed under this restraint, most notably with regard to their forced participation in the containment of the People's Republic of China. If the new Japan was not really new, neither was the sovereign Japan of the post-1952 period truly sovereign. Within Japan, this outcome of the occupation was criticized as "dependent independence." This was a perception with wide currency and a long, still burning, fuse.

Yoshida Shigeru, the dominant conservative politician of the first postsurrender decade, once wrote of a "thirty-eighth parallel" running through the heart of postwar Japanese society. He was referring to the polarization between those who accepted his own "realistic" policies and the progressive and radical forces who opposed rearmament and partisan alignment in the cold war and continued to espouse the cause of democratic reformism. Like Yoshida himself, these opposition forces did not suddenly appear full-grown on the postwar scene; they had prewar roots and reflected tensions starkly evident in the prewar society. At the same time, however, the size of the opposition, its diversity and articulateness, and its ability to exist without fear of crass government repression were all greater than had been the case in the prewar period. This development reflected both an ex-

panded consciousness forged by self-reflection on the war and the expanded arena of civil liberties instituted during the early period of the
occupation.

In a sense, the many ironies of the occupation are reflected in this
impression of a divided country in a divided world. By 1950, Yoshida,
spokesman for the old guard and a consistently outspoken critic of virtually the entire gamut of occupation reforms, had become the pre-
eminent Japanese symbol of the new U.S.–Japan partnership—while
defense of the original reformist ideals had fallen to a constituency
which had once been America's firmest supporter but now stood
among its severest critics. Neither side was monolithic, but the broad
lines of confrontation were clear enough. Neither side was really new,
although both had undergone changes. Unlike official Washington,
neither side had greatly altered its position since the surrender. The
pressures of past and present, of internal and impinging forces, had
reshaped both state and society—but in channels which in retrospect
seem less epochal and more conservative than many declared them to
be at the time.

A Question of Paternity

Sodei Rinjirō

Lose a modern war, and you probably will experience occupation by the victor. Failure to occupy casts doubt upon the victor's will and limits that nation's ability to influence the postwar development of the defeated country.

What is an occupation? An occupation is a process whereby the victor nation enforces its will on the vanquished nation. The military power of the victor forms the backdrop. Hence, to paraphrase von Clausewitz, an occupation is the continuation of war by other means. The dynamics generated between occupier and occupied determine the form and content of the occupation. By carrying out an occupation, the victor nation realizes the goals of the war.

The occupation of Japan by the Allied Powers—in reality, by the United States—espoused enormous intentions: not simply to destroy Japan's military power so that she could not again emerge as a militaristic state and become a threat to the world, but also to transform Japan into a democratic nation. This aim of the victor was a crucial factor in determining Japan's political direction. Nor should this fact surprise us, for Japan has a history of being shaped by forces from the outside, forces which at times have been no less important than pressures from within.

Of course, it is one thing to declare one's intentions and quite another to realize one's goals. How true is the occupier to his intentions? How much actual force does he expend in the realization of his goals? As these factors vary, so too will the fruits of an occupation and thus its significance.

In the case of the American occupation of Japan, there was a vast gap between the announced goals and the actual results. Several factors created this gap, among them the personality of General Mac-

Arthur, the person in the driver's seat, and the propaganda excesses of his underlings. As the cold war deepened, moreover, America changed the course of its occupation policies—from creating a democratic though weak Japan to creating an economically strong Japan though perhaps not so democratic. This development precluded the realization of many of the early aims of the occupation.

Nevertheless, we cannot deny that the occupation shaped the mold in which postwar Japan was cast. For one very simple example, take the new constitution. Among the political leaders of Japan in the immediate postwar era there existed neither the intent nor the capability to draft so liberal and so democratic a document. Had the new constitution not been imposed from above, by the occupation's Government Section, it would not have come into existence. Yet in its first thirty years this constitution was not revised in any way. It has managed to survive until the present, and the Japanese people are living with it today. These facts alone indicate the great significance of the occupation.

Some people suggest that history eventually would have decreed that Japan have a democratic constitution even without the occupation. But that is only simplistic historical determinism—like suggesting that fathers are not an essential part of the reproductive process. Today antidemocratic forces within Japan are seeking to restrict the fundamental rights of the people, and the people are able to protect those rights by relying on the constitution. Clearly the constitution has sunk its roots among the people.

Land reform too would have been impossible without the occupation. Among the nations of Asia which have not experienced the liberation of farmland, the Philippines and Indonesia suffer from political unrest among the rural population and—until a few years ago—so did South Vietnam. What a contrast with Japan! Japan succeeded in her economic recovery and achieved prosperity by abolishing rural hardship through land reform and by turning her villages into a vast domestic consumer market. What made this drastic change possible? The power of the occupation.

Most of the farmers who received land through land reform were not able to survive as "independent capitalists" (MacArthur's phrase) in the economic growth of the postwar years; the ultimate solution may lie in some form of collectivization. But to have asked that of the American occupation would have been to ask the impossible. In the main, the occupation reforms corrected past abuses through the exercise of political power. The occupation had no power to stop the future play of economic forces. Thus the reforms of the occupation bore that limitation.

Labor legislation offers a further example. The workers sought to extend their right to organize; and had it not been for the power of the occupation forces, it is certain that workers would not have been able to acquire their rights in such orderly fashion. Today these rights are a given; no matter what force one applied, it would be impossible now to wrest these fundamental rights from the hands of Japan's workers. They realize that these rights have brought them economic prosperity and thus would never let them slip from their grasp. If the drastic reforms of the occupation had not taken place, the postwar labor scene would have been characterized by disorder. Workers would have resorted to such techniques as the wildcat strike to achieve their rights. In that case it is certain that Japan would not have succeeded in achieving today's economic prosperity.

The same thing goes for women's rights. It is true that the males of that day had lost much of their traditional authority. Still, without the irresistible compulsion of the occupation forces, there is little likelihood that Japanese would have given equal rights to women. Having achieved equality, the women of today are defending those rights. They may work to strengthen and extend them, but they will never let them go.

Thus most of the pillars supporting democracy in Japan today—the fundamental human rights of all citizens, the land of the farmers, the rights of the workers, the equal rights of women—were established by the occupation. This fact alone speaks volumes about the significance of the occupation. Although the occupation represented external pressure, although it acted from above, its significance for Japan's postwar history was enormous.

What enabled these successes to take root was the indigenous cooperation and understanding the reforms received. At the risk of sounding somewhat crude, let me suggest that most reforms carried out by occupations resemble rape. Reforms carried out from above by force usually cause resentment. Such reforms usually take unfortunate forms and have unfortunate fates. They tend not to last long.

The reforms of the occupation of Japan were not pushed through by one-sided force, however. For the wartime leaders, the economic combines, and the landlords, these reforms did mean the loss of powers and rights they had enjoyed for some time. But for the people in general, the reforms of the occupation were a blessing. In place of the husbands of old, obstinate and barbarous, there appeared the reformers, handsome and rich. The masses of the people, delighted, jumped into bed with their conquerors, cooperated, and gave birth . . . to the reforms. The reforms which have taken root in Japan today are those—and only those—which had support at the level of the masses. These included the four reforms upon which we have focused: fundamental human rights, land reform, the basic rights of workers, women's rights.

Not all reforms did take root. The dissolution of the economic combines ran into fierce opposition and sabotage on the part of the capitalists. Most of the combines, though broken up, were able to survive until American policy changed and this reform was discarded. Thereafter they recovered their former strength. Given the fact that the occupiers pursued a policy of half-measures and that the occupied showed little cooperation, it is not surprising that this reform never took root.

Article 9 of the new constitution symbolizes the pacifism at which the early occupation aimed. The Japanese people responded and, despite the Americans' later change of heart, today pacifism has deep roots in Japan. Seizing the occasion offered by the Korean War, the United States urged the remilitarization of Japan; and so Japan came to maintain a military establishment which the constitution does not formally recognize. Thus demilitarization stopped in midstream; but even this abortive reform played its role. Witness the widespread antagonism today to the maintenance of a strong military force. This antagonism is characteristic particularly of the young people and women; and it is the women who form the largest force for peace in Japan today.

Before the war the Japanese people were warlike. But in the postwar era the slogan has been "Economic Expansion, Not Expansion Through Military Means." Once again, the occupation's peace constitution is a prime agent of this change. Today, when voices from the political and financial worlds call for strengthening the military to protect Japan's enormous investments in Korea and Southeast Asia, popular opposition is strong enough to block such a development.

The reforms which America carried out in occupied Japan were on the model of "guided democracy." Democracy delivered in this manner has its internal weaknesses. The history of democracy worldwide indicates that the fundamental rights of the people cannot be bestowed from above or from the outside. They must be earned through the struggle of the masses themselves against the old power structure —from below, from within. But in Japan under the occupation, the old power structure which should have been the target of the struggle of the masses had already fallen victim to the power of the allied armies. Hence the masses could only accept with gratitude the rights bestowed upon them from above. It is perhaps only natural that rights won without struggle do not inspire the same devotion as rights written in blood.

For the masses themselves to strengthen the rights which had been bestowed upon them, it probably would have been necessary for them to fight head-on against the occupation forces whenever the occupier acted unreasonably. To strengthen democracy, it is not enough simply to accept these rights. At times one should fight against all rulers, even those who are merciful. But the occupation authorities did not permit movements from below to challenge them. Even slight opposition was suppressed mercilessly. The mass media were subjected to censorship in every detail. Controls like these are probably the essence of the business of being occupied, and reforms imposed by an occupation undoubtedly have their limits. Even so, the occupation of Japan did bestow democratic rights on the Japanese people.

More than a quarter-century has passed since Japan regained independence, and today there is a tendency for the leading classes in Japan to give the occupation less than its due. In the textbooks used in Japan's compulsory education, there are virtually no accounts of the occupation. Political and bureaucratic leaders tend to look upon the occupation as another episode in the past—not because they think that the occupation has no significance at all in Japanese history but because they are reluctant to admit that the very structure of Japan was remodeled through the agency of a foreign power.

The leaders are not alone in their discomfiture. The masses too face embarrassment. It is not pleasant for them to be reminded how they cooperated all too readily with the occupation forces, which were, after all, the former enemy. In the early days of the occupation, the Japanese people did in fact get drunk on the democracy bestowed on them. They gladly hopped into bed with those in power. Today, when the baby from that union has grown up, they prefer not to recognize the existence of the father. Just as one cannot deny the significance of the father for the child, one cannot deny the significance of the occupation in Japanese history.

Some Questions and Answers

Takemae Eiji

First: a problem of terminology. Does the word "Japan" in "the Allied Occupation of Japan" mean only the main islands? Or does it include Okinawa? Until quite recently, most historians have dealt with the occupation primarily as it affected the four main islands. But now many people have come to realize that we must include Okinawa, a realization which has caused consternation among many of the experts.

On the main islands the reforms of the occupation included demilitarization, democratization, and respect for fundamental human rights. But the reforms on the main islands could take the forms they did only because policies of a very different nature were carried out on Okinawa. Okinawa was compelled to become a military base; its democratization was sharply limited; and its people's fundamental human rights were neglected. The progressive reforms on the main islands and the radically different policies in Okinawa were two sides of the same coin, and any evaluation of the occupation as a whole must take both sides into account. Still, our topic here is primarily to discuss the historical significance of the occupation of the four main islands.

Second: a question of time frame. How long a sweep of history do we intend to consider? Our judgment of the occupation's significance will depend on the answer to this question. If we think in terms of a hundred years or two hundred years, of looking backward from the year 2052 or the year 2152, we may find ourselves concluding that the occupation was not so significant. Even then, however, we could expect lively debate on the subject. Remember, for example, the energetic discussions which accompanied the Meiji Centennial of the late 1960s. But if we think in terms of thirty years, or perhaps of fifty years, our judgment will be quite different.

Third: a matter of approach. Does it help much to break everything down into continuities and discontinuities? The continuities in question are the legacy of presurrender Japan; the discontinuities are the changes brought about by occupation decree. Indeed, it is tempting to plot Japan's postwar historical evolution simply in terms of these two vectors.

But this dichotomy obscures as much as it reveals. For one thing, absolute discontinuity—a complete break with the past, a wholly new culture—is utterly impossible. There is always continuity; it is only the degree of continuity which is in question. For another thing, a judgment in favor of continuities leads easily to the corollary that the occupation was insignificant (and a judgment in favor of discontinuities leads just as easily in the opposite direction). But the issue is not so simple. It may not be a question of either/or. It may well be a question of both/and.

This leads us to our major assertion: that speaking in terms of a period of thirty or fifty years, and conceding the importance of various continuities in Japanese history before and after the war, the policies of the occupation had an enormous influence on the development of postwar Japan. Scholars who focus on "modernization" and see the occupation largely in that context have suggested that the occupation reforms simply accelerated changes which were going to happen anyway—that the occupation merely hastened modernization. The reforms of the occupation did not simply accelerate changes which were predetermined in nature. In significant measure they determined the character and direction of postwar changes. In effect, they were the gas pedal but also the steering wheel. Without the reforms of the occupation, the postwar changes might have led in a very different direction.

Now for some evidence in support of this assertion. In the occupation of Germany and Korea, divided jurisdictions led to divided countries. But in the occupation of Japan, the United States exercised virtually sole jurisdiction and no division arose. Here is one instance of the power of occupation policies to determine the direction of postwar developments.

Occupation policies were often decisive in shaping the politics, the economics, and the culture of postwar Japan. Without the power of the occupation army, for example, it would not have been possible to establish the concept that the emperor's role is symbolic. Further, in the absence of orders from the occupation army there would not have developed the constitutional order we know today: the liberalization of the old constitution, the abolition of the special police, the end of antileftist legislation, the growth of local self-government. Today popular sovereignty, pacifism, respect for fundamental human rights, and local self-government have become the essence of the new constitutional order. They also represent a bulwark against the revival of the old emperor system, remilitarization, and against a return of the police state.

Not all occupation reforms were equally successful or unequivocally successful, of course. Economic deconcentration was implemented only incompletely. Its purpose, like that of many reforms of the occupation, was to undermine the competitive position of Japanese capitalism; and the occupation soon moved in another direction. Ironically, however, the overall result of the limited deconcentration which took place was to strengthen Japan's competitive position and facilitate the growth of Japanese capitalism. A limited deconcentration and severe restrictions on military spending (the renunciation of war in article 9 of the constitution) gave the economy a major boost.

Land reform, most observers agree, was the greatest success of occupation policy. It served the cause of social justice by giving poor tenant farmers their own land, and the class of poor tenant farmers disappeared. In this sense, land reform was unequivocally good. Once that judgment is behind us, however, ambiguities begin to creep in. For the land reform weakened the farmers' movement. It cost the Socialist Party, whose fortunes were closely linked with the farmers' movement, its electoral base in the countryside. Why? Because the cultivators who had just become proprietors of the land they worked tended to support the conservatives rather than the socialists. Thus land reform strengthened the power of the conservatives and weakened the socialist challenge.

Indeed many of the landlords, stripped of their holdings by the reform, came to wonder what land reform was all about. After all, they watched as land values rose dramatically with the rapid economic growth of the postreform years; then they watched as their former tenants, who had become cultivator-owners thanks to the reform, sold the land that had cost them virtually nothing and became wealthy. Viewed from the perspective of the present day, land reform created a new and affluent class: the ex-tenants who sold the land that came to them through the reform. But that development must be laid at the door of the postwar economic growth, not at the door of the occupation.

As the years have passed, the influence of occupation reforms has penetrated into the very core of Japanese society. Economists often speak of trickle-down effects and say that tax breaks or subsidies for business eventually have a positive effect on labor, too. But what happened in Japan as the years passed was more of a drenching than a trickle. The drenching of the roots of Japanese society by the waters of occupation policies has led in recent years to the emergence in local politics of progressive officials—some prefectural governors and virtually all big-city mayors—and of progressive self-government bodies. Since nothing comparable happened in prewar Japan, we are forced to attribute enormous significance to occupation era changes.

There are some, of course, who do not accept this assertion. They come from a number of viewpoints and put forward a number of arguments. Many of these critics belong to the group which focuses on the modernization of Japan. They emphasize the continuities more than the discontinuities, the legacy of prewar Japan more than the impact of occupation reforms. Or they emphasize the influence of wartime conditions. But on closer examination we find that the facts do not support their arguments.

Take the issue of continuities. Indeed there existed in prewar Japan precursors of the various postwar reforms. Examples are easy to find. A labor union law was presented to the Imperial Diet in prewar days on a number of occasions, only to be defeated. Land reform was proposed as a means of combatting unrest among tenant farmers. There were proposals for the rationalization of the great economic combines. An educational reform extending compulsory education from six years to eight had gone into effect briefly (and then was suspended) even before the end of the war.

Moreover, once the war was over but before the occupation pushed through its radical reforms, the Japanese government drafted some lukewarm proposals of its own to forestall action by the occupation. There were, for example, the proposals of November 1945 dealing with the partial reform of the bureaucracy, the labor union law submitted to the Imperial Diet in December, an electoral reform proposal, a land reform proposal, and others. These reforms failed in their purpose, of course, for they did not keep the occupation from taking more radical action; but they indicate that there were in fact domestic precedents for most occupation reforms.

The picture changes when we take a closer look at the reform proposals themselves. They give us some indication of what postwar changes would have been like had the occupation authorities not had the last word, and we are forced to the conclusion that the occupation mattered enormously. Proposed labor legislation, for example, differed from both prewar proposals, which sought to recognize labor unions as a means of preserving order, and from occupation reforms, which were predicated on modern industrial relations. Similarly, the proposed educational reforms adhered to the prewar ideology of the emperor system. They differed entirely from the occupation reforms, which took individualism as their keynote.

Consider now the suggestion that wartime conditions played an important role. During the war, for example, patriotic labor organizations were set up in almost every industry. These organizations were horizontal in form; that is, they were industrywide. Some people have suggested that these patriotic labor organizations paved the way for the rapid expansion of labor federations in the postwar era. To some extent, they have a point. But the patriotic labor organizations of the wartime years served also as negative role models, for they discredited the principle of horizontal organization and thus turned the postwar unions in the direction of vertical organizations (one union per factory). Similarly, the wartime shortage of labor led to the appearance of women in large numbers in the workplace. This development in turn formed the point of takeoff for the postwar movement to improve the status of women. But the postwar women's movement was dramatically different from any of the wartime developments.

Some scholars approach the occupation from a very different direction and yet wind up with arguments not so different from the ones we have just examined. They emphasize that many occupation reforms were aborted after 1947 and that the conservative Liberal Democratic party has continued to rule in the postwar years. In other words, the occupation reforms were not radical enough; the basic pattern of Japanese politics did not change. To be sure, the reverse course was important. (In general, I believe that the occupation started out well and then, after 1947, went steadily downhill.) Had the reverse course not taken place, the occupation reforms would have had a still greater impact than they in fact had. The Katayama cabinet, for example, Japan's first and only social democratic government, had only a brief life; and as the reverse course took hold, the conservatives reasserted control. They have held power ever since.

But we must not overlook two points. First, this development originated in a change in occupation policy, a change which suppressed the mass movement which otherwise would have played a major role in bringing about democratization. Hence occupation policy played a major role even in this apparent continuity. Second, the fact of continued control by the conservatives should not blind us to the fact that there were important differences between prewar conservatives and postwar conservatives. They bore the same label; but they were quite different.

Thus the argument in favor of continuities falls short on all counts. It overlooks certain fundamental facts: that the occupation reforms covered a very broad front; that many of them lasted the full six years of the occupation; that many were not reversed after the occupation army left; that because the Americans ruled indirectly, through the Japanese government, there was less resentment than there might have been against a more visible occupying army. The argument in favor of continuities fails also to account for measures which are inconceivable without the occupation. The release of political prisoners is one of these. Given the power structure of the time as well as the strength of the special police, the release of political prisoners depended entirely on the occupation. Most important, the argument in favor of continuities fails to account for the nature of the changes which came to postwar Japan. It is this aspect, the content of the reforms, which is the keystone of my assertion that the reforms of the occupation were decisive in shaping postwar Japan.

Since my specialty lies in the field of labor reform, let me comment in conclusion on two aspects of occupation labor policy on which opinions are sharply divided. These are the general strike of 1 February 1947 and the Red Purge of 1950.

The decision to forbid the general strike called for 1 February 1947 marks a turning point in the occupation. As the first move in the direction of suppressing the labor movement, it was the object of widespread resentment among the working class. By forbidding the strike, the occupation authorities denied public employees the right to strike. (Public employees included the workers of the national railroad and the postal system.) That resentment may be misdirected, however. What would have happened had the strike not been forbidden? Given the conditions of the day, is it not probable that occupation authorities would have called out their troops? The result would have been the direct control of labor by the occupation army. Viewed in this light, the decision to forbid the general strike may have been unavoidable.

The issue of the Red Purge is slightly different. Although there existed within the union movement in 1950 a spontaneous drive for the expulsion of communists from the unions, the occupation pushed through its Red Purge relying on power alone. Therein lie the problems. For one thing, the constitution and the basic labor law prohibited discrimination on the basis of thought or belief. For another, many anticommunists fell victim to the clean sweep. As a result, resentment against the Red Purge has not died out yet. Moreover, the Red Purge was used by various domestic political forces for their own ends. The communists used it in their campaign against the occupation and in favor of an early peace treaty. One faction of the Socialist Party used it to establish its own control within the labor unions. The conservatives, firmly in power, used it to suppress the left in the name of the occupation army; they also used the widespread antagonism against this arbitrary use of power as a weapon against the occupation. In this way the Red Purge became the focus of extremely complex political maneuvering. Viewed in the light of today's political conditions, the Red Purge merits further analysis.

Nevertheless, these are relatively minor matters. On the basic issue there is really no question: the occupation reforms did exercise a decisive influence on Japanese history in the postwar era.

PART XII

Japan:
East or West?

THE QUESTION ASKED in this final part may seem ambiguous or even silly. Yet it is the kind of question that will occur to Western students or travelers to Japan *after* they have become acquainted with Japanese society. It is the kind of unspoken question that remains when it has been decided that people in the modern world are all alike. People *look* different—because of "race" and the "epicanthic fold" and all that—but these skin-deep differences are significant only to unsophisticated observers from uniracial areas. These differences otherwise lack cultural, social, and political significance.

Indeed, only determined racists continue to focus on skin-deep differences. I was raised in central Illinois and had little contact with Japanese. After studying Japan for some years my race consciousness disappeared at a tennis club in Tokyo while watching a dozen or so Japanese players at tennis, a favorite game of mine. I became aware of comparing them individually to American tennis players I had observed, finding exact counterparts to one who always foot-faulted, one who blamed every miss on his racket, one who sweat like a Turk or was cool as a cucumber, one who hogged the court in doubles or had to inspect the net when he missed a few serves. All the idiosyncrasies and idiocies I knew so well from my tennis playing youth were there before me and suddenly the fact that each Japanese player was more like an American in my experience than like the other Japanese was crystal clear. That the range of difference among Japanese was far greater than the range of difference between Japanese and Americans was subsequently observed so frequently and repeatedly in a great variety of contexts that it became almost an article of faith with me.

Life is long, however, and experiences are many. A few of the latter, coming in recent years, have rather surprised me and, I confess, shaken this "one world" faith just a little. One such experience is my observation of Japanese who revert to some earlier and certainly non-Western tradition in meeting various contingencies. "Scratch a Japanese businessman and meet a samurai," some would say. (Of course, one can also say, "Scratch an American banker and find a Jesse James.") Such crude sayings are not only unkind but untrue in the normal course of events. And yet the samurai heritage remains in the background of modern Japan just as the frontier heritage lies behind twentieth-century America, celebrated respectively in ever-popular samurai films and western movies. Both are cruel and violent traditions, but they are different. Japan's samurai tradition is haughty and class conscious; America's frontier tradition is egalitarian.

Francis L. K. Hsu, the anthropologist, some twenty years ago published a polemical book called *Americans and Chinese: Two Ways of Life* in which he contrasts an American individual-centered tensely emotional lifestyle tradition with a Chinese situation-centered less emotional one. Quite clearly he favored the latter. But regardless of that, Hsu held that the differences were real and, moreover, that in situations of stress and/or inebriation these differences would come to the surface and even determine behavior. Though this book was controversial in many ways and a revised edition (1981) has appeared, Hsu's evidence that East remains East and West remains West underneath the veneers of commonality and modernity is quite convincing.

Japan is not China, of course, but in certain ways the grip of the traditions stemming from Japanese insularity may provide an even stronger hold than those of China, while being quite as different as China's from those of the Western world, especially America.

The essayists in this part are, again, Edwin O. Reischauer of Harvard, whose recent book *The Japanese* should be read in full by anyone seriously studying Japan; Charles B. Fahs, one of the pioneers of Japanese studies in the United States; and Miwa Kimitada of Sophia University. Though Reischauer thinks the question as posed rather silly, his answers invoke other questions which demand attention: Isn't "West" rather "North"? And isn't there a unique Japanese element? Fahs depicts a Japan which is able to be both East and West in quite exemplary fashion. In general these Western experts find much to admire in Japan. But the concluding essayist, Japanese scholar Miwa, argues that Japan has been too long and too much a peripheral country, unwilling or unable to accommodate herself smoothly to international relations.

—HILARY CONROY

Not Westernization But Modernization

Edwin O. Reischauer

We all know the wisecrack about silly questions receiving silly answers. The question set for these essays—"Japan: East or West?"—runs this risk. That is because it asks a false question based on a mistaken concept of the alternatives. One problem with our question is that its terminology is not clear. "West" itself is no longer a clear-cut category, and "East," as everything that is not "West," is even less meaningful. At one time the "West" may have seemed easy to identify, a term applied to the lighter-skinned members of the so-called white race who lived in a well-defined corner of the world, adhered to the Christian religion, and drew culturally from a Greco-Roman tradition. Since then, however, bewildering technological advances, rampant secularism, geographic sprawl, some degree of racial mixing, and the democratic-communist bifurcation of political systems have made the "West" a very fuzzy term indeed. In fact, "East-West" now is commonly used to describe the political division that exists within what was once the old West.

"East" as the rest of the world has, of course, always been an even vaguer term. All it could ever be was a handy way to designate the bulk of the world's population that was not Christian and Greco-Roman in tradition or lighter-skinned white in race. Within this vast non-West, there have always been diverse cultural and racial groupings, each comparable to the West in size and significance. The largest of these groupings and perhaps the most distinctive historically has been the East Asian cultural area, inhabited by people of the Mongoloid race and deriving most of its higher civilization from that of ancient North China. There can be no doubt in anyone's mind that Japan derives racially and historically from this East Asia. If the question of our title is simply asking to what racial-cultural group Japan historically belongs, the answer is too obvious to need statement.

But the question clearly is meant to signify something more than this. I take it to mean the following: Is Japan as she is now developing becoming essentially like the countries of the West, meaning the Western half of the old West, or will she remain at heart Eastern, meaning either East Asian or perhaps a more general and amorphous non-Western "East"? A second question is possibly also implied: Do Japan's interests lie more with the so-called Northern industrialized lands of Western Europe and North America—what is often called the First World but might be termed the "New West"—or with the preindustrial or industrializing lands of the so-called South in Asia and also Latin America and Africa—that is, the Third World which might also be termed the "New East"?

Even these questions, however, seem to me somewhat simpleminded. The answers to both would be much too complex to allow for any either/or sort of response. Perhaps the only simple answers that could be given would have to be "both" or "neither," but even these do not satisfy. Japan undoubtedly shares many characteristics both of surface phenomena and deeper attitudes with various other modern countries both East and West. At the same time she puts these features together in ways that are often *sui generis*. Japan is extremely "Japanese," and undoubtedly will remain so, even though sharing much with other lands. This is the way it has been for a long time, and I see no signs of it changing now.

The reason why the question of our title is posed at all, I think, is because of two basic misperceptions of modern times. All people have tended to identify themselves and their kind as civilized and to see all others as barbarian. Perhaps the Chinese have held longest and most adamantly to this view of the world. But it took on a new meaning during the past few centuries when the industrialization of parts of Europe suddenly made the West incomparably richer and stronger than the rest of the world and set up a dichotomy in people's thinking between a prosperous, dynamic, all-powerful West and an impoverished, seemingly static, and floundering East. Westerners in their arrogance could easily see all other peoples as sharing a common ignorance, perversity, and stultifying fatalism which, contrasting as it did with the Western self-image, permitted the lumping together of all these varied peoples as "Eastern."

What is more surprising than this Western attitude is the fact that at least parts of the rest of the world accepted the assumption that it belonged to a unitary East. Perhaps this reaction was a natural drawing together for strength against the domineering West. The solidarity sought by the extraordinarily diverse nations and cultures of the present so-called Third World is a typical example. In the case of Japan, generations of thinkers have been stirred by certain concepts—that "Asia is one," for example, or that Japan would remain true to "Eastern ideals" however much she might make use of Western techniques.

The "East" and "Asia" these Japanese had in mind was usually China, with which Japan indeed did share much: a strong work ethic, Confucian concepts of morality, a politically centered society, a common writing system, and deep artistic, literary, and philosophic traditions. Some tried to broaden the concept to include India, where a once shared Buddhism and some artistic and philosophic survivals of that time did produce a small area of shared experiences, attitudes, and artifacts, though the differences between Indian and Japanese culture remained vastly greater. All the way from basic philosophic premises to mundane life-styles, the contrasts between Indian and East Asian civilizations could hardly be sharper. Almost no Japanese attempted to stretch the unity of the "East" to include Islamic West Asia, which, as the Near East, was the East that Europeans had first and foremost in mind. To East Asian eyes the contrasts between East and West Asia were simply too evident and the Islamic world was too obviously related to the West as a sibling culture deriving from ancient Mediterranean civilization.

Still, the concept of Japan as part of a unitary East or Asia persisted, and it was compounded by a second mistaken notion—that any aspect of modern industrialization and technology or anything derived from them is now and forever Western and therefore not Eastern. Such a concept, of course, is a gross misunderstanding of the nature of history. Technologies are in one sense culturally dominant, but in another sense culturally neutral. The invention of paper and printing in China had tremendous cultural impact on China and in time on all lands to which they spread, but they did not make most other lands in any way culturally Chinese. The invention of the steam engine or the discovery of the modern uses of electricity have had comparable cultural impact but have not meant that the lands that borrowed these innovations necessarily became Anglicized, or Americanized, or even Westernized.

In the past, technological breakthroughs, such as agriculture, the wheel, bronze, iron, and the like, became in time the common property of all humanity. This is obviously happening also in the case of the modern scientific method and the vast number of technological innovations it has helped spawn. They started in the West and helped give it a temporary predominance. One could even argue that certain characteristics of Western culture made their first appearance there more probable than in other civilizations. (The same argument might be put forward for the invention of paper and printing in China.) But this is irrelevant. Modern technology is not to be classed as forever "Western." It is simply a new technological level in the world in which the West happened to pioneer but which inevitably will spread in time to the whole world.

If we first admit the falsity of the East-West dichotomy and then drop the definition of modern technology as forever Western, most of what lies behind the question of our title evaporates into thin air. Obviously modern technology has had a profound impact on Japan as on other non-Western lands to which it has spread. But the same thing has happened in the West too. New technologies brought with them new institutions and new values. Most of the characteristics that modern technology and its accompanying institutions and values have brought to the West contrast sharply with what the West had been before—affluence with poverty, democratic and communist egalitarianism with feudal privilege, mass culture with elitism, secularism with rigid religious attitudes, and so on ad infinitum.

There should be no surprise that similar changes are taking place in the rest of the world. In the case of Japan it was not the traditional characteristics of the West that transformed the nation. Nothing could be more central to traditional Western culture than Christianity and the emphasis on the individual, but both of these have been largely rejected by the Japanese. Instead they have adopted the modern innovations of the West with enthusiasm—railroads, airlines, television, mass sports, modern newspapers, modern legal and political processes, and the like, all clearly the outgrowth of modern technological innovations and their accompanying institutions and value systems. These have had a great impact on Japan in much the same way that they have changed the lands of the West, though sometimes with subtle differences. Seen in this light, it seems more reasonable to describe Japan's great changes as a process of modernization rather than westernization.

In the great process of modern change, even culturally close countries like England and France have remained quite distinct from each other. There can be no doubt that culturally more different lands, such as Japan and India, will remain even more distinctly themselves. It is in this sense, I believe, that when people have more perspective on the time we are now going through it will appear to have been a time of great technological and also institutional change everywhere but not a time when the whole world was westernized.

The great technological change of modern times, however, does carry with it special psychological burdens for the latecomers. The fact that others have led the way in the change creates a greater realization of what may be happening and therefore a greater sense of loss of what once was. With more advanced models to follow, changes may be forced at a more rapid pace and are likely to appear to be simply imitations of alien cultures rather than natural changes of technology and its accompanying institutions and value system. This makes the inevitable clash between the old and the new take on the more emotional tones of a struggle between native and foreign.

Moreover, the temporary dominance of the areas which led in the great technological change of modern times did result in a great deal of superficial imitation of nonessential Western traits by the others. Japan as she emerged into the world from her long seclusion was forced to conform to a Western-dominated international system and therefore sought to appear as Western as possible in Occidental eyes. Western things also appeared stylish. The Japanese in developing their modern form of life would probably have abandoned the less practical clothing of an earlier, more leisurely age, as virtually all other people have, but there was no need for them to have adopted instead Dior styles and none too practical white shirts and neckties. Mass participation and spectator sports would probably have developed in the new age, but there was no need that they should have included baseball and skiing.

Japan on the whole, however, seems to be moving past these particular psychological problems of the late starter. The Japanese are now completely at home with the styles and fads of international culture, mixing them at will with their own traditional traits and proving themselves a prolific source of cultural influences on other countries both West and East. They wisely examine what others are doing in facing the problems of modern times (the countries of the West could learn a lot from them on this score), but they are not blindly imitative and usually come up with a result superior to what can be found abroad. Only in their fear that somehow change means a loss of identity do they show the old anxieties. But even this may be passing as it becomes ever more clear that a thoroughly industrialized and modernized Japan operates its economy, society, and politics in ways not only quite distinct from the lands of the West but in most ways probably more efficiently. As of the present writing the Japanese are still engaged in the great *Nihonjin-ron* debate over the meaning of being a Japanese and the special role of Japan in the world, but this debate may prove to be the last great outbreak of this particular sort of worry.

In closing, let me return to the two specific questions formulated earlier in this essay, simpleminded though they may be. First, is Japan becoming essentially like the countries of the West or will she remain Eastern at heart? As I said, the answer cannot be a simple choice between the two but something much more complex. Among the great shaping forces of Japan as she now exists are characteristics deriving from the past, some shared with the rest of East Asia but some uniquely Japanese. Among these are the strong work ethic, a pervasive esthetic sense, an intense feeling for decorum and orderly processes, and above all a strong orientation toward group identification and group activity, albeit with a matching sense of individual endeavor, achievement, willpower, and personal improvement. These are but a few examples of strong survivals from the past which, when manifested in modern institutions, make Japan different from the countries of the West and the rest of the world as well. They are hardly to be identified as Eastern traits in general, though some could be called East Asian. But basically they are Japanese. Japan is and will remain very Japanese.

On the other hand, there can be no doubt that the technological, institutional, and intellectual modernization of Japan has brought the style of life in Japan quite close to life-styles in parts of the West. Young Japanese and young Westerners mix with little sense of strangeness. As other parts of the non-West go through the technological changes Japan has already experienced, they too become more like Japan. One sees this already in places like South Korea, Taiwan, Hong Kong, and Singapore, which share some cultural roots with Japan and have experienced some of the same technological modernization.

In summary, one might attempt to answer our question by saying that Japan shares a great deal that is both fundamental and superficial with the West and that she will increasingly share some of these characteristics with other non-Western countries as they modernize. But underneath these shared features, one must add, lie some very distinctive and fundamental Japanese traits which are certainly not to be called Eastern and are only in part East Asian: these traits are wholly Japanese and will probably always make Japan distinctly Japanese.

The other question is where Japan's chief interests lie—with the West (or "North") or with the East (or "South"). The simple answer is, of course, with both. Japan's very life today depends on a massive worldwide exchange of goods, and for this exchange to continue and grow there must not only be world peace but an effectively operating world system of trade. With the one very important exception of oil, Japan's chief source of energy, the greater part of Japan's economic relations at present are with the West rather than the East. Moreover, as a thoroughly industrialized nation, Japan's interests and points of view lie closer to those of the industrialized lands of the West than to the industrializing lands of the East. Japan will naturally continue to play a major role as one of the leading members of the First World of industrialized, trading democracies. Still, both for Japan and the other First World nations, relations with the less industrialized countries of the Third World will in the long run be crucial. There can be no choice between East and West or alignments of the two against each other without bringing catastrophe not only to Japan but in the long run to the whole world.

Thus even our two more specific questions turn out to be not very meaningful. In itself Japan is neither East nor West but simply Japanese—a changing mixture of many elements all blended together in Japan's unique way. Japan cannot be allied exclusively or even primarily to either East or West but must be an integral part of a globally unitary world. The real questions about Japan's future are, first, whether Japan can learn to play the major role her great economic size demands of her if a peaceful worldwide system of trade is to be achieved and maintained and, second, whether such a world is really possible however well Japan may play her role. If either answer proves to be in the negative, the prospects for Japan's future are dismal.

In any case, however, the sharp dichotomy of East or West throws little light on our understanding of Japan or her future. Its inclusion in this volume as one of the great questions of the period we now call modern Japanese history may some day seem a quaint survival of a nineteenth-century world view that still distorted our vision in the late twentieth century.

A Combination
of East *and* West

Charles B. Fahs

Since we live on a globe, "East or West?" is an ambiguous question. East or west of what? Greenwich? The international date line? The Urals? Better defined, the question is whether Japan's cultural and political orientation has been, is, or will be "east" (primarily toward the neighbors to her west in Asia) or "west" (toward the economically advanced and democratic countries of Western Europe, North America, and the South Pacific). In this sense, which is the one I shall adopt here, the question has been a traumatic one for modern Japanese thought and foreign policy. The supposed dilemma has become increasingly misleading since at least the nineteen twenties, however. It is based on too short a perspective of world history. For Japan today choice between East and West is not desirable, not necessary, and not possible.

"Asia" too is an imprecise concept. The traditional boundaries in the Urals, the Caucasus, the Bosphorus, Suez, and the waters of Southeast Asia are arbitrary and artificial. When Japanese talk or write of Japan's ties to Asia they are usually even more imprecise as to what area is meant. That Japan is geographically part of some "Asia" is not debatable. Her island chains have been pushed up or extruded as the Pacific plate has been subducted under the eastern edge of the Eurasian plate. In the distant past there were land connections to the mainland, and Japan's flora and fauna are therefore related to those on the continent. Human conditions apparently came relatively late. The origins of the Japanese people and their language are obscure but certainly Asian. Cultural influence in the prehistoric period must have been Asian. The little that can be proved suggests, however, that outside influence was attenuated and indigenous development important. For example, pottery excavated in Japan has been dated earlier than any thus far found elsewhere in the world. In the historical period cultural imports from Korea and China, notably writing, literature, Buddhism, philosophy, and art, became important indeed. Until the age of Vasco da Gama and Magellan all Japan's external cultural contacts were of necessity with Asia. But two things should be remembered.

First, Japan's cultural sources were almost exclusively in Northeast Asia—the Chinese culture zone. Contacts with Southeast Asia were far less extensive and those with the rest of Asia were remote, indirect, or nonexistent. Japan, Korea, and China are the only nations today using writing systems which, as far as we know, developed independently of Middle Eastern influences. All the other writing systems of Asia are related distantly to those of the West. Japanese, until quite recently, shared with Chinese and Koreans a distaste for milk and its products—in sharp contrast to Asian countries such as India where much of the diet is based on milk. Buddhism came from India, but Japan received it from Korea and China in the Mahayana version most fully developed there. Physically Japanese are close enough to the statistical range of Koreans and Chinese for a Japanese with sufficient knowledge of the local language and customs to pass in either country. This is more difficult in Southeast Asia and virtually impossible in most other parts of Asia. Japanese society and behavior are distinctive but such Asian resemblances as exist are with China and Korea. Nakane Chie of Tokyo University uses Indian society as the sharpest contrast to the vertical society she sees in Japan. Thus the idea that Japanese are Asian is meaningful only in the narrow sense of the Chinese cultural watershed. As the concept of Asia expands beyond this, the argument for Japan's affinity with Asia becomes artificial and weak.

Second, each of the imported cultural elements has been transformed in Japan into something distinctly Japanese. Even before the impact of Western culture, Japanese society, thought, and artistic expression were all well differentiated from those of Korea and China, the parts of Asia with which Japan had closest links. In those days Japanese were more conscious of being separate and different from the rest of Asia than of being a part of it.

The arrival of the Portuguese in the sixteenth century, followed by the Spanish and Dutch, for the first time made a choice between East and West conceivable by extending Japanese international contacts beyond Asia. When the reaction came under Hideyoshi and the Tokugawa, however, it was nationalistic and neither particularly anti-

West nor pro-Asia. Exclusion reduced contacts with Asia almost as drastically as it did contacts with the West. Japan kept small and carefully controlled doors open to Europe, China, and Korea. Until the nineteenth century the question "East or West?" hardly occurred.

Exclusion was possible because in the seventeenth century the three great modern revolutions of science, technology, and democracy had only begun. While the power of the Western European countries was growing, it was not yet disproportionately greater than that of countries which had not experienced any of those revolutions. Moreover, in East Asia that power was attenuated by distances not yet greatly shrunk by technology.

By the nineteenth century the situation had changed. Science, technology, and broader political participation had given the Western nations disproportionate power. Great Britain was in firm control in India and Malaya, the Netherlands in Indonesia, and Russia had extended its authority to the Pacific. By the time of Perry's expedition to Japan both Russia and Great Britain had imposed treaties on China by force. Russia was showing interest in Hokkaido. Japan ended her isolation because she could not defend herself against Western pressures. The principal motivation for the Meiji Restoration was the need for a stronger government to defend Japan against the West. Western incursions in other parts of Asia were repeatedly cited as auguries of what would happen to Japan if she did not act. Modern Japan was born under a threat from the West which Japanese perceived as also involving the other peoples of East Asia. Japanese felt that the threat would have to be repulsed in those other countries too if Japan was to be safe. Japanese leaders accurately recognized that the Western elements of science, technology, and broad political participation would have to be adopted if Japan was to gain the strength needed for defense; but this recognition did not prevent resentment against the West for the pressures and the resulting dislocations of Japanese interests and customs. Indeed a healthy nationalism made such resentment entirely normal.

In this way strong sentiments of both military and cultural resistance to the West and a special Japanese role in East Asia became embedded in modern Japanese thought. These sentiments were initially grounded in the reality of the expansion of Western power in East Asia and were therefore useful in Japan's evaluation of the world around her and the policy alternatives available to her. The sentiments were not confined to the autocratic statesmen of the Meiji period, to the military, or to the conservatives but were widely shared in

Japanese society. They were reflected in the writings of Fukuzawa Yukichi, a liberal and sharp critic of the government, in the views of the leaders of the popular rights movement opposing the Satsuma–Chōshū oligarchy, and even in the thinking of the American-trained Christian leader Uchimura Kanzō. Japanese public opinion, even university opinion, from time to time demanded actions in Asia more aggressive than the government thought expedient. Because these sentiments were vaguely delineated they did not offer clear guidance for policy. Because they were widely felt they were seldom questioned.

While Japan's "Asian-ness" is, in a limited sense, indubitable, it was then and is now no guarantee that Japan's interests and those of other countries of Asia coincide or that mutual understanding, respect, and confidence are more likely with Asian countries than they are with countries in other parts of the world. (Just as the vague concept of "American-ness" underlying the Monroe Doctrine offers no assurance of mutuality of interests, understanding, or confidence between the United States and the countries to her south.) Such vague concepts easily become mystiques—seductive but misleading and a dangerous basis for thinking on foreign policy.

That is what happened to the sentiment of a special Japanese mission to save Asia from the West. While idealistic in origin, it rapidly deteriorated into Japanese imperialism. Saigō Takamori, in his unsuccessful advocacy in 1873 of an unarmed mission to Seoul for the opening of Korea, may have been idealistic. But the government-sponsored punitive expedition to Formosa in 1874 was carefully calculated to serve Japanese interests as were the Sino-Japanese War in 1894 and the Russo-Japanese War in 1904. Japanese adventurers roamed East Asia. Some of the "China *rōnin*" were genuinely motivated by unselfish concern for China. Miyazaki Torazō, who sought Sun Yat-sen out in Canton in the 1890s and brought him to Tokyo, was one such, judging from his "Dream of Thirty-three Years" *(San-jū-san nen no yume)*. In contrast, Uchida Ryōhei, founder and president of the Black Dragon (Amur) Society, in the introduction to his "Japan's Asia" *(Nihon no Ajia)*, derived the very word "Asia" from "Ahihara" (as it occurs in the *Kojiki*) and concluded that it was Asia which Amaterasu had bequeathed to the Japanese imperial line.

Cultural resistance to the West at home was also an ambivalent goal. Much of what the West offered certainly had to be accepted in order to gain the economic and military strength necessary for defense and was welcomed for that reason. Additional changes, particularly

legal ones, were necessary to secure the revision of the unequal treaties, which remained a major goal of Japanese foreign policy until finally accomplished after 1900. But what of Western culture was essential and what was not? Could one not take Western technology but
retain Japanese spirit? Japan's strong feeling of national identity was
helpful in preventing blind acceptance of everything Western. To it is
due Japan's success in retaining so many of her own rich traditions.

While national identity provided a will to resist, it offered little
guidance in the difficult process of selection. The most critical issue
was democracy. Was democracy technology or spirit? Fundamental or
nonessential? While welcomed by some early Meiji writers such as Fukuzawa, democracy seemed to run counter not only to an aristocratic
tradition but also to the vertical lines of authority which are so important throughout Japanese society, to the Confucian ideal of the moral
scholar-administrator, to the bureaucratic legacy of the shogunate,
and to the personal interests of the Sat–Chō oligarchs. Moreover, the
need for stability and continuity in a period of rapid change was genuine and suggested caution in the adoption of new institutions. So
there was both a temptation and a tendency to treat democracy as
nonessential—to underestimate, that is, the deeper connections between individualism and intellectual, economic, and social development. Democracy was not easily accepted. But in the perspective of
the slow development of democracy in the West, the progress made in
Japan from 1868 to the enactment of the universal suffrage law in
1927 was remarkable.

Before democracy could be consolidated, however, it came under
attack from a new quarter. Anarchism, Marxism, and Leninism,
though Western in origin, were radical critiques of Western culture.
They offered their Japanese adherents an opportunity to condemn
Western individualism, private business, and representative government, just as Japanese traditionalists were doing, but at the same
time to enjoy the illusion that they were in the vanguard of history instead of bringing up the rear. Lenin's doctrines on the role of the colonial peoples also offered the lure that a socialist Japan could have an
important Asian role. While left-wing parties were weak and soon
suppressed, their ideologies penetrated deeply and widely, particularly among intellectuals and students. These doctrines influenced a
younger generation of bureaucrats and army officers. They confirmed
traditionalists in their prejudices against democracy but, at the same
time, alarmed them with threats to the imperial institution and to social stability. That traditionalists and radicals simultaneously dispar-

aged individualism and parliamentary institutions helps to explain why the very real progress which Japan had made toward democracy in the few decades since the granting of the Meiji Constitution was brought to a halt in the late twenties and early thirties. Their parallel reaction against the West and toward Asia is one reason why there was so little effective opposition to the drift to war and why there were so many conversions to collaboration with the expansion policy.

In the young officers' movement and related patriotic societies traditional and radical thought were substantially merged. Kita Ikki's proposals for a planned, collectivist bureaucratic government and economy, for example, were not very different in essence from what the left was advocating. If a self-appointed governing elite was desirable, it was more Japanese to have it operate in the name of the emperor than in the name of a diffuse and poorly defined proletariat. Certainly the military could not be expected to accept the leadership of groups which looked for guidance to Moscow—the capital of Japan's traditional military enemy. Just as certainly, if the goals were similar and the choice was between a nationalist and an internationalist formulation of them, the nationalists would win out. Marxism helped spread the canard that democracy was passé and thereby helped to undermine parliamentary government, but inevitably it was the nationalists who took control.

At the same time that anti-West and pro-Asia sentiments were becoming stronger in Japan in the 1920s and 1930s they were becoming less and less appropriate to the wider world situation. After the First World War imperialism of the kind which had threatened Japan and her neighbors in the nineteenth century was already in retreat. The diffusion of science, technology, and democratic ideas, a diffusion which colonialism had itself facilitated, was making the retention of colonial empires more difficult, increasingly expensive, and less acceptable to voters at home. By the thirties the United States was committed to leaving the Philippines, significant progress was being made toward self-government in India, and the United States and the United Kingdom were both prepared to cooperate with the efforts of China to achieve unification, revision of unequal treaties, and economic development. Had Japan been content with the original goal of independence for Asia and less ready to write off Western democracy, patience might have enabled her to avoid war by cooperation with the West in these developments.

Japanese attention was diverted from the trends toward decolonization and democracy, however, which now appear to have been the basic trends, by the world depression and the trade crisis which accompanied it, by discrimination in the United States and elsewhere against "Asiatics," by the continuing expansionist ambitions of a Russia now communist, and by the initial successes of Hitler. Under these circumstances, Japan's sentiments of resistance to the West, her mystique about Asia, and her resulting desire to settle Asian problems single-handed led her deeper into China until the Pacific War became unavoidable. In the 1930s, as in the postrestoration period, these sentiments were not confined to the military, the industrialists, the conservatives, or to any one group. They were widespread in the Japanese population—so widespread that it was possible to mobilize public opinion behind the war effort with far less coercion and thought control than was normal at that time in Nazi Germany and is still normal in the Soviet Union. They made Ishihara Kanji's thesis of The Final War and the later doctrine of a Coprosperity Sphere seem plausible.

Military failure discredited the war but not ipso facto the sentiments which had made it possible. Japanese showed great realism in accepting defeat when it came. The occupation was more humane than most. But it was only natural that many Japanese of all persuasions resented both defeat and occupation and that the feeling of cultural resistance to the West was thus prolonged.

The mystique about Japan's special relation to Asia was weakened but not destroyed. The Second World War in fact hastened decolonization in Asia and, for that reason, some Japanese today justify Japan's role in the war. But the number of such persons is small— the costs of the war to both Japan and the countries she overran too obviously exceeded any benefits.

The Asian mystique has survived principally among Marxists who, encouraged by communist successes in China, North Korea, and Vietnam, still dream of a major Japanese role in a socialist Asia. There has been a postwar crop of China *rōnin*, just as there was a prewar crop, but they carry somewhat different ideological baggage. In this pattern of thought the belief in a coming socialist millennium plays much the same role that The Final War did in the thought of Ishihara Kanji—a justification for all present sacrifices.

But the sentiments of resistance to the West and special ties to Asia are even less appropriate now than they were when the China War began. That science, technology, democracy, and the economic and social benefits they bring were pioneered in the West is history, but the patents have long expired. Through cultural diffusion these goals have become part of the aspirations of all mankind. They are a common world heritage, not something imposed by the West. Having adopted and naturalized them Japan is free to continue to evolve her own style of political and economic institutions. But Japanese have now experienced a wide range of political, economic, and intellectual freedoms and have found those freedoms enjoyable. Japan's institutions will never mirror America's, but Japan is unlikely soon again to welcome dictatorship—either military or proletarian.

Asia is not threatened by the West. Nor is it a promising frontier for exclusive development by any country. Despite Asia's enormous population its potential as a market is limited by poverty. It can supply only a part of the raw materials Japan needs—even if, using the traditional definition of Asia, we include the Persian Gulf, a region with which Japan certainly has had few cultural or historical connections. Aside from the oil-rich countries of West Asia, the few prosperous areas, such as South Korea, Taiwan, Hong Kong, and Singapore, will increasingly become export competitors of Japan. The larger areas, beset by overpopulation, have periodic food shortages which threaten to become chronic and which Japan has no way to meet. Capital needs are enormous; but with population growth still out of control, there is likely to be considerable instability throughout the area in the next several decades making investment precarious and economic growth sporadic. As a special responsibility for Japan, Asia is a potential disaster area. Moreover, there is no exclusively Asian solution to Asian problems. Asia needs what the West has to offer. If Japan has a responsibility to help it is because, like the other countries of the West, she has the technological and economic means to do so, not because she is Asian. Japan herself needs the markets, technology, agricultural products, and science found in the West.

Japan herself now combines East and West. She has maintained the continuity and vitality of her ancient cultural heritage far better than have most other peoples. But, at the same time, she has become an exemplar of the scientific, industrial, and democratic revolutions which, though long regarded as Western, are now part of the world's heritage. It is this combination—preservation of national culture together with the benefits of modernization, particularly freedom—to which most of the peoples of the developing countries, Asian or not, aspire. If Japan wishes to help them, she can do so most effectively in cooperation with the other developed countries which share these goals. I think this is the direction which Japan will continue to choose in the decades immediately ahead.

Neither East nor West But All Alone

Miwa Kimitada

In this essay I wish to shed new light upon modern Japan's international conduct as related to her location between East and West. Two views are commonly held: (1) that modern Japan felt a great sense of national inferiority when faced with Western countries and (2) that this inferiority complex necessitated Japan's overcompensation in the form of arrogance and superiority toward her East Asian neighbors. Such may have been the case, but it appears to me that this tells only half the truth at most.

The other half is that the Japanese applied different approaches to East and West. They retained traditional patterns of international conduct when they dealt with their East Asian neighbors. As long as these Asiatic countries remained tradition-bound and held Western models in total disdain, there was no reason why the Japanese should deal with them in a Western style. When faced with Western nations, however, the Japanese tried as best they could to apply Western ways correctly. Since they had mastered the intricate system of international law, the basic principle for order in the international relations of the European world, they could do this effectively. In other words, the difference in attitudes as modern Japanese handled affairs with East Asian countries on the one hand and Western countries on the other was a result of their discriminating application of different international systems to produce desired ends.

This essay, then, has two purposes: first, to indicate the conditions that gave rise to such differentiating Japanese attitudes and, second, to demonstrate how the practices derived from them affected some of the significant events in Japan's modern history. In my opinion the most basic condition influencing Japanese international relations was a structural one: the fact that Japan was located on the fringe of the traditional East Asian world. By the East Asian world I mean the historical world in which the common denominator was the use of Chinese ideographs. It is not quite the same as calling it a "Chinese cultural world," for although Chinese ideas were carried by the ideographs, non-Chinese ideas too were disseminated through the use of the ideographs, as with Buddhism, which originated in India. The structural significance of this East Asian world was the fact that it was a hierarchical order of states, with the Chinese empire at its apex and countries like Korea and Vietnam forming the middle layer. Below these were China's outlying territories and the habitats of barbarians.

According to ancient Chinese records, Japan both in name and fact was for a few isolated short periods on the same level as Korea and Vietnam. But from a Japanese point of view what is important is that Japan had earlier developed a sense of detachment from China and Chinese cultural preponderance. Yet this did not mean the total rejection of things Chinese. On the contrary, the Japanese kept borrowing from Chinese ways to manage their foreign affairs long after they had stopped doing so in domestic affairs.

China provided the form and manner for Japan's own empire. This empire began to take shape after the failure of Toyotomi Hideyoshi's expeditions to conquer Korea in the 1590s. Hideyoshi's failure meant the collapse of his plan for establishing himself as the founder of a dynasty to command the East Asian world as a whole—not only Japan and Korea, but even the Chinese empire itself. Japanese imperial control of the historical world of East Asia had become a lost cause, at least for the moment. Yet somehow Japanese zeal for building an empire in the image of the Chinese empire was definitely more than a mere dream; it remained a force.

Thus there emerged by the beginning of the Tokugawa period (1603–1868) a miniaturized empire built in the image of the Chinese empire on the periphery of China's East Asian world. Japan was at its apex; the kingdoms of the Ryukyus and Korea and even some outlying countries to the south were tributary states. Yet this miniature empire remained part of the general state system of the East Asian world and not outside it. Here the imperial benevolence of the Chinese emperor was the guilding norm, and a feudalistic relationship was the principle of order.

In contrast the state system which had come into existence since the treaties of Westphalia (1648) in Europe was based upon the idea of the sovereignty and equality of each state. Order within this Western system was to be maintained by honest observance of international law; disputes were to be resolved through peaceful judicatory procedures. Such was the world system into which Japan was led with the conclusion of the Treaty of Kanagawa in 1854 with the United States. In principle this historical event signified that Japan too could in due course enjoy the same privileges as a sovereign state as soon as she met all the qualifications to become an equal member of that European society of nation-states. The qualifications demanded of the Japanese by their Western "treaty powers" were, externally, the strict observance of international law and, within the country, full adoption and practice of a Western-type legal system. Also deemed important were religious freedom and other rights constitutionally guaranteed among advanced Western countries.

What were the immediate effects of all this? To put the answer simply, the Japanese response was a call for the modernization of the country along Western lines. They wanted to transform their country into a modern nation-state as quickly as possible so that equality as a sovereign state would be theirs too. To do so, apart from the adoption of Western legal practices, they had to be concerned with the defense of their own existence, saving whatever remaining portion of independence they still enjoyed.

Here lay really substantial problems. For the first time in their national history the Japanese had to concern themselves with the unprecedented need of clearly delineating their "national" borders, for example, an indispensable attribute of a sovereign state in the Western scheme. Were all the extreme territorial limits of countries like Korea and the Ryukyus, which were included in the traditional Japanese empire, to come within the national demarcation of Japan as a modern—Western-type—nation-state?

In this connection, some peculiarly Japanese phenomena of overlapping and sometimes contradicting regional and national identities began to surface. The ambiguity of Japanese national consciousness as to national borders was definitely a cause for an earlier origin of Pan-Asianism, or Eastern Asian identity, which some Japanese leaders distinctly came to possess. In fact practically all modern Japanese leaders, even before the opening of the country in the mid-nineteenth century, were possessed with both national and regional self-identities as Japanese and at the same time as East Asians. This identity continued even after Japan severed herself from the fringe of East Asia and attached herself instead to the periphery of the European world. But the implications of this matter will be discussed later. For the moment I am concerned with the discussion just begun: the problem of defense against Western nations as related to Japanese awareness and management of "national" borders.

Where there was direct territorial contact with a Western nation, in this case Russia, the demarcation was promptly decided upon in the north as part of the first treaty between Japan and Russia. But in the south and west, where Korea and the Ryukyus were involved, traditional practices within that East Asian state system worked as a staying force, and Japanese moves toward establishing a Western-type border were either ignored or met with a mere structural, as distinct from political, resistance. Thus the Ryukyus were made a prefecture within Japan as a nation-state by 1879. As for Korea, the first significant step was taken to terminate the hereditary function the lord of Tsushima had performed as a go-between in Korean–Japanese relations of the Tokugawa period; the second step was for the new Tokyo government to begin handling affairs with Korea directly. The first substantial achievement in the Western style was the conclusion of a treaty in 1876 which stipulated that Korea was an "independent" state. This step was to remove Korea from traditional Chinese suzerainty, thereby purporting to draw a Western-style "international" border between China and Korea, and eventually make Korea attach itself of its own accord to form an imperial unity with Japan, just as the unity of England and Scotland had materialized in 1707.

As long as China appeared strong to the Japanese, they thought in terms of mutual destiny and defense in the new age of Western preponderance in world affairs. This attitude was clearly demonstrated in the case of Formosa. The strategic value of this island was well appreciated by the Japanese. Some naturally wanted to take it over from China. But for the most part it mattered very little whether China held onto it or not, because Formosa was considered a common asset and basis for defense of the East Asian world as a whole. In fact it was not until 1884 when China proved ineffective in its defense of Vietnam against France that a man like Fukuzawa would openly suggest Japanese occupation of Formosa.

We come now to the most telling example in which the Japanese used traditional forms from the East Asian world system and modern Western legal practices to deal with an act of grave significance: Japan's annexation of Korea in 1910. The act of annexation was consummated when the Japanese emperor sent out an imperial message to authorize the Korean king to become a prince of the Japanese empire in that long-established Chinese practice of international feudalism, even though a formal treaty of Western form had been adopted and signed.

What was the significance of these differing measures? One action was definitely meant for Western nations. They should accept the change of Korean status in the world system as thoroughly legal. The other measure was meant for the transition of Korea from independence to colonial status. It was not so revolutionary a change as the Western-style treaty might have suggested. In practice it was not to be so much different from that Sino-Korean relationship in the traditional East Asian world with which the Confucian bureaucrats of the Korean aristocracy had always identified themselves with a degree of pride and comfort, as well as a sense of peace and security. But the military rule of Korea by Japan that began in 1910 proved a great disillusionment to the Koreans. Their sense of betrayal must have been profound and their resentment acute. Only when we consider the Korean situation in those terms can we appreciate the rapid and forceful spread of anti-Japanese demonstrations for national liberation covering a greater part of the country in 1919.

The determined suppression and severe punishment meted out to those disillusioned, discontented, and nationalistic Koreans were immediate and sweeping. Then the Japanese tried to reconstruct their moralistic front with the introduction of a civilian governor-general as an imperial benevolence per se—instead of oppressive occupation by militant terror. Yet there was no denying that here was definitely emerging an empire not much different from European counterparts in theory, practice, and rhetoric.

But a more catastrophic moment was yet to come when Japan would consider herself not only on the periphery of the European world, having removed herself from the fringe of the traditional East Asian world order, but brazenly at the center of a new world order she was to create in the Pacific area. This was the Greater East Asia Co-prosperity Sphere proposed by Japan in 1940. Somehow it retained the traditional values of the premodern agrarian "anarchism" of the East Asian world, extolled as a countermeasure to overcome the ills of modernizing forces of industrialized nationalistic countries. There was a ring of idealism and a nostalgic utopianism to the message. Samples of antimodern ideas, purporting to reconstruct a closed economy of self-sufficiency to guarantee continued prosperity, are not difficult to find. In today's parlance the message could have been that Japan was seeking the sustenance of a carefully planned and managed ecological balance of recycling industrialization and agriculture. The values of the frugal life-style were still there—and, coupled with a nationalistic sense of self-sacrifice and devotion, these values were to make the new order work. At least most of the Japanese had come to believe this to be true, and they were driven into war for the reconstruction of the decadent, European-centered, modern world order.

The Japanese self-image had shamelessly come to assume the grand proportions of illusory self-esteem. This delusion was eloquently and symbolically manifest in the designation the Japanese emperor used for himself in signing the declaration of war against the British and Americans. Emperor Hirohito called himself *Tennō* whereas his grandfather, the Meiji emperor, and father, the Taishō emperor, had called themselves *Kōtei* as they signed the declarations of war against China and Russia in 1894 and 1904, respectively, and against Germany and its allies in 1914.

The difference is truly significant, because *Kōtei* was a common noun used in East Asia to designate the emperors of China and even at times Korean kings. Even monarchs of European empires from ancient times down to the contemporary period, including the Mexican Emperor Maxmilian, were all referred to as *Kōtei*. But *Tennō* was totally different. It had been used once by the Chinese in ancient times and then was discarded. But as far as the Japanese were concerned, this word simply signified the Japanese emperor and nobody else. In 1894, 1904, and 1914, wars were declared in the name of *Kōtei* and the Japanese fought them as a modern Western-type nation, meticulously abiding by international law. Japan then was just one of many similar nation-states. But in 1941 Japan declared war on two major Western nations in the name of a monarch who was not only distinct in designation but represented a whole set of distinctly different values.

By 1941 Japan had become ethnocentric in ideas and egocentric in external affairs. While Japan was posing as the big brother of all Asian nations whom she meant to liberate from the shackles of Western colonialism, she was imposing on them a more severe self-conceited order of particularistic nationalist orientation.

Thus a full cycle was closed in the reorientation of the Japanese in modern history. First there was the mastery and effective application of the international legal system which was the spirit and structure of the world system the modern European nation-states had established. Simultaneously in the East Asian world there was the discerning application of traditional East Asian ways where useful. Finally came self-conceited Japanism as a paramount order bestowed with universal applicability and abundant benefits to replace both earlier systems. Japan, then, at least in her recent past, has been neither East nor West but all alone: proud, militant, and aggressive.

Suggested Readings

I. When Does Modern Japan Begin?

Black, C. E. *The Dynamics of Modernization*. New York, 1966.
Borton, Hugh. *Japan's Modern Century*. New York, 1970.
Dore, R. P., ed. *Aspects of Social Change in Modern Japan*. Princeton, 1967.
Duus, Peter. *The Rise of Modern Japan*. Boston, 1976.
Eisenstadt, S. M. *Modernization: Protest and Change*. Englewood Cliffs, 1966.
Jansen, Marius B., ed. *Changing Japanese Attitudes Toward Modernization*. Princeton, 1965.
_____. *Japan and Its World: Two Centuries of Change*. Princeton, 1981.
Kimbara Samon. *"Nihon Kindaika" Ron no Rekishi zo* [History of the "modernization of Japan"]. Tokyo, 1968.
Lockwood, William P., ed. *The State and Economic Enterprise in Japan*. Princeton, 1965.
Najita Tetsuo. *Japan*. Englewood Cliffs, 1974.
Shively, Donald, ed. *Tradition and Modernization in Japanese Culture*. Princeton, 1971.
Smith, Thomas C. *The Agrarian Origins of Modern Japan*. Stanford, 1959.
Taira Koji. *Economic Development and the Labor Market in Japan*. New York, 1970.
Ward, Robert E., ed. *Political Development in Modern Japan*. Princeton, 1968.
Ward, Robert E. and Darkwart A. Rustow, eds. *Political Modernization in Japan and Turkey*. Princeton, 1964.

II. Have "Modern" and "Modernization" Been Overworked?

Bellah, Robert. *Tokugawa Religion: The Values of Pre-Industrial Japan*. Glencoe, 1957.
Black, C. E. *The Dynamics of Modernization*. New York, 1966.
Burks, Ardath. *Japan: Profile of a Post Industrial Nation*. Boulder, 1981.
Craig, Albert. *Chōshū in the Meiji Restoration*. Cambridge, Mass., 1961.
Dore, R. P., ed. *Aspects of Social Change in Modern Japan*. Princeton, 1967.
Dower, John, ed. *Origins of the Modern Japanese State*. New York, 1975.
Eisenstadt, S. M. *Modernization: Protest and Change*. Englewood Cliffs, 1966.

Fukutake Tadashi. *Asian Rural Society: China, India and Japan.* Tokyo, 1967.
———. *Japanese Rural Society.* Ithaca, 1972.
Hall, John W. "The New Look of Tokugawa History." In J. W. Hall and M. B. Jansen, eds., *Studies in the Institutional History of Early Modern Japan.* Princeton, 1965.
Harootunian, H. D. *Toward Restoration: The Growth of Political Consciousness in Tokugawa Japan.* Berkeley, 1970.
Jansen, Marius B., ed. *Changing Japanese Attitudes Toward Modernization.* Princeton, 1965.
Kimbara Samon. *"Nihon Kindaika" Ron no Rekishi zo* [History of the "modernization of Japan"]. Tokyo, 1968.
Lockwood, William P., ed. *The State and Economic Enterprise in Japan.* Princeton, 1965.
Maruyama Masao. *Studies in the Intellectual History of Tokugawa Japan.* Tokyo and Princeton, 1974.
Moulder, Frances. *Japan, China, and the Modern World Economy.* Cambridge, England, 1977.
Nakamura, James I. *Agricultural Production and Economic Development of Japan: 1873-1922.* Princeton, 1966.
Najita Tetsuo. *Japan.* Englewood Cliffs, 1974.
Sato Seisaburo, Shumpei Kato, and Yasusuke Murakami. "Analysis of Japan's Modernization." *Japan Echo* 3(2)(1976).
Shively, Donald, ed. *Tradition and Modernization in Japanese Culture.* Princeton, 1971.
Smith, Thomas C. *The Agrarian Origins of Modern Japan.* Princeton, 1968.
Taira Koji. *Economic Development and the Labor Market in Japan.* New York, 1970.
Ward, Robert E., ed. *Political Development in Modern Japan.* Princeton, 1968.
Ward, Robert E. and Darkwart A. Rustow, eds. *Political Modernization in Japan and Turkey.* Princeton, 1964.

III. The Meiji Restoration: Product of Gradual Decay, Abrupt Crisis, or Creative Will?

Beasley, W. G. *The Meiji Restoration.* Stanford, 1972.
Bolitho, Harold. *Treasures Among Men: The Fudai Daimyō in Tokugawa Japan.* New Haven, 1974.
Craig, Albert M. *Chōshū in the Meiji Restoration.* Cambridge, Mass., 1961.
Dower, John W., ed. *Origins of the Modern Japanese State.* New York, 1975.
Harootunian, Harry. *Toward Restoration: The Growth of Political Consciousness in Tokugawa Japan.* Berkeley, 1970.
Ishii Takashi. *Zōtei Meiji Ishin no kokusaiteki kankyō* [The international environment of the Meiji Restoration]. Tokyo, 1973.
Jansen, Marius B. *Sakamoto Ryoma and the Meiji Restoration.* Princeton, 1961.
Sakata Yoshio and John W. Hall. "The Motivation of Political Leadership in the Meiji Restoration." *Journal of Asian Studies* 16(1956):31–50.
Smith, T. C. "Japan's Aristocratic Revolution." *Yale Review* 56(1961):370–383.
Totman, Conrad. *The Collapse of the Tokugawa Bakufu: 1862-1868.* Honolulu, 1980.
Toyama Shigeki. *Meiji Ishin.* Tokyo, 1951.

IV. The Meiji Government and Its Critics: What Is Best for the Nation?

Akita, George. *Foundations of Constitutional Government in Modern Japan.* Cambridge, Mass., 1967.

Beckmann, George M. *The Making of the Meiji Constitution.* Westport, 1957.

Blacker, Carmen. *The Japanese Enlightenment.* Cambridge, England, 1964.

Bowen, Roger. *Rebellion and Democracy in Meiji Japan.* Berkeley, 1980.

Braisted, William R., Yasushi Adachi, and Kikuchi Yuji, translators. *Meiroku Zasshi: Journal of the Japanese Enlightenment.* Cambridge, Mass., 1973.

Craig, Albert and Donald Shively, eds. *Personality in Japanese History.* Berkeley, 1970.

Davis, Sandra T. W. *Intellectual Change and Political Development in Early Modern Japan.* Cranbury, 1980.

Fukuzawa Yukichi. *The Autobiography of Fukuzawa Yukichi.* Trans. Eiichi Kiyooka. New York, 1966.

Hackett, Roger F. *Yamagata Aritomo in the Rise of Modern Japan.* Cambridge, Mass., 1971.

Hall, Ivan. *Mori Arinori.* Cambridge, Mass., 1973.

Havens, Thomas R. H. *Nishi Amane and Modern Japanese Thought.* Princeton, 1970.

Ike Nobutaka. *The Beginnings of Political Democracy in Japan.* Baltimore, 1950.

Livingston, Jon, Joe Moore, and Felicia Oldfather, eds. *The Japan Reader.* Vol. 1: *Imperial Japan 1800-1945.* New York, 1973.

Najita Tetsuo. *Hara Kei in the Politics of Compromise: 1905-1915.* Cambridge, Mass., 1967.

Norman, E. H. *Japan's Emergence as a Modern State.* New York, 1940.

Notehelfer, Fred. *Kōtoku Shūsui: Portrait of a Japanese Radical.* Cambridge, England, 1971.

Pittau, Joseph. *Political Thought in Early Meiji Japan: 1868-1889.* Cambridge, Mass., 1967.

Pyle, Kenneth B. *The New Generation in Meiji Japan.* Stanford, 1969.

Scalapino, Robert A. *Democracy and the Party Movement in Prewar Japan.* Berkeley, 1953.

Scheiner, Irwin. *Christian Converts and Social Protest in Meiji Japan.* Berkeley, 1970.

Shively, Donald H. "Nishimura Shiseki: A Confucian View of Modernization." In Marius B. Jansen, ed., *Changing Japanese Attitudes Toward Modernization.* Princeton, 1965.

V. Meiji Imperialism: Planned or Unplanned?

Chen, Edward I-te. "Japan's Decision to Annex Taiwan: A Study of Itō-Mutsu Diplomacy: 1894-95." *Journal of Asian Studies* 37(1)(November 1977):61.

Conroy, Hilary. *The Japanese Seizure of Korea: 1868-1910.* Philadelphia, 1960 paperback ed., 1974.

Goodman, Grant, ed. *Imperial Japan and Asia.* New York, 1967.

Iriye Akira. *Pacific Estrangement: Japanese and American Expansion, 1897-1911.* Cambridge, Mass., 1972.

———. "Imperialism in East Asia." In James B. Crowley, ed. *Modern East Asia: Essays in Interpretation.* New York, 1970.

_____, ed. *The Chinese and the Japanese*. Princeton, 1980.

Jansen, Marius B. *The Japanese and Sun Yat-sen*. Cambridge, Mass., 1954.

Kim, C. I. Eugene and H. K. Kim. *Korea and the Politics of Imperialism: 1876–1910*. Berkeley, 1967.

Kim, Key-Hiuk. *The Last Phase of the East Asian World Order*. Berkeley, 1980.

Mayo, Marlene. "The Korean Crisis of 1873 and Early Meiji Foreign Policy." *Journal of Asian Studies* 31(4)(August 1975).

_____. *The Emergence of Imperial Japan*. Lexington, 1970.

McWilliams, Wayne C. "East Meets East: The Soejima Mission to China, 1873." *Monumenta Nipponica* 30(3)(August 1975).

Nish, Ian. *The Anglo-Japanese Alliance*. London, 1966.

Okamoto Shumpei. *The Japanese Oligarchy and the Russo-Japanese War*. New York and London, 1970.

Totten, George et al. "Japanese Imperialism and Aggression: Reconsiderations." *Journal of Asian Studies* 22(4)(August 1963): 469–472.

VI. The Russo-Japanese War: Turning Point in Japanese History?

Arima Tetsuo. *The Failure of Freedom: A Portrait of Modern Japanese Intellectuals*. Cambridge, Mass., 1969.

Dore, R. P. "The Modernizer as a Special Case: Japanese Factory Legislation, 1882–1911." *Comparative Studies in Society and History* 11(4)(October 1969): 433–450.

_____. "Mobility, Equality and Individuation." In Ronald P. Dore, ed., *Aspects of Social Change in Modern Japan*. Princeton, 1967.

Dower, John W. *Empire and Aftermath*. Cambridge, Mass., 1979.

Fridell, Wilbur M. *Japanese Shrine Mergers: 1906–12*. Tokyo, 1973.

Harootunian, H. D. "A Sense of an Ending and the Problem of Taishō." In Bernard S. Silberman and H. D. Harootunian, eds., *Japan in Crisis: Essays on Taishō Democracy*. Princeton, 1974.

Marshall, Byron. *Capitalism and Nationalism in Prewar Japan: The Ideology of the Business Elite, 1868–1941*. Stanford, 1967.

Mitani Taichiro. *Nihon seitō seiji no keisei* [Establishment of Japanese party politics]. Tokyo, 1967.

Miyachi Masato. *Nichiro-sengo seijishi kenkyu* [Study on post–Russo-Japanese war politics]. Tokyo, 1973.

Notehelfer, Fred. *Kōtoku Shūsui: Portrait of a Japanese Radical*. Cambridge, England, 1971.

Pyle, Kenneth B. "Advantages of Followship: German Economics and Japanese Bureaucrats, 1890–1925." *Journal of Japanese Studies* 1(1)(Autumn 1974): 127–264.

_____. "The Technology of Japanese Nationalism: The Local Improvement Movement, 1900–1918." *Journal of Asian Studies* 33(1)(November 1973):51–65.

_____. *The New Generation in Meiji Japan*. Stanford, 1969.

Roden, Donald T. *Schooldays in Imperial Japan*. Berkeley, 1980.

Silberman, Bernard S. "Taishō Japan and the Crisis of Secularism." In Bernard S. Silberman and H. D. Harootunian, eds., *Japan in Crisis: Essays on Taishō Democracy*. Princeton, 1974.

Smethurst, Richard. *A Social Basis for Prewar Japanese Militarism.* Berkeley, 1974.

Taira Koji. *Economic Development and the Labor Market in Japan.* New York, 1970.

Wray, Harold J. "A Study in Contrasts: Japanese School Textbooks 1903 and 1941–45." *Monumenta Nipponica* 27(1)(Spring 1973).

VII. How Democratic Was Taishō Democracy?

Arima Tetsuo. *The Failure of Freedom: A Portrait of Modern Japanese Intellectuals.* Cambridge, Mass., 1969.

Beckmann, George and Okubo Genji. *The Japanese Communist Movement: 1922–1945.* Stanford, 1969.

Bernstein, Gail Lee. *Japanese Marxist: A Portrait of Kawakami Hajime.* Cambridge, Mass., 1978.

Bikle, George. *The New Jerusalem: Aspects of Utopianism in the Thought of Kagawa Toyohiko.* Tucson, 1976.

Duus, Peter. *Party Rivalry and Political Change in Taishō Japan.* Cambridge, Mass., 1968.

————. "The Era of Party Rule." In James B. Crowley, ed., *Modern East Asia: Essays in Interpretation.* New York, 1970.

Havens, Thomas. *Farm and Nation in Modern Japan.* Princeton, 1974.

Large, Stephen S. *The Rise of Labor in Japan: The Yūaikai, 1912–1919.* Tokyo, 1972.

————. "Nishio Suehiro and the Japanese Social Democratic Movement, 1920–1940." *Journal of Japanese Studies* 36(1)(November 1976):37–56.

Marshall, Byron. *Capitalism and Nationalism in Prewar Japan: The Ideology of the Business Elite, 1868–1941.* Stanford, 1967.

Mitchell, Richard. *Thought Control in Prewar Japan.* Ithaca, 1976.

Morley, James, ed. *Dilemmas of Growth in Prewar Japan.* Princeton, 1971.

Najita Tetsuo. *Hara Kei in the Politics of Compromise: 1905–1915.* Cambridge, Mass., 1967.

Pyle, Kenneth. "State and Society in the Interwar Years." *Journal of Japanese Studies* 3(2)(Summer 1977).

Scalapino, Robert. *Democracy and the Party Movement in Prewar Japan: The Failure of the First Attempt.* Berkeley, 1962.

Silberman, Bernard S. and H. D. Harootunian, eds. *Japan in Crisis: Essays on Taishō Democracy.* Princeton, 1974.

Smith, Henry. *Japan's First Student Radicals.* Cambridge, Mass., 1972.

Taira Koji. *Economic Development and the Labor Market in Japan.* New York, 1970.

Titus, David Anson. *Palace and Politics in Prewar Japan.* New York, 1974.

Totten, George. *The Social Democratic Movement in Prewar Japan.* New Haven, 1966.

VIII. Japanese Colonialism: Enlightened or Barbaric?

Chang Han-yu and Ramon H. Myers. "Japanese Colonial Development Policy in Taiwan, 1895–1906: A Case of Bureaucratic Entrepreneurship." *Journal of Asian Studies* 22(4)(August 1963).

Chen, Edward I-te. "Japanese Colonialism in Korea and Formosa: A Comparison of the Systems of Political Control." *Harvard Journal of Asiatic Studies* 30(1970).

Kim, Han-kyo. "The Japanese Colonial Administration in Korea: An Overview." In Andrew C. Nahm, ed., *Korea Under Japanese Colonial Rule*. Kalamazoo, 1973.

Kublin, Hyman. "The Evolution of Japanese Colonialism." *Comparative Studies in Society and History* 2(1)(October 1959).

Lee, Chong-sik. *The Politics of Korean Nationalism*. Berkeley, 1965.

Myers, Ramon H. and Adrienne Ching. "Agricultural Development in Taiwan Under Japanese Colonial Rule." *Journal of Asian Studies* 23(4)(August 1964).

Nahm, Andrew C., ed. *Korea Under Japanese Colonial Rule: Studies of the Policies and Techniques of Japanese Colonialism*. Kalamazoo, 1973.

Tsurumi, E. Patricia. *Japanese Colonial Education in Taiwan: 1895–1945*. Cambridge, Mass., 1977.

IX. The 1930s: Aberration or Logical Outcome?

Berger, Gordon Mark. *Parties Out of Power in Japan: 1931–1941*. Princeton, 1977.

Dore, R. P., ed. *Aspects of Social Change in Modern Japan*. Princeton, 1967.

Ishida Takeshi. *Kindai Nihon seiji kōzō no kenkyū* [A study of the political structure of modern Japan]. Tokyo, 1956.

Maruyama Masao. *Thought and Behaviour in Modern Japanese Politics*. London, 1963.

Masumi Junnosuke, *Nihon seitō shiron* [On the history of Japanese political parties]. 4 vols. Tokyo, 1965–1968.

Maxon, Yale Candee. *Control of Japanese Foreign Policy: A Study of Civil-Military Rivalry, 1930–1945*. Berkeley, 1957.

Mitani Taichirō. *Nihon seitō seiji no keisei* [The political development of Japanese political parties]. Tokyo, 1967.

Mitchell, Richard H. *Thought Control in Prewar Japan*. Ithaca and London, 1976.

Morley, James W., ed. *Dilemmas of Growth in Prewar Japan*. Princeton, 1971.

Morris, Ivan I. *Nationalism and the Right Wing in Japan*. London, 1960.

Ōuchi Tsutomu. *Fuashizumu e no michi* [The road to fascism]. *Nihon no rekishi* [Japanese history], vol. 24. Tokyo, 1967.

Smethurst, Richard. *A Social Basis for Prewar Japanese Militarism: The Army and the Rural Community*. Berkeley, Los Angeles, and London, 1974.

Spaulding, Robert M., Jr. *Imperial Japan's Higher Civil Service Examinations*. Princeton, 1967.

Titus, David Anson. *Palace and Politics in Prewar Japan*. New York and London, 1974.

Totten, George O. *The Social Democratic Movement in Prewar Japan*. New Haven and London, 1966.

———, ed. *Democracy in Prewar Japan: Groundwork or Facade?* Lexington, Mass., 1965.

X. Japan's Foreign Policy in the 1930s: Search for Order or Naked Aggression?

Bergamini, David. *Japan's Imperial Conspiracy*. New York, 1971.

Berger, Gordon M. *Parties Out of Power in Japan: 1931–1941*. Princeton, 1977.

Blaker, Michael A. *Japan's International Negotiating Style.* New York, 1977.

Borg, Dorothy and Shumpei Okamoto, eds. *Pearl Harbor as History.* New York and London, 1973.

Butow, Robert J. C. *Tōjō and the Coming of the War.* Princeton, 1961.

Coox, Alvin D. and Hilary Conroy. *China and Japan: Search for Balance Since World War I.* Santa Barbara, 1978.

Crowley, James B. "A New Deal for Japan and Asia: One Road to Pearl Harbor." In J. B. Crowley, ed., *Modern East Asia: Essays in Interpretation.* New York, 1970.

_____. *Japan's Quest for Autonomy.* Princeton, 1966.

Elsbree, Willard H. *Japan's Role in Southeast Asian Nationalist Movements: 1940-45.* Cambridge, Mass., 1953.

Iriye Akira. *After Imperialism.* Cambridge Mass., 1965.

_____. *The Japanese-American War.* Cambridge, Mass., 1981.

Lebra, Joyce C. *Japanese-Trained Armies in Southeast Asia.* Hong Kong, 1977.

Lu, David J. *From the Marco Polo Bridge to Pearl Harbor.* Washington D.C., 1957.

Maxon, Yale Candee. *Control of Japanese Foreign Policy: A Study of Civil-Military Rivalry, 1930-1945.* Berkeley, 1957.

Morley, James W., ed. *Deterrent Diplomacy, Japan, Germany and the USSR: 1935-1940.* Selected translations from *Taiheiyō sensō e no michi: kaisen gaikō shi.* Studies of the East Asian Institute, Japan's Road to the Pacific War Series. New York, 1976.

_____. *Dilemmas of Growth in Prewar Japan.* Princeton, 1971.

_____. *Japan's Foreign Policy: 1868-1941.* New York, 1974.

Nish, Ian. *Japan's Foreign Policy: 1869-1942.* London, 1977.

Ogata, Sadako N. *Defiance in Manchuria.* Berkeley and Los Angeles, 1964.

Oka Yoshitake. *Konoe Fumimaro: "Unmei" no Seijika* [Konoe Fumimaro: Fate's Politician]. Tokyo, 1972.

Peattie, Mark R. *Ishiwara Kanji and Japan's Confrontation with the West.* Princeton, 1975.

Pelz, Stephen E. *Race to Pearl Harbor.* Cambridge, Mass., 1974.

Pluvier, J. M. *Southeast Asia from Colonialism to Independence.* Kuala Lumpur, 1974.

Royama Masamichi. *Foreign Policy of Japan: 1914-1939.* Tokyo, 1941.

Titus, David A. *Palace and Politics in Prewar Japan.* New York and London, 1974.

Thorne, Christopher. *The Limits of Foreign Policy: The West, the League, and Far Eastern Crisis of 1931-1933.* New York, 1972.

Togo Shigenori. *The Cause of Japan.* New York, 1956.

Takemoto Toru. *Failure of Liberalism in Japan.* Washington D.C., 1979.

Toland, John. *The Rising Sun: The Decline and Fall of the Japanese Empire, 1936-1945.* New York, 1970.

Tsunoda Jun, ed. *Taiheiyō no sensō e no michi* [The road to the Pacific war]. 8 vols. Tokyo, 1962.

XI. The Allied Occupation: How Significant Was It?

Allinson, Gary D. *Suburban Tokyo.* Berkeley, 1979.

Dazai Osamu. *No Longer Human.* Trans. Donald Keene. New York, 1958.

_____. *The Setting Sun*. Trans. Donald Keene. New York, 1956.

Dore, R. P. *Land Reform in Japan*. Oxford, 1958.

Dower, John W. "Occupied Japan and the American Lake." In Edward Friedman and Mark Selden, eds., *America's Asia: Dissenting Essays on Asian-American Relations*. New York, 1971.

_____. *Empire and Aftermath: Yoshida Shigeru and the Japanese Experience, 1879-1954*. Cambridge, Mass., 1979.

Kawai Kazuo. *Japan's American Interlude*. Chicago, 1960.

Kosaka Masatake. *100 Million Japanese: The Postwar Experience*. Tokyo, 1972.

Manchester, William. *American Caesar*. Boston, 1978.

Minear, Richard H. *Victor's Justice: The Tokyo War Crimes Trial*. Princeton, 1971.

Osaragi Jirō. *Homecoming*. New York, 1955.

Passin, Herbert. *The Legacy of the American Occupation: Japan*. New York, 1968.

Reischauer, Edwin O. *The United States and Japan*. 1st ed. Cambridge, Mass, 1950.

Sodei Rinjirō. *Makkaasaa no nisennichi* [The two thousand days of MacAuthur]. Tokyo, 1974.

Takemae Eiji. *Nihon senryō hishi* [The untold history of the Allied Occupation of Japan]. Tokyo, 1977.

Tsurumi Kazuko. *Social Change and the Individual: Japan Before and After Defeat in World War II*. Princeton, 1970.

Ward, Robert E. *The American Occupation of Japan 1945-1952: An Annotated Bibliography of Western-Language Materials*. Chicago, 1974.

Yoshida Shigeru. *The Yoshida Memoirs*. Trans. Kenichi Yoshida. Boston, 1962.

XII. Japan: East or West?

Beardsley, Richard K. and John Hall. *Twelve Doors to Japan*. New York, 1965.

Brzezinski, Zbigniew. *The Fragile Blossom*. New York, 1972.

Fairbank, John King, ed. *The Chinese World Order: Traditional China's Foreign Relations*. Cambridge, Mass., 1968.

Gibney, Frank. *Japan: The Fragile Superpower*. New York, 1975.

Hearn, Lafcadio. *Japan: An Interpretation*. New York, 1904.

Hsu, Francis L. K. *Iemoto: The Heart of Japan*. New York, 1975.

Ienaga Saburo. *The Pacific War*. New York, 1978.

Kahn, Herman. *Japan: The Emerging Superstate*. Englewood Cliffs, 1970.

Keene, Donald. *Living Japan*. New York, 1959.

Miwa Kimitada. "Fukuzawa Yukichi's 'Departure from Asia': A Prelude to the Sino-Japanese War." In Edmund Skrzypczak, ed., *Japan's Modern Century*. Rutland, 1968.

_____. "Nashonarizumu to gurobarizumu" [Nationalism and globalism]. In Kinhide Mushakoji and Michio Royama, eds., *Kokusai gaku: Riron to tembō* [International studies: theories and prospects]. Tokyo, 1976.

Nakamura Hajime. *Ways of Thinking of Eastern Peoples: India, China, Tibet, Japan*. Honolulu, 1964.

Nakane Chie. *Japanese Society*. Berkeley, 1970.

Nishijima Sadao. "Higashi Ajia sekai" [The East Asian world]. In Mitsusada Inoue, ed., *Sōgō kōza Nihon no shakai bunka shi* [Lectures on the sociocultural history of Japan]. Vol. 1. Tokyo, 1973.

Reischauer, Edwin O. *The Japanese*. Cambridge, Mass., 1977.

Sato Seizaburo. "Japan's World Order." In Irwin Scheiner, ed., *Modern Japan*. New York, 1974.

Vogel, Ezra. *Japan as Number One*. Cambridge, Mass., 1979.

The Contributors

AKASHI YOJI is professor of history at Nanzan University and director of the Center for Japanese Studies. Interested in Japan's relations with Southeast Asia, he has had published numerous articles and chapters in scholarly journals and monographs, among them "Japanese Occupation of Malaya: Interruption or Transformation" (*Southeast Asia under Japanese Occupation,* Alfred W. McCloy, ed., Yale University Southeast Asia Studies, 1980) and "Bureaucracy and the Japanese Military Administration, with Specific Reference to Malaya" (*Japan in Asia,* William H. Newell, ed., Singapore University Press, 1981). Akashi received the Most Outstanding Educator of the Year award in 1971.

JACKSON H. BAILEY is professor of history and director of the East Asian Studies Program at Earlham College. He has done research on modern Japanese political history and written interpretive articles on Meiji politics and contemporary Japanese culture. He also directed the team of scholars and TV professionals that conceived and developed the award-winning thirty-program series of films for public television, "Japan: The Living Tradition" and "Japan: The Changing Tradition."

BANNO JUNJI is an associate professor at the Institute of Social Science, University of Tokyo. His main subject of interest is the political history of the Meiji and Taishō periods (1868–1925). He has written two books, *Meiji Kempo Taisei no Kakuritsu* (University of Tokyo Press, 1971) and *Meiji Shiso no Jitsuzo* (Sobunsha, 1977), on the Meiji period, and a third, *Taishō Seihen* (Mineruba Shobo, 1982) on the time of the Taishō political crisis.

MICHAEL A. BARNHART is assistant professor of history at the State University of New York at Stony Brook. He has had published "Japan's Economic Security and the Origins of the Pacific War," in *The Journal of Strategic Studies,* and recently completed a manuscript on the economic dimensions of U.S.–Japanese relations before Pearl Harbor. He is currently working on a study of America's acquisition of military bases overseas, primarily in Asia and the Mediterranean, during the decade after the Second World War.

HAROLD BOLITHO, an associate professor in the Department of Japanese at Monash University, is a native of Australia and founding president of the Japanese Studies Association of Australia. He obtained his B.A. at the University of Melbourne and his Ph.D. at Yale University. He is the author of *Treasures Among Men* (Yale University Press, 1974) and *Meiji Japan* (Cambridge University Press, 1977) and co-editor of *A Northern Prospect: Australian Papers on Japan* (Australian National University Press, 1981). He is currently researching the regional background to the Meiji Restoration. He has also written articles on early Tokugawa history and, most recently, the history of sumō wrestling.

THOMAS W. BURKMAN is associate professor of history at Old Dominion University, where he has taught Japanese history since 1976. He has also taught at Colby College, Michigan State University, and Kwansei Gakuin University. He has been a post-doctoral Fulbright fellow and visiting research scholar at the University of Tokyo (1978), visiting lecturer at the University of California at Davis (1981–1982), and has edited *The Occupation of Japan: Educational and Social Reform,* published by the MacArthur Memorial in 1982. He is active in organizing international symposia on the Allied Occupation and is interested in intellectual issues attending diplomatic questions. His project on Japan, the League of Nations, and world order covers the years 1914 to 1938 and has taken him to archives in Tokyo, London, and Geneva.

ARDATH W. BURKS is professor emeritus of Asian Studies at Rutgers University. He has been chairman of the Department of Political Science, director of International Programs, and associate and acting vice-president for Academic Affairs. A specialist on contemporary Japanese politics, Burks did postdoctoral research at the University of Michigan Center for Japanese Studies, Okayama, and he was a member of the *Kindaika* (Modernization) Seminar at the Institute for Humanistic Studies, Kyoto University. He has also served on the staff of the International House of Japan, Tokyo. In recent years he has made frequent trips to Japan, Korea, and China to carry out research, acquire materials for the Rutgers Library, and act as a consultant. Burks is a former member of the Board of Directors of the Association for Asian Studies.

VICTOR CARPENTER is presently an assistant at the Faculty of Law, Tohoku University, Sendai, Japan. He is a graduate of Macalester College (1972) and has done intensive Japanese language work at Cornell University

(1972–1973) and the Tokyo Inter-University Center (1975–1976). He is a Ph.D. candidate in East Asian history at Stanford University. The subject of his dissertation is localism and the implementation and fate of American sponsored local autonomy reforms in post–World War II Japan.

EDWARD I-TE CHEN, associate professor of Japanese history, is the director of the Asian Studies Program at Bowling Green State University in Ohio. Specializing in Japanese colonialism, he has contributed many articles to important journals, including the *Harvard Journal of Asiatic Studies* and *Journal of Asian Studies*. He is preparing an interpretive study on Gotō Shimpei, Japan's civil administrator on Taiwan from 1898 to 1906.

HILARY CONROY is currently professor of Far Eastern history and co-chairperson of the International Relations and East Asian Studies programs at the University of Pennsylvania. He was a Japanese language officer during the occupation of Japan and subsequently acquired several distinguished positions and honors. These include Fulbright research scholar at Tokyo University, director of International Seminars in Tokyo and the Kansai areas, president of the Conference on Peace Research in History, and senior specialist at the Institute of Advanced Projects at the East-West Center (Honolulu) to name but a few. His most recent publications are *History of Asia, East Across the Pacific,* and *China and Japan: Search for Balance.*

JOHN W. DOWER, professor of Japanese history at the University of Wisconsin, Madison, received his Ph.D. in history and Far Eastern languages from Harvard University. He is the author of *The Elements of Japanese Design* and *Empire and Aftermath: Yoshida Shigeru and the Japanese Experience, 1878–1954,* and the editor of *Origins of the Modern Japanese State: Selected Writings of E. H. Norman* and, most recently, *A Century of Japanese Photography.* Dower has been a research associate at Kyoto University and Tokyo University and was affiliated for a year with the Postwar Financial History Project of the Japanese Ministry of Finance. His current major research focuses on the United States and Japan between 1941 and 1952, the years of war and occupation.

PETER DUUS, professor of history at Stanford University, has taught at Harvard University, Washington University, and Claremont Graduate School. He is the author of *Party Rivalry and Political Change in Taishō Japan, Feudalism in Japan,* and *The Rise of Modern Japan,* as well as numerous book reviews and articles. He is currently at work on a study of the Japanese colonization of Korea.

DAVID G. EGLER is assistant professor of history at Western Illinois University. He has received Ford Foundation, NDFL, and Fulbright fellowships and a grant from the Yoshida International Educational Foundation in Tokyo. He has written reviews and conference papers and has had published "The Ideology of Racial Co-operation among Manchurian Resident Japanese as a Prologue to the Manchurian Incident, 1929–1931" (*Asian Profile*, December 1976). He is currently exploring more fully the political and ideological efforts put forth by both Japanese and Chinese before World War II to create a viable pan-Asian common ground.

CHARLES B. FAHS studied and taught at Kyoto and Tokyo Imperial universities and was a research analyst and subsequently chief of Far East Division research for the Office of Strategic Services. After the Second World War he joined the Rockefeller Foundation and was director of its Humanities Division from 1950–1962. He also taught at Pomona College, Claremont Graduate School, Muhlenberg College, and Miami University.

JERRY K. FISHER is professor of history at Macalester College, and he is involved in programs designed to increase knowledge of East Asia among secondary school teachers. He has had published several articles; among them are "Han chisei jidai yocho suru chikyu shimin no shi" [The death of a world citizen signals the coming of an anti-intellectualism] in *Asahi Journal* and "Chugoku no kyoiku ni tsuite" [Notes on Education in China] in *Gendai Kyoiku Kagaku* [Contemporary education].

JOHN WHITNEY HALL received his Ph.D. from Harvard University in 1950. He is A. Whitney Griswold Professor of History at Yale University and has also taught at the University of Michigan. Between 1960 and 1966 he served as chairman of the Association of Asian Studies' Conference on Modern Japan, an organization that brought out six volumes of studies between 1965 and 1971. On behalf of this group he organized the 1960 Hakone Conference on Japan's modernization. *Government and Local Power in Japan, 500–1700* (1966), *Studies in the Institutional History of Early Modern Japan* (with Marius B. Jansen, 1968), *Japan from Prehistory to Modern Times* (1970), and *Japan Before Tokugawa* (with Nagahara Keiji and Kozo Yamamura, 1981) are some of his published works.

MIKISO HANE was born in California but spent his teens in a small village in prewar Japan. He served as an assistant in Japanese at Yale University, where he enrolled and received a B.A. degree (1952) and Ph.D. (1957). During 1959–1961 he taught history at the University of Toledo and since 1961 has been at Knox College. He received Fulbright, Japan Foundation, NEH, and other grants to conduct research in Japanese history. He has had published a number of articles on Meiji liberal thought, and is the author of the following books: *Japan, A Historical Survey* (Scribner's, 1972); *Peasants, Rebels and Outcastes* (Pantheon, 1982); a translation of Masao Maruyama,

Studies in the Intellectual History of Tokugawa Japan (Princeton and Tokyo university presses, 1974); and *Emperor Hirohito and His Chief Aide, The Honjō Diary* (Tokyo University Press, 1982).

ANN M. HARRINGTON is assistant professor of history and chairperson of the Department of History at Mundelein College, Chicago. She coordinates the Asian Studies Program and teaches Chinese and Japanese history. She has done extensive research on the *kakure* Kirishitan of Japan. Her article, "The *Kakure* Kirishitan and Their Place in Japan's Religious Tradition" appeared in the December 1980 issue of the *Japanese Journal of Religious Studies*. Harrington is currently doing research on women in the Japanese empire.

HATA IKUHIKO, who received his Ph.D. in 1974 from the University of Tokyo, is professor of history at Takushoku University. He was research associate at Columbia and Harvard universities (1963–1965), chief historian at the Ministry of Finance (1971–1976), visiting lecturer at Princeton University (spring 1978), and fellow at The Woodrow Wilson Center (fall 1978). Some of his many publications are *Shiroku Nippon Saigumbi* [History of Japan's rearmament] (Tokyo, 1976), *Taiheiyo Kokusai Kankeishi* [The hidden crisis between Japan, the U.S. and the U.S.S.R.] (Tokyo, 1972), and "Japan Under the Occupation" (*The Japan Interpreter,* Winter 1976).

THOMAS R. H. HAVENS teaches history at Connecticut College.

THOMAS M. HUBER is assistant professor of history at Duke University. He was a research associate at the University of Tokyo and taught at Stanford University and the University of California, Berkeley. His main interests lie in the institutional and intellectual history of modern Japan. He is the author of *The Revolutionary Origins of Modern Japan,* as well as of several scholarly articles that deal with political issues of the 1860s and 1870s.

JAMES L. HUFFMAN is associate professor of history at Wittenberg University in Springfield, Ohio. He is the author of *Politics of the Meiji Press: The Life of Fukuchi Gen'ichirō* (University Press of Hawaii, 1980). As former journalist for the *Minneapolis Tribune,* he has also had published several articles on the history of Japan's press. His current research interests focus on the impact of the Meiji press-government struggle and on the social costs of Meiji modernization policies. Huffman also has served as senior translator-editorial consultant for *The Japan Interpreter.*

HAN-KYO KIM, professor of political science at the University of Cincinnati since 1963, has taught courses on politics and international relations of Japan, China, and Korea. His research interests are in the field of Korean studies. He is co-author of *Korea and the Politics of Imperialism* (University of California Press, 1967) and editor of *Essays on Modern Politics and History* (Ohio University Press, 1969), *Reunification of Korea: Fifty Basic Documents* (Institute for Asian Studies, 1972), and *Studies on Korea: A Scholar's Guide* (University Press of Hawaii, 1980). He has also had published articles and book reviews in *Journal of Asian Studies, Comparative Politics, American Political Science Review,* and others. He has received research grants from Social Science Research Council/American Council of Learned Societies, University of Cincinnati, U.S. Department of Health, Education, and Welfare, and Asian Research Foundation (Tokyo). In 1980 he was a visiting professor in the Department of International Relations, University of Tokyo.

KISAKA JUNICHIRŌ teaches at Ryukoku University and is a contributor to the Iwanami series on Japanese history. He has recently edited and contributed to the publication *Nihon, fuashizumu no hakuritsuto hokai* [The establishment and the collapse of Japanese fascism] (Tokyo, 1979). In his essay he introduces the period from the 1930s to 1945 as a "fifteen-year war," a concept much utilized by Japanese historians of the era.

STEPHEN S. LARGE, educated at Harvard University and University of Michigan, is reader in history at the University of Adelaide in South Australia. He has served as councillor for Japan and Northeast Asia in the Asian Studies Association of Australia and as president of the Japanese Studies Association of Australia. His publications include *The Rise of Labor in Japan: The Yūaikai, 1912-1919* (Sophia University Press, 1972) and *Organized Workers and Socialist Politics in Interwar Japan* (Cambridge University Press, 1981). His current research is on Buddhism and political dissent in prewar Japan.

BYRON K. MARSHALL, who did his graduate work at Stanford University, is currently professor of history and chairperson of the East Asian Studies Department. He was president of the Midwest Conference on Asian Affairs and a member of the Northeast Asian Council of the Association for Asian Studies. Most recently he has been involved in a study of the intellectual elite as represented by academics at the Imperial Universities of Tokyo and Kyoto, and he has had published "Growth and Conflict in Japanese Higher Education, 1905–1930" (*Conflict in Japanese History,* Koschmann and Najita, eds., Princeton University Press, 1982).

MARK C. MICHELSON is the area manager for North Asia with Business International Asia/Pacific Ltd. in Hong Kong. He recently directed a Business International study entitled *Taiwan to 1987: Economic and Political Outlooks for Political Planners.* Michelson holds a B.A. from Carleton College, a Ph.D. from the University of Illinois at Urbana-Champaign, and a special certificate from the New York University Graduate School of Business. He was a visiting researcher at the University of Tokyo and Sophia University during 1975–1976 with the support of a Fulbright-Hays Dissertation Fellowship. Most of his scholarly research and writing has been concerned with Japan's international relations in the first half of the twentieth century.

RICHARD H. MINEAR, professor of history at the University of Massachusetts, Amherst, is a graduate of Yale University (B.A., 1960) and Harvard University (Ph.D., 1968). The American war in Indochina, which occurred during his late twenties, had a major impact on his thinking about Japan. Author of two books and editor of a third, *Through Japanese Eyes,* a reader for high-school use, he has also written about American attitudes toward Japan. He teaches courses on Japan, Vietnam, Asia through film, and historical reasoning. His most recent projects are translations of Japanese literature of the World War II era.

MIWA KIMITADA, professor of international history at Sophia University since 1957, was born and raised in Matsumoto-shi, Japan. He received his B.S. and M.A. degrees from Georgetown University and Ph.D. from Princeton University, where he also was a visiting professor. His published works include *Matsuoka Yosuke, Gendai Kokusai Kankei ron* [Contemporary international relations] and *Postwar Trends in Japan* (co-author). Currently he is interested in the intellectual continuity in modern Japanese history from the prewar to postwar periods.

BONNIE B. C. OH is assistant professor of history at Loyola University of Chicago. She has had published several articles in scholarly journals in the United States and abroad, including the *International History Review,* and contributed chapters to symposia volumes such as *The Chinese and the Japanese: Essays in Political and Cultural Interactions* (Princeton University Press, 1980). Her research interests range from the late Ch'ing China to the late nineteenth-century relations among China, Japan, and Korea, to women in East Asia. She is co-editor of a forthcoming volume on "Women in the Japanese Empire, 1895–1945," to which she is contributing a chapter on Korean women. She has also begun to work on "China as Korea's First Modernizer, 1882–1894: a Reassessment of China's Role in Korea."

SHUMPEI OKAMOTO, professor of history at Temple University, received his B.A. from Aoyama Gakuin University and Anderson College, and his M.I.A. and Ph.D. from Columbia University. He is the author of *The Japanese Oligarchy and the Russo-Japanese War* and co-editor, with Dorothy Borg, of *Pearl Harbor as History: Japanese-American Relations, 1931–1941.* He is interested in Japanese war literature and is currently engaged in a study of writings on Hiroshima.

MARK R. PEATTIE is associate professor of history and director of the East Asian Studies program at the University of Massachusetts, Boston. After twelve years with the United States Information Agency in the Far East, most of which were spent in Japan, he earned a doctoral degree in modern Japanese history at Princeton University and then taught at Pennsylvania State University and the University of California at Los Angeles. His research in the history of the Japanese military culminated in the publication of his study *Ishiwara Kanji and Japan's Confrontation with the West* (Princeton University Press, 1975). More recently he has been engaged in a study of Japanese colonialism and is the co-editor of *The Japanese Colonial Empire, 1895-1945* (Princeton University Press, forthcoming).

EDWIN O. REISCHUAER, born in Tokyo in 1910, was on the faculty of Harvard University from 1938 to 1981, teaching Japanese and Chinese language and history and modern Japanese politics. He is now retired with the title of University Professor Emeritus. He served as American Ambassador to Japan from 1961 to 1966. Among his works are *Japan Past and Present; The United States and Japan; Ennin's Travels in T'ang China; Ennin's Diary; Wanted: An Asian Policy; East Asia: Tradition and Transformation* (co-author); *Beyond Vietnam: The United States and Asia; Japan: The Story of a Nation; Toward the 21st Century: Education for a Changing World;* and *The Japanese.*

RICHARD J. SMETHURST is associate professor of history at the University of Pittsburgh. His primary publication, *A Social Basis for Prewar Japanese Militarism: The Army and the Rural Community* (Berkeley, 1974), deals with the military's pre–World War II efforts at mobilizing the countryside for war. Currently he is studying the growth of commercial agriculture and its effects on landlord–tenant farmer relations in Japan from 1870 to 1940.

HENRY D. SMITH II is associate professor of history at the University of California, Santa Barbara. He is the author of *Japan's First Student Radicals* (Harvard University Press, 1969), and editor and co-author of *Learning from SHOGUN: Japanese History and Western Fantasy* (University of California, Santa Barbara, 1980). His present interest in the history of Japanese urban culture is reflected in an essay entitled "Tokyo and London: Comparative Conceptions of the City" (*Japan: A Comparative View*, Albert Craig, ed., Princeton University Press, 1979). He is currently preparing a study of landscape views of the city of Edo.

SODEI RINJIRŌ is professor of political science at Hosei University and specializes in American politics and U.S.–Japanese relations. He has frequently been on national television and radio and written numerous articles for *Asahi Journal, Chuo Koron,* and many other periodicals. His major publications are winner of a Mainichi Award for the Distinguished Publications of the year 1974, *Makkaasaa no Nisennichi* [Two thousand days of MacArthur] published by Chuo Koron-sha in 1974; *Watakushitachi wa Tekidattanoka: Zaibei Hibakusha no Mokushiroku* [Were we the enemy?—a saga of Hiroshima survivors in America] published by Ushio Shuppan-sha in 1978 and a nominee for the Nippon Non-fiction Award of that year; and *Yureru Amerika, Moeru Amerika* [America in turmoil] published by Gendaishi Shuppankai in 1972.

ROBERT M. SPAULDING is on the faculty of the Department of History at Oklahoma State University. His major field of specialization is the Japanese civil service since 1868, and he has had published the first detailed history of the civil service examination system before 1945, *Imperial Japan's Higher Civil Service Examinations* (Princeton University Press). He is now completing work on a book of quantitative analysis of the careers of all men who held managerial positions in the Japanese civil service between 1919 and 1943. He has also had published research on the so-called new bureaucrats of the 1930s.

KOJI TAIRA is professor of economics and industrial relations at the University of Illinois at Urbana-Champaign. He teaches labor economics, economic development, and Japanese economy. He is the author of *Economic Development and the Labor Market in Japan* (New York, 1970), of articles on a wide range of topics in journals and anthologies, and of a few books written in Japanese. Taira is also co-author of *An Outline of Japanese Economic History* (Tokyo, 1979). His M.A. degree is from the University of Wisconsin and his Ph.D. degree is from Stanford University. He has taught at the University of the Ryukyus, the University of Washington, Stanford University, Keio University, and Hokkaido University.

TAKEMAE EIJI has presided over the Japan Association for Studies on the History of the Occupation since its founding in 1972. Following studies in the United States funded by East-West Center grants, he graduated from the Law School of Tokyo Metropolitan University in 1968 and received his Ph.D. in 1970. He is currently professor of law and political science at Tokyo Keizai University. Among his works published in Japanese are "Postwar labor reform in Japan: history of GHQ labor policy" (Tokyo University Press, 1982), "Occupation and the Japanese postwar history: whole picture of allied control policy" (Soshi-sha, 1980), and "Study of the U.S. labor policy for Japan" (Nihon Hyoron-sha, 1970).

DAVID A. TITUS, professor of government at Wesleyan University, specializes in comparative politics with a focus on Japan, Britain, China, and the Soviet Union. He is author of *Palace and Politics in Prewar Japan* (Columbia

University Press, 1974) and numerous articles on Japan. Having lived in Japan for over four years, he has directed the Associated Kyoto Program at Doshisha University, as well as conducted research in Tokyo. In 1975 he was program chairman for the Association for Asian Studies. His current research is on Watsuji Tetsuro's "emperorism" and democracy in postwar Japan.

CONRAD TOTMAN, professor of history at Northwestern University, has had published *Politics in the Tokugawa Bakufu, 1600-1843* (Harvard University Press, 1967); *The Collapse of the Tokugawa Bakufu, 1862-1868*, (University Press of Hawaii, 1980) winner of the John K. Fairbank Prize, and *Japan Before Perry* (University of California Press, 1981). He has recently completed a biography of Tokugawa Ieyasu and is currently engaged in a study of the history of forests and forestry in pre-industrial Japan. He has written several articles on the fall of the Tokugawa regime, most recently "Ethnicity in the Meiji Restoration" (*Monumenta Nipponica*, Autumn, 1982).

GEORGE OAKLEY TOTTEN III, chairman of the Department of Political Science at the University of Southern California, served as the first director of the USC–UCLA Joint East Asia Language and Area Center and founded the Year-in-Japan program at USC. His fields of interest are comparative government, political philosophy, and Japanese studies. Some of the books he has written, edited, and/or contributed to include *Democracy in Prewar Japan: Groundwork or Facade?; The Social Democratic Movement in Prewar Japan; Socialist Parties in Postwar Japan; The Whaling Issue in U.S.-Japan Relations; Aspects of Social Change in Modern Japan; Japan in Crisis: Essays on Taishō Democracy;* and *Sources of the Japanese Tradition.*

E. PATRICIA TSURUMI is associate professor of Japanese history at the University of Victoria, where she also teaches women's studies. She is the author of *Japanese Colonial Education in Taiwan, 1895-1945* (Harvard University Press, 1977), and has had published articles on Japanese colonialism, the history of Japanese education, and Japanese women. Currently she is engaged in a study of Meiji women, education, and industrialization, and she is also writing a critical biography of Takamure Itsue, 1894-1964.

TAEKO WELLINGTON is an instructor in Japanese at the Kamehameha Schools in Honolulu, Hawaii. Her main research interest is in the area of interaction between language and culture. She is currently a member of the team engaged in a project for strengthening and maintaining ethnic languages in the United States, funded by the National Endowment for the Humanities.

HARRY WRAY is associate professor of history at Illinois State University and specializes in the history of modern Japanese education. His avid interest in Japan has taken him there nine times, and he has taught at Sophia University and Nanzan University. His essays have appeared in *Monumenta Nipponica, Asian Forum,* and the *Malaysian Journal of Education,* and he has contributed chapters to *Chinese-Japanese Relations: The Search for Balance* and *Tenno ga Baiburu o yonda Hi* [The day the Emperor read the Bible]. He is currently involved in research dealing with educational reform of occupied Japan. His M.A. degree in history is from the University of Nebraska and his Ph.D., from the University of Hawaii.

CPSIA information can be obtained
at www.ICGtesting.com
Printed in the USA
JSHW021627271219
3190JS00008B/34

9 780824 808396